LIBRARY IN A BOOK

ANIMAL RIGHTS

REVISED EDITION

Lisa Yount

Facts On File
An imprint of Infobase Publishing

To Frodo, Leo, Bertha, Midnight Louise, and Mira

and in memory of Mary, Frodo I, Panzer, Richard,

and King Kong, beloved companions all

ANIMAL RIGHTS, Revised Edition

Copyright © 2008, 2004 by Lisa Yount
Graphs copyright © 2008, 2004 by Infobase Publishing

Facts On File, Inc.
An imprint of Infobase Publishing
132 West 31st Street
New York NY 10001

Library of Congress Cataloging-in-Publication Data

Yount, Lisa.
    Animal rights / Lisa Yount. — Rev. ed.
      p. cm. — (Library in a book)
    Includes bibliographical references and index.
    ISBN 978-0-8160-7130-2 (alk. paper)
    1. Animal rights. I. Title.
    HV4708.Y84 2008
    179'.3—dc22   2007027687

Facts On File books are available at special discounts when purchased in bulk quantities for businesses, associations, institutions, or sales promotions. Please call our Special Sales Department in New York at (212) 967-8800 or (800) 322-8755.

You can find Facts On File on the World Wide Web at http://www.factsonfile.com

Text design by Ron Monteleone
Graphs by Sholto Ainslie

Printed in the United States of America

MP Hermitage 10 9 8 7 6 5 4 3 2 1

This book is printed on acid-free paper.

CONTENTS

PART I
OVERVIEW OF THE TOPIC

Chapter 1
Issues in Animal Welfare and Animal Rights   **3**

Chapter 2
The Law and Animal Rights   **85**

Chapter 3
Chronology   **119**

Chapter 4
Biographical Listing   **141**

Chapter 5
Glossary   **151**

PART II
GUIDE TO FURTHER RESEARCH

Chapter 6
How to Research Animal Rights Issues   **163**

Chapter 7
Annotated Bibliography   **180**

Chapter 8
Organizations and Agencies   **240**

PART III
APPENDICES

Appendix A
Animal Welfare Act, 1970   **269**

Appendix B
Endangered Species Act, 1973   **278**

Appendix C
Animal Legal Defense Fund v. Glickman I, 154 F.3d 426, 1998   **288**

Appendix D
Animal Legal Defense Fund v. Glickman II, 204 F.3d 229, 2000   **300**

Appendix E
Animal Enterprise Terrorism Act (PL 102-346), 2006   **307**

Appendix F
Tables and Graphs   **310**

Index   **316**

PART I

OVERVIEW OF THE TOPIC

CHAPTER 1

━━━━━━━━━━

ISSUES IN ANIMAL WELFARE
AND ANIMAL RIGHTS

It has been hailed as "the civil rights movement of the twenty-first century."[1] It has been criticized as the domain of sentimental cranks, wild-eyed terrorists, or simply spoiled city people with no real understanding of nature. Whether praised or damned, the quest for better treatment of animals—even perhaps extending to granting them some form of legal rights—has already made significant changes in Western society and law, and it may well make more profound ones in the decades to come.

Humans have always had a close but complex, even what animal rightist attorney Gary Francione calls "schizophrenic," relationship with other species. On one hand, the myths of most cultures show ancestors, spirits, or even gods in animal form and describe animals as worthy of respect and sometimes awe. People have valued domesticated animals as working partners and companions for thousands of years. At the same time, humans throughout history have killed animals to obtain food and clothing, bought and sold them as property, and exterminated them as vermin.

Although theologians and philosophers occasionally discussed human responsibilities to the "brute creation," systematic attempts to change or legislate people's treatment of animals arose only in the 19th century. Ironically, and perhaps tellingly, as several historians of the animal protection movement have pointed out, these efforts came mainly from the group whom the Industrial Revolution had separated most completely from daily contact with animals (except pets and some working animals): the upper classes in the cities of Europe and America. These early crusades, which focused on cruelty to horses and other working animals and on the use of animals in scientific experiments, produced the first organizations and the first laws aimed at protecting animals from mistreatment.

By the end of the century, however, social concern for animals was waning. It remained in the background until shortly after World War II, when

3

an upsurge in the use of animals, particularly in farming and medical research, raised new issues and spurred the formation of new organizations. Then, in 1975, Australian philosopher Peter Singer published a book called *Animal Liberation*, which inspired some members of the ongoing crusade for animal welfare to spawn a new social movement with different goals: the movement for animal liberation (as Singer called it) or animal rights. Most animal welfarists had focused on caring for homeless animals and trying to prevent "unnecessary" cruelty, leaving unquestioned the morality of confining or killing animals for socially accepted purposes such as the production of meat. Singer and his followers, however, boldly asked whether humans had a right to hurt or kill animals for any reason.

During the rest of the 20th century and into the 21st, the animal rights movement, along with the broader-based and more moderate animal welfare movement from which it sprang, used a variety of attention-getting and frequently controversial methods to produce major changes in public (and, to a lesser extent, legislative and judicial) thinking about the treatment of companion animals, wildlife, and animals in agriculture, science, and entertainment. It made many people examine, often for the first time, the morality of their relationship to animals as a whole.

THE PHILOSOPHY OF ANIMAL RIGHTS

In the King James Version, Genesis, the first book of the Bible, states that God told the first humans, "Be fruitful, and multiply, and replenish the earth, and subdue it: and have dominion over the fish of the sea, and over the fowl of the air, and over every living thing that moveth upon the earth."[2] In general, the Judeo-Christian tradition taught that, although "brute beasts" should be treated gently and respected as part of God's creation, they were made for humans to use.

Thirteenth-century theologian and philosopher Thomas Aquinas, echoing ideas found in ancient Greek and Roman writings, stated that animals deserve no consideration in themselves because they lack reason. The Bible prohibited cruelty to animals, Aquinas said, only "lest through being cruel to other animals one becomes cruel to human beings."[3] French philosopher René Descartes expanded on Aquinas's view in the early 1600s by saying that animals were essentially living machines. He maintained that they could not really suffer because they did not possess reason, soul, or feeling. The cries they made when scientists operated on them, he said, had no more significance than the squealing of ungreased machine parts. Some thinkers in the second half of the 18th century began to question this picture of animals, however. In 1789, British philosopher Jeremy Bentham wrote, "The question is not, Can [animals] *reason?* nor, Can they *talk?* but, Can they *suf-*

fer?"[4] He even speculated that "the day may come when the rest of the animal creation may acquire those rights which never could have been withholden from them but by the hand of tyranny."[5]

Philosophical consideration of the nature, purpose, and value of animals, as well as of the nature of rights and their possessors, is at the heart of the modern animal rights movement. Indeed, Richard Ryder, a British psychologist who became a leader in shaping the philosophy of the animal rights movement, has written that "animal liberation is possibly unique among liberation movements in the extent to which it has been led and inspired by professional philosophers."[6] Many of these philosophers' (and their opponents') discussions center on abstract, often dauntingly abstruse, questions such as "What are rights?," "What are the requirements for having rights?," and "If two rights conflict, how does one decide which is the more important?" No one has answered these questions definitively in regard to human beings, so it is certainly no surprise that they provoke disagreement when applied to animals.

PETER SINGER

Peter Singer's 1975 book, *Animal Liberation*, has been repeatedly called "the Bible of the animal rights movement." Nonetheless, Singer did not use the term *animal rights* in the book except, as he puts it, as a "convenient political shorthand," and he felt that "in the argument for a radical change in our attitude to animals, [this term] is in no way necessary."[7] Furthermore, unlike Tom Regan and some later writers in the movement, Singer does not demand (or at least does not expect) that all human uses of animals be abolished. His book chiefly urges people to expand their range of moral concerns to include animals. He says that humans should stop discriminating against animals simply because animals are not members of the human species.

Singer is a utilitarian, a follower of Jeremy Bentham and other philosophers who hold that the goal of all sentient beings—those who can feel pleasure and pain—is to maximize pleasure and minimize pain. Because animals (mammals, at least) can feel pleasure and pain, Singer says, they are sentient beings and therefore have an interest in avoiding pain and achieving pleasure that humans should respect. "Pain is pain," he writes, "and the importance of preventing unnecessary pain and suffering does not diminish because the being that suffers is not a member of our own species."[8]

As a utilitarian, Singer calculates value in terms of the total amount of pleasure and pain resulting from an action. This way of thinking permits causing pain to a few if it brings pleasure or cessation of pain to a far greater number. Singer therefore grants that using animals in medical research can be considered moral if the research can be done in no other way and is likely to save many human lives, because the good that will probably result from the research outweighs the harm done to the animals. Using animals for meat or to test cosmetics, on the other hand, is not moral because the good resulting from those uses is relatively slight and can be achieved in other ways.

Singer sees animals as having inherent value, or value in themselves, not merely as means to human ends. Nonetheless, he does not say that all animals should have the same rights or that any animals should have all the rights granted to humans. A living thing's level of inherent value depends on its level of sentience, he believes, and he admits that normal adult humans can suffer in ways that animals cannot—by imagining future pain, for example. Such humans therefore have a greater value than other animals. He maintains, however, that animals should be treated the same as humans who have a capacity for suffering similar to their own, such as people with severe brain damage or human babies. He has said that no experiment is right to perform on an animal that would be wrong to perform on a three-year-old human child.

Valuing humans more highly than other creatures simply because they are human is what Singer calls speciesism. (Richard Ryder coined this term in 1973, but Singer adopted it, and it is often associated with him.) He equates speciesism with racism and sexism, saying that neither race, gender, nor species is a justifiable reason for discrimination. He compares human use of animals to slavery and the animal liberation movement, as he terms it, to 19th-century crusades to free African slaves.

Tom Regan

Another philosopher, Tom Regan, formerly of North Carolina State University (he retired in 2001), went beyond Singer's ideas in a 1984 book, *The Case for Animal Rights*. This book defines many beliefs of the animal rights movement's more radical wing.

Unlike Singer, Regan explicitly uses the term *rights* in connection with animals. Furthermore, eschewing Singer's pragmatic or utilitarian notions, Regan states that all human uses of animals that cause suffering are morally wrong and should be abolished, no matter how much benefit they might bring to humans. He writes, "It is not larger, cleaner cages that justice demands in the case of animals used in science, but empty cages; not traditional animal agriculture, but a complete end to all commerce in the flesh of dead animals."9

Regan sees animals—mammals, at least—as "subjects of a life," meaning that they are conscious beings with some concept of self-identity and of goals that they wish to pursue. He goes further than Singer by stating that animals' inherent value, and, therefore, their moral standing, is the same as that of humans. Because animals and humans have the same inherent value, Regan believes that they are entitled to the same basic rights, including rights to life, bodily integrity, and respectful treatment. Unlike many philosophers, he does not feel that they need to be able to understand these rights in order to possess them. Some animal rights activists have carried Regan's line of thinking to striking—some would say shocking—extremes, as when Michael Fox, a bioethical scholar who in 2007 was chief consultant and veterinarian for the India Project for Animals and Nature, said, "The life of an ant and the life of my child should be granted equal consideration."[10]

EVALUATING ANIMALS

One area of major disagreement between animal rights philosophers such as Singer and Regan and their critics concerns the criteria for having rights and the evaluation of whether any animals—and, if so, which ones—meet those criteria. Interpretation of scientific data as well as philosophical terminology is involved in these discussions. Common criteria for having rights include the ability to reason and understand abstract concepts, the ability to distinguish between right and wrong, the ability to use language, and possession of some concept of self.

Whatever Descartes may have thought, few modern observers would deny that birds and mammals, at least, and possibly all animals with a central nervous system, can feel physical pain. When treated in ways that humans would call painful, other animals show the same behaviors that people in pain do: They cry out, writhe and make facial contortions, avoid the painful stimulus if they can, and so on. Thus, they are clearly sentient beings in the sense that Singer used the term. Whether they can also "suffer" in the way that humans do is more debatable. Most people familiar with mammals such as cats, dogs, and horses have observed behavior suggesting that these animals experience emotions that go beyond immediate physical needs and that they can remember, predict, and learn. However, critics such as Michael P. T. Leahy, former senior lecturer in philosophy at the University of Kent in Britain (now deceased), said that people's own emotions often lead them to anthropomorphize, or ascribe human mental processes to, animals and that there is no real way to know what mental experiences animals have.

The intellectual powers of animals, especially of great apes (chimpanzees, bonobos, gorillas, and orangutans), relative to those of humans are especially hard to evaluate. Animal rights supporters point to behavioral studies that appear to break down most, if not all, of the distinctions usually made between the intellects of humans and apes. For instance, primatologist Jane Goodall observed chimpanzees in Africa not only using but making tools. Other researchers have taught chimpanzees, gorillas, and bonobos to communicate with humans through sign language or computer keyboards. Some of these scientists report that the animals produced novel signs, such as combining the signs for *water* and *bird* to indicate a swan, and that they demonstrated some understanding of syntax (grammar and word order). Chimpanzees have also demonstrated the ability to recognize themselves in a mirror, which has been held to indicate that these apes have some concept of themselves as unique beings. Animal behaviorist Frans de Waal, for one, claims that apes can transmit cultural knowledge. (Some scientists have claimed that a few other mammals, including elephants and dolphins, possess some of the same humanlike characteristics that apes are said to have, such as a sense of self and the ability to use language.) Because apes seem to have intellectual capacities that overlap those of humans so closely, animal rightists say they should be allowed a similar overlap of rights.

Critics such as Clive D. L. Wynne, associate professor in the Department of Psychology at the University of Florida, Gainesville, dispute some of the conclusions of the ape scientists and their followers. Wynne says it is by no means clear whether chimpanzees who use signing or computers are really thinking linguistically or have merely learned elaborate tricks to please their human testers and obtain rewards. Similarly, he believes that apes' ability to recognize themselves in mirrors does not necessarily indicate self-awareness.

In any case, critics say, none of the ape experiments shows the capacity for abstract thought or the ability to understand such concepts as right and wrong, which many philosophers require for possession of rights. British philosopher Roger Scruton, for instance, has written that "the notion of a right . . . is an expression of the sovereignty that human beings claim over their own lives, and is only doubtfully applied to creatures who do not understand moral ideas, and who have no conception of their duties."[11] Similarly, another British philosopher David S. Oderberg claims that even if animal rights supporters are correct in saying that some animals possess consciousness, self-concept, memories, desires, and even the ability to use language— which he is by no means convinced is the case—these characteristics do not entitle them to rights. "A right holder must, first, know that he is pursuing a good, and secondly, he must be free to do so," he writes in *Human Life Review*. Neither of these things applies to animals: "No animal knows why it lives the way it does; no animal is free to live in one way or another."[12]

Philosophers who deny that animals are entitled to rights frequently emphasize that they are not thereby saying that treating animals cruelly is morally acceptable. Conservative Christian Matthew Scully writes, for instance, that "we are called on to treat [animals] with kindness, not because they have rights or power or some claim to equality, but in a sense because they don't; because they all stand unequal and powerless before us."[13]

In addition to questioning whether animals can have rights, some philosophers and scientists disagree with Peter Singer's classification of speciesism as an evil equal to racism and sexism. For instance, Lewis Petrinovich, an emeritus professor of psychology at the University of California, Riverside, claims that there is no biological basis for discrimination on the basis of race or gender, but a desire to help members of one's own species—the pool of potential partners for reproduction—is built into humans (and all other animals) by evolution. He believes that humans incapable of abstract thought, such as babies and severely brain-damaged people, can justifiably be given more rights than animals because they are part of the social community that nature drives morally active humans to value.

THE LAW OF ANIMAL RIGHTS

Because so much disagreement and confusion exist about philosophical, moral, and ethical definitions of rights, some commentators say that the term should be used only in the context of law. In *Animals and the Law: A Sourcebook*, St. Cloud State University professor Jordan Curnutt defines legal rights as benefits that the law protects and defines as being owed to the holders of those rights.

Focusing on animal rights as defined by law certainly simplifies the issue in one way. Commentators such as Curnutt say that Western laws, from ancient Babylonia to the present day, present a clear and unanimous view of the rights of animals: They have none. In the eye of the courts, animals are things, or property—period. As such, they have no legal standing or value in their own right. Laws have protected animals only in order to benefit humans, for instance by safeguarding economic interests or guaranteeing that meat is fresh and therefore is likely to be safe to eat. Curnutt writes that judges have almost unanimously interpreted even laws against cruelty to animals as being intended "not really to protect animals . . . [but] to protect humans from harm and prevent the decay of their moral character."[14]

STANDING TO SUE

Because animals have no legal standing, attorneys cannot file suits on their behalf, even when the animals are treated in ways that appear to violate existing laws. Organizations attempting to use lawsuits to compel government agencies to enforce animal protection laws therefore must use human plaintiffs, and finding plaintiffs that courts will accept has proved extremely difficult. This is because "standing to sue," as opposed to legal standing as a whole, refers to a person's relationship to a particular legal situation, and the rules governing it are extremely complex. *Black's Law Dictionary* explains that, in order to be acceptable plaintiffs in a lawsuit, individuals or groups must show that the actions of the defendant(s) "invade a private substantive legally protected interest" belonging to them.[15] In several landmark court cases, the Supreme Court has spelled out further requirements that animal protection groups, like the environmental groups involved in the cases, have found extremely hard to meet.

Animal Rights

In *Sierra Club v. Morton* (1972), the first of these cases, that well-known environmental organization filed suit against Rogers Morton, then secretary of the interior and head of the U.S. Forest Service, in an attempt to force the Forest Service to stop a development in a California wilderness area that the group claimed would violate several laws governing the preservation of national forests. A district court granted a preliminary injunction against the development, but the Ninth Circuit Court of Appeals removed it, saying that the Sierra Club had not proved that the project would violate any of its members' legally protected interests. Reviewing the case, the Supreme Court upheld the ruling of the appeals court. It granted that "esthetic and environmental well-being are important ingredients of the quality of life in our society, . . . deserving of legal protection through the judicial process." Nonetheless, it held that the Sierra Club's lawyers had not demonstrated that the development would violate club members' esthetic and environmental interests because the lawyers had not shown that the members visited that particular area.[16] The group therefore lacked standing to sue.

In a 1992 case, *Lujan v. Defenders of Wildlife*, the Supreme Court, in a majority opinion written by Justice Antonin Scalia, defined the requirements for standing more precisely. In order to obtain standing to sue, Scalia wrote, a plaintiff's lawyers must prove three things:

1. that a "concrete and particularized" injury (invasion of legally protected interests) to the person or to one or more members of the group has occurred "in fact"—in a manner "actual or imminent, not conjectural or hypothetical";
2. that the injury is "fairly traceable" to (clearly caused by) the actions of the defendant (not those of some third party) that are alleged to be illegal; and
3. that a legal decision in favor of the plaintiff is likely to stop the injury or prevent further injury of the same kind.

Scalia concluded that the Defenders of Wildlife, like the Sierra Club in the previous case, lacked standing to sue because the group had not shown exactly how and when the development it wanted to stop would cause "actual or imminent" injury to its members. Courts threw out several animal rights groups' suits for alleged violations of the Animal Welfare Act (AWA) for the same reason.

In a key 1998 case, *Animal Legal Defense Fund v. Glickman*, however, the District of Columbia Circuit Court of Appeals granted Animal Legal Defense Fund (ALDF) member Marc Jurnove standing to sue then Secretary of Agriculture Dan Glickman, who, as head of the U.S. Department of Agriculture (USDA), was responsible for enforcing the AWA. Among other things, the AWA governs the treatment of animals by zoos or other exhibitors, and Jurnove claimed to have suffered aesthetic injury when he repeatedly saw conditions at a Long Island (New York) zoo that, he alleged, violated the AWA's requirements for treatment of primates.

In the court's majority opinion, Judge Patricia Wald ruled that Jurnove had established that he had been injured "in a personal and individual way . . . by seeing with his own eyes the particular animals whose condition caused him aesthetic injury."[17] He had also shown that the vagueness of the USDA's AWA regulations permitted the conditions that caused the injury. Finally, Wald wrote, it was reasonable to believe that more specific rules would prevent future injury because Jurnove had testified that he planned to revisit the zoo frequently to monitor the animals.

ALDF v. Glickman was the first AWA case in which standing to sue was granted. Rob Roy Smith, then a student at the Northwestern School of Law of Lewis and Clark College, wrote soon after the appeals court decision that it "la[id] a foundation for animal welfare litigation to follow" and potentially would "spark a legal and political revolution in animal law."[18] The appeals court later rejected Jurnove's case on its merits, however, showing that standing to sue is far from the only obstacle that animal rights attorneys must overcome.

ANIMALS AS LEGAL PERSONS

Some animal rights activists in the legal profession, most notably Gary Francione, who teaches law at Rutgers University, and Steven Wise, who teaches law at Harvard University, hope to progress well beyond ALDF's qualified victory. It seems unjust to them that cruelty to animals can be redressed only through reference to the emotional distress of human beings observing it. They maintain that the intellectual and emotional capacities of chimpanzees and bonobos should entitle these animals, at least, to some of the legal rights of humans—enough to end most medical experimentation on them and prohibit their being kept in zoos, for instance. Wise calls the present rigid legal distinction between humans and animals "arbitrary, unfair, and irrational."[19]

Wise and the Great Ape Project, a group of scientists, scholars, and activists working for great ape rights, believe that apes should be granted legal personhood, which would allow human representatives to bring suits on their behalf, just as a suit can now be filed on behalf of a small child or an incompetent adult. They note that categories of legal persons that are not persons in the usual sense, such as corporations and ships, already exist and that the definition of legal persons has been broadened in the past, for instance when Africans and their descendants in the United States were reclassified as persons rather than property. Thus, they believe, there is no fundamental reason why animals could not be defined as legal persons.

Not surprisingly, the proposal that apes and perhaps other animals be made legal persons has aroused considerable criticism, even ridicule. "Would even bacteria have rights?" queries University of Chicago law professor Richard A. Epstein, who terms the concept of animal rights "intellectually dangerous."[20] Even some supporters of animal rights think that establishment of legal personhood may not be necessary to protect apes. Eric Glitzenstein, part of a husband-and-wife legal team in Washington, D.C., that has represented many animal rights and environmental protection groups, feels that "you can take existing law and accomplish much of the same thing."[21] Gary Francione, however, says that "we have had 'humane' laws for 200 years now; yet we use more animals, in more horrific ways, than ever before." Such laws, Francione claims, "may make us feel better, but they do little for animals."[22]

At the very least, books by Francione and Wise have attracted considerable attention both within and outside the legal community to the subject of animal law, which includes all laws relating to human activities that affect animals, not just those supported or envisioned by the animal rights movement. The law schools of Harvard University and of Georgetown University in Washington, D.C., began offering courses in animal law in 1999. In 2007, law schools in the United States were offering at least 86 courses in animal law. Several journals and a number of books were devoted to the subject, and hundreds of attorneys had made it their specialty.

THE ANIMAL RIGHTS MOVEMENT, ITS OPPONENTS, AND THEIR TACTICS

Peter Singer's *Animal Liberation* was a call to action as well as a philosophy treatise, and action resulted, partly because his ideas fell on fertile ground already plowed by other social movements, such as the African-American Civil Rights movement and the feminist movement, and drew on a common distrust of capitalism, large industries, and science. By the end of the 1980s, through a series of memorable and often controversial campaigns, what came to be called the animal rights movement had branded itself on the consciousness of the public—not to mention that of its opponents in agriculture, research, and other fields—as a mainstream grassroots movement. Targeted industries began to form their own advocacy and lobbying groups to counter the animal groups' actions.

The animal rights movement declined in strength and visibility during the 1990s, but it by no means disappeared. In 2001, Lyle Munro, a sociologist at Monash University in Australia (where Peter Singer also formerly taught), estimated that 10 to 15 million people worldwide belonged to the "animal movement," although it is not clear whether he meant just the animal rights movement or all animal protection movements combined. The

United States and Britain each have several hundred organizations devoted to one aspect or another of animal protectionism (which includes both animal rights and animal welfare). People for the Ethical Treatment of Animals (PETA), which claims to be the largest animal rights organization in the world, says that it alone has 1.6 million members.

MEMBERS OF THE ANIMAL RIGHTS MOVEMENT

Even more than most social movements of the late 20th century, the animal rights movement in both the United States and Europe has been characterized by grassroots activity, with many campaigns and demonstrations planned independently by local groups and small organizations. Most animal rights groups consist of a handful of professional leaders, backed by far larger numbers of volunteer activists. "Professionals keep the movement organized," says animal rights activist Stephen Fox. "Amateurs keep it honest."[23]

Several surveys conducted in the 1990s painted a statistical portrait of the typical animal rights activist. In one such survey, done in the United States in 1990, 97 percent of the activists interviewed were white, 78 percent were women, 57 percent were between ages 30 and 49, 33 percent had higher education degrees (as compared to 7.6 percent of U.S. citizens as a whole at the time), and 39 percent had incomes of $50,000 or more (when only 5 percent of the U.S. population had incomes at this level). About 70 percent had no living children, and 90 percent shared their homes with at least one animal (the national figure was about 40 percent).

Lyle Munro extensively interviewed about 350 animal rights activists and supporters in Australia, Britain, and the United States in the mid-1990s. Most of the interviewees told him that they had joined the movement because of close relationships with individual animals or a powerful emotional encounter with animals—what sociologist James Jasper calls a "moral shock." An Australian named Roger, for example, said he had become an activist after treating ducks injured in a wildfire.

> *I can remember the heartbeat. I can remember the calming effect of covering the bird's head. . . . I felt I had done something constructive, something positive to relieve the terror and the horror that bird was experiencing.[24]*

Supporters, critics, and animal rightists themselves agree that most people in the movement feel a powerful emotional attachment to their cause. Lawrence and Susan Finsen, who wrote about the animal rights movement in America in the mid-1990s, said that the moral foundation of the movement is compassion. Hunting supporter Ward M. Clark, an opponent of the movement, describes this compassion as "misplaced" and accompanied by "intellectual laziness," but animal rights activists see their emotions, which include anger as well as compassion, as literally the heart of their crusade.[25] Tom Regan, the quintessential animal rights philosopher, wrote that "philosophy can lead the mind to water but only emotion can make it drink."[26]

For most animal rights activists, Lyle Munro found, "animal protection had become a way of life."[27] They generally ate a vegan diet, excluding animal products such as milk and eggs as well as meat, and tried to avoid all other uses of animal products. They felt an extremely strong moral commitment to their cause and belief in its rightness. This conviction—Ward Clark calls it "arrogance"—helped them endure disapproval from family and friends, but it also sometimes made them impatient with slow, incremental changes in laws and public opinion. On occasion, it led them to criticize more moderate animal protectionists who, for example, still ate meat.

TACTICS OF THE ANIMAL RIGHTS MOVEMENT

Both traditional animal welfare groups such as the American Society for the Prevention of Cruelty to Animals (ASPCA) and more aggressive animal rights groups such as PETA employ the standard tactics used by virtually every social or political advocacy group: fund-raising and member recruitment, education (including programs aimed at children), direct mail and letter writing campaigns, and, in recent years, web sites and e-mail contact lists. Animal rights groups, like other organizations working vigorously for social change, also use high-profile media campaigns, boycotts, lobbying of legislators, sponsorship of ballot initiatives, and lawsuits (usually aimed at pressuring government agencies to enforce animal protection laws). PETA and a few other groups also sometimes buy shares in companies they oppose, such as large drug companies, in order to gain the right to introduce shareholder resolutions at company meetings; the resolutions almost never pass, but they gain publicity for the rights groups' point of view. A few extremist animal rights organizations resort to threats, vandalism, arson, and occasionally physical assault against those they consider to be abusers of animals.

Animal rightists' tactics have worked better in some areas than others. Most commentators probably would agree with Andrew N. Rowan of the Humane Society of the United States (HSUS), who wrote in 2000 that "the movement has enjoyed greater success in reshaping cultural attitudes than in securing laws."[28] Difficulty in meeting legal requirements such as those for standing to sue has often caused animal rights groups' lawsuits to be thrown out, and powerful opponents in Congress with ties to agriculture or other industries that the groups attack usually block their efforts to have new laws passed or gain more funding to enforce existing ones. Animal rights publicity campaigns, on the other hand, have frequently been highly effective in gaining attention and, sometimes, in changing public opinion and persuading businesses to adopt more animal-friendly policies. At the same time, some of these campaigns have created considerable controversy.

Ranging from appearances by supermodels clad only in banners proclaiming that they would rather go naked than wear fur to distribution of "Unhappy Meals" featuring pictures of dead cattle and toys in the shape of wounded farm animals, the campaigns launched by PETA have become particularly famous—or infamous—for their flamboyance. "Probably everything we do is a publicity stunt," PETA's cofounder, Ingrid Newkirk, said in a 1991 interview. "We are not here to gather members, to please, to placate, to make friends. We're here to hold the radical line."[29] Even PETA's numerous critics admit that they have done so very successfully. "Think what you want, but PETA's approach is working," Betsy Cummings, then executive editor of *Sales and Marketing Management*, wrote in 2001, calling the group's tactics "forceful, persistent, pointed, and attention-getting."[30]

Some of PETA's nervy broadsides have produced strong complaint. College students may have liked PETA's 2000 "Got Beer?" campaign, which claimed that beer was more healthful than milk, but Mothers Against Drunk Driving was not amused. A 2001 billboard advertisement reading "Eat the Whales," intended to point out what PETA saw as the hypocrisy of environmentalists who protested whaling but still ate meat, alienated groups who might have become PETA's allies. The Center for Consumer Freedom, a nonprofit coalition of restaurants, food companies, and consumers who oppose animal rights groups, objected to "Your Mommy Kills Animals," a comic book–like pamphlet that PETA distributed as part of an antifur campaign in 2004, saying that the booklet was unnecessarily frightening and attempted to indoctrinate children and teens with PETA's "radical" philosophy. "Milk Gone Wild," another PETA campaign to publicize the alleged health risks of milk that was launched in early 2006, drew similar criticism for depicting young women with cows' udders.

PETA and some other animal rights groups have become famous for using language and pictures to make their audience feel intense emotions. "We have to shock and mesmerise and entice, and tell powerful stories about the suffering of animals," Andrew Tyler of Britain's Animal Aid has said.[31] PETA's Newkirk has compared the killing of chickens for meat to the murder of Jews in Nazi concentration camps. Other groups have used pictures of animals that the public finds attractive or "cute," such as tigers, pandas, and big-eyed baby seals, to elicit sympathy. Videotapes of alleged animal abuse create shock.

However, as Lyle Munro points out, "the politics of emotion . . . have to be carefully managed if they are to avoid alienating potential supporters."[32] The Jewish Defense League has objected to the Holocaust comparison, and opponents within the movement say that the sympathy campaigns ignore animals that are just as endangered or abused as the featured ones but are less appealing. Researchers and meat industry spokespeople have claimed that "abuse" photos and tapes are often used out of context (photographs may not have been taken at the places mentioned in accompanying text, for instance, or may be decades old) or are altered to create a false impression.

The greatest debate has arisen over the tiny number of animal rights groups who employ threats and violence, particularly the shadowy organization called the Animal Liberation Front (ALF), which began in Britain in the 1970s but now also has representatives in the United States, Canada, Australia, New Zealand, and several European countries. Both Scotland Yard in Britain and the Federal Bureau of Investigation (FBI) in the United States have classified the ALF as a domestic terrorist group. Indeed, John Lewis, the FBI's deputy assistant director for counterterrorism, told Congress in May 2005 that the ALF and other extremist animal rights and environmental groups were the greatest domestic terror threat in the United States. He estimated that such groups have caused about $100 million in damage through arson and vandalism. The Foundation for Biomedical Research, which defends research on animals against animal rights critics, reported in 2006 that 363 violent or otherwise illegal acts were committed by environmental and animal rights activists in the early 2000s, as compared to only 220 such acts in all of the 1980s and 1990s.

Most of the ALF's activities, such as firebombing cars, "liberating" experimental animals, and smashing equipment in laboratories, have caused only property damage, but that damage has often been extensive. The ALF and a related environmental group, the Earth Liberation Front (ELF), have claimed responsibility for more than 600 acts of arson and vandalism in the United States alone since 1996, producing damages totaling more than $43 million, according to FBI Domestic Terrorism section chief James Jarboe. The ALF has repeatedly insisted that it takes "all necessary precautions against hurting any animal, human and nonhuman,"[33] and Jarboe admitted in March 2002 that "so far—knock on wood—they haven't [actually harmed anyone in the United States]." Jarboe feared, however, that "that may not last."[34] Certainly the ALF and related groups have at least threatened to cause injury, as when a group calling itself the Justice Department mailed razor blades and threats to 87 American scientists who did research on primates in 1999. In 2003, a group calling itself Revolutionary Cells set off bombs at Chiron and Shaklee, two corporations indirectly involved in animal testing, and threatened to do the same to similar firms. No one was injured in the blasts, but the group warned similar businesses that employees and their homes might be targeted next.

A second group whose activities have caused concern, both in the United States and Britain, is Stop Huntingdon Animal Cruelty (SHAC). British animal rights activists Greg Avery and Heather James founded this organization in November 1999 to shut down Huntingdon Life Sciences (HLS),

Europe's largest contract animal testing laboratory, which had been accused by PETA and others of abusing animals in its facility. After SHAC published the names of Huntingdon shareholders, leading to the harassment of some, HLS moved its financial center to the United States because U.S. securities laws allow greater anonymity of shareholders. SHAC in turn set up its own United States branch, SHAC-USA. Although SHAC spokespeople have denied the allegation, opponents of SHAC and SHAC-USA say that these groups have close ties to the ALF. They point out, for example, that the ALF has attacked a number of people associated with HLS.

On September 7, 2005, the New York Stock Exchange (NYSE) abruptly postponed a planned listing for trade of shares in Life Sciences Research, the name used by HLS in the United States. NYSE made no public statement about the reason for the postponement, but the action was widely attributed to animal rights groups' harassment of individuals and companies involved in the sale or purchase of HLS/Life Sciences Research stocks. For example, less than two weeks earlier, on August 26, the Manhasset Bay Yacht Club, in Port Washington, New York, had been covered with red paint and animal rights slogans. The ALF claimed that it had carried out this vandalism because the club's members included two executives of Carr Securities, a stock trading firm that had begun to make a market in shares of Life Sciences Research. The ALF warned that anyone else who traded or purchased such shares would be at risk of similar or worse harassment.

The attack on the yacht club was an example of "tertiary targeting," a tactic that ALF and other extremist animal rights groups began using in the late 1990s. In tertiary targeting, activists threatened and destroyed property, not only of employees of HLS and other animal testing laboratories, but of individuals and companies whose ties to the laboratories were indirect at best and often tenuous. Tertiary targets have included a roofer, a bakery, and a nursery that provided care for children of some contract workers for Huntingdon, for example. In mid-2004, protesters surrounded and vandalized the home of a California man named Mitchell Lardner, whose only connection with animal research was that he directed an investment subsidiary of Japan's Sumitomo Corporation, and the chemicals division of Sumitomo had done business with Life Sciences Research. (Lardner later quit his job.)

Britain, too, has seen increasingly violent protests, particularly against research on animals. According to the country's national policing unit for domestic extremism, 86 serious attacks on research facilities or individuals occurred there in 2005, more than in any other country in Europe. Animal rights groups succeeded in stopping the building of a primate research laboratory at Cambridge University in January 2004 and temporarily halted construction of a new animal research center at Oxford University as well. The construction at Oxford began in January 2004, but in July, Montpellier PLC, the major contractor scheduled to build the laboratory, withdrew from the project after animal rights activists harassed and threatened its stockholders. Construction resumed in November 2005, after Oxford obtained several injunctions forbidding protesters from coming near the unfinished facility or the homes of anyone involved in the project, as well as from publishing the names of researchers or construction workers on the Internet.

By far the most bizarre animal rights attack against people associated with animal research occurred in October 2004, when protesters stole the remains of Gladys Hammond from a grave in Yoxall, England. Hammond had been the mother-in-law of Christopher Hall, who, with his brother, David, ran a farm called Darley Oaks, where they raised guinea pigs for medical research. The protesters offered to return Hammond's body if the Halls would shut down Darley Oaks. The Halls gave in and closed their farm, located in Newchurch, England, in August 2005. Police recovered the body in early May 2006 and arrested three activists, who were sentenced on May 11 to 12 years in prison for the theft. (A fourth activist, arrested separately, was sentenced to four years.)

Extremist groups such as SHAC and SHAC-USA, in turn, have been the targets of stepped-up prosecution by law enforcement agencies. Earlier concern about activities of groups such as ALF had led to the passage in 1992 of the Animal Enterprise Protection Act, which makes physical disruption of animal production and research facilities a violation of U.S. federal law. On May 27, 2004, Kevin Kjonaas (sometimes spelled Jonas), then president of SHAC-USA, and six other members of the organization were indicted on charges of violating this and other federal laws by using the Internet to terrorize employees and business associates of HLS and Life Sciences Research. According to the indictment, the SHAC-USA web site had published contact information for HLS employees, including their home addresses and telephone numbers and, in some cases, the names, ages, and schools of their children. The site also posted a list of "top 20 terror tactics," including numerous forms of personal assault, property destruction, and vandalism.

At the group's trial in a federal district court in Trenton, New Jersey, attorneys for the defendants claimed that Kjonaas and the others had simply been exercising their right to free speech. After hearing testimony from HLS employees describing intimidation and vandalism that they had suffered following the postings, however, the jury rejected that argument and found six of the "SHAC Seven," as supporters called them, guilty on March 2, 2006. On September 12, three of the six, including Kjonaas, were sentenced to jail terms of up to six years. SHAC-USA, as a corporation, was placed on five years probation and ordered to pay a $1 million restitution fine. Although the Animal Enterprise Protection Act had been strengthened in May 2002 as part of the Public Health Security and Bioterrorism Preparedness and Response Act, this case represented the first trial and conviction for violation of the law.

Although most animal rights groups, even radical ones such as the ALF and SHAC, have so far usually limited themselves to threats, harassment, and property damage, a few incidents of physical violence have occurred. British ALF members kidnapped documentary filmmaker Graham Hall (no relation to the guinea pig farm owners), who had made an exposé film of the group, and burned the organization's initials into his back in 1999. In February 2001, animal rightists armed with baseball bats attacked Brian Cass, the managing director of HLS, producing a broken rib and a head injury that required 10 stitches. SHAC denied involvement in the incident.

ALF member Keith Mann, convicted of terrorist activities in Britain, said in 1998, "No one has died yet [as a result of animal rightists' attacks], but that time will come."[35] In fact, it may have come already. On May 6, 2002, a popular Dutch politician named Pim Fortuyn was shot to death in a radio station parking lot in Amsterdam, and Volkert van der Graaf, founder of a group called Environmental Offensive, was arrested and charged with the crime. Van der Graaf admitted the killing, and in April 2003 he was sentenced to 18 years in prison for it. Although van der Graaf said he was chiefly concerned about the effects of Fortuyn's philosophy, which he compared to Nazism, on weak groups in human society, van der Graaf also opposed animal agriculture and may have been stirred to action partly because Fortuyn had expressed support for breeding animals for fur.

Both the United States and Britain have passed new laws to rein in animal rights extremists. The Animal Enterprise Terrorism Act, passed by the U.S. Senate on September 30, 2006, and the House of Representatives on November 13, 2006, was signed into law by President George W. Bush on November 27, 2006. This law expanded the definitions of "animal enterprise" and "economic damage" from those used in the similarly named 1992 law and raised penalties for those who cause, or threaten to cause, economic or personal damage to people or businesses directly or indirectly connected with animal enterprises. Animal rights groups decried it as a limitation on free speech and legitimate civil disobedience that unfairly singled them out.

The British Parliament, for its part, passed amendments to the Serious Organised Crime and Police Act that made it a criminal offense to use intimidation campaigns to cause economic damage to individuals or companies directly or indirectly associated with research on animals. The law, like its U.S. counterpart, gave police increased powers to act against groups who carry on such campaigns. The amendments, proposed in November 2004, became law on July 1, 2005.

Some animal rights activists feel that extreme tactics are necessary because nothing else will bring about the results they desire. Speaking of the ALF, British activist Tim Dailey said, "In a war you have to take up arms and people will get killed. . . . It's a war, and there's no other way you can stop vivisectors [people who operate or experiment on living animals]."[36]

Some groups who say they do not use or advocate violence themselves have supported ALF's actions morally and sometimes financially. PETA, for example, contributed more than $45,000 in 1995 toward the cost of defending ALF member Rodney Coronado, who was convicted of a firebombing at Michigan State University. PETA's web site has compared the ALF to the Underground Railroad and the French Resistance.

Most animal rights groups, however, strongly disavow the use of violence. In a joint resolution published in the *New York Times* in 1991, for instance, the ASPCA, the HSUS, and more than 100 other animal protection groups stated that they opposed "threats and acts of violence against people and willful destruction and theft of property."[37] This disapproval may be as much strategic as moral. A 1994 editorial in the magazine *Animal People* complained that "the ALF and imitators are practically singlehandedly responsible for rationalizing the organized backlash against the animal rights movement,"[38] and HSUS's Andrew Rowan points out, "As a matter of historical fact, threats of bodily harm and acts of destruction . . . are nearly always counterproductive in the long term."[39] Most of Lyle Munro's interviewees said that legal tactics were more effective, as well as more justifiable, than illegal ones.

In contrast to the ALF or even PETA, many animal rights groups choose tactical approaches that encourage dialogue and compromise with those whose behavior they seek to change. For example, the late Henry Spira, founder of Animal Rights International and leader of a successful campaign against product testing on animals in the 1980s, was famous for his willingness to meet opponents halfway and his refusal to verbally attack them as individuals, no matter how strongly he might criticize their actions. According to Lyle Munro, Spira claimed that

> *his strategy of accommodation, a version of reintegrative shaming that favours reinforcement and forgiveness, leads to less animal suffering and is more effective than the vilification and stigmatisation of opponents is. . . . According to how the theory of reintegrative shaming [by Australian criminologist J. Braithwaite] works, the crime, not the offender, is the focus of the moralising effort.[40]*

OPPONENTS OF THE ANIMAL RIGHTS MOVEMENT

Lyle Munro writes that "one measure of a social movement's success is the intensity of opposition to it," and by that standard, the animal rights movement has been successful indeed.[41] At first, farmers, scientists, hunters, and others targeted by animal rights protests often simply ignored what they regarded as fringe activity. As the protests stirred up increasing public pressure, however, groups opposing them faced the fact that, as critic Marlene

Halverson said in 1991, "social concerns regarding the treatment of animals are [not] going to go away or . . . continue to be answer[able] by denial and resistance," and they began actively fighting back.[42] Existing trade associations such as the Animal Agriculture Alliance set up committees and campaigns to respond to animal rightists' attacks, and some new organizations, such as the National Association for Biomedical Research, were established solely for the purpose of defending particular industries.

Particularly since the 1990s, anti–animal rights groups have used many of the same tactics as the animal rightists in campaigns to defend their treatment of animals. They publish pamphlets and videotapes, present position statements on their web sites, and offer fact packets to teachers and journalists to counteract what they say is misrepresentation or outright lying by animal rights organizations. "For years scientists have not been good at informing the public about the benefits of what they do. A lot of propaganda has been allowed to fill the gap," says Andrew Gay, marketing director of HLS.[43] Similarly, Duane Thurman and Bob Fountain write in *Feedstuffs*, an agribusiness newspaper, "The issue of how [food] animals are raised and slaughtered has become more important than availability, price, and quality of . . . animal protein foods to many urban consumers. . . . The industry [needs to adopt] . . . a more aggressive, comprehensive, open, national consumer education program about protein foods and confinement animal production."[44]

Following the example set by animal rights organizations, opposition groups have learned to appeal powerfully to emotion. For instance, to counter antivivisectionists' pictures of what Andrew Gay calls "cuddly animals with things sticking out of their heads," animal research advocacy groups such as the British Research Defence Society have published testimonials from seriously ill people who say they would not be alive if research on animals had not taken place.[45] "We have now realized the issue is about people," not scientific information, says Mark Matfield, the society's former executive director.[46]

Just as with some animal rights groups, a few opposition groups have allegedly resorted to underhanded or even illegal tactics, although none has been accused of physical violence. Janice Pottker, a freelance writer who published material critical of the Ringling Bros. and Barnum & Bailey Circus and its head, Ken Feld, sued Feld and the circus in 1999, claiming that Feld had hired (among others) a former head of covert operations at the Central Intelligence Agency (CIA) to spy on her and attempt to derail her career. According to court records, the ex-CIA official, Clair George, admitted overseeing operations against Pottker and also against animal rights groups that opposed the circus, including the Performing Animal Welfare Society (PAWS) and PETA. Pottker's suit was still pending as of late 2005. Meanwhile, PETA filed a similar suit against Feld and some of his employees in 2001, alleging that they carried out covert operations against and infiltration of the animal rights group between 1988 and 1998. On March 15, 2006, a jury in Fairfax County, Virginia, ruled in favor of Feld in this suit, concluding that if any illegal acts occurred, he did not know about them. The circuit court judge then dismissed the suit.

ANIMALS AS COMPANIONS

The chief way in which most people consciously interact with animals is by having pets—or, as some animal rights activists urge others to call them, "companion animals." According to a survey conducted in 2005 and 2006 by the American Pet Products Manufacturers Association, 63 percent of households in the United States include at least one animal, and 45 percent of households have more than one. U.S. citizens spent $36.3 billion to care for their animal companions in 2005.

James Serpell wrote in *In the Company of Animals* that people are drawn to share their lives with animals because "they do not judge us, criticize us, lie to us or betray our trust."[47] Trained companion animals help some physically disabled people lead independent lives, and elderly or mentally disabled people often respond to animals when they have all but lost the ability to respond to other humans. The companionship of animals has even been credited with healing powers. In turn, many human "guardians" pamper and cherish their companion animals and view them as members of their family.

Some animal welfare organizations, as well as individual attorneys and private citizens, are trying to raise companion animals' status in law to match the high place they hold in the hearts of those whose households they share. The idea that pets are more than mere property is reflected, for instance, in attempts to change the word *owner* to *guardian* in city and state laws relating to pets. By 2007, such efforts had succeeded in 15 cities, towns, and counties and in one state, Rhode Island.

Groups are also working for changes in state laws that will allow people to establish valid, enforceable trusts for the care of pets or other animals, to obtain visitation rights in custody disputes over pets that stem from divorce, and to sue for loss of companionship and infliction of emotional distress when a pet is deliberately or negligently injured or killed. Twenty-three states had statutes regarding trusts for pets by March 2004. As of early 2007, no state had accepted loss of a pet's companionship as a tort, or grounds for a civil lawsuit, but six states (Alaska, Florida, Hawaii, Idaho, Kentucky, and Louisiana) allow monetary recovery for infliction of emotional distress by killing or injuring a pet. Some veterinary associations support creation of a legal status for pets that would allow, but limit, noneconomic awards in malpractice lawsuits against veterinarians.

Of all relationships between humans and animals, the companion animal one surely comes the closest to being symbiotic, or equally beneficial to both partners. Nonetheless, some radical animal rightists consider even the keeping of companion animals to be a kind of slavery because the animal usually has no choice about whether to be part of the relationship. Ingrid Newkirk, for instance, calls it an "absolutely abysmal situation brought about by human manipulation"[48] and says it should be "phased out" and be replaced by "enjoyment at a distance."[49] Similarly, John Bryant, author of a 1990 British book called *Fettered Kingdoms*, wrote, "Pet animals are slaves and prisoners, and I am opposed to both slavery and imprisonment."[50]

Most animal protectionists do not share this view, however. On the contrary, as Lyle Munro writes, "the keeping of companion animals is one of the distinguishing characteristics of animal protectionists."[51] Surveys have shown that some 90 percent of self-identified animal rights supporters or activists in the United States share their household with one or more animals, and each household has an average of 4.7 animals, about five times the national average. Many animal rightists cite an experience or relationship with a companion animal as the reason they were drawn to the cause.

THE FIRST ANIMAL PROTECTION SOCIETIES

The public's close relationship with companion animals, Lyle Munro believes, "is . . . the basis for the reservoir of good will that the animal movement depends on in its campaigns."[52] It was also the basis for the animal protection movement itself. Concern for companion animals, or at least for domesticated working animals, was the reason for the formation of the first animal protection laws and organizations.

England passed the first national animal protection law, the Ill Treatment of Horses and Cattle Bill, or Martin Act (named after Richard Martin, the Irish minister of Parliament, who introduced it), in 1822. It forbade "any Person [from] wantonly and cruelly beat[ing], abus[ing] or ill treat[ing] any Horse, Mare, Gelding, Mule, Ass, Ox, Cow, Heifer, Steer, Sheep or other Cattle."[53] The law was expanded to cover all domestic animals, including the bulls used in bullbaiting (which judges had not considered to be cattle) and the cocks used in cockfighting, in 1835. These common lower-class amusements thus became illegal.

Two years after the original Martin Act was passed, Britisher Arthur Broome founded the Society for the Prevention of Cruelty to Animals (SPCA), the West's first national animal protection organization. (It had been preceded by the Liverpool Society for Preventing Wanton Cruelty to Brute Animals, founded in 1809, which is said to be the world's oldest known animal welfare group.) The group worked to make sure the Martin Act was enforced, particularly in regard to the treatment of the horses that filled the streets of British cities. Queen Victoria lent the society her patronage, allowing it to add *Royal* to its name, in 1840.

The group was influential, probably because, according to historian B. Harrison, it kept its views and tactics firmly in line with middle- and upper-class Victorian mores. By the end of the century it had persuaded British legislators to pass laws that protected wild and domestic animals in a variety of situations, from use in scientific laboratories to drawing of carts, and had made kindness to animals a widely accepted concept, at least among relatively affluent people in the cities. The idea was much less well received in rural England, where activities such as fox hunting remained popular and the slaughter of animals on farms was a daily occurrence.

The United States followed England's example thanks to Henry Bergh, a wealthy New Yorker whose thoughts had been turned toward animals by experiences during his career as a diplomat. In Russia he had been greatly disturbed by the sight of peasants beating their horses, and in England he observed the RSPCA and decided to establish a similar group in America. He founded the American Society for the Prevention of Cruelty to Animals (ASPCA) in 1866 and, a mere year later, succeeded in persuading the New York legislature to pass an anticruelty law that became a model for most later laws. Numerous similar groups (despite its name, Bergh's organization at that time was active only in New York) and laws sprang up in the following decades in the United States, Britain, and other nations that followed the traditions of these countries. By 1921, every state in the United States had some sort of law forbidding cruelty to animals, and most countries in Europe did too.

BREEDING AND SALE OF COMPANION ANIMALS

State anticruelty laws are still the chief laws that protect companion animals, but some other laws also affect them. For instance, the federal Animal Welfare Act, passed in 1966 and amended in 1970, covers (among many other things) breeding facilities that sell dogs to pet stores. So far, however, this law has proved unable to control what animal rightists call "puppy mills": large kennels in which purebred puppies are crowded together in unsanitary housing, sometimes given inadequate food and veterinary care, and taken away from their mothers at an early age to be sold through brokers or dealers. Because of the conditions in which they have been raised, these animals frequently have health problems. According to an article in the July–August 2007 issue of a magazine published by Best Friends, an animal welfare group, animal welfare organizations estimate that between 4,000 and 5,000 puppy mills exist in the United States. Some contain more than 1,000 breeding dogs.

Animal protectionists say that the USDA's lax enforcement of the AWA has allowed puppy mills to continue. They also have criticized the American Kennel Club (AKC) for accepting money from breeders to certify the ancestry of purebred dogs regardless of the animals' health, a practice that they say encourages puppy mills. Some animal welfare groups have worked for the passage of federal or state laws that would force more strict control of dog breeding, such as specifying how many litters a mother dog would be allowed to have each year. (In puppy mills, female dogs are kept pregnant almost constantly.) The AKC has expressed disapproval of puppy mills, but it opposes laws that restrict breeding and states that establishing the health of a dog is the buyer's responsibility. Several states have passed "lemon laws" that require businesses that sell dogs to replace, pay for treatment of, or refund the purchase price of any dog found to have a serious disease or congenital defect soon after purchase.

Animal protectionists' criticism extends to pet stores, which are not covered by the AWA. PETA launched a campaign against the large pet store chain PETCO in 2003, for example, but ended it in April 2005 after PETCO agreed not to sell large birds, such as parrots and cockatoos, in its stores. PETA claimed that such birds are exceptionally stressed by captivity. Some animal protectionists disapprove of pet stores because, they say, people should adopt homeless animals from shelters rather than adding to pet overpopulation by buying specially bred animals in stores.

CRUELTY TO COMPANION ANIMALS

State animal cruelty laws differ in their level of detail, but all specify to some degree the kinds of animals protected, the actions prohibited, the mental state required to establish liability, and the uses of animals that are exempted. Most do not cover socially approved uses of animals, such as killing certain animals for meat or using them for experiments in licensed laboratories.

However they are defined, laws against animal cruelty have resulted in few prosecutions and even fewer convictions. One estimate in the late 1990s stated that about 50,000 complaints of cruelty are probably filed in the United States each year, but they produce only about 500 prosecutions and 50 convictions. When a conviction does occur, punishments are usually what many animal protectionists consider woefully inadequate. Even the most egregious examples of animal torture and murder have been classified as misdemeanors in many states, punishable by seizure of the animals plus a fine or, at most, perhaps a year in jail.

In the last 10 or 20 years, however, thanks in part to the activities of animal protection groups, the public has become much less tolerant of companion animal abuse. This change in opinion was shown clearly during a nationally publicized California case in 2000, in which animal rights groups and concerned citizens established a $120,000 reward for the identification and capture of a man who threw a woman's dog into traffic, causing its death—a far greater sum, critics pointed out, than was offered for information on most kidnapped children. The man was eventually found, arrested, convicted, and given the state's maximum sentence for cruelty to animals, three years in prison. In 1998, a Wisconsin judge meted out an even harsher sentence, a prison term of 12 years, to a man who had tortured and killed numerous kittens and puppies. By April 2006, 43 states, the District of Columbia, Puerto Rico, and the U.S. Virgin Islands classified severe animal abuse as a felony.

Sociologists and law enforcement officers, meanwhile, are paying increasing attention to abuse of companion animals because research has shown that many people who become serial killers or other violent criminals as adults abused animals as children. The relationship between cruelty to animals and violence to humans remains complex and poorly understood, but evidence for some link between the two has become strong enough to warrant the founding of programs in which animal control officers, law enforcement officers, and social workers cooperate to uncover cases of childhood animal abuse and obtain psychiatric help for young offenders. In addition, experts say that animal abuse often occurs in the same households as child abuse and domestic violence, and the discovery of any one of these crimes should prompt a search for the others.

Britain's Animal Welfare Act, which became law in England and Wales on November 8, 2006, goes well beyond (critics say too far beyond) punishment of obvious cruelty, attempting to prevent animal suffering before such suffering occurs. The Department of Environment, Food, and Rural Affairs (DEFRA), the government department that introduced the bill, called it the most significant animal welfare legislation since the Protection of Animals Act, which was passed in 1911. The Animal Welfare Act applies not only to pets but to all vertebrate animals, including farmed animals (although it focuses on nonfarmed animals)—but not, to the dismay of animal rights activists, to animals used in research. Supporters of the exclusion say that the welfare of these animals is protected by other laws.

The new British law boosts penalties for animal cruelty and neglect to a maximum of 51 weeks in prison, a fine of £20,000, or both. More expansively, it states that keepers of animals have a legal duty to do everything reasonable to ensure the welfare of those animals, including providing them with a suitable environment, a suitable diet, and housing that allows them to be either with or apart from other animals as their needs dictate. It guarantees all vertebrate animals "five freedoms": freedom from hunger and thirst; freedom from discomfort; freedom from pain, injury, and disease; freedom from fear and distress; and freedom to express normal behavior. Critics such as George F. Will, writing in the February 13, 2006, issue of *Newsweek*, complain that these "freedoms," originally defined by the European Union's Farm Animal Welfare Council, comprise one more than the "four freedoms" that U.S. president Franklin D. Roosevelt granted to human beings in a famous 1941 speech. Opponents of the new British law fear that it will allow the RSPCA and the police to invade citizens' privacy to search for even minor infractions in treatment of their pets.

Issues in Animal Welfare and Animal Rights

SHELTERS FOR HOMELESS COMPANION ANIMALS

Unfortunately, many potential companion animals do not have human guardians. They may be born on the streets, run away or become lost, or be surrendered or abandoned by people who can no longer keep them or have simply grown tired of them. According to one estimate, some 8 million to 12 million dogs and cats arrive at pounds or shelters in the United States every year. (Facilities for homeless animals are often called pounds when they are managed by cities and shelters when they are managed by private groups, but in reality the two often overlap, as when cities hire local SPCAs or humane societies to run their animal control facilities.) These facilities, originally set up in the early 1800s to prevent public nuisances and the spread of diseases such as rabies by rounding up stray dogs, began to be overwhelmed with animals in the years following World War II, when postwar prosperity allowed the pet population to burgeon.

In an attempt to stem the growing tide of homeless dogs and cats, shelters started aggressive adoption outreach programs. In addition, in the late 1970s, the animal welfare groups that ran many shelters began to promote the idea that companion animals should be spayed or neutered as early in their lives as possible. Since the operations (spaying especially) were expensive, some shelters opened low-cost spay and neuter clinics to help low-income people afford them. This action produced an outcry from veterinarians, who felt that the shelter groups were unfairly using the tax advantages of their nonprofit status to offer services at a lower price than the veterinarians could. Some veterinarians, as well as some pet owners, also questioned whether sterilization was good for the animals.

Today, virtually all animal protection groups, and many people who adopt companion animals as well, agree that the animals should be sterilized. Veterinarians now say that the operations can be safely performed when the animals are as young as eight weeks old, so many shelters sterilize even the youngest animals before making them available for adoption. Alternatively, shelters may require adopters to sign a contract promising to have the animals neutered within a certain time period or even to pay a deposit, which is returned when the adopters present a signed certificate from a veterinarian saying that the operation has been done. No state law forces owners to spay or neuter their animals, but at least 30 states require all animals adopted from shelters or pounds to be sterilized. (Some groups have urged the passage of legislation that would prohibit the breeding of dogs and cats until shelter populations are considerably reduced, but this move has not been popular.) In addition to sterilizing animals turned in to them, some shelters work with feral cat colony caregivers to have adult feral cats sterilized and rereleased and kittens collected for socialization and adoption.

Spay/neuter campaigns have had a substantial effect on the companion animal overpopulation problem, especially in reducing the population of very young animals, but they have by no means eliminated it. In addition to promoting spaying and neutering, therefore, many shelters now seek ways to keep more adopted animals in their existing homes. They may guide people to landlords who accept pets, help to pay animal care costs for low-income families or senior citizens, provide dog training programs, or hire animal behaviorists to work with owners to find solutions to problems such as barking, house soiling, and clawing furniture.

Once animals are turned in to a shelter or picked up by animal control officers and taken to a pound, their lives are likely to be short. If an animal is not reclaimed by its original owner or adopted by a new one within a week or two, it probably will be euthanized, even if it is healthy. Estimates say that more than half of the animals turned in to or collected by pounds and shelters—4 to 9 million a year—are killed there.

In an attempt to change this depressing state of affairs, some animal welfare organizations around the mid-1980s began to establish no-kill shelters, in which animals, once accepted, remain until they are adopted—no matter how long that takes. These shelters keep their populations at a manageable size by limiting the number of animals they accept, taking only the most adoptable ones, and usually rejecting those that are old, ill, or have behavior problems. The no-kill shelter movement is still relatively small—an estimate in late 2006 stated that out of about 5,000 shelters in the United States, a mere 800 were considered no-kill—but it is growing.

Perhaps surprisingly, not all animal rights or welfare groups support no-kill shelters. Critics such as PETA say that these shelters simply force someone else, such as a pound, to do their killing for them or indirectly encourage owners to abandon the animals that the shelters reject. Even the "lucky" animals that the shelters accept may spend months or years in small, barren cages if they are not adopted quickly.

More controversially, rather than euthanizing animals considered unadoptable, some shelters sell such animals to laboratories for research or education, or to dealers who, in turn, sell them to laboratories. Supporters of this practice say that since the animals are slated to die anyway, they might as well benefit science first, but because of fears, justified or otherwise, about what might be done to animals in a lab, many shelter organizations and members of the public oppose this practice. By early 2003, 14 states had passed laws barring shelters from selling animals directly for research or education. Even in those states, however, shelters can still sell to "middleman" animal dealers.

THEFT OF COMPANION ANIMALS

The dealers who buy animals from shelters are classified by the AWA as class B dealers, meaning that they buy animals from "random sources" rather than breeding them specifically for sale as so-called class A dealers do. The AWA stipulates that class B dealers must be licensed by the USDA and must keep careful records showing the sources of their animals, but animal rights groups such as the American Anti-Vivisection Society claim that these records are sometimes incomplete or falsified.

Animal rightists say that some class B dealers or the "bunchers" they buy from (who are not licensed or inspected by the USDA) do not limit themselves to purchasing animals from shelters. According to these critics, bunchers may send people masquerading as families, sometimes complete with children, to claim animals described in "free to good home" advertisements, or they may steal pets outright. Shelters and pounds as well as animal protection organizations estimate that hundreds of thousands of pets are stolen each year, and Patricia Jensen, a former USDA assistant secretary, stated in 1996 that laboratories' (usually unknowing) use of "stolen and fraudulently acquired pets . . . [is] one of the most egregious problems in research."[54] The National Association for Biomedical Research, however, says the accusation that laboratories frequently buy stolen animals is a "myth."

The latest attempt to counteract misappropriation of pets for use in laboratories was the Pet Protection Act, passed in 1990. This amendment to the AWA requires pounds and shelters to hold animals for at least five days before selling them to dealers. (Dealers were already required to hold animals for five days, but owners are not likely to know where to find animal dealers, whereas shelters and pounds are easy to locate.) Some state and local laws also specify holding periods. These laws are seldom enforced, however, and, even on the rare occasions when conviction is obtained, penalties are small.

Because of class B dealers' often dubious sources, as well as the fact that the genetics and health of the animals they supply are unknown, many laboratories avoid such dealers, and animal protection groups and even some USDA officials have recommended that this category be eliminated entirely. The Society for Animal Protective Legislation, a division of the Animal Welfare Institute, has urged Congress to pass the Pet Safety and Protection Act, a federal law that would prohibit class B dealers, unlicensed individuals, and pounds from selling dogs and cats to laboratories. Researchers defending class B dealers, however, say that small scientific facilities often cannot afford to buy purpose-bred animals from class A dealers. Furthermore, they point out, requiring laboratories to buy research animals only from breeders unnecessarily adds to the overpopulation of cats and dogs.

ANIMALS IN AGRICULTURE

Although 19th-century anticruelty laws such as Britain's Martin Act forbade farmers to beat cattle or other farm animals, they did not regulate the way the animals were raised or the methods by which those intended for meat or other destructive uses were killed. Concern about these issues arose only in the 1950s and 1960s, following the growth of large, intensive farms after World War II. Today, many animal rights activists see the issue of animals in agriculture as equally or perhaps even more important than the ever-popular subject of animals in research.

RAISING OF FARM ANIMALS

The Food and Agricultural Organization of the United Nations (FAO) stated in its *Livestock Report 2006* that the world's people consumed 244,000,000 metric tons of animal meat in 2002, the most recent year for which statistics were available. In 2004, according to the National Agricultural Statistics Service, the United States alone slaughtered 9,310,023,000 animals for food, including 31,515,000 cattle, 98,416,000 hogs, and 8,895,748,000 chickens. The number of fish and other aquatic creatures being raised for food is also substantial.

Animal rightists claim that most of these animals, along with others being raised for eggs, milk, and fur, live under abysmal conditions. One of the first descriptions of these conditions appeared in a 1964 British book called *Animal Machines*, in which Ruth Harrison described life on what she called factory farms:

> *The old lichen covered barns are being replaced by . . . industrial type buildings into which the animals are put. . . . The sense of unity with his stock which characterizes the traditional farmer is condemned as being uneconomic and sentimental. . . . The factory farmer . . . uses new systems . . . which subject the animals to conditions to which they are not adapted . . . characterized by extreme restriction of freedom, enforced uniformity of experience, the submission of life processes to automatic controlling devices and inflexible time scheduling.*[55]

Farms of the type Harrison described began to replace the classic family farm of Old MacDonald and childhood readers in the United States and other developed countries in the late 1940s, when agricultural and shipping technology advanced and a rising population increased the demand for meat. Today they are becoming common in certain developing countries, as well as China. A study of world livestock production systems published by the FAO in 1996 estimated that 79 percent of the poultry, 68 percent of the eggs, and 39 percent of the pork produced worldwide came from intensive farms. These large farms permit economies of scale and efficiency that make their survival possible on the low profit margin that exists in agriculture.

Although interpretations of the conditions' effects differ, the nature of the conditions under which animals are raised on intensive farms usually is not disputed. For instance, egg-laying hens are housed in wire cages with three to six birds to a cage, allowing each hen about 55 square inches of space. By comparison, the cover of a big-city telephone book is about 102 square inches. The cages, few of which contain nesting material, slant downward slightly so that the hens' eggs can roll onto a conveyor belt for easy removal. The cages are stacked in rows and tiers to make a huge battery that may hold thousands or even tens of thousands of birds. A layer house, or warehouse full of such batteries, may contain 80,000 hens.

Once a year the hens are forced to begin molting, or dropping their feathers, usually by being deprived of food, water, and sometimes light for several days. Molting, during which the hens do not lay eggs, is a natural part of the birds' yearly cycle. The purpose of forcing it is to make all the hens molt at once and make the process last as short a time as possible so that its effect on egg production is minimized. Kept on this schedule and bred for high production volume, battery hens may lay 280 or more eggs a year, as opposed to the 12 to 20 eggs that hens would lay during the same period in their natural state.

Most of the eggs are sold, but some are kept to produce new chickens. Since they cannot be egg layers, males are killed almost immediately after birth. Females, which will become new laying hens, usually have the ends of their beaks and sometimes their toes cut off with a hot blade so that they will not be able to peck or scratch one another, a natural aggressive tendency that can develop into cannibalism in the close confines of the battery cages.

Broiler chickens—those intended to be sold as meat—are bred from different lines and raised on different farms. Most are males. They, too, are kept in huge warehouses, with 10,000 to 20,000 birds in a building. Unlike laying hens, they are not caged, but instead stay on the floor of the warehouses. Broiler chickens are genetically selected to grow rapidly and reach a relatively large weight, four to five pounds, in about six weeks. Broiler breeders, which produce new broilers, are kept much like broilers except that, as with laying hens, their beaks and toes are trimmed to prevent aggressive behavior. To prevent fertility problems associated with the obesity to which they are genetically prone, they are often fed very restricted diets.

Cattle, too, lead lifestyles that depend on the purpose for which they have been bred. Those intended for consumption as beef are usually males. A few weeks after birth they are branded and castrated, and the buds on their heads that would normally grow into horns usually are burned so the animals will not develop weapons that can be used against other cattle or people. Anesthesia is seldom used during these procedures. The cattle are allowed to graze in pastures for about nine months, after which they are shipped to feedlots for "finishing." Some 10,000 animals may be crowded together on the packed dirt surface of a feedlot. For several months the cattle in feedlots are fed high-calorie corn and soy meal, sometimes treated with growth promoters, to make them gain weight rapidly. When they reach their market weight of 1,000 pounds or so, they are sent to slaughter.

Dairy cattle (of which there were 9,005,000 in the United States in 2005) are treated differently from beef cattle. Cows on some large farms are allowed to graze in pastures, but many dairy cattle spend part or all of their time in packed dirt lots or concrete-floored stalls, where they are mechanically milked two or three times a day. They must be made pregnant once a year to keep their milk flowing, but their calves are removed right after birth.

Male calves born into a dairy herd are either killed at birth or raised as veal. Animal rights groups publicizing the treatment of veal calves, with pictures of calves imprisoned without bedding in stalls so small that the animals could not lie down or turn around, caused considerable public outrage in the 1980s. The animal rightists also reported that the calves were deliberately fed iron-poor diets to make them anemic so that their flesh would remain desirably pale. This kind of treatment is still legal in the United States, but veal producers say that calves today are less tightly confined, fed adequate diets, and kept under more sanitary conditions.

Pigs have their own version of intensive farming. Like broiler chickens, they are kept in large, warehouselike buildings. Sows, or female pigs, used for breeding (and therefore kept pregnant or nursing almost constantly) spend most of their adult lives in gestation stalls (when they are pregnant) and farrowing crates (in the weeks around the time they give birth), some of which are so narrow that they cannot turn around. Their piglets, if they are male, are castrated about two weeks after birth. The teeth of both males and females are clipped and their tails are cut short, or docked, to keep them from injuring or being injured by other pigs. Nonbreeding pigs spend about 20 weeks in a growing building or sometimes in a pasture before being sent to slaughter. The growing buildings usually lack bedding and have slatted floors so that the animals' manure can fall into a pit below.

As intensively farmed animals go, sheep and lambs lead a relatively easy life. They are the only major food animal still allowed to live normally outside for most of their lives.

Not all farmed animals are raised for food, of course. Sheep provide wool as well as meat, and other animals, primarily mink, a relative of the weasel, are farmed for their fur. Mink and other fur animals, such as foxes, are usually raised in pens or cages, then killed and skinned.

Efforts to control problems resulting from intensive farming conditions can sometimes create other problems. Crowding, for instance, can make animals unusually susceptible to disease because of easy transmission of microorganisms and to immune suppression due to stress. Many intensive farmers therefore dose their animals with antibiotics, both to prevent disease and to stimulate growth by allowing the animals to digest their feed more completely. In the late 1990s, the World Health Organization and the U.S.

National Academy of Sciences' National Research Council reported studies showing a link between the use of antibiotics in food animals and the development of antibiotic-resistant bacteria in those animals. The Animal Health Institute, a trade organization for the makers of animal health care products, says that the National Research Council study found the incidence of human disease caused by such bacteria to be very low. Animal rights groups and other critics of the practice reply, however, that these bacteria can easily pass their resistance genes to other bacteria that cause human illness.

Intensive farmers also sometimes give animals hormones or other substances to promote growth and productivity. An article in the January 5, 2002, issue of *Science News* stated that two-thirds of the beef cattle in the United States were given hormones for this purpose. According to the Humane Farming Association, which opposes the practice, bovine growth hormone (BGH) was given to 30 percent of dairy cows in the United States in 2000 to increase milk production. These measures, combined with genetic selection for economically desirable traits, have proven very effective, but animal rights organizations say that they also increase the likelihood of disability and illness in the treated animals.

Pigs and broiler chickens bred for fast growth and laying hens and dairy cattle bred for high output, the Animal Protection Institute says, often become so heavy or develop such fragile bones that walking becomes painful or even impossible. The likelihood of lameness is increased by the bare concrete or slatted floors common in animal warehouses and by the packed dirt of paddocks and feedlots. Dairy cows treated with BGH are more likely than others to develop mastitis, a painful udder inflammation. Pigs genetically selected for fast growth and leanness are highly excitable and, therefore, are likely to damage themselves or suffer stress reactions during transport. Turkeys must be artificially inseminated because the males are too fat to mate normally. "One of my biggest concerns is the possibility that producers are pushing animals beyond their biological limits," writes livestock expert Temple Grandin.[56]

Animal rights groups claim that intensive farming causes unimaginable suffering. Close confinement and crowding prevent animals from indulging in natural behaviors, resulting in boredom, frustration, and abnormal aggression. This aggression, in turn, must be prevented by physical mutilations such as debeaking and dehorning, which can produce lifelong pain.

Some intensive farming practices also endanger human health, animal rightists say. In addition to the possible increase in drug-resistant bacteria caused by feeding healthy animals antibiotics, they point out, a deadly human brain disease may have sprung up because some ranchers in Europe and North America fed cattle feed that contained the ground-up remains of other cattle and sheep. In the late 1980s, a form of fatal brain infection called bovine spongiform encephalopathy (BSE), dubbed "mad cow disease" by the media, became widespread in Britain, where the use of such feed was common. The disease, caused by poorly understood malformed proteins called prions, proved to be spread when cattle ate brain or nerve tissue in animal feed that had come from animals with the illness.

Worse still, the British government admitted in March 1996 that about 10 people had died of a similar disease, called variant Creutzfeldt-Jakob disease in humans, and they might have caught it from eating beef from cattle afflicted with BSE. Rancher Howard Lyman's warnings that the disease might also appear in the United States caused a group of Texas cattlemen to sue him and Oprah Winfrey, host of a 1996 television talk show on which he appeared, for product defamation. (The suit failed.)

By the end of 2006, 162 people in Britain had died of variant Creutzfeldt-Jakob disease. At least 23 people had died of the disease elsewhere in the world as well, including one in the United States in 2004. That patient, however, was thought to have contracted the disease in Britain, where she grew up.

Once it became clear that "mad cow disease" was widespread and could occasionally be transmitted to humans, Britain quickly outlawed the use of ruminant remains in cattle feed, and in August 1997 the United States and Canada did so as well. U.S. agriculture officials admit, however, that only about 75 percent of ranchers complied with the ruling at first. (They claim that more than 99 percent had complied by 2003.) Furthermore, the disease takes years to develop, and cattle that could have eaten tainted feed before the ban were still alive in the early 2000s. Critics of this feeding practice, and of intensive farming in general, thus were not surprised when a cow with BSE was discovered in Alberta, Canada, in May 2003 and another, also apparently born in Canada, was found in the state of Washington in December 2003. Even more disturbing to U.S. citizens, the Department of Agriculture confirmed in June 2005 that a cow born and raised in Texas had died of BSE—the first native case of the disease. Four other BSE cases have also been identified in Canada.

Reports about the Canadian animals led to widespread concern both in the United States and abroad. Some 30 countries, together making up about 90 percent of the U.S. beef export market, halted their importation of American beef within a week of the December 2003 report. (The United States, similarly, had banned importation of Canadian beef after the May 2003 report.) Although they admitted that the U.S. cow had been processed as meat before its illness was diagnosed and recalled some meat, government officials played down the risk to the human food supply, as well as announcing numerous changes in testing and slaughtering rules aimed at eliminating future threats. Nonetheless, numerous animal rights and vegetarian groups seized on this highly publicized occurrence as another reason why people should give up eating meat.

Trade organizations such as the American Meat Institute say that animal rightists exaggerate the problems caused by intensive farming. Many of the worst conditions the animal groups cite, they claim, occur on only a small number of farms or no longer occur on any farms. Industry organizations such as United Egg Producers (UEP), a trade organization that represents 85 percent of egg producers in the United States, maintain that the way animal facilities are managed has more effect on animals' welfare than the type of housing used. Furthermore, the trade groups say, there is no verifiable way to tell what emotions—if any—intensively farmed animals experience.

Animal rights organizations never mention the positive features of intensive farming, supporters of the practice point out. Keeping animals indoors protects them from weather, attacks by predators, and some diseases. Intensive farming technology has produced more nutritionally balanced feeding and more effective veterinary care than was possible on traditional farms. Confinement systems can be kept cleaner than open lots. Confining hens or pigs in separate enclosures protects them from attacks by other animals and ensures that each receives an appropriate amount of food. Farrowing stalls keep sows from accidentally crushing their piglets. Industry trade groups point out that the American Veterinary Medical Association approves of most of the practices that animal rightists criticize, including beak trimming and stalls or tethers for sows, as long as they are monitored carefully. Farmers have a powerful economic incentive to keep their animals healthy and productive, these supporters say, and therefore will care for the animals as well as possible.

Canadian animal welfare professor David Fraser and his coauthors, writing in *The State of the Animals: 2001*, may provide the best summary of the situation. "Proponents of each of these highly simplified [pro and con] views can cite facts and examples to support their claims," they say, "yet neither one provides an adequate or accurate description of animal agriculture."[57] Even within a small region, they point out, farms and agricultural practices can be quite diverse.

ATTEMPTS TO CHANGE CONDITIONS ON INTENSIVE FARMS

For the most part, animal rights groups have had little success in persuading state or federal governments to regulate, let alone ban, intensive farming practices in the United States. Both federal laws such as the AWA and most state animal cruelty laws specifically exempt animals in agriculture treated in accordance with "normal practice."

There have been a few exceptions. Florida passed a law banning sow gestation stalls in 2002—the first U.S. law to limit means of confining farm animals—and, after a fierce contest between animal rights groups and the meat and livestock industries, voters in Arizona did the same in November 2006. The Arizona measure, which also outlawed veal crates for calves but did not affect farrowing stalls, will not take effect until the end of 2012. On April 27, 2006, too, the city council of Chicago passed a measure barring the sale of the gourmet delicacy foie gras. Foie gras is made from the livers of geese or ducks force-fed grain to make their livers fatty, a practice that animal welfare groups decry as cruel.

Animal rightists have had better luck in using public opinion to persuade businesses to require certain changes. Some of the groups' most effective campaigns have targeted large restaurant and supermarket chains, particularly fast food chains such as McDonald's. These campaigns publicized the alleged misery of factory farmed animals and urged the public to boycott the chains unless the chains insisted that their meat suppliers make certain improvements in the conditions of the animals they raise. Following such campaigns, McDonald's issued revised guidelines for its suppliers in August 2000, and Burger King and Wendy's did likewise in June 2001.

In its August 2000 settlement, McDonald's agreed to buy eggs only from producers who do not use starvation to force molting and who provide 72 square inches of space for each hen in a battery cage. Wendy's also agreed to these conditions, as well as requiring that chickens be stunned with electricity before they are slaughtered. Meanwhile, in October 2000, UEP issued new guidelines that promised to gradually increase the size of battery cages by up to 40 percent, make debeaking less painful, and develop ways to force molting without starvation. Al Pope, then president of the organization, said the guidelines were issued partly in response to animal rights protests but chiefly because "it is the right thing to do" and "will benefit the industry in the long run."[58] The McDonald's and UEP guidelines were similar, although McDonald's demanded that the changes be implemented sooner than UEP wished.

Animal rights groups' crusade against fur farming and the fur trade has also been cited as one of the movement's success stories. Beginning in the 1970s, organizations such as PETA waged attention-getting campaigns against the wearing of fur, using tactics ranging from pictures of supermodels such as Naomi Campbell saying (and showing, to a limited extent) that they would rather go naked than wear fur to spraying red paint on the fur coats of women in the streets. The protests appeared to work. There were more than 1,200 mink farms in the United States in 1968, for instance, but by 2003 the number had dropped to 307. However, it is not really clear whether the apparent decline in fur use in the United States is due to a change in public feeling brought about by the rights organizations or simply to changes in fashion. The International Fur Trade Federation claimed that global sales of fur in 2005 were valued at $12.77 billion, representing an increase of 9.1 percent over the previous year and marking the seventh yearly increase in a row.

Europe has been a more fertile ground than the United States for legislative control of intensive farming. As far back as 1964, in response to Ruth Harrison's book about "factory" farming, the British Parliament set up a committee to investigate conditions on intensive farms. The so-called Brambell Committee's report, issued in 1965, set standards for treatment of farm animals and inspired Parliament to pass the Agriculture (Miscellaneous Provisions) Act in 1968, which put some of these standards into law.

The European Union (EU) has banned hormonal growth promoters since 1988 and BGH since 2000. Switzerland outlawed battery cages for laying hens in 1991, and Sweden did the same in 1998; the EU decided in 1999 to phase out such cages in all member nations by 2012. Britain banned crates for veal calves in 1990 and confinement for sows in 1999 and, in 2003, even passed a law requiring farmers to put balls in pigsties to give the animals "environmental enrichment." Sweden, Finland, and the Netherlands have made sow gestation crates illegal, and the EU is phasing them out on a schedule similar to that for battery cages. The EU has agreed to ban forced molting outright and phase out veal crates by 2007. Britain outlawed fur farming in November 2000.

On January 23, 2006, the European Commission adopted the ambitious Community Action Plan on the Protection and Welfare of Animals. The plan, which covers the years between 2006 and 2010, features a number of steps that would affect the welfare of farm animals, including upgrading of current minimum welfare standards, more careful inspection of farms, and help for developing nations in improving their treatment of livestock. Specific parts of the plan address treatment of broiler hens, maximum journey times for animals in international transport, and use of certain types of fur, including cat and dog fur. Representatives of some member countries complained that implementing the plan would be too expensive for farmers, however, and in June, agriculture ministers from eight member states blocked adoption of a resolution that would have supported the plan.

Future success of efforts to modify intensive farming in either Europe or the United States is likely to depend on animal rights groups and the animal agriculture industry being willing to meet each other halfway. Such compromise may be hard to achieve. Some industry spokespeople claim that the rightists' ultimate agenda is not merely improving conditions for farm animals but completely destroying animal agriculture, and some rightist groups admit to this. PETA spokesman Bruce Friedrich, for instance, says that PETA will not be satisfied until "no corporations are serving up animal products."[59]

Because they feel that animal rights organizations will not compromise with them, some animal industry members take a hard line against the rightists' attacks. A few have tried using lawsuits to stop criticism, but so far these attempts have not been very successful. In 1998, after seven years of litigation in the so-called McLibel case, a judge in England ruled against McDonald's, which had sued two London activists for libel for distributing pamphlets that accused the chain of the "torture and murder" of millions of animals.[60] The judge said that the activists had not proved all their claims, but a number of the factory farming practices they described could be considered cruel. Similarly, when cattlemen sued American talk show host Oprah Winfrey and others under a Texas food disparagement law after a guest on a 1996 Winfrey program warned of possible health dangers from American beef, allegedly causing a sharp drop in beef prices, a jury acquitted the defendants in 1998 because they concluded that the guest's claims, while possibly exaggerated, were not false.

Other representatives of both sides of the animal agriculture controversy are willing to work toward compromise goals, if only because each side has faced the fact that the other is not going to go away. Animal rights groups realize that, whatever they might desire, most people are not likely to stop eating or wearing all animal products. Similarly, the agriculture industry understands that, whether justified or not, public concern about how farm animals are treated can have a significant effect on its sales figures, and it hopes that voluntarily making changes will help it avoid what it sees as overly restrictive government regulation. Some industry members also agree with animal agriculture expert Temple Grandin, who stresses that humane treatment is profitable as well as moral: "Good stockmanship can improve productivity of pigs and dairy cattle by more than 10 percent," she writes, and "costs very little."[61]

Whatever their motives, animal agriculture and related industries are continuing to develop both improved practice standards and better methods of making sure the standards are followed. For instance, in 2003 the National Chicken Council adopted a new list of best practices and an audit checklist, and the American Meat Institute made a similar change in 2005. The USDA's Agricultural Research Service is working on new ways to measure and control stress in farm animals. Animal agriculturists are trying to design more humane housing for confined animals, such as cages for laying hens that are not only roomier but include perches, nest boxes, and nesting material. Improvements in electronic systems may allow dairy cows to be kept in open pens and come into milking stations at will to be milked by robotic milkers.

Some animal rights groups, in turn, are telling people that if they must eat meat, they should buy it from sources that treat their animals relatively well. Consumers can purchase "organic" or "free-range" meat at health food stores, for instance, or buy meat from farms with verified high standards of animal care. The American Humane Association has created a "free farmed" label to designate food that comes from animals raised under conditions deemed likely to leave them free of fear, stress, and disease and able to enjoy normal behaviors and the companionship of other animals. However, some critics both within and outside the animal rights movement say that terms such as *free range* can be unclear or misleading and that it is often hard to determine which methods of keeping animals actually contribute to improved animal welfare.

Regardless of who instigates them, improvements in farm animal care are likely to raise the cost of meat and other animal products. Commentators disagree on both the probable amount of increase and the willingness of consumers to accept it. "In 1999 we succeeded in having sow stalls banned [in Britain], and the extra cost now for a meal that includes pork or ham is less than a penny," maintains Peter Stevenson, political and legal director of the British anti–factory farming group Compassion in World Farming.[62] On the other hand, an executive of a leading hog-producing company in the United States said that British pork producers were "decimated" by the ban because retailers imported cheaper meat from countries with less strict welfare standards and consumers bought it. UEP said in 2005 that converting all laying hen facilities to cage-free housing, a typical change demanded by animal rights groups, would cost between $3 billion and $5.8 billion—and it is by no means clear that such costs could be successfully passed on to consumers. In a survey published in 2004 by the National Corn Growers Association, only 31 percent of those surveyed said they would pay even 5 percent more than they currently do for meat and poultry in order to obtain products labeled "humanely raised."

TRANSPORTATION AND SLAUGHTERING

The only two federal laws that apply directly to farm animals affect them near the end of their lives. The first law, the Twenty-eight-Hour Act, governs shipping of live animals to feedlots and slaughterhouses. It grew out of the fact that in the late 19th century, when shipping livestock by railroad for long distances first became common, cattle, sheep, and pigs were jammed together into boxcars and sent on journeys of three to six days, usually without food, water, or bedding. Not surprisingly, by the time they arrived at slaughterhouses, 30 to 40 percent of these animals were already dead, and most of the others were in poor condition.

When newspapers in Boston and Chicago publicized this situation, animal welfare organizations such as the Massachusetts Society for Prevention of Cruelty to Animals, as well as some members of the public, demanded changes. In 1873, therefore, after two years of debate and resistance from representatives of the railroad and livestock industries, Congress passed a law requiring that cattle, sheep, and pigs be rested and given access to food and water on any rail or ship journey that lasts more than 28 hours. In *Animals and the Law*, Jordan Curnutt explains that this was the first federal law intended, at least in part, to mitigate cruel conditions for animals.

The Twenty-eight-Hour Act was revised and expanded in 1994 to cover "vehicles" in general rather than just railroad cars, regulate conditions during loading and unloading, and specify five hours for the rest period. In November 2006, at the urging of the Humane Society of the United States, the USDA confirmed that the term *vehicles* includes trucks. As with most other federal laws affecting animals, the USDA's Animal and Plant Health Inspection Service (APHIS) has the job of enforcing this law. The law appears to be enforced rarely, and fines for violation are minor. It does not apply to poultry.

The second federal law governs slaughterhouses. In a normal slaughterhouse, cattle or pigs are run along a chute into a restraint device where each animal is supposed to be stunned (rendered unconscious), usually by a blow to the head. It is then hoisted by its legs onto a conveyor line and killed by having its throat slit, causing it to bleed to death within seconds. In the first half of the century, however, stunning methods were sometimes ineffective, resulting in animals being bled out or even occasionally dismembered or skinned while still conscious.

Animal welfare groups such as the Humane Society of the United States, as well as prominent senator Hubert Humphrey, protested against this state of affairs, and in 1958 their complaints finally produced passage of the Humane Slaughter Act, which required that pigs, cattle, and sheep be made unconscious by some rapid method before being cut, chained, hoisted, or knocked down. The law was revised and somewhat expanded in 1978, at which time it became the Humane Methods of Slaughter Act. It is enforced by a branch of the USDA called the Food Safety and Inspection Service (FSIS).

Articles published in the *Washington Post* in 1997 claimed that the Humane Methods of Slaughter Act was being violated routinely. Since then, however, Congress has increased the USDA's budget for slaughterhouse inspections, and large meat purchasers such as the McDonald's fast food chain have demanded improvements. A 2001 audit of 44 beef plants and 20 pork plants revealed that almost all animals were successfully stunned the first time, and animal handling expert Temple Grandin said in 2006 that the figure was then 99 to 100 percent. Grandin added that she had seen more improvement in slaughterhouse treatment since 1999—when McDonald's began auditing meat suppliers to enforce its new guidelines—than in the preceding 25 years of her career.

The Humane Methods of Slaughter Act does not apply to animals killed by the methods of Jewish (kosher) and Muslim (halal) ritual slaughter, which require animals to be conscious at the time of killing, and some animal rights organizations say that this exemption has permitted unnecessary abuse. On November 30, 2004, PETA released a video that it said had been taken secretly at AgriProcessors, Inc., in Postville, Iowa, the largest kosher slaughterhouse in the world. (AgriProcessors claimed that most of the video in fact could not have been filmed at their plant.) The video showed cattle being shocked with electric prods and having their tracheas (windpipes) and esophaguses ripped from their throats while they were fully conscious. Although the USDA says that when properly done, the throat-slitting method of Jewish religious slaughter renders cattle unconscious within seconds, animals in the videotape sometimes appeared to live and have some awareness for up to three minutes after their throats were cut. The Jewish Orthodox Union, which certifies AgriProcessors as kosher, and USDA put pressure on AgriProcessors to correct its procedures, and after an audit in 2005, the USDA concluded that it had done so satisfactorily.

Animal rightists have also complained that the Humane Methods of Slaughter Act does not cover another practice of which they disapprove, the killing of "downer" animals—those too sick or injured to walk into a slaughterhouse on their own. The animals are pushed, carried, or dragged to slaughter, causing great suffering, according to groups such as Farm Sanctuary. In the early 2000s the National Cattlemen's Beef Association maintained that less than 1 percent of cattle slaughtered for meat were downers and that most downer cattle did not suffer from conditions that made them a threat to the food supply, and for years the cattle and meat industries successfully fought off animal rights groups' attempts to persuade Congress to ban the use of downer cattle as meat. On December 30, 2003, however, a week after a slaughtered downer cow in Washington State was found to have BSE ("mad cow disease"), which may be transmissible to humans who eat meat from sick animals, Agriculture Secretary Ann Veneman announced that downer cattle would no longer be allowed to enter the human food supply.

Techniques involved in slaughtering chickens, which, as the USDA confirmed in September 2005, are not covered by the Humane Methods of Slaughter Act, have also aroused controversy. The standard method of stunning the birds before slaughter uses electrical current, but PETA, HSUS, and some other animal rights organizations say that this technique is often ineffective, leaving some birds still conscious when their throats are slit or even when they are thrown into baths of scalding water to remove their feathers. These groups have urged the substitution of controlled-atmosphere stunning, which uses a mixture of gases to render the birds unconscious by depriving them of oxygen. After a review of both techniques, however, McDonald's Corporation decided in July 2005 that the two were equally acceptable. The review stated that the World Organisation for Animal Health (OIE) had come to a similar conclusion. Meanwhile, HSUS and five poultry consumers filed suit against the USDA in December 2005 in an attempt to force it to include poultry in the protections granted by the federal slaughter law.

Most other industrialized countries have laws similar to the Twenty-eight-Hour Act and the Humane Methods of Slaughter Act, some of which were passed or strengthened because of massive public protests. Such protests broke out in Australia in the 1980s and in Britain in 1995, for example, following publicity about the stressful conditions during long-distance (especially overseas) transport of live animals. On November 22, 2004, the European Council adopted a new regulation on the protection of animals during international transport, which introduces stricter rules for journeys of more than eight hours and inaugurates more efficient monitoring techniques, including checks on vehicles by means of a satellite navigation system. Further EU-wide restrictions on transport were made in May 2006. The World Organisation for Animal Health, meanwhile, established the first worldwide standard for animal transport on May 25, 2005. The standard also covers treatment during slaughter.

ANIMALS IN SCIENCE

Australian sociology professor Lyle Munro writes that "for many people inside or outside of the [animal protection] movement, . . . experimentation [on animals] remains the most important moral dilemma, as well as the most controversial question."[63] It is also, after cruelty to working and companion animals, the issue that has concerned the movement longest.

RESEARCH

Ancient Greek thinkers such as Hippocrates made the first systematic explorations of anatomy and helped to lay the foundations of Western medicine more than 2,000 years ago by performing surgical experiments on living animals, a practice called vivisection. Vivisection was common in Rome and, after languishing during the Middle Ages, revived during the Renaissance. Major medical advances such as English physician William Harvey's discovery of the circulation of the blood, which he first described in 1628, grew out of vivisection (Harvey cut open dogs, snakes, and deer captured in hunts by his friend and patron, King Charles I). By the early 18th century, research on animals was widespread in Europe.

Concern about vivisection began in Britain in 1875, when a scientist named George Hoggan published an account of his time in the laboratory of famed French physiologist Claude Bernard that included descriptions of Bernard's many painful experiments on unanesthetized animals. When the RSPCA refused to take a strong stand against vivisection, several animal protectionists formed a new group, the Victoria Street Society for the Protection of Animals from Vivisection, specifically to combat the practice.

In 1876, following the recommendations of a commission set up by Queen Victoria, Parliament passed the Cruelty to Animals Act, the first law to regulate the use of animals in research. It required anyone planning to experiment on living vertebrates to obtain a license from the home secretary, which would be granted only after the experimenter described the laboratory and proposed procedures and showed that the research would be likely to produce significant new medical knowledge.

Antivivisectionist societies were also established in the United States, but they failed to obtain any legislation against the practice, and interest in the subject faded away after World War I. Then, just as happened with animal agriculture, a surge of activity brought on by the prosperity following World War II revived American concern about vivisection. In this case the activity was government-supported medical research, and its rise produced a corresponding increase in the demand for laboratory animals. By 1957, U.S. laboratories were using some 17 million animals a year, and their activities were almost completely unregulated. No federal law covered laboratory animals, and, like farm animals, they were explicitly exempted from most state anticruelty laws.

Then, as now, the vast majority of laboratory animals were rats and mice, but some were cats and dogs, and researchers began to ask pounds and shelters to supply these. When some private shelters refused to surrender their animals, groups such as the National Society for Medical Research persuaded several states and cities to pass laws requiring them to do so. The American Humane Association (AHA), then the largest animal welfare organization in the United States, made little attempt to fight these pound seizure laws, so some disaffected AHA members left to form more active groups such as the Animal Welfare Institute (1951) and the Humane Society of the United States (1954).

These organizations had little luck in reversing the pound seizure laws or obtaining any other research regulations, however, until a case in which a Pennsylvania family's dog was stolen and sold to a laboratory received considerable publicity in 1965. A few months later, in February 1966, an exposé in *Life* magazine revealed the filthy conditions under which one animal dealer kept dogs before selling them. The combination of these two events caused the American public to flood Congress with more letters than it was receiving about civil rights or the Vietnam War. Faced with this outcry, legislators quickly passed the Laboratory Animal Welfare Act (LAWA), which became law in August 1966.

Perhaps not surprisingly given its background, the LAWA was designed chiefly to protect family pets. It focused on animal dealers, requiring them to obtain licenses from the USDA, which was given responsibility for enforcing the law (after 1972 this duty fell to APHIS), and to keep records of all dogs and cats they sold. The law also ordered the secretary of agriculture to "promulgate standards to govern the humane handling, care, treatment, and transportation of animals by dealers and research facilities" but stated that no rules were to be made affecting the handling or care of animals "during actual research or experimentation."[64]

Congress expanded LAWA in 1970 and renamed it AWA. Among other things, the new law required the USDA to monitor records and perform inspections to verify that facilities were meeting the act's standards of animal care. The USDA set forth those standards in regulations issued in 1972.

Public concern about the conditions under which animals are kept in laboratories and about the nature of the experiments carried out on them skyrocketed in the early 1980s because of two widely publicized scandals, both centering on videotapes made clandestinely inside laboratories by members of animal rights groups. The first of these horror stories began in May 1981, when Alex Pacheco, who had recently joined Ingrid Newkirk in founding PETA, obtained a volunteer position in Dr. Edward Taub's laboratory, part of the Institute for Behavioral Research in Silver Spring, Maryland. In an effort to discover whether regrowth of nerves and perhaps restoration of function was possible following injuries or strokes, Taub had cut nerves leading from the spinal cords to the arms of macaque monkeys so that the animals could no longer feel pain or other sensations in the limbs. He then tried to force the monkeys to use the numbed limbs (over which they still had muscle control) to see whether such use would stimulate regrowth in the cut nerves.

APHIS had inspected Taub's laboratory, as the AWA required, and had found it to be in compliance with the law. Pacheco, however, saw the monkeys living under what he described as truly horrible conditions.

The smell was incredible. . . . I saw filth caked on the wires of the cages, feces piled in the bottom of the cages, urine and rust encrusting every surface. There, amid this rotting stench sat seventeen monkeys, their lives limited to metal boxes just 17 ¾ inches wide.[65]

Perhaps worst of all, the monkeys apparently no longer recognized their treated limbs as part of their bodies and had viciously bitten and chewed them, producing wounds that often became infected and were left untreated.

Working alone in the laboratory at night, Pacheco videotaped the monkeys and their miserable surroundings. He also brought in local primate experts to witness what he had seen. He then took his film, notes, and the experts' sworn statements to local police. On September 11 the police searched the laboratory, confiscated 17 monkeys, and charged Taub with 17 counts of animal cruelty, one for each monkey—the first time a federally funded researcher had been charged under a state animal cruelty law. Taub was convicted of six counts of animal cruelty in December 1981, but the convictions were overturned on appeal in 1982 and 1983, partly because the higher courts ruled that the animals' sufferings were not "unnecessary or unjustifiable," as the law required, but rather were part of the "purely incidental and unavoidable pain" that can occur during research.[66]

The second scandal, revealed in a similar way, took place at the University of Pennsylvania's Head Injury Clinical Research Laboratory in Philadelphia in

1984. In this case the incriminating videotape was made by the researchers themselves. Members of ALF stole 60 hours of it when they broke into the laboratory in May, and PETA edited the footage into a half-hour documentary, which it distributed widely. The PETA video (which researcher Adrian Morrison calls "cleverly edited" and "grossly distorted") showed live baboons being used essentially as crash test dummies, with helmets glued to their heads and then struck with pistons.[67] It also pictured the baboons being operated on without anesthesia, under clearly nonsterile conditions, while the surgeons smoked pipes and cigarettes. For many viewers, the most unsettling aspect of the footage was the apparently callous attitude of the experimenters and technicians, some of whom were shown making fun of the writhing animals.

Public outrage about these two high-profile cases played a part in persuading Congress to expand and toughen the AWA in 1985. The new amendments, collectively called the Improved Standards for Laboratory Animals Act, emphasized the importance of "minimiz[ing] pain and distress" to animals during experiments.[68] It also mandated exercise programs for dogs and "a physical environment adequate to promote the psychological well-being of primates."[69]

Finally the 1985 AWA amendments required institutions using animals to set up Institutional Animal Care and Use Committees (IACUCs) to review proposals for all new experiments that used animals and to monitor ongoing experiments and the overall care of animals in the institution. Each committee was to have a minimum of three members, one of whom was a veterinarian and one of whom was a person who represented "general community interests in the proper care and treatment of animals" and was not affiliated with the institution or related to anyone who was.[70] Animal rightists, however, have complained that people with ties to their organizations are very rarely chosen to serve on IACUCs and that IACUC meetings or their records are seldom open to the public. "Their effectiveness in screening inappropriate, redundant, and/or inhumane experiments is questionable," animal rights advocate Martin Stephens maintains.[71]

In general, animal rights groups have not been happy with either the AWA's standards or the USDA's enforcement of them. In the 1990s, for instance, some groups filed a series of petitions and lawsuits aimed at forcing the USDA to remove a controversial feature of its 1972 AWA regulations that explicitly excluded rats, mice, and birds from coverage by the law, even though these species make up about 85 to 95 percent of all vertebrate animals used in laboratories. The USDA claimed that it lacked the funds and staff to handle the paperwork and inspections that covering this huge number of animals would require. Furthermore, it said, including rats, mice, and birds in the AWA was unnecessary because their care was already regulated by guidelines published by the Public Health Service and the National Institutes of Health, which all federally funded researchers must follow.

The groups' early lawsuits were thrown out, either directly or on appeal, because the organizations could not demonstrate standing to sue, but in September 2000 a district court judge granted standing to one plaintiff, a student who worked in a college psychology laboratory and claimed aesthetic injury from seeing mistreatment of the rats there. After the USDA's legal counsel advised the agency that a judge might well rule against it if the suit came to trial, it settled the suit out of court by promising to remove the controversial exemption. Former Secretary of Agriculture Dan Glickman, writing in the *Journal of the American Medical Association* in February 2001, claimed that the USDA's decision "was in the best interest of all involved . . . and will not jeopardize important research,"[72] but an opposing article in the same issue called the move "a complete capitulation . . . to the demands" of the rights groups.[73]

Before the animal rightists had finished celebrating, scientists and others who supported the use of animals in experimentation, represented by such groups as the National Association for Biomedical Research (NABR), persuaded Congress that this change would drown researchers in paperwork, cost $280 million or more per year, and impede research necessary to improve human health. The legislature therefore blocked the proposed alteration, first for a year and then, in May 2002, permanently. Animal rights groups have vowed to continue fighting for the change.

Even when the law is held to apply, enforcement can be lax. A 2005 report from the USDA's Office of the Inspector General (OIG) complained that the eastern region management of the Animal Care division of APHIS, which is responsible for inspecting laboratories to discover violations of AWA, had cut its referrals of suspected violators to the Investigative and Enforcement Services (IES) unit by more than half between 2002 and 2004. Even when cases were referred, the IES often either took no action against the reported violators or assessed fines that the OIG considered "minimal." The OIG also stated that the inspections made by the agency's veterinary medical officers were frequently incomplete.

As with intensive farming, public feeling against the use of animals in experiments has been stronger in Europe than in the United States, and legislation has been more strict and appeared sooner. Britain began to regulate laboratory animal use 90 years before the United States did, for example. In 1986 that country replaced its 1876 act with the Animals (Scientific Procedures) Act, which covers all experiments using vertebrates, including rats and mice, and this act was further expanded in 1999. Numerous commentators have said, approvingly or otherwise, that British regulations governing use of laboratory animals are the most comprehensive in the world.

In 1986, the same year that Britain passed its new act and a similarly rigorous law took effect in West Germany, the EU approved the Animal Experiments Directive (86/609/EEC), which established uniform animal welfare provisions for all member countries and required member countries to develop legislation promoting alternatives to laboratory animal use. In June 2002, after 10 years of debate, Germany went even further by becoming the first EU country to guarantee protection to animals in its constitution. (Switzerland, which is not a member of the EU, passed a constitutional amendment in 1992 that recognized animals as beings rather than things.)

Making regulation of animal experiments more stringent may backfire, however. Some British scientists have complained that the rules governing experiments in that country are so complex and bureaucratic that they force animal researchers to go elsewhere, to Britain's scientific and economic loss. Similarly, a firm called Bridge Pharmaceuticals has established a market in helping United States–based drug companies outsource their animal testing to China, where they are welcomed eagerly. Glenn Rice, Bridge's CEO, says that his company adheres to U.S. standards for animal welfare when carrying out research overseas, but representatives of both Chinese and U.S. animal rights groups claim that China is a popular destination for animal research because its standards are relatively lax and it muzzles protesters who might complain about animals' treatment.

The issue of animal use in science continues to produce confrontational rhetoric on both sides. The more extreme animal rightists maintain that the use of animals in science, like every other human use of animals, is simply wrong, no matter how great its potential benefit for humans. "Even if animal research produced a cure for AIDS, we'd be against it," says PETA's Ingrid Newkirk.[74] Not surprisingly, statements such as Newkirk's produce equally intransigent reactions from some scientists. For instance, Frederick Goodwin, a former director of the National Institute of Mental Health, has said that attempting to compromise with animal rightists is a mistake because they see doing so as an admission of guilt.

Both sides of the debate often present arguments that rely on science (as they interpret it) as well as emotion. Animal rights groups claim that experiments and drug tests on animals are invalid and even dangerously misleading because of biological differences between animals and people. They point out that some widely used drugs such as aspirin are poisonous to animals but not to humans, for instance, and other drugs have passed animal tests but have later had to be withdrawn because they proved to have dangerous side effects in people. They say that lack of supporting evidence from animal studies held up campaigns linking smoking and lung cancer in the late 1950s and early 1960s, long after clinical studies of human patients strongly suggested such a link. "Not a single animal test has gone through a validation process [to demonstrate relevance] to human health," claims Jessica Sandler, a spokesperson for PETA.[75]

Scientists who support animal research, on the other hand, say that two-thirds of the Nobel Prizes in physiology or medicine were awarded for discoveries that grew at least partly out of experiments on animals. Major scientific organizations, including the Institute of Medicine of the National Academy of Sciences and the American Medical Association, also unequivocally support the use of animals in research. Scientists admit that comparisons between animals and humans are not perfect, but most maintain that the anatomy and physiology of mammals are similar enough to make animal experiments a highly accurate means of testing drugs and learning about diseases. To be sure, this line of reasoning brings up what animal rights philosopher Peter Singer calls the researcher's central dilemma:

> *Either the animal is not like us, in which case there is no reason for performing the experiment; or else the animal is like us, in which case we ought not to perform an experiment on the animal which would be considered wrong if performed on one of us.*[76]

Animal rightists also claim that most of the health gains of the last hundred years have come about because of improvements in sanitation and diet, not because of the drugs and vaccines developed through animal experiments. Similarly, they believe that scientists who wish to improve human health today should concentrate more on methods of disease prevention, such as lifestyle changes, than on the creation of new drugs or other treatments. Animal research supporters such as Adrian Morrison and Frederick Goodwin reply that many preventive methods, like methods of treatment, were and are developed on the basis of animal experiments.

Responding to accusations that they are indifferent to the suffering of the animals they use, some researchers admit to being emotionally torn when they must hurt or kill animals. Others point out that, whatever their feelings, they have practical incentives to use as few animals as possible and to treat them gently. Animals are expensive, they say, and animals that are excessively stressed or sick with any disease other than the one being studied are worthless as experimental subjects. "We have to have them in exquisite health," says Michael Hayre, vice president of comparative medicine at St. Jude Children's Research Hospital in Memphis. "Any stress in the animal will throw off the study results."[77]

One issue within the subject of animal research that has proved particularly difficult to settle is the use of primates (monkeys and apes), particularly great apes such as chimpanzees, in medical experiments. On the one hand, these animals' close biological similarity to human beings makes them seemingly essential for certain types of experiments. Chimpanzees, for instance, are the only nonhuman animals that HIV, the virus that causes AIDS, will infect, so a number of them have been used in attempts to develop a vaccine against the disease. (They do not actually develop AIDS, however. Animal rightists say this fact makes them useless for studying the disease, but some scientists feel that discovering how they are able to resist the virus could be very valuable.) On the other hand, these animals' intelligence and seemingly humanlike emotions and behaviors make many people see experimenting on them as perilously close to experimenting on, say, brain-damaged children. Chimpanzees are also endangered in the wild, which makes capturing them for use in experiments problematic at best.

Because of these concerns, most European countries, Japan, and New Zealand have banned research on chimpanzees, and most other countries are trying to phase out ape experiments. Countries that regulate animal research, including the United States, usually have particularly strict rules about housing primates, including requirements for their psychological well-being such as allowing contact with other members of their species and providing objects for play. In December 2000, Congress passed the Chimpanzee Health Improvement, Maintenance, and Protection (CHIMP) Act, which authorizes the secretary of health and human services to set up and operate a system of sanctuaries to which chimpanzees no longer needed for research can be "retired." Animal rightists have criticized this act, however, because it allows the animals to be reclaimed for further experiments if there is a good scientific reason for doing so. The USDA reported that 54,998 nonhuman primates were used in experiments in 2004.

In June 2007, the National Center for Research Resources (NCRR), part of the National Institutes of Health, announced that it would no longer breed chimpanzees for research. This ruling, prompted (the agency said) by the high cost of caring for the animals, made permanent a moratorium on breeding that had existed since 1995. An article about the decision that appeared in *The Scientist* online on June 5 stated that NCRR owned or supported about half of the estimated 1,000 research chimpanzees remaining in the United States. NCRR said that it would continue to pay for the care of these animals.

PRODUCT TESTING

A second way of using animals in science, product testing, has also been the subject of major animal rights campaigns. The U.S. Food and Drug Administration (FDA) and similar agencies in most other industrialized countries require drugs and other medical treatments to be tested on animals before being tried on humans. Even when animal tests are not legally required, as is the case with most cosmetics and household products, many companies use them as a way to guarantee the safety of their products and protect themselves against lawsuits. Products are often tested for acute toxicity (their ability to act as poisons with immediate effects) and the ability to irritate the eyes and skin. Product testing today accounts for between a fifth and a quarter of all animals used in science. Most of these animals are used to test drugs.

Animal Rights

In the 1970s, almost all safety testing of products was done on living animals, using several standard procedures. The usual test for acute toxicity was the LD50 ("lethal dose for 50 percent") test, in which groups of about 100 animals (usually rats) were given (usually by force feeding) varying doses of the test substance until half of one group died. The other animals were killed after two weeks so they could be autopsied to determine sublethal toxic effects of the substance. This test, invented in Britain in 1927, produced numerical data from which the toxic dose of a substance could be computed. It was popular because it was easy to carry out and produced the kind of quantitative data that regulatory agencies liked. However, its critics have said that it not only causes great suffering in the animals but is too crude to provide much useful information.

The two standard irritancy tests were called Draize tests, after their inventor, John Draize of the FDA, who created them in the 1940s. In the skin irritation test, a patch of skin on the body of a rabbit was shaved and then scraped to create a slight abrasion. The substance being tested was placed on a piece of gauze and taped over the abrasion. The spot was examined for redness, blistering, or other signs of irritation after one day and again after three days. In the Draize eye irritation test, rabbits were restrained in devices that kept them from touching their heads, and the tested material was placed in their eyes. The eyes were examined at varying intervals, ranging from one to seven days, to find out whether they were irritated. (Signs of irritation could range from mild reddening to complete destruction of the eye.) Rabbits were preferred for this test because, unlike humans and many other mammals, they have no tear ducts to produce fluid that can wash irritating substances out of their eyes. Like the LD50 test, the Draize tests have been criticized for their inaccuracy as well as their cruelty.

Animal rights activist Henry Spira established the Coalition to Abolish the Draize Test in the late 1970s. In 1980, the group targeted Revlon, the leading company in the cosmetics industry, by placing a full-page advertisement in the *New York Times* showing a rabbit with bandaged eyes and asking, "How Many Rabbits Does Revlon Blind for Beauty's Sake?" Most readers had never heard of these tests and were shocked to learn about them. After further campaigns and an outpouring of letters from the public, Revlon and several other cosmetics companies agreed not to test new products on animals. Spira's campaign, which grew to involve 400 animal protection organizations, also generated more than $1.75 million in funding for research into alternatives to animal tests within its first year. Probably largely because of Spira's and similar campaigns, use of the Draize test fell by 87 percent during the 1980s.

Campaigns against the testing of cosmetics and household products on animals continued to be successful during the 1990s. Gillette agreed to stop testing its products on animals in 1997, and Mary Kay Cosmetics and Procter and Gamble followed suit in 1999. The LD50 test has been refined to reduce the number of animals used and to use nonfatal doses, and increasing numbers of government regulatory agencies are accepting nonanimal alternatives to this and other animal tests for nondrug products. Britain, Austria, and the Netherlands have banned all testing of cosmetics on animals, and in January 2003 the EU voted to ban all such tests and the sale of cosmetics tested on animals anywhere in the world by 2009.

Nonetheless, some companies still test cosmetics and household products, or ingredients that go into such products, on animals. The HSUS estimates that safety testing of chemicals and consumer products accounts for 10 to 20 percent of laboratory animal use in the United States, amounting to 2 to 4 million animals a year. Furthermore, some regulatory agencies still require or at least encourage animal tests for certain products. Neither the FDA nor the Consumer Product Safety Commission, another U.S. government agency, require animal testing for most cosmetics or household products; however, the FDA insists on such tests for eye care products as well as drugs, and the Consumer Product Safety Commission accepts (but does not insist on) animal tests for some toxic products.

A third government agency, the Environmental Protection Agency (EPA), was the focus of a major campaign by animal rights groups. In 1998, the agency asked manufacturing companies to provide health and environmental safety information for 2,800 high-production-volume (HPV) chemicals—those manufactured at the rate of 1 million pounds or more per year. These substances are everywhere in the environment, the EPA said, yet many of them have never been tested in ways that meet current safety standards, or else data from the tests is not available to the public. Companies could fulfill the agency's request either by releasing existing test data or by performing new tests.

PETA and other animal rights organizations attacked the EPA proposal, claiming that tests it requested would kill 1.3 million animals. The groups also stated that standard animal tests were unreliable and that "modern, reliable, non-animal tests are available but are being ignored."[78] On this issue, as on some others such as wildlife management, animal rights and environmental protection organizations have found themselves on opposite sides, since many environmental groups feel that at least some animal tests of potentially toxic chemicals are necessary. "We would prefer that a small number of lab rats are used to save the rest of us," Gina Solomon, a senior scientist with the National Resources Defense Council, said in 2002.[79]

Responding to the animal groups' pressure, the EPA and the Clinton administration agreed in late 1999 to permit nonanimal tests in part of the EPA program, to provide funding for development and validation of non-animal tests, and to delay acute toxicity testing for two years so that alternatives to the LD50 test could be developed. Animal rights organizations are still critical of the program, however, maintaining, for instance, that many proposed new tests are unnecessary because the information demanded by the EPA already exists in some form. PETA and others have tried to use lawsuits to stop the HPV testing program, but they were not successful. A 2005 article in the *Washington and Lee Law Review* stated that, although the EPA agreed to change the rules of its HPV Challenge program to minimize the amount of animal testing it required, tests on animals remained a substantial part of the program's testing protocol.

EDUCATION

The use of animals in education, which accounts for about 10 percent of all laboratory animal use, is also controversial. College, high school, and sometimes even elementary school students are frequently required to dissect the bodies of animals such as frogs in their biology classes, and some medical and veterinary students practice surgical and medical techniques on living or dead dogs and other animals. The HSUS estimates that about 6 million vertebrate animals are dissected each year in U.S. high schools alone. Most of the animals are frogs, which are usually taken from the wild. Most of the remaining corpses or body parts come from animals that would have been killed anyway, such as euthanized dogs and cats (or those scheduled to be euthanized) from pounds and parts of cattle, sheep, and pigs from slaughterhouses.

Many animal rights groups maintain that killing animals for educational purposes is unnecessary, and some students have protested or even sued to be relieved of dissection requirements because they felt that killing an animal in order to dissect it was morally wrong. Several states now require that students be allowed to use alternative methods, such as "virtual dissection" computer programs, if they ask to.

Opinions differ, however, about whether these alternatives are as effective as actual dissections. "Repetition is the most important aspect of learning, and you can only dissect an animal once," Jonathan Balcombe of the Physicians Committee for Responsible Medicine points out.[80] However, the National Association of Biology Teachers and the National Science Teachers Association say that real dissection still has its place in schools. "Dissection gives students a unique opportunity to observe how animals are structured to function the way they do," says Adrian Morrison, a strong supporter of the use of animals in science.[81] Similar differences of opinion exist about computer programs or other alternatives to the use of animals in surgery practice for medical and veterinary students.

THE SEARCH FOR ALTERNATIVES

Just as many animal rights groups would like all eating and wearing of animal products to cease, so many ultimately hope to see all research and testing on animals end. Most of these, however, recognize that neither aim is likely to be achieved in the foreseeable future and, therefore, are willing to work toward lesser but more practical goals. The most commonly accepted path toward reduction of animal use in science and improvement of conditions for animals in laboratories was first laid out in 1959 by two British scientists, W. M. S. Russell and Rex Burch. In *The Principles of Humane Experimental Technique*, Russell and Burch described what they called the "three Rs" of alternatives to animal research: Replace—substitute tests and experiments using such things as cultured cells or computer simulations for tests and experiments on whole animals; reduce—redesign tests and experiments so that they can be performed on smaller numbers of animals; and refine—redesign tests or experiments to cause less pain and distress to animals.

For the most part, both scientists and animal protectionists ignored Russell and Burch's book when it was first published. When the animal rights movement became active in the 1970s, however, some antivivisection groups began promoting the three Rs as a way of weaning scientists and regulators away from reliance on animals.

Some scientists and legislators embraced this approach as well. The governments of the Netherlands and some other European countries began promoting and funding the search for alternatives to animal research as early as the late 1970s. The EU established the European Centre for the Validation of Alternative Methods (ECVAM) in 1991. In the United States, the National Institutes of Health (NIH) Revitalization Act, passed in 1993, ordered the director of the NIH, the federal government's chief research facility, to develop, validate, and support tests that fulfill the three Rs. To carry out this mandate, the NIH established the Interagency Coordinating Committee on the Validation of Alternative Methods (ICCVAM) in 1994. Temporary at first, the ICCVAM was made a permanent standing committee in December 2000. Similarly, the British government opened the National Centre for the Replacement, Refinement and Reduction of Animals in Research (NC3Rs) in May 2004.

Today, the three Rs are a mainstream concept. Most countries' legislation governing laboratory animals incorporates this approach, and most research institutions and IACUCs have written it into their policy. Many regulatory agencies also accept the word of ICCVAM and ECVAM regarding the validity of alternative tests and have substituted nonanimal methods for the LD50, Draize, and similar tests under at least some circumstances. Scientists and businesses such as drug companies are often willing, even eager, to adopt alternative tests because they are usually cheaper, faster, and easier to execute than animal tests. "The beauty of the three Rs is that they provide a way for all parties to work together to advance the cause of both animals and humans," Richard Smith wrote in an editorial in the *British Medical Journal* in 2001.[82]

"The prospects for making steady progress [in having alternatives substituted for animal tests] is very good," Michael Balls, the former director of ECVAM, said in 1999, but he added that "many individuals, especially in government and in animal welfare, have unrealistic expectations of the rate at which progress can be made in replacing current animal procedures."[83] Alternatives work better for some purposes than others. Drug companies find computer programs and cell culture techniques useful for initial screening of possible new drugs, for instance, but tests carried out later in the development of a drug still usually involve animals, to meet regulatory requirements if nothing else. Although some animal rights groups claim that most animal research can now be replaced by methods that do not use whole animals, most scientists disagree. A spokesperson for the National Association for Biomedical Research, for instance, says, "Many of the processes that occur within the human body remain too complex to be simulated by a computer or a cell culture."[84]

In addition to replacing animal tests with ones that do not use animals and reducing the number of animals needed in certain tests, scientists are trying to refine experiments on animals by developing better ways to define, measure, and relieve pain and stress, including stress caused by inadequate housing. For one thing, they increasingly recognize that stress can change animals' physiology enough to invalidate the results of some experiments. University of California, Davis, animal behaviorist Joseph Garner, for one, maintains that animals kept in barren conditions show signs of actual brain damage. Hanno Wurbel of the Institute of Laboratory Animal Sciences in Zurich adds:

> *It took some time for scientists to realize that using 'dirty' animals [animals exposed to disease-causing microorganisms] can compromise the validity of experiments. Today, we are about to realize that the same could hold true if we use animals with impaired welfare. It is time to improve housing conditions for scientific, if not for ethical reasons.*[85]

Even identifying pain and stress, let alone determining the most effective ways to minimize them, can be difficult, however. For one thing, as Jane Salodof MacNeil points out in an April 2004 issue of *The Scientist*, prey animals such as mice tend to hide distress so that they will not appear vulnerable to predators. Enriching laboratory animals' environments can cause problems when scientists attempt to compare recent experiments with older ones in which animals lacked the enrichment, MacNeil says. Experts also disagree on whether an enriched environment—or which type of enrichment—really makes animals "happier."

At least partly because of the new emphasis on alternatives, the number of animals used yearly in experiments declined sharply. In the United States, according to the Foundation for Biomedical Research's citation of USDA statistics, the number of dogs used in research declined by 61 percent, the number of cats by 62 percent, and the number of rabbits by 35 percent between 1973, about the time laboratory animal use is thought to have peaked, and 1998. Similar decreases occurred in Britain, Germany, the Netherlands, and Switzerland.

Nonetheless, an estimated 50 to 100 million animals are still used in some 50 million research and testing procedures worldwide each year. The USDA reported that 1,101,958 mammals other than rats and mice were used in the United States in 2004; if rats and mice make up about 90 percent of total research animals, the total would be a little more than 11 million animals— not counting birds and invertebrates such as worms and fruit flies.

Statistics indicate, furthermore, that in the early 2000s the number of animals used in research in developed countries such as Britain has started to rise once again. Much research in the rapidly growing field of biotechnology and genetic engineering, for instance, is done on mice, including transgenic mice, which have been engineered to carry genes from other species, usually humans. According to the Coalition for Medical Progress, a British group that supports research on animals, 33 percent of animal experiments done in Britain in 2004 involved transgenic or genetically modified animals, of which 96 percent were mice (almost all the rest were fish). REACH (Registration, Evaluation, and Authorisation of Chemicals), an EU-wide program for chemical testing that was adopted by the European Commission on October 29, 2003, and is scheduled to begin in 2007, may also demand the use of millions of animals.

On the other hand, new genetic technology may also offer more ways around animal experiments. DNA microarrays, or "chips," which contain hundreds or even thousands of short strands of DNA that act as probes for different genes, are held to be a likely tool for toxicity testing, for example. Even more advanced are "animals on a chip," silicon or plastic wafers containing cells from different organs or tissues of a particular species, connected by fluid "blood"; these could be used to test the effects of new drugs on different parts of the body. New methods of freezing and storing mouse embryos could allow special genetic strains to be preserved that way rather than by breeding stock, thus greatly reducing the number of adult animals that must be housed in laboratories. New methods of imaging and recording data from animals without operating on or killing them could also reduce suffering.

ANIMALS IN ENTERTAINMENT

What could be more wholesome and innocent than a day at the circus or a zoo? Plenty of things, animal rights supporters say. Many animal rights organizations claim that animals in circuses are abused to make them perform tricks for the public and, in between performances, spend their lives in confining, uncomfortable cages. Some zoos provide better habitats for their animals than others, the groups admit, but they believe that no benefits in even the best zoos justify keeping wild animals in captivity. There is even less excuse, they believe, for most other forms of animal "entertainment," such as animal fighting, rodeos, and even racing. "To treat animals as objects for our amusement is to treat them without the respect they deserve," states a fact sheet published by the animal rights magazine *Animals Voice*.[86] Nonetheless, many people continue to enjoy being entertained by animals and say that doing so can have educational as well as aesthetic value.

ANIMAL FIGHTING

Watching animals fight each other (or humans), and often betting on the outcome, has been a popular form of entertainment since ancient times. Most people have read about the Roman emperors' famous displays of lions and other beasts in arenas such as the Circus Maximus (from which the term *circus* comes). Ordinary people could not afford lions, but in many societies they enjoyed watching pairs of dogs or roosters (the latter often with knife-sharp spurs, called gaffs, tied to their legs) fight one another in open pits. Bullbaiting, in which dogs were allowed to attack a bull tethered to a stake, was the target of the world's first attempt at passage of an anti–animal cruelty law, proposed in Britain in 1800. Opponents defeated the measure, arguing that ending this "sport" would deprive the working class of one of its few forms of amusement. Bullbaiting, however, was finally outlawed in Britain in 1835.

Most people in North America and Europe today, whether animal rightists or not, disapprove of animal fighting. The Protection of Animals Act outlawed all animal fighting in Britain in 1911. Animal fighting is also prohibited by the federal Animal Fighting Venture Prohibition Act, a 1976 amendment to the AWA, although an exception is made for cockfighting in states where it is legal.

Other laws forbid specific types of animal fighting. Cockfighting is illegal in all U.S. states except Louisiana and New Mexico, and it is a felony in 28 of those states. Watching a cockfight is also against the law in about 40 states, and a federal law that took effect on May 14, 2003, makes "knowingly sell[ing], buy[ing], transport[ing], deliver[ing], or receiv[ing] a bird in interstate commerce for purposes of participation in a fighting venture" punishable by a fine of up to $15,000 and/or a jail term of up to one year. Cock breeders may get around this law by claiming that they breed their birds only for bird shows, however, and cockfighting remains popular enough in some U.S. cultures to make breeding and fighting, by some estimates, a multimillion dollar industry. Similarly, dog fighting is illegal in all 50 states and a felony in most, yet it is still a common underground activity.

Animal rightists point out that in addition to causing obvious pain and injury to the animals—the losers, if not killed outright, are often abandoned to die of their wounds—fighting, at least in the case of dogs, presents potential danger to humans as well, since dogs bred to fight other dogs (a process that often involves systematic abuse) are also likely to attack people. Certain breeds used frequently for fighting or aggressive guarding, such as pit bulls (bull terriers), have become so notorious that some cities, such as Denver, Colorado, ban anyone from keeping them. Some dog owners and animal protectionists have protested such breed-specific legislation, emphasizing that dogs of any breed can be gentle and loving if given proper training and socialization.

RODEOS

Some people see rodeos as exciting contests of cowboy skill and a symbol of America's wild frontier past, but animal rights groups say that rodeos are almost as hard on animals as fighting. In roping contests, calves or even full-grown steers are brought to a sudden halt and then thrown to the ground, sometimes breaking bones or dislocating joints. Leather straps tied tightly around their loins irritate horses and bulls into bucking so that riders will face a thrilling challenge in trying to stay on them.

The Professional Rodeo Cowboys Association (PRCA), which oversees major rodeos and sets standards for the treatment of animals during them, claims that injury to animals in modern rodeos is uncommon. The group has done its best to eliminate some cruel practices, such as the addition of spikes to bucking straps (indeed, it requires that the leather straps be padded to minimize tissue damage). However, animal rightists point out, less than half of all American rodeos are accredited by the PRCA or any other standard-setting organization.

Most animal rights groups would like to see rodeos legally banned, but they have had little success in obtaining such legislation. Rodeos are exempt from the AWA, and no other federal law affects them, although the Twenty-eight-Hour Law applies to the transportation of animals to and from rodeos. No one connected with rodeos apparently has ever been convicted of violating this law or any state animal cruelty law. Only two states, Rhode Island and Ohio, regulate rodeos.

SHOWING AND RACING

Animals are not usually visibly injured during horse and dog showing or racing, but some animal rights organizations say that these activities have a hidden abusive side as well. Most notorious was the practice of "soring," in which the high-stepping gait of a breed called the Tennessee walking horse was accentuated by blistering the horses' front legs with chemicals and then wrapping chains or wires around the blisters to irritate them further, making the legs so painful so the animals took their weight off their feet as often as possible. One of the few federal laws specifically governing animals in entertainment, the Horse Protection Act, was passed in 1970 to outlaw this practice. USDA regulations let managers of horse events choose their own soring inspectors, however, and critics say that lax inspection and enforcement allow soring to continue.

In another form of abuse now illegal in many states, live animals, usually rabbits, were used as lures to train greyhounds to race, and the dogs were allowed to tear the animals apart when they caught them. Greyhound racing spokespeople say that live lures are now seldom used, but an investigator from HSUS claimed that 90 percent of greyhound trainers used them in 1991.

One would think that, for economic reasons if nothing else, racing animals themselves would be well cared for, but animal rightists say that this is not always the case. Although the practice is illegal, horses are sometimes given excessive doses of painkillers before a race so they will continue to run even when injured. Between races, dogs or horses may be kept in crowded, unsanitary facilities. Furthermore, except for champions kept for breeding purposes, the lives of racing horses and dogs often come to an abrupt end when the animals stop winning. Some horses go to slaughterhouses, while other, somewhat luckier ones begin "second careers," for instance working in riding stables or pulling carriages for tourists. Greyhounds are usually killed or sold to laboratories after about two years of racing unless they are taken in by protection organizations, which try to find homes for them.

Like rodeos, horse and dog races and shows are exempted from the AWA, although the Twenty-eight-Hour Act governs the transportation of racing animals. Most states leave control of racing to state racing commissions, which are more concerned with gambling at the races than with animal welfare. Racing personnel have rarely been charged under state anticruelty laws and even more rarely convicted.

In the mid-2000s, the greatest racing-related concern of animal rights organizations was the slaughter of horses considered unfit for racing or other activities. Horses are seldom used for human or even animal food in the United States, but there is a strong demand for horse meat in countries such as France, Belgium, and Japan, where people consider it a delicacy. The United States contains three horse slaughter plants, one in Illinois and two in Texas, all foreign-owned, and the USDA says that 91,757 horses were killed there in 2005. Other horses are transported, under what animal protection organizations such as the Society for Animal Protective Legislation (SAPL, a division of the Animal Welfare Institute) say are miserable conditions, to Canada or Mexico to be slaughtered. SAPL claims that the killing methods also are often inhumane.

Rightist groups succeeded in having a bill banning the slaughter of horses for human consumption, the American Horse Slaughter Prevention Act (an amendment to the Horse Protection Act), introduced into the House of Representatives in February 2002. The bill would also prohibit import, export, and interstate trade and transport of horseflesh or live horses for human consumption. The House passed the bill, then HR 503, on September 7, 2006, by a vote of 351 to 40. A companion bill, S 311, was introduced into the Senate on January 17, 2007. The Committee on Commerce, Science, and Transportation reported favorably on it on April 25, but as of mid-2007, the Senate as a whole had not acted on it.

Organizations such as SAPL celebrated the House's action, but meat industry spokespeople and other opponents of the bill say that it would make conditions worse for unwanted horses if it became law. The legislation contains no financial provision for caring for the animals, so many would be neglected or abandoned to die of starvation, they claim. Rights groups say that these problems can be offset by strengthening and enforcing animal cruelty laws and by supporting horse sanctuaries and rescue organizations, which find people who will adopt and care for the horses.

CIRCUSES AND ANIMAL SHOWS

Most people probably think of a trip to the circus as a harmless family outing, but animal rights groups such as PETA say that circuses are anything but harmless to their animals. These organizations claim that many smaller circuses lack the funding, expertise, and sometimes the will to care for exotic animals properly. Furthermore, they point out, even well-cared-for circus animals cannot live in a natural environment or carry out most normal behaviors and social relationships. Conditions are even worse when circuses travel, requiring tight confinement and sometimes other hardships for the animals. "When I look at animals held captive by circuses, I think of slavery," says comedian and social activist Dick Gregory.[87]

Animals in circuses, zoos, and other exhibitions (with the exception of rodeos, races, and dog, horse, and cat shows) are protected by the AWA, but animal rightists say that the law's regulations often are not followed, and the USDA's APHIS lacks sufficient inspectors to check up on exhibition conditions regularly. Animal groups claim that the same spotty enforcement hampers the Twenty-eight-Hour Act, which governs care of exhibited animals during transportation, and state anticruelty laws as applied to circus animals. Animal rights supporters have persuaded a few cities to ban circuses and other exhibitions that include animals, but no states have done so.

Some animal rights groups claim that trainers of performing animals regularly use whips, electric prods, or other pain-inducing devices. Most animal trainers vehemently deny this charge, saying that they train the animals by means of food and other rewards and maintain close, affectionate relationships with them. Sara the Tiger Whisperer, a performer with Ringling Bros. and Barnum & Bailey Circus, says, "I have an awesome relationship with my tigers, and we spend lots of time together even when we're not performing. I do everything I can to make their lives as comfy as possible."[88] If nothing else, trainers maintain, reward is a more effective tool for shaping behavior than punishment, and it is also safer for the trainer.

The truth is almost surely that, as in every other area of human-animal relationships, a wide range of training situations exists. In one highly publicized case, PETA publicly claimed that a popular Las Vegas entertainer, Bobby Berosini, abused the orangutans in his animal act. The animal rights group distributed a videotape taken by a dancer at the hotel where Berosini worked that appeared to show the entertainer hitting one of the animals backstage. In 1989, Berosini sued PETA and other animal rights organizations that had attacked him for invasion of privacy and defamation of character. He claimed that the dancer had deliberately upset the orangutans, making it necessary for Berosini to control them, and that the videotape had been heavily edited to produce a false effect. A jury supported Berosini in 1990, but in 1994 the Nevada Supreme Court ruled that the videotape did show abuse and required Berosini to pay some of the animal groups' trial costs.

On the other hand, a jury in San Jose, California, took less than two hours in December 2001 to bring an acquittal in a PETA suit against Mark Gebel, an elephant trainer for the Ringling Bros. and Barnum & Bailey Circus, who was accused of violating a state law against abusing elephants. A San Jose policewoman and an officer of the Humane Society of Santa Clara claimed that they had seen Gebel strike an elephant with an ankus, or bullhook (a device with a blunted tip that is frequently used for controlling elephants), during a parade in the preceding August. They said they saw a dime-sized red spot, which appeared to be blood, on the elephant's leg shortly afterward. Under cross-examination, however, they admitted that they had not actually witnessed the ankus touching the elephant but had only seen Gebel lunge at the animal. The "blood" spot disappeared after the elephant was bathed, and a circus veterinarian testified that he found no injuries. The attorney representing Gebel and the circus did not even present a defense because, he said, the prosecution's case was so weak that none was needed. The jury apparently agreed, and the jury foreman said afterward that the case never should have been brought to trial.

Several individuals and organizations have established sanctuaries for former performing animals that have been sold after becoming too old, injured, or ill to work. For example, Jonathan Kraft, a former Las Vegas showman, has established a refuge for big cats and other wild predators in the Arizona desert. Carol Buckley, a former circus trainer and performer, has set up the Elephant Sanctuary in Tennessee for Asian elephants. Some sanctuaries are better than others, however. Big Cat Rescue, a sanctuary in Tampa, Florida, warns that only 42 of the thousands of places that claim to be animal refuges are accredited by the Association of Sanctuaries. Some of the others, Big Cat Rescue claims, simply breed big cats and other wild animals for sale at animal auctions or on the Internet.

Some sanctuaries also take in exotic animals that ill-advised people had adopted as pets, usually when the animals were babies, and then either abused or abandoned when the animals grew up and began to be destructive rather than cute. Although private ownership of tigers, lions, and other big cats was banned completely in 12 states and limited or regulated in 25 others by 2006, protection groups such as Big Cat Rescue maintain that adoption of such animals as pets remains widespread, usually resulting in death within two years of adoption for the animals and presenting a significant threat to humans who encounter them as well. The Captive Wildlife Safety Act, an amendment to the Lacey Act that became federal law on December 19, 2003, bans interstate transport of big cats and other large predators for private use as pets, but animal rights groups would like to see private ownership of exotic pets outlawed entirely.

ZOOS

Zoos and aquariums have an even better public reputation than circuses—but Richard Farinato, director of the captive wildlife program of the HSUS, claims it is "a better reputation than they deserve."[89] Many zoos stress the naturalistic environments in which they house their animals, their captive breeding programs for endangered species, and their efforts to educate the public about animals and nature, but animal rightists say that all of these are inadequate at best and actually harmful at worst.

Even critics admit that the best zoos today offer their occupants state-of-the-art veterinary care and nutrition as well as attendance by well-educated, devoted keepers, resulting in a longer life than the animals usually would have in the wild. No matter how well cared for they are, however, a fact sheet published by *Animals Voice* claims that "keeping animals in zoos harms them, by denying them freedom of movement and association, which is important to social animals, and frustrates many of their natural behavior patterns, leaving them at least bored, and at worst seriously neurotic."[90] A study from Oxford University published in late 2003 states that animals with large home ranges in the wild, such as polar bears, elephants, and lions, do particularly poorly in captivity, showing high infant mortality and incidence of pacing, a neurotic behavior.

Following ideas first presented by German zoo builder Carl Hagenbeck in 1907 and Heini Hediger, director of the Basel Zoo in Switzerland, in the

1950s, state-of-the-art zoos try to make their animal habitats as natural looking as possible and offer plenty of room for animals to roam or hide from the public. Landscape architect Grant Jones, who designed the first of these new habitats for Seattle's Woodland Park Zoo in the mid-1970s, called this approach "landscape immersion." As Hediger recommended, it includes features of the animals' native habitat that help them engage in normal behaviors, such as trees for them to rub against or sharpen their claws upon. It is also intended to make visitors appreciate the grandeur of the world's natural landscapes, in which they are supposed to feel immersed.

Critics such as David Hancocks, director of the Open Range Zoo in Victoria, Australia, say, however, that even these naturalistic environments may be more restrictive than they seem. Some are made chiefly of plastic and concrete rather than natural materials. In other cases, the animals are restricted to a small part of these beautiful landscapes by electric fences or other invisible barriers. Even when that is not true, animals may spend much of their time, such as the night hours, "off display" in small holding cages.

Furthermore, plenty of zoos still house their animals in the traditional and depressing barred, barren, concrete-floored cages, limiting their activities so severely that the animals resort to abnormal, stereotyped behaviors such as pacing or chewing the bars. The AWA prescribes minimum housing requirements for zoos as well as circuses and other animal exhibits, and it was the primate housing at a zoo that drove New Yorker Marc Jurnove and others to sue for violation of the AWA in the late 1990s, resulting in the first granting of standing to an individual in an AWA case. The European Commission also has a directive setting standards for zoos, 1999/22/EC, which includes a requirement for research and education programs as well as appropriate housing conditions for the animals.

Zoos say that their captive breeding programs offer one of the best hopes for preserving endangered species, most of which have lost their habitats through land clearing or are threatened by poaching in the wild. Animal rights groups claim, however, that although these programs have reduced the numbers of animals taken from the wild to replenish zoo stock, they are of little use in preserving rare species. Some breeding efforts (such as those for pandas) have failed, requiring importation from the wild to continue. Others are forced to work with a limited pool of animals, contributing to increases in birth defects and genetic problems related to inbreeding.

Still other breeding programs, such as the ones for tigers and other big cats, apparently have been entirely too successful, creating more animals than the zoos can afford to house or exhibit. Richard Farinato of HSUS says there are now more tigers in private hands or unregulated facilities—at least 13,000 in the United States alone in early 2007—than in the wild. Guidelines established in 2000 by the Association of Zoos and Aquariums (AZA), which accredits the most respected zoos, require zoos to give or sell "surplus" animals only to other zoos with AZA accreditation or equivalent standards, but an investigation by *U.S. News & World Report* in 2002 revealed that this does not always happen. Even much-admired zoos such as those in the Bronx (New York) and San Diego (California) sell some animals to substandard facilities or dealers, who in turn may auction them off to roadside zoos, owners of game ranches that provide so-called canned hunts, or people looking for exotic pets.

The AZA began addressing some of these problems in the 1980s with its Species Survival Plan. Even zoo critic David Hancocks admits that the plan has been an overall success and that "animals in accredited zoos are now bred sensibly and wisely."[91] He is not sure how useful even the best breeding programs are in the long run, however, because "the problem is not loss of species but loss of entire habitats and the eradication of complete, functioning, balanced ecosystems."[92] Furthermore, only a small percentage of zoos are accredited by the AZA and follow their regulations.

Richard Farinato also questions the conservation value of zoo-sponsored scientific research, which, he says, "has limited application to the conservation of free-living populations" and chiefly "addresses husbandry techniques or other issues specifically aimed at the management of animals in captivity."[93] However, the AZA says that in 2006, 166 of its member organizations participated in and/or spent more than $16 million on 1,719 conservation, research, and education projects in 97 countries or regions.

Hancocks and other animal rightists doubt the educational benefits of zoos as well. Hancocks says that by emphasizing the colorful and cute rather than trying to present whole natural ecosystems, most zoos produce "a kindergarten view of the natural world" that is "upside down" because it stresses big mammals rather than the tiny invertebrates that constitute the bulk of nature.[94] Zoo critics claim that people can learn more about animals by watching them in their natural habitats on television nature documentaries or reading articles in magazines like *National Geographic* than they can from any zoo or animal show. "What we . . . teach children in a place like Connyland [a marine park in Switzerland that displays captive dolphins] is a lesson in domination, a lack of respect for other living things," says Noelle Delaquis, an animal rights activist who is trying to end the keeping of dolphins in captivity.[95]

Some animal rights groups believe that it would be better to maintain endangered animals in large wilderness reserves or sanctuaries than in zoos, although they do not say where such reserves might be found or created or who would pay for them. Alternatively, David Hancocks suggests, zoos could be redesigned to be part of "natural history institutions that can reveal the connectedness . . . of the natural world," including complex interdependencies between plants and animals.[96] Such institutions, he says, would represent partnerships between traditional zoos, botanical gardens, natural history and geology museums, aquariums, science centers, and even perhaps libraries and art galleries. Some of the most farsighted zoos today, in fact, are pursuing just such a goal.

ANIMALS IN THE WILD

The idea of protecting wild animals for their own sake, like most aspects of what is now called animal rights, is a product chiefly of the late 20th century. It is an outgrowth at least as much of the environmental movement as of the animal rights movement, and it has produced both some of the most striking instances of cooperation and the deepest disagreements between the two.

ENDANGERED SPECIES

The killing of wild animals, especially in the United States, was seldom restricted before the 20th century, and as the country expanded, excesses frequently occurred. Hunters on the Great Plains shot bison ("buffalo") by the millions for meat, hides, and other products. The last passenger pigeons and Carolina parakeets died in zoos in 1914, victims of the fashion for putting feathers on women's hats. Sealers, feeding another fashion of the 1870s, reduced the northern fur seal population in Alaska's Pribiloff Islands, the animals' primary breeding ground, from about 3 million when the United States bought Alaska from Russia in 1868 to about 800,000 by 1890. Whalers made similar incursions into whale populations during the same period.

The threatened or actual extinction of wildlife species, along with loss of their wilderness habitats, began to attract government attention around the end of the 19th century as even some hunters realized that, unless they employed some degree of restraint, their "geese that laid golden eggs" would soon cease to exist. With the encouragement of sport hunters, many of whom were also pioneer conservationists, states started to establish permanent agencies to regulate hunting and manage wildlife populations to produce a sustained yield of game animals for future hunters.

Regulation of hunting and wildlife was at first considered to be the province of the states. The Supreme Court spelled this out in its ruling on an 1896 case called *Geer v. Connecticut*, in which Justice Edward White wrote that each state had the right to regulate its "common property in game" in order to "preserve for its people a valuable food supply," even if doing so affected the movement of animals out of the state.[97] The federal government, however, banned hunting in Alaska's Afognak Island and in Wyoming's Yellowstone National Park in the 1890s, and in 1900 Congress passed the Lacey Act, which prohibited interstate movement of birds or other animals killed or captured in violation of state laws (or parts of their bodies, such as feathers), invoking the federal legislature's constitutional right to regulate interstate commerce. The Lacey Act, one of the first laws to protect nongame species, was an attempt to stop market hunters' wholesale slaughter of birds to provide feathers for women's hats.

This schizophrenic state of legal affairs continued until 1928, when the Supreme Court ruled in *Hunt v. United States* that the federal government could regulate activity on federal lands such as national forests, even if its regulations contradicted hunting laws in the states where the lands were located. The court based this authority on the Constitution's Property Clause (Article IV, Section 3), which states that "Congress shall have the Power to dispose of and make all needful Rules and Regulations respecting the Territory or other Property belonging to the United States." In a second decision, *Kleppe v. New Mexico* (1976), the court extended the power of the Property Clause to wildlife on public land.

Meanwhile, international treaties entered the wildlife conservation picture in the early 20th century. The first one involving the United States was the Fur Seal Treaty of 1911, which was signed by the United States, Britain (for Canada), Russia, and Japan, the four nations responsible for most of the decimation of northern fur seals that had taken place in the late 19th century. In this treaty, the countries agreed not to hunt fur seals on the open ocean, a practice recognized as wasteful because the dead animals usually sank before they could be collected. When the United States signed such agreements, Congress eventually passed laws to implement them within the country. The Migratory Bird Treaty Act, passed in 1918, was the first such law, passed to execute an agreement made with Canada in 1913 to protect nongame migratory birds and limit the hunting of game birds. (No law was made regarding sealing until 1966, when the Fur Seal Act was passed.)

The Lacey Act, the Migratory Bird Treaty Act, and the Fur Seal Act all protected particular groups of species. The same was true of several other federal wildlife laws: the Bald Eagle Protection Act (1940), the Whaling Convention Act (1949), the Wild Free-Roaming Horses and Burros Act (1971), and the Marine Mammal Protection Act (1972). The idea of preserving all endangered or threatened species as such, on the other hand, did not arise until the 1960s, when the writings of Rachel Carson and others made Americans realize the extent to which human activities were destroying not only animals themselves but their habitats through such activities as logging and land clearing.

Extinction—the complete disappearance of particular species—has always been a part of nature, but humans, it appeared, were speeding up tremendously the rate at which extinction occurred. Preservationists argued that some vanishing species might contain materials valuable for medicine or other human uses. More important, they said, all species contribute to the complex interactions that scientists were beginning to recognize in ecosystems, and the loss of biological diversity brought about by the increased extinction rate might doom other species or even whole ecosystems.

Wildlife-oriented animal protection groups such as Friends of Animals joined general-purpose environmentalist organizations in helping to persuade Congress to pass the Endangered Species Preservation Act in 1966, an expanded version of the act in 1969, and, finally, the Endangered Species Act (ESA), which President Richard Nixon signed into law in December 1973. This law states that its purpose is to protect species of plants and animals classified as endangered ("in danger of extinction throughout all or a significant portion of its range") or threatened ("likely to become endangered . . . in the foreseeable future"), along with "the ecosystems upon which endangered and threatened species depend."[98] Although the act was amended in 1978, 1982, and 1988, the 1973 version is still in force today. Jordan Curnutt calls the ESA "the most comprehensive, controversial, and perhaps the most complicated wildlife protection law in the world."[99]

The ESA provides elaborate procedures for classifying a species, subspecies, or population as endangered or threatened. Any species of plant or animal, anywhere in the world, is potentially eligible. In 1973, 109 species were listed; by January 2007, 1,879 species worldwide, including 1,311 found in the United States, were on the list, and only 42 had been removed, including 17 that were considered to be recovered and nine that had become extinct. (The rest were removed because of errors in the data that had led to their being listed.) The law forbids anyone to take ("harass, harm, pursue, hunt, shoot, wound, kill, trap, capture, or collect") or attempt to take members of listed species in the United States, its territorial waters, or the open ocean and to export, import, possess, sell, or transport endangered species or any part of their bodies.[100] It also forbids government agencies to authorize, fund, or carry out projects that will harm a listed species or damage its so-called critical habitat. The U.S. Fish and Wildlife Service (FWS), part of the Department of the Interior, is in charge of enforcing this law.

The ESA also implements a major international agreement, the Convention on International Trade in Endangered Species of Wild Fauna and Flora (CITES), as it applies to the United States. This agreement was established in March 1973 and signed by 80 countries. By 2007, 169 countries were signatories, making CITES one of the largest conservation agreements in existence. CITES maintains its own list of endangered and threatened species worldwide, numbering more than 39,000 species (7,000 species of animals and 32,000 species of plants) in 2007. The signatory countries have agreed to limit or ban trade in these plants and animals or any materials made from them to the degree CITES determines. CITES has achieved some notable triumphs, such as an international ban on the sale of ivory from elephants in 1989, but certain plants and animals are still in grave danger from aspects of international trade, including trade in animal parts used in traditional Asian medicine, such as bear gall and gallbladders, and general trade on the Internet. In 2005, the International Fund for Animal Welfare (IFAW) reported that during a one-week period it found online listings for more than 9,000 live animals or wildlife products, 70 percent of which were from threatened or endangered species.

One of the most important parts of the ESA from the standpoint of environmental and animal welfare groups is its citizen suit provision, which states that any person can file a civil suit against another person, organization, or government entity claiming violations of the act. Citizens may also charge the secretary of the interior with failure to list a species as threatened or endangered or to remove a recovered species from the list. The Supreme Court ruled in 1997 that landowners who feel that actions taken to protect species have damaged their interests can also sue under this provision.

Environmental and animal rights groups have frequently attempted to use the ESA's citizen suit provision. The courts have often ruled that they did not have standing to sue, but in a few cases, judges have granted standing to the wildlife species themselves. One such species was a Hawaiian native bird, the palila, which, the Ninth Circuit Court of Appeals wrote in 1988, "as an endangered species under the Endangered Species Act . . . [has] a legal status and wings its way into federal court as a plaintiff in its own right."[101]

One aspect of the ESA that has caused considerable conflict between conservation groups and businesses such as logging companies is the question of how a species's critical habitat is to be determined and protected. A 1975 FWS regulation stated that "environmental modification or degradation [that] . . . disrupts essential behavior patterns" was to be included in the definition of *harm* in the act.[102] In 1992, however, after logging projects in Oregon's old-growth forests had been halted because they degraded the habitat of the endangered northern spotted owl, a pro-logging group called the Sweet Home Chapter of Communities for a Great Oregon sued the secretary of the interior, claiming that Congress had never intended the ESA to cover habitat degradation, or at least that it had intended that such damage should be prevented by purchase of land rather than halting of activities. The district court for the District of Columbia rejected the suit, but the D.C. Circuit Court reversed the decision on appeal. In 1995 the Supreme Court upheld the inclusion of environmental degradation in the definition of *harm*.

Determination of the critical habitat that must be protected for particular species (defined as geographic areas "on which are found those physical or biological features essential to the conservation of the species and which may require special management considerations or protection") is also a contentious issue, particularly when the economic impact of setting lands aside or halting projects on those lands is large.[103] The ESA does require that economic impacts be considered before designating an area as critical habitat, and the FWS says that it tries very hard to work with project designers and landowners to resolve conflicts and find ways for projects to proceed or land to be used without harming species, but some landowners have complained that they are not compensated for loss of use of their land or reduction in property values resulting from actions taken to conserve species.

Conflicts between human economic needs and the needs of endangered species have frequently produced both headlines and landmark court cases, as when a three-inch-long endangered fish called the snail darter nearly stopped the building of the gigantic Tellico Dam in Tennessee in the mid-1970s. Congress attempted to reduce these conflicts in 1982 by amending the ESA to make it less threatening to developers and landowners. These amendments allowed the FWS to grant permits for "incidental take" of an endangered species—harm to such a species occurring as a byproduct of an activity that does not otherwise violate the ESA or any other applicable laws. To obtain such a permit, a developer or landowner must file a habitat conservation plan (HCP), which specifies ways in which the predicted damage will be minimized and mitigated, for example by conservation efforts elsewhere on the land in question. The amendments also included a so-called No Surprises rule, which states that once the landowner and the FWS have agreed on the actions and expenditures required by an HCP and an incidental take permit has been granted, the government cannot demand any additional money, actions, or limitations of actions, even if unforeseen circumstances arise at a later time that might call for new measures to protect the species in question. Many environmental and animal protection organizations criticized the No Surprises rule, but the FWS defended it as a necessary incentive to encourage the private sector to cooperate in efforts to preserve endangered species.

Conflict between the ESA and property rights supporters continued, however, resulting in additional court cases. One recent suit questioned FWS's method of determining the numbers of a species in order to decide whether it was endangered, a far from academic matter to the farmers and fishermen in the basin of the Klamath River, which flows through southern Oregon and northern California. The Klamath was once the third-largest producer of salmon on the West Coast, and it is still considered prime habitat for king (Chinook) and coho (silver) salmon and steelhead and rainbow trout. However, according to the Pacific Coast Federation of

Fishermen's Associations, the combination of six dams, constructed for hydroelectric power between 1908 and 1962, and diversion of water from Upper Klamath Lake to provide irrigation for farms in the arid upper Klamath valley left the water remaining in the river so reduced in volume, hot, and laced with harmful chemicals from agricultural runoff that it was often fatal to the fish, cutting salmon runs to less than 10 percent of their former size.

Numbers of naturally spawned coho salmon in the Klamath River became so low that in 1998 the National Marine Fisheries Service (NMFS) classified the Oregon Coast coho salmon as threatened, placing that group of fish under the protection of the ESA. In doing so it followed the "hatchery policy" that the agency had set forth in 1993, which stated that salmon spawned in hatcheries would be counted along with wild-spawned fish to determine population size only "sparingly" and when the hatchery-spawned fish were considered "essential to recovery" of the species. NMFS felt that this was not true of hatchery-spawned coho salmon, which made up the bulk of salmon in the Klamath, so it did not count them in making its determination to list the Oregon Coast coho.

During the next several years, a number of actions in the Klamath valley, including federal timber sales, road building, and diversion of irrigation water from Upper Klamath Lake, were halted at least partly in order to protect the Oregon Coast coho as required by the ESA. These moves greatly angered farmers and industrialists in the area. In 2001, therefore, the Alsea Valley Alliance, a local property rights group, sued to challenge the validity of the listing of the Oregon Valley coho under the ESA.

In its suit, *Alsea Valley Alliance v. Evans*, the alliance pointed out that NMFS had earlier defined wild-spawned and hatchery-spawned coho in the Klamath as belonging to the same evolutionarily significant unit (ESU), a term the agency had introduced in 1991 to substitute for the smallest group that the ESA allowed to be given separate consideration, the "distinct population segment" (which Congress did not define). If the two groups of fish were part of the same ESU, the alliance's attorneys said, NMFS's decision to count one and not the other was "arbitrary and capricious" and therefore forbidden by the Administrative Procedures Act.

On September 10, 2001, U.S. District Court Judge Michael Hogan accepted the alliance's reasoning and ruled in its favor. He set aside the 1998 listing of the Oregon Coast coho salmon and ordered NMFS to reconsider its hatchery policy and reexamine all the listings that had stemmed from the policy's application. The NMFS received its first petition to have the Oregon Coast coho delisted before the month was out, and actions halted because of the coho's protected status were resumed. The Bush administration announced on November 9, 2001, that NMFS would not appeal Hogan's decision. Instead, it would conduct a review of 23 of its 25 salmon and steelhead listings, in which hatchery-bred fish had not been counted.

- Fisheries and environmental groups did appeal, however, and on December 14 the Ninth Circuit Court of Appeals halted all changes until it had ruled on the appeal, thus effectively restoring protection to the salmon. On February 24, 2004, the higher court rejected the environmental groups' appeal because, the three-judge panel said, Hogan's ruling was not a "final order" and therefore could be appealed only by NMFS.

The judges made no comments about the merits of Hogan's decision, but their rejection of the appeal reinstated that decision and thus, in effect, confirmed the delisting of the Oregon Coast coho salmon. Pacific Legal Foundation, a property-oriented legal group that had provided attorneys for the Alsea Valley Alliance, said that the ruling was the most groundbreaking environmental decision of the decade. Brian J. Perron, writing in the Summer 2003 issue of *Environmental Law*, expressed fear that the coho delisting, which he called misguided, would profoundly impact salmon recovery efforts in the Northwest.

- The 30th anniversary of the ESA in 2004 brought many attempts to evaluate the law's effectiveness over the span of its existence. Supporters pointed out that only a handful of species had gone extinct since being listed under the ESA; detractors noted that not many more than that had recovered enough to be delisted. Commentators on both sides emphasized the controversy that the law has aroused throughout its history, setting environmentalists against developers and landowners and requiring numerous court interpretations of the statute's meaning and scope. Writing in *Bioscience* in April 2004, science writer Scott Norris said that the ESA was probably the most divisive environmental policy issue in the United States. Far from encouraging preservation of endangered species and their habitat, Daniel R. and Randy T. Simmons wrote in the Winter 2003 issue of *Regulation*, the ESA's broad reach and potential for producing onerous restrictions spurred many landowners to destroy habitats on their properties so that endangered species would not move in, or, if they found such creatures, to take covert direct action against them (often described as "shoot, shovel, and shut up").

Opinions on ways to "improve" the ESA and its enforcement were just as divided as views of its performance to date. Supporters called for more funding, prompter listing of species, and more support from Congress and the president (support that had been notably lacking, they said, from the George W. Bush administration). Critics called for more clarity in the ESA regulations and the science underlying them, more incentives to encourage landowners to cooperate with programs to preserve endangered species and their habitat, and more input from the private sector in designing such programs.

The most important attempt to turn suggestions for revision into legislation was the Threatened and Endangered Species Recovery Act (TESRA, or HR 3824), a revision of the ESA sponsored by former Republican Representative Richard W. Pombo. Pombo, a rancher from Tracy, California, introduced the bill to the House of Representatives on September 19, 2005, and the House passed it by a vote of 229 to 193 on September 29. Pombo's bill aroused the ire of environmentalists and animal welfare groups, who said that it weakened the ESA, for instance by repealing some of the requirements for protecting critical habitat, and strongly favored landowners, for instance by allowing property owners to obtain compensation from the government for forgoing a merely proposed use of their land that, if carried out, would threaten listed species or their habitat. Pombo's critics rejoiced when he lost his seat in Congress to Democrat Jerry McNerny in the November 2006 election. As of late 2007, the Senate had not taken up Pombo's bill.

HUNTING

Among wildlife issues addressed by animal rights groups, by far the strongest emotions seem to be stirred up by hunting. Most such groups see modern hunting as completely indefensible. The Fund for Animals, for example, terms recreational hunting "a piteously unfair and cruel slaughter of innocent animals," and one animal rights ethicist called it the equivalent of child abuse.[104] Hunters, for their part, have an almost religious devotion to their sport, describing it as their way of expressing a bond with nature. Hunting supporter Ward Clark calls it "a matchless experience, a communion,"[105] and British baroness Anne Mallalieu, head of the British pro-hunting group Countryside Alliance, writes that hunting is "our [rural people's] music, it is our poetry, it is our art, it is our pleasure. . . . It is our whole way of life."[106]

As hunters and their supporters never tire of pointing out, humans have hunted throughout their evolution; humanity's closest animal relatives, chimpanzees, also hunt and eat meat. Traditionally, the chief purpose of hunting was to provide meat, clothing, and other materials necessary for survival. Today, although almost half of hunters in the United States are said to eat what they kill, few rely on hunting as a major food source. They hunt primarily for enjoyment, and it is chiefly this sport aspect of hunting that rouses animal rightists' ire.

In England, the most common form of sport hunting is the pursuit of foxes, deer, or hares with dogs. According to the Burns Report, a report on hunting with dogs that was commissioned by the British Parliament and released in June 2000, hunts are an important and sometimes "dominant" feature of social life in rural Britain. In the United States, hunting is usually done with guns, and the most common prey animals—amounting to about half of the 134 million animals killed in the country by hunters each year—are birds, mainly doves, ducks, grouse, quail, and partridges. Another third of the animals killed are squirrels, rabbits, and raccoons. Larger prey include deer (more than 6 million a year), elk, and bears.

Hunting in both countries is largely a rural pursuit, whereas most of the people who oppose hunting come from cities. The animosity between hunters and their opponents is therefore increased by mutual misunderstanding and clashes between urban and rural cultures. Ted Kerasote, an American supporter of hunting, complains that the sport "stands in jeopardy at the hand of a mostly urban society that has come to know wildlife largely through TV and computer screens."[107] In Britain, class is involved in the hunting dispute as well because many Britons see fox hunting as primarily an upper-class activity, although British hunters and their supporters maintain that hunting is popular with all classes in the countryside.

Especially in the United States, hunters claim that hunting is a form of wildlife management. Because settlers killed most wolves and other natural predators of game animals such as deer in the 18th and 19th centuries, hunting supporters say, these prey animals overpopulate if not culled by their only remaining predator, humankind. When such overpopulation occurs, the animals consume all the edible plant matter in their habitat, depriving other animals of food and damaging the ecosystem as a whole. They then succumb to starvation and disease, a far more painful and lingering death than one brought about by a skilled hunter's bullet. Hunting, its defenders say, controls animal populations the same way nature does.

Animal rights groups grant that deer and some other animals tend to overpopulate and that this can be destructive to the animals and their environment. They point out, however, that doves, ducks, and squirrels, the most commonly hunted animals in the United States, do not usually overpopulate. Hunters even shoot animals whose populations have reached all-time lows, such as black ducks. Furthermore, animal rightists question whether hunting is the best, let alone the only, way to control overpopulation when it does occur. Other possibilities exist, including reintroduction of natural predators, relocation, and contraception. (One contraception method is PZP or porcine zona pellucida vaccine, a vaccine against part of the mammalian egg developed in the 1970s, which can be injected by means of a dart.) Hunters say that at least at present, all these methods are expensive, labor intensive, and unreliable. Instead, they promote "sustainable use"—that is, regulated hunting and related activities, such as trapping and fishing—as the best way to manage wildlife populations, conserve habitat, and bring benefits to local economies at the same time.

Discussions about the value of hunting as a wildlife management tool highlight a philosophical disagreement that sometimes divides animal rights organizations from environmental ones. Environmental groups usually try to preserve species and habitats rather than individuals. Some environmental and wildlife preservation organizations, such as the National Wildlife Federation, therefore accept sport hunting under some conditions or want government agents to hunt, trap, or otherwise kill certain types of animals in order to prevent overpopulation or excessive predation on endangered species. Animal rights groups, on the other hand, focus on individual animals and thus usually oppose all hunting and trapping.

This disagreement about management techniques often underlies a deeper clash about whether wildlife should be "managed" at all. Whether as a responsibility entailed by humankind's traditional dominion over other animals or as an attempt to correct the damage already done to ecosystems by human activities such as land clearing, many environmental groups, as well as many scientists and most government wildlife agencies, feel that scientists and wildlife experts should closely monitor wild animal populations and take whatever steps seem necessary to keep them healthy and in balance with their food supply. In line with their hands-off policy on other human-animal interactions, however, many animal rightists say that people should interfere with nature as little as possible, especially when the interference involves killing.

Hunters also argue that, at least in the United States, they are among the foremost preservers of wildlife habitat. They must purchase licenses from their states in order to hunt legally, and the money from license fees is used to buy wilderness land and support wildlife management programs. State fish and wildlife agencies, in fact, receive most of their funding from hunters. (For this very reason, such agencies tend to support hunters' interests.) Hunters of waterbirds must also buy so-called duck stamps as a sort of secondary license or tax, and the revenue from these is used to maintain duck habitat. Money to preserve and restore wildlife habitat comes from federal taxes on sporting guns, handguns, ammunition, and archery tackle as well. Finally, private hunting groups such as Ducks Unlimited spend considerable money to buy, preserve, or even create habitats for their chosen game animals. No one has more motivation than hunters themselves, hunting supporters say, to maintain healthy, sustainable populations of game animals—and when game animals benefit, other animals that live in the same ecosystem usually do as well. In the mid-2000s, at least some hunters and environmentalists were rediscovering shared goals and forming new alliances to protect wildlife and its habitat against such threats as global warming. For example, Carl Pope, executive director of the well-known environmental organization Sierra Club, is himself a hunter and has sought alliances with hunting groups.

Hunters and animal rights activists disagree about how cruel hunting is. Hunters maintain that they usually accomplish a clean kill, in which the animal dies instantly, whereas animal rights organizations say that at least one animal is wounded and escapes, to die a lingering death from blood loss and infection, for every one that dies on the spot. Similarly, British anti-hunting web sites frequently feature pictures of foxes being torn to bits by dogs, but hunt supporters say that this occurs only after the fox has been killed by the hunters and its dead body is thrown to the dogs as a reward. Britain's Burns Report concluded that the killing in a fox hunt is no more cruel than most other methods used to dispose of foxes, which many farmers see as pests. Hunting advocates say that hunters who eat their kill are at least as moral as people who buy meat at the supermarket—perhaps, in fact, more so because, until they are taken, hunted animals live free and natural lives, whereas animals on factory farms are tightly confined and may be abused in other ways. Food animals that come from the wild also do not contribute to pollution and habitat destruction, as farmed food animals are said to do.

Certain practices have caused controversy within the hunting community as well as between it and animal rights groups. Most hunters feel that high-technology devices such as laser sights, spotlights, explosives, automatic weapons, and aircraft are not sporting, and most states have outlawed the use of such devices in hunting. Hunters are more divided over the use of bait to attract game animals, particularly bears and waterbirds. In the United States, federal FWS regulations have forbidden the use of bait in hunting migratory birds since the 1920s, but baiting bears is permitted. About a third of the states completely outlaw the use of bait, and many others limit it. The use of dogs, too, is sometimes outlawed. Many hunters feel that any practice that virtually guarantees a kill is not fair to the prey. Naturally, animal rights groups feel even more strongly that such activities should be banned.

Another practice that has garnered much disapproval from hunters as well as animal rights activists is the canned hunt, in which hunters pay for the chance to shoot game animals, often exotic ones such as African antelopes, zebras, or tigers, and take home their heads, horns, or skin as trophies. The animals frequently are half-tame creatures raised on the game ranch or preserve where the hunt takes place or purchased from circuses or zoos. Although some game preserves have large acreages through which the hunters may pursue their prey, others pen the animals in small enclosures where they cannot escape. They guarantee a kill to any hunter who pays their fee. "That ain't hunting. That's a slaughter," says Florida hunter Perry Arnold.[108] A new version of the canned hunt, introduced by Texas-based LiveShot.com in the mid-2000s, caused even greater outrage than the standard version because it allowed paying customers to use their computers to shoot captive animals by remote control. (In 2007, the site was no longer available.) At least 20 states have restricted or banned canned hunting (including seven that had banned Internet hunting by mid-2005), and animal rights groups and some pro-hunting groups such as the Izaak Walton League have tried to obtain a federal law against it as well, though so far without success.

Animal rights groups have used a variety of tactics in efforts to stop hunting. The League Against Cruel Sports (LACS), founded in Britain in 1924 to stop fox hunting, concentrated on trying to have the sport banned by law. It also bought large tracts of land in hunting territory and used them as wildlife sanctuaries. When these approaches failed to have much effect on hunting, a new group called the Hunt Saboteurs Association (HSA) split off from the LACS in 1964, becoming the first British animal rights group to focus on direct action. It broke up hunts nonviolently, usually by distracting dogs with bait, scents, or noise. In the early 1970s, disgruntled members of the HSA formed a still more radical group called the Band of Mercy, which damaged cars and other property of hunters and their supporters with vandalism and even bombs. This group later became the highly controversial Animal Liberation Front, which targets anyone it classifies as an animal abuser.

Sabotaging hunts and harassing hunters also became popular in the United States in the late 1960s and 1970s. There, the preferred technique was to frighten prey animals away by such methods as talking loudly or playing music. Although these methods were nonviolent, they irritated hunters into demanding help from their legislators. States began to pass laws against harassment of hunters, beginning with Arizona in 1981, and by 1995, every state had such a law. In addition, a pro-hunting group, the Wildlife Legislative Fund of America (now the U.S. Sportsmen's Alliance), began working for a federal antiharassment law. In 1994 the group obtained passage of the Recreational Hunting Safety and Preservation Act, which makes it illegal to "engage in any physical conduct that hinders a lawful hunt."[109]

Not content with sabotage, violent or otherwise, antihunting groups in Britain fought for years to have hunts with dogs outlawed, and, despite powerful opposition from organizations such as the Countryside Alliance, they finally succeeded. Scotland passed a bill prohibiting the hunting of mammals with hounds in March 2002, and (after, according to an anecdotal history of foxhunting, 120 hours of debate in 2004 alone—as compared to a mere 11 hours spent that year on the war in Iraq) the British Parliament voted in a similar ban for England and Wales on September 16, 2004. The ban, which covered foxes, deer, mink, and hares, went into effect on February 17, 2005.

Reports differ about how effective the ban, called the Hunting Act, has been or will be. Police lack funding and, many say, the desire to enforce the prohibition; they rely on the public and organizations such as the HSA to provide videotapes or other evidence that the law has been broken. The antihunting groups, meanwhile, have moved on to the new target of game bird shooting, which was not affected by the Hunting Act. Rather than banning shooting itself, they are working to modify the country's new Animal Welfare Act to outlaw the breeding and rearing of birds for shooting. (A ban of this type already exists in the Netherlands.) Some groups target fishing as well, claiming that fish feel pain when they are hooked.

The United States is unlikely to outlaw hunting as a whole, although federal and state laws ban or limit the hunting of certain species, and thousands of other laws, administered by state wildlife agencies or commissions, regulate the sport in various ways. Common types of laws limit the times of year during which hunting is allowed (open and closed seasons), the number of animals of particular types that each hunter can kill (bag limits), and the kinds of weapons that may be used. Hunters must normally purchase both hunting licenses and permits to kill particular kinds of animals; the number of permits issued depends on the number of animals that a state wildlife agency thinks can be safely harvested. Many states also require hunters to take education courses that cover gun safety, hunting ethics, and principles of wildlife management and conservation.

Although hunting remains legal in the United States, its popularity seems to be declining. The number of hunting licenses sold dropped by 11 percent between 1982 and 1997, according to the FWS. Some 14 million Americans, about 6 percent of the U.S. population, bought hunting licenses in 2000, the most recent year for which statistics are available. Paul G. Irwin, former president and CEO of HSUS, claimed that "the decline in hunting has [chiefly] to do with . . . a growing rejection of the idea of killing for fun." Other commentators say that many factors probably are involved, including a growing lack of leisure time and a decrease in hunting areas that can be reached without spending considerable time and money.[110]

TRAPPING

About 4 million animals were estimated to have been trapped, primarily for their fur, in the United States in 2000. (Some trapping is done for food or to remove animals that humans regard as nuisances, such as coyotes.) In the United States, 150,000 to 200,000 trappers were registered in 2004. Animals trapped commercially include rabbits, foxes, raccoons, and beavers. Like fur farming, trapping has declined since animal rights groups began attempting to persuade people not to wear fur. In the late 1980s, for instance, about 20 million animals were trapped yearly.

Animal rights groups have protested trapping as well as hunting. The National Trappers Association claims that "the professional wildlife conservation community universally endorses traps and trapping as critical and essential wildlife management tools" to keep populations at optimum size and prevent the spread of disease, but animal rightists say that almost all traps cause terribly painful injuries and deaths.[111] They also estimate that for every targeted animal, from two to five "nontargeted" ones, including endangered species and family pets, are caught in traps. The National Trappers Association denies this.

The type of trap that has caused the most controversy is the steel-jawed leghold trap, which is used in about 80 percent of trappings in the United States. Of 15 practices that could be considered harmful to animals, both Australian and American animal activists indicated in surveys that they considered use of these traps the worst. The National Trappers Association claims that fish and wildlife agencies regularly use steel-jawed leghold traps to capture animals for study or transportation to other sites and that they would not do so if the traps usually harmed the animals caught in them. However, the American Veterinary Medical Association and the American Animal Hospital Association both say that the traps can cause severe tissue damage.

A second type of trap, the Conibear or body-gripping trap, is supposed to kill animals quickly by snapping shut on their necks and breaking them. Opponents of the traps say that the traps sometimes close on an animal's chest or hips instead, producing a slow death from shock and suffocation as the trap crushes its body. Snares, a third type of trap, are wire loops that tighten around an animal's leg or neck. The National Trappers Association compares them to "a dog collar and leash," but if the wire is uncoated, as is often the case, it can cut through flesh to the bone.[112] The only kind of trap that dependably does not injure an animal is the live trap, in which food bait essentially lures an animal into a cage with a door that then shuts, but commercial trappers seldom use such traps because they are expensive.

No federal law governs trapping as a whole, but many states have laws or regulations that limit the activity. Like hunting, trapping requires a license in all states, and some states limit trapping by season, bag limit, size and placement of trap, or all of these. Steel-jawed leghold traps have been outlawed in eight states (as well as in 89 other countries, including all members of the EU) and are restricted in most others. (A bill to ban these traps nationwide, the Inhumane Trapping Prevention Act, was introduced into the House of Representatives on July 26, 2005, but as of early 2007 it had not passed.) Four states have outlawed body-gripping traps, nine have banned snares, and some others restrict size or placement of these devices. Forty-five states also have laws that require trappers to check their traps at stated intervals so that animals caught in them can be either killed or released. Other state laws specify minimum distances by which traps must be separated from roads or human habitations, to minimize the capture of pets or other disturbance to humans. California stands alone in banning all trapping of furbearing animals for either commercial purposes or sport.

THE FUTURE OF ANIMAL RIGHTS

Although the ideas and tactics of its more extreme members have caused considerable controversy and its basic aims are still far from being achieved, the animal rights movement has certainly succeeded in establishing itself as a social and political force during the past 30 years. It has made people think about subjects that most had never considered before, such as the conditions under which cattle and chickens live before reaching their dinner tables. As a result, the public has begun to examine the ethical implications of lifestyle choices ranging from eating meat to buying eye makeup and taking their children to the zoo.

Polls show that public opinion in the United States and Europe on many issues involving human treatment of animals has become more animal-friendly since the crusade for animal rights began. To some extent, behavior has changed as well. Robert Garner wrote in the British magazine *Parliamentary Affairs* in 1998, for instance, that because of the animal rights movement, "a social stigma is now attached to the wearing of fur; the number of vegetarians has increased markedly, creating a new marketing niche; [and] the demand for 'cruelty free' cosmetic products has played an important role in the decision of many manufacturers to seek alternative testing methods."[113]

Nonetheless, most people still eat meat, wear at least some animal products (such as leather shoes), and approve of research on animals if it seems likely to contribute substantially to human health and safety. Intensive farming and widespread habitat destruction continue worldwide. Although there has been some tightening of laws and regulations governing treatment of animals, especially in Europe, the animal rights movement has had much less effect on government and law than on the public, and many uses of animals remain virtually unregulated (or are regulated by laws that are seldom enforced).

Most commentators doubt that animal rightists will achieve their more extreme aims, such as full legal rights for animals, in the next 50 years. However, the influence of the animal rights crusade is likely to continue to bring changes as people increasingly examine their consciences about what uses of animals they can accept and what sacrifices of effort and money they will make to improve animals' lot. Futurist Lee Shupp, strategic director of Cheskin Research in Redwood Shores, California, said in an interview published in *American Demographics* in 2001 that he believes that

> *within the next 10 to 20 years, the idea that animals . . . have some indi-*
> *vidual rights will become a generally accepted notion. . . . I don't think we're*
> *going to become a nation of vegetarians [but] I think it's likely that we're*
> *going to pay a lot more attention to how animals are treated, not only as*
> *pets, but as sources of food.*[114]

Animal rights activists and their opponents will continue to compete for the hearts and minds of the public as each side increasingly recognizes that the other is here to stay. Corporations and individuals who work with or use animals will try harder to explain their activities as they realize that responding to consumers' concerns about treatment of animals makes good business sense. All but the most extreme animal rightists, for their part, most likely will face the fact that some human relationship with, and probably some human use of, animals will continue for the foreseeable future, and they will concentrate on shaping that relationship rather than trying to end it. Both sides of the animal rights debate may come to understand that willingness to respect each other's point of view, discuss issues rationally, and make compromises will work better than moral intransigence in advancing their aims.

Many observers both within and outside the animal rights movement say that the movement's future success will depend to a very large extent on whether it forms alliances with other social movements and groups that share some of its goals. Possible allies include groups devoted to consumer issues, human health, and the environment, as well as academics and even representatives of business and industry. Such alliances could greatly increase the movement's ability to influence governments as well as the public. Andrew Rowan and Bernard Unti of the HSUS write that the relationship between animal protection and environmentalism will be particularly important because "among all new social movements, environmentalism elicits the most support and the greatest degree of consensus" and "has emerged as the pivotal foundation of new social movements worldwide."[115]

Indeed, whatever their position on the many debates within the area of animal rights, it seems likely that increasing numbers of people will come to recognize that humans' treatment of animals is simply one aspect of their treatment of nature as a whole. In a much-quoted statement, Mohandas Gandhi said, "The greatness of a nation and its moral progress can be judged by the way its animals are treated."[116] More than greatness or even morality may be at stake, however. The way human beings treat the other creatures with whom they share the planet, as a reflection of the way they treat the planet itself, may be what determines their own survival.

[1] Gary Francione, quoted in Harold D. Guither, *Animal Rights: History and Scope of a Radical Social Movement.* Carbondale: Southern Illinois University Press, 1998, p. 23.

[2] Genesis, 1: 28.

[3] Thomas Aquinas, quoted in Frank R. Ascione and Randall Lockwood, "Cruelty to Animals: Changing Psychological, Social, and Legislative Perspectives," in Deborah J. Salem and Andrew N. Rowan, eds., *The State of the Animals: 2001.* Washington, D.C.: Humane Society Press, 2001, p. 39.

[4] Jeremy Bentham, quoted in Lyle Munro, *Compassionate Beasts: The Quest for Animal Rights.* Westport, Conn.: Praeger, 2001, p. 17.

[5] Jeremy Bentham, quoted in Jordan Curnutt, *Animals and the Law: A Sourcebook.* Santa Barbara, Calif.: ABC-CLIO, 2001, p. 435.

[6] Richard Ryder, quoted in Edward Skidelsky, "Nonsense upon Stilts," *New Statesman,* vol. 129, June 5, 2000, p. 53.

[7] Peter Singer, quoted in Adam Kolber, "Standing Upright: The Moral and Legal Standing of Humans and Other Apes," *Stanford Law Review,* vol. 54, October 2001, p. 193.

[8] Peter Singer, quoted in Lewis Petrinovich, *Darwinian Dominion: Animal Welfare and Human Interests.* Cambridge, Mass.: MIT Press, 1999, p. 211.

[9] Tom Regan, quoted in Guither, *Animal Rights,* p. 20.

[10] Michael Fox, quoted in Ward M. Clark, *Misplaced Compassion: The Animal Rights Movement Exposed.* San Jose, Calif.: Writers Club Press, 2001, p. 13.

[11] Roger Scruton and Andrew Tyler, "Do Animals Have Rights?" *The Ecologist,* vol. 31, March 2001, p. 24.

[12] David S. Oderberg, "The Illusion of Animal Rights," *Human Life Review,* Spring–Summer 2000, p. 42.

[13] Matthew Scully, quoted in Michael Mountain, "Speaking for the Animal Right," *Best Friends Magazine,* January–February 2003, p. 22.

[14] Curnutt, *Animals and the Law,* p. 29.

[15] *Black's Law Dictionary,* quoted in Guither, *Animal Rights,* p. 163.

[16] Antonin Scalia, quoted in Curnutt, *Animals and the Law,* p. 48.

[17] Patricia Wald, quoted in Curnutt, *Animals and the Law,* p. 62.

[18] Rob Roy Smith, "Standing on Their Own Four Legs: The Future of Animal Welfare Litigation after *Animal Legal Defense Fund, Inc. v. Glickman,*" *Environmental Law,* vol. 29, Winter 1999, p. 990.

[19] Steven Wise, quoted in Josie Glausiusz, "He Speaks for the Speechless," *Discover,* vol. 22, September 2001, p. 18.

[20] Richard A. Epstein, "The Next Rights Revolution? It's Bowser's Time at Last," *National Review,* vol. 51, November 8, 1999, p. 44.

[21] Eric Glitzenstein, quoted in Shawn Zeller, "Counsel for a Menagerie of Clients," *National Journal,* vol. 32, March 4, 2000, p. 715.

[22] Gary L. Francione and Lee Hall, "Confused Animal Rights Movement," *San Francisco Chronicle,* August 21, 2002, p. A21.

[23] Stephen Fox, quoted in Munro, *Compassionate Beasts*, p. 73.

[24] Roger, quoted in Munro, *Compassionate Beasts*, p. 95.

[25] Clark, *Misplaced Compassion*, p. 41.

[26] Tom Regan, quoted in Munro, *Compassionate Beasts*, p. 39.

[27] Munro, *Compassionate Beasts*, p. 5.

[28] Bernard Unti and Andrew N. Rowan, "A Social History of Postwar Animal Protection," in Salem and Rowan, eds., *The State of the Animals: 2001*, p. 29.

[29] Ingrid Newkirk, quoted in Clark, *Misplaced Compassion*, p. 36.

[30] Betsy Cummings, "Shock Treatment," *Sales and Marketing Management*, vol. 153, January 2001, p. 64.

[31] Andrew Tyler, quoted in Munro, *Compassionate Beasts*, p. 131.

[32] Munro, *Compassionate Beasts*, p. 190.

[33] Animal Liberation Front, quoted in Mike Weiss, "Eco-Terrorists Frustrate FBI," *San Francisco Chronicle*, February 3, 2002, p. A1.

[34] James Jarboe, quoted in Sean Higgins, "The Terrorist Tactics of Radical Environmentalists," *Insight on the News*, vol. 18, April 22, 2002, p. 45.

[35] Keith Mann, quoted in Terry O'Neill, "Bambi's Vigilantes," *The Report Newsmagazine*, vol. 28, February 5, 2001, p. 25.

[36] Tim Dailey, quoted in Guither, *Animal Rights*, pp. 159–160.

[37] Joint resolution, quoted in Guither, *Animal Rights*, p. 57.

[38] *Animal People*, quoted in Guither, *Animal Rights*, p. 161.

[39] Unti and Rowan, "A Social History of Postwar Animal Protection," p. 31.

[40] Munro, *Compassionate Beasts*, p. 165.

[41] Munro, *Compassionate Beasts*, p. 31.

[42] Marlene Halverson, quoted in Guither, *Animal Rights*, p. 22.

[43] Andrew Gay, quoted in Ed Shelton, "New Comms Tactics Test Animal Research Groups," *PR Week*, January 25, 2002, p. 9.

[44] Duane Thurman and Bob Fountain, "Burning Issues in Future for Animal Ag," *Feedstuffs*, vol. 78, November 6, 2006, p. 24.

[45] Andrew Gay, quoted in Shelton, "New Comms Tactics Test Animal Research Groups," p. 9.

[46] Mark Matfield, quoted in Shelton, "New Comms Tactics Test Animal Research Groups," p. 9.

[47] James Serpell, quoted in Munro, *Compassionate Beasts*, p. 178.

[48] Ingrid Newkirk, quoted in Guither, *Animal Rights*, p. 68.

[49] Ingrid Newkirk, quoted in Clark, *Misplaced Compassion*, p. 38.

[50] John Bryant, quoted in Munro, *Compassionate Beasts*, p. 177.

[51] Munro, *Compassionate Beasts*, p. 176.

[52] Munro, *Compassionate Beasts*, p. 178.

[53] Martin Act, quoted in Curnutt, *Animals and the Law*, p. 71.

[54] Patricia Jensen, quoted in Judith Reitman, "From the Leash to the Laboratory," *Atlantic Monthly*, p. 17.

[55] Ruth Harrison, quoted in Guither, *Animal Rights*, pp. 2, 87.

[56] Temple Grandin, "Progress in Livestock Handling and Slaughter Techniques in the United States, 1970–2000," in Salem and Rowan, eds., *The State of the Animals: 2001*, p. 108.

[57] David Fraser, Joy Mench, and Suzanne Millman, "Farm Animals and Their Welfare in 2000," in Salem and Rowan, eds., *The State of the Animals: 2001,* p. 98.

[58] Al Pope, quoted in Sally Schuff, "Inside Washington," *Feedstuffs,* vol. 74, May 20, 2002, p. 5.

[59] Bruce Friedrich, quoted in Megan Steintrager, "Duty and the Beast," *Restaurant Business,* vol. 101, June 15, 2002, p. 24.

[60] Animal rights pamphlet, quoted in Curnutt, *Animals and the Law,* p. 164.

[61] Grandin, "Progress in Livestock Handling and Slaughter Techniques in the United States, 1970–2000," p. 108.

[62] Peter Stevenson, quoted in Tessa Fox, "Animal Passions," *Caterer & Hotelkeeper,* June 13, 2002, p. 20.

[63] Munro, *Compassionate Beasts,* p. 157.

[64] Laboratory Animal Welfare Act, quoted in Curnutt, *Animals and the Law,* pp. 442–443.

[65] Alex Pacheco, quoted in Charles Patterson, *Animal Rights.* Lincoln, Neb.: iuniverse.com, 2000, pp. 52–53.

[66] Quoted in Curnutt, *Animals and the Law,* p. 52.

[67] Adrian R. Morrison, "Personal Reflections on the 'Animal-Rights' Phenomenon," *Perspectives in Biology and Medicine,* vol. 44, Winter 2001, p. 62.

[68] 1985 revision of Animal Welfare Act, quoted in Curnutt, *Animals and the Law,* p. 446.

[69] 1985 revision of Animal Welfare Act, quoted in Curnutt, *Animals and the Law,* p. 447.

[70] 1985 revision of Animal Welfare Act, quoted in Curnutt, *Animals and the Law,* p. 446.

[71] Martin Stephens, quoted in Lisa Yount, *Issues in Biomedical Ethics.* San Diego, Calif.: Lucent Books, 1998, p. 70.

[72] Dan Glickman, "Regulations for the Use of Laboratory Animals," *Journal of the American Medical Association,* vol. 285, February 21, 2001, p. 941.

[73] Estelle A. Fishbein, "What Price Mice?" *Journal of the American Medical Association,* vol. 285, February 21, 2001, p. 939.

[74] Ingrid Newkirk, quoted in Clark, *Misplaced Compassion,* p. 37.

[75] Jessica Sandler, quoted in Glen Martin, "It's PETA vs. Greens in Tiff over Lab Rats," *San Francisco Chronicle,* July 22, 2002, p. A6.

[76] Peter Singer, quoted in Yount, *Issues in Biomedical Ethics,* p. 62.

[77] Michael Hayre, quoted in Scott Shepard, "Animal Protection Law Targets 70,000 Mice in St. Jude Labs," *Memphis Business Journal,* vol. 22, November 17, 2000, p. 1.

[78] PETA advertisement, quoted in Deborah Rudacille, *The Scalpel and the Butterfly.* Berkeley: University of California Press, 2000, p. 299.

[79] Gina Solomon, quoted in Martin, "It's PETA vs. Greens in Tiff over Lab Rats," p. A6.

[80] Jonathan Balcombe, quoted in Virginia McCord, "More Frogs Live to Croak," *Insight on the News,* vol. 14, March 30, 1998, p. 42.

[81] Adrian Morrison, quoted in Patterson, *Animal Rights,* p. 33.

[82] Richard Smith, "Animal Research: The Need for a Middle Ground," *British Medical Journal*, vol. 322, February 3, 2001, p. 248.

[83] Michael Balls, quoted in Robert Koenig, "European Researchers Grapple with Animal Rights," *Science*, vol. 284, June 4, 1999, p. 1604.

[84] National Association for Biomedical Research, quoted in Guither, *Animal Rights*, p. 80.

[85] Hanno Wurbel, "Better Housing for Better Science," *Chemistry and Industry*, April 16, 2001, p. 237.

[86] "Animal Rights FAQ: Section 9, Animals for Entertainment," www.animalrights.com/arsec9q.htm, p. 3, downloaded on January 9, 2003.

[87] Dick Gregory, quoted in Catherine Gourley, "Animal Welfare or Animal Rights?" *Writing!*, vol. 24, January 2002, p. 9.

[88] "Sara the Tiger Whisperer," quoted in Denise Martin, "Ringling Bros. Waging a Campaign to Combat Allegations of Animal Abuse," *Orange County Register*, July 26, 2002, p. K3830.

[89] Richard Farinato, "Another View of Zoos," in Salem and Rowan, eds., *The State of the Animals: 2001*, p. 145.

[90] "Animal Rights FAQ: Section 9, Animals for Entertainment," p. 2.

[91] David Hancocks, "Is There a Place in the World for Zoos?" in Salem and Rowan, eds., *The State of the Animals: 2001*, p. 143.

[92] Hancocks, "Is There a Place in the World for Zoos?" p. 143.

[93] Farinato, "Another View of Zoos," p. 147.

[94] Hancocks, "Is There a Place in the World for Zoos?" p. 138.

[95] Noelle Delaquis, quoted in "When Dolphins Cry," *Swiss News*, March 2001, p. 10.

[96] Hancocks, "Is There a Place in the World for Zoos?" p. 139.

[97] Edward White, decision in *Geer v. Connecticut*, quoted in Curnutt, *Animals and the Law*, p. 318.

[98] U.S. Fish & Wildlife Service, "ESA Basics," http://www.fws.gov/ downloaded December 2002, p. 1.

[99] Curnutt, *Animals and the Law*, p. 369.

[100] Endangered Species Act, quoted in Curnutt, *Animals and the Law*, p. 373.

[101] Ninth Circuit Court of Appeals decision in *Palila v. Hawaii Department of Land and Natural Resources (Palila II)*, quoted in Curnutt, *Animals and the Law*, p. 35.

[102] Fish and Wildlife Service ESA regulation, quoted in Curnutt, *Animals and the Law*, p. 374.

[103] Endangered Species Act, quoted in Fish and Wildlife Service, "ESA Basics," p. 2.

[104] Fund for Animals, quoted in Clark, *Misplaced Compassion*, p. 94.

[105] Clark, *Misplaced Compassion*, p. 68.

[106] Anne Mallalieu, quoted in Munro, *Compassionate Beasts*, p. 205.

[107] Ted Kerasote, "Straight Talk on Hunting," *Sports Afield*, vol. 223, August 2000, p. 34.

[108] Perry Arnold, quoted in Jeffrey Kluger, "Hunting Made Easy," *Time*, vol. 159, March 11, 2002, p. 62.

[109] Recreational Hunting Safety and Preservation Act, quoted in Curnutt, *Animals and the Law*, p. 305.

[110] Paul G. Irwin, "Overview: The State of Animals in 2001," in Salem and Rowan, eds., *The State of the Animals: 2001*, p. 4.

[111] National Trappers Association, "Trapping Facts," www.nationaltrappers.com/ Facts.html, downloaded on February 8, 2003, pp. 3–4.

[112] National Trappers Association, "Trapping Facts," pp. 1–2.

[113] Robert Garner, "Defending Animal Rights," *Parliamentary Affairs*, vol. 51, July 1998, p. 459.

[114] Lee Shupp, quoted in "Futurespeak," *American Demographics*, May 1, 2001, p. 56.

[115] Unti and Rowan, "A Social History of Postwar Animal Protection," p. 31.

[116] Mohandas Gandhi, quoted in Margaret C. Jasper, *Animal Rights Law*. Dobbs Ferry, N.Y.: Oceana Publications, Inc., 2002, p. vii.

CHAPTER 2

THE LAW AND ANIMAL RIGHTS

LAWS AND REGULATIONS

Hundreds of pieces of state and local legislation, and a handful of federal laws, affect humans' treatment of animals in the United States. Compared to rulings in other areas of legislative interest, however, laws concerning animals are scant.

The roles of federal and state legislation differ depending on the situations in which animals are kept. Virtually all laws against cruelty to cats and dogs as companion animals are state laws, for example, but treatment of those same species in laboratories is governed almost entirely by federal law. The states normally regulate hunting and trapping unless endangered species are involved, in which case the federal Endangered Species Act (ESA) takes over.

The amount of legal regulation also varies in different industries and in different aspects of the same industry. For instance, the federal Humane Slaughter Act regulates the way food animals are killed, but their treatment before that time is hardly regulated. The Animal Welfare Act (AWA) and its regulations describe in some detail the minimum housing and care required for different kinds of animals in laboratories and animal exhibitions, but the act specifically forbids any direct regulation of experimental procedures performed on the animals. The same act covers zoos, circuses, and animal shows but not animal races or rodeos.

This section describes the federal and state laws that have had the most significant effects on the animal welfare issues discussed in Chapter 1. The laws are arranged by date, with the oldest first.

ANIMAL WELFARE ACT (1970)

Government-funded medical research in the United States increased substantially in the late 1940s, and so did the demand for laboratory animals, including cats and dogs. Stories in the mid-1960s about the theft of pets and the miserable conditions in which some dealers held animals destined for sale to laboratories produced a public outcry that made Congress pass the Laboratory Animal Welfare Act (LAWA) in 1966.

The LAWA's chief purpose was clearly the protection of family pets. It required dealers who sold dogs and cats (but not other animals) to obtain licenses from the U.S. Department of Agriculture (USDA), which was given responsibility for enforcing the law, and to identify and keep records of all animals they sold. Similarly, laboratories that used dogs and cats, but no others, had to buy the animals from licensed dealers and keep records of the purchases. The law also ordered the secretary of agriculture to "promulgate standards to govern the humane handling, care, treatment, and transportation of animals by dealers and research facilities," including primates, cats, dogs, rabbits, guinea pigs, and hamsters, but no rules were to be made affecting the handling or care of animals "during actual research or experimentation."

In 1970, Congress gave the LAWA a shorter name, the Animal Welfare Act (AWA), and expanded it considerably. The AWA (7 U.S.C. 2131-2157) is the only significant federal law that regulates the use of animals in research, product testing, and education. It applies to all laboratories carrying out research supported in whole or in part by federal funds or using animals that have been transported across state lines, which, according to Jordan Curnutt's *Animals and the Law*, means "virtually all research using laboratory animals" of the covered types in the United States.[1]

Unlike its predecessor, the AWA regulated animal exhibitors as well as wholesale dealers and laboratories. It also covered "any warm-blooded animal," not just the six species mentioned in the LAWA. The new law specified the meanings of certain terms and the penalties for violation more clearly than the old one had, and it required monitoring and inspections to verify that research and exhibition facilities were meeting its standards of animal care, which the LAWA had not. These inspections, along with other aspects of implementing and enforcing the AWA, were assigned to the USDA's Animal and Plant Health Inspection Service (APHIS) in 1972.

APHIS issued regulations implementing the AWA later in 1972. They provide minimum requirements (which are sometimes, though not always, quite detailed) for the housing of different species of laboratory animals, specify the kinds of records that dealers and laboratories must keep, and so on. They also require training programs for all personnel who handle animals. Probably the most controversial aspect of these regulations is their redefinition of "animal" to exclude rats, mice, and birds, which make up about 95 percent of all laboratory animals. Farm animals are also exempted from the AWA.

The AWA was revised in 1976, 1983, 1985, 1990, and 1991, with the 1985 amendments (collectively termed the Improved Standards for Laboratory Animals Act) being the most significant. Partly in response to two high-profile cases of apparent animal abuse in laboratories in the early 1980s, the AWA's 1985 amendments specifically require scientists to "minimize pain and distress" to animals during experiments, to consult with a veterinarian about pain control as well as general care, and to provide anesthesia or analgesia unless withholding such medication is deemed "scientifically necessary." They also mention for the first time the desirability of seeking nonanimal alternatives to animal testing and of avoiding unnecessary duplication of animal experiments. They mandate exercise programs for dogs and "a physical environment adequate to promote the psychological well-being of primates," but they let the regulated institutions and the veterinarians decide how to fulfill these requirements.

The 1985 revision of the AWA also requires institutions using animals to set up Institutional Animal Care and Use Committees (IACUCs). Each committee must have at least three members, including a veterinarian and a person who represents "general community interests in the proper care and treatment of animals" and is not affiliated with the institution or related to anyone who is. The IACUC reviews proposals for all new experiments using animals at its institution as well as monitoring ongoing experiments and the overall care of the institution's animals. It is supposed to judge whether each use of animals is scientifically necessary and to evaluate steps taken to minimize the animals' pain and distress. However, although it can reject a research plan completely (which apparently rarely happens), it cannot prescribe or alter such a plan.

The Pet Protection Act is a further amendment to the AWA made in 1990. It requires all animal control facilities (pounds and shelters) to hold cats and dogs brought to them for at least five days before selling them to dealers who may sell them to laboratories. This is similar to the requirement for dealers in the original 1966 LAWA, but it is more useful because pet owners are more likely to be able to find animal control facilities than animal dealers and thus should have a better chance of retrieving lost or stolen pets. The requirement also gives animals a somewhat better chance to be adopted. The Pet Protection Act increases record-keeping requirements for dealers and animal control facilities as well.

ENDANGERED SPECIES ACT
(1973—AMENDED 1978, 1982, 1988)

Several federal laws, such as the Bald Eagle Protection Act (1940) and the Marine Mammal Protection Act (1972), protect particular wildlife species or groups of species. In addition, calls for a law to protect all endangered or threatened species began in the 1960s, when Americans started to realize the extent to which human activities were destroying not only animals themselves but their habitat through such activities as logging and clearing land for agriculture or housing. The result of this destruction was a rapid rise in the rate at which species were vanishing completely, or becoming extinct.

Congress passed the first federal law aimed at protecting endangered species, the Endangered Species Preservation Act, in 1966. It directed the secretary of the interior to identify every endangered native fish and wildlife species and preserve the species and their habitats where possible, but, amazingly, it did not prohibit hunting of identified species, except on federal lands, or their commercial transportation across state borders. In 1969, this weak act was replaced by the Endangered Species Conservation Act, which expanded the types of animals covered and extended the range of the endangered species list to the entire world. However, the new act still did not cover plants, and it left most species protection up to the states.

Environmental groups demanded that these acts be strengthened, and the final result was the Endangered Species Act (ESA), signed into law in December 1973. It appears in the U.S. Code as 16 U.S.C. 1531-1544. The ESA's purpose is to protect species of plants and animals classified as endangered ("in danger of extinction throughout all or a significant portion of its range") or threatened ("likely to become endangered . . . in the foreseeable future"), along with "the ecosystems upon which endangered and threatened species depend." Such species should be preserved, the act said, because they are of "aesthetic, ecological, educational, historical, recreational, and scientific value to the Nation and its people." The act covers all plant and animal species worldwide, including subspecies and, in the case of vertebrates, populations (thus a vertebrate species may be declared to be endangered in a particular area, even though it is thriving elsewhere). Although the ESA was amended in 1978, 1982, and 1988, the 1973 version is basically still in force today. In 1978, the Supreme Court called this law "the most comprehensive legislation for the preservation of endangered species ever enacted by any nation."[2]

The ESA provides elaborate procedures for classifying a species, subspecies, or population as endangered or threatened. Individuals or groups may petition to have a species considered for listing, or the department of the interior's Fish and Wildlife Service (FWS), which is in charge of implementing the law except in the oceans, may determine on its own that a species needs to be added to the list. The law forbids anyone to take ("harass, harm, pursue, hunt, shoot, wound, kill, trap, capture, or collect") or attempt to take members of listed species in the United States, its territorial waters, or the open ocean and to export, import, possess, sell, or transport endangered species or any part of their bodies. It also forbids government agencies to authorize, fund, or carry out projects that will harm a listed species or damage its "critical habitat" unless they receive an exemption from a cabinet-level committee. Violation of the law can result in fines of up to $100,000 and jail terms of up to six months.

The FWS, the Commerce Department's National Marine Fisheries Service (which administers the ESA in the oceans), and the USDA's Forest Service are required to devise plans for helping endangered species "recover" to the point where they are no longer endangered or threatened. These agencies work with the states and private landowners to develop conservation programs. As authorized by the ESA, they also administer the provisions of the Convention on International Trade in Endangered Species of Wild Fauna and Flora (CITES) as these apply to the United States. This international agreement was signed in 1973.

One of the most important parts of the ESA from the standpoint of environmental and animal welfare groups is its so-called citizen suit provision, which states that any person can file a civil suit against another person, organization, or government entity, claiming violations of the act. Citizens may also charge the secretary of the interior with failure to list a species as threatened or endangered or to remove a recovered species from the list. Environmental and animal rights groups have attempted to use the citizen suit provision frequently, although courts have usually ruled that they did not have standing to sue. Landowners who feel that actions taken to protect species have damaged their interests can also sue under this provision.

FWS regulations and, sometimes, court challenges have refined the definition of particular terms in the ESA. For instance, a 1975 regulation specified that "environmental modification or degradation [that] . . . disrupts essential behavior patterns" was to be included in the act's definition of "harm." The Supreme Court upheld this inclusion in a 1995 case, *Babbitt v. Sweet Home Chapter of Communities for a Great Oregon*. Determination of the "critical habitat" that must be protected for particular species (defined as geographic areas "on which are found those physical or biological features essential to the conservation of the species and which may require special management considerations or protection" has also been a contentious issue. The ESA specifies that economic impacts are not to be considered when deciding whether to list a species as threatened or endangered, but they must be considered when determining critical habitat.

Some of the 1982 amendments to the ESA addressed complaints from developers and landowners and attempted to provide incentives for them to cooperate with the law. Among other things, the amendments allowed the FWS to grant permits for "incidental take" of an endangered species—harm to such a species incidental to an activity that does not otherwise violate the ESA or any other applicable laws. To obtain such a permit, a developer or landowner would have to file a habitat conservation plan (HCP), which specifies ways in which the predicted damage will be minimized and mitigated, for example by conservation efforts elsewhere on the land in question. Another amendment, known as the No Surprises rule, stated that, once the landowner and the FWS have agreed on the actions and expenditures required by the HCP and the incidental take permit has been granted, the government cannot demand any additional money, actions, or limitations of actions, even if unforeseen circumstances arise at a later time that might call for new measures to protect the species in question.

The 30th anniversary of the ESA in 2004 brought many evaluations of the law's effectiveness over the span of its existence and put attempts to revise it into high gear as well. One revision, signed into law in 2004, exempts lands owned by the military from some of the requirements of the ESA regarding critical habitat. This law also requires the FWS to consider the impact on national security when making critical habitat designations that might affect military activities.

HUMANE METHODS OF SLAUGHTER ACT (1978)

In the first half of the 20th century, large meat animals (cattle, sheep, and pigs) slaughtered at meatpacking plants were normally stunned, usually by being hit over the head with a hammer, before their throats were slit. The stunning sometimes failed, however, resulting in animals being bled out or even occasionally dismembered or skinned while still conscious. In response to pressure from prominent senator Hubert Humphrey and several national animal welfare groups, Congress passed the Humane Slaughter Act in 1958 to end this cruel state of affairs. The law, which covered pigs, cattle, and sheep killed in U.S. packing plants that supplied meat to the federal government, required that these animals be "rendered insensible to pain by a single blow or gunshot or an electrical, chemical or other means that is rapid and effective" before being cut, chained, hoisted, or knocked down. It also specified procedures for handling the animals just before slaughter. The USDA was given the job of implementing and enforcing the law.

The slaughter law was revised in 1978, at which time it became the Humane Methods of Slaughter Act, 7 U.S.C. 1901-1906. This version of the law covers all U.S. plants subject to federal inspection (required for plants engaging in interstate commerce)—about 95 percent of all U.S. meatpackers—and plants in all foreign countries that export meat to the United States. Unlike its predecessor, it provides a way for the government to verify that meatpackers are following its regulations. Inspectors working for a branch of the USDA called the Food Safety and Inspection Service (FSIS) are stationed in slaughterhouses and have the authority to stop the production line if they see either violations of handling and slaughter regulations or signs of diseased animals or meat. FSIS inspectors also periodically examine plants in countries that export meat to the United States, although they do not remain there all the time.

The Humane Methods of Slaughter Act, like the earlier slaughter law, has two important and controversial exceptions. First, it does not apply to birds, which make up more than 95 percent of the animals killed in slaughterhouses. Chickens and turkeys therefore may legally be killed while they are still conscious. Many poultry slaughterhouses dip their birds in a tank of electrically charged water to stun them (a method that some animal rights groups say is sometimes ineffective), but only California has a law that requires them to do so.

The Humane Methods of Slaughter Act also does not apply to Jewish kosher slaughter, which requires that animals be conscious and standing when they are killed. (The original purpose of this religious rule was probably to ensure that people ate fresh meat from healthy animals.) Kosher killing is done by slitting the throat with an extremely sharp knife and, properly carried out, is said to be almost painless and to induce unconsciousness within seconds. However, a videotape allegedly taken at AgriProcessors, Inc., of Postville, Iowa, the largest kosher slaughterhouse in the world, and released by People for the Ethical Treatment of Animals (PETA) in November 2004, suggests that techniques for keeping the slaughter humane are not always followed. The exemption to the federal act also covers halal, rules of slaughter in the Muslim religion that are similar to kosher. Although this exception has been challenged in court as showing favoritism to particular religions, the Supreme Court in a 1974 case, *Jones v. Butz*, affirmed a district court ruling that the law is constitutional.

ANIMAL ENTERPRISE PROTECTION ACT (1992)

Congress passed the Animal Enterprise Protection Act (P.L. 102-346) in 1992 in response to the violent activities of a handful of extremist animal rights groups such as the Animal Liberation Front (ALF). The act makes physical disruption of animal production and research facilities a violation of federal law. Facilities covered under the law include "commercial or academic enterprise[s] that use animals for food or fiber production, agriculture, research, or testing" as well as zoos, aquariums, circuses, rodeos, fairs, and competitive animal events such as races. Disruption is defined as "intentionally stealing, damaging, or causing the loss of, any property (including animals or records) used by the animal enterprise, . . . thereby caus[ing] economic damage exceeding $10,000 to that enterprise." The law specifies monetary restitution and other penalties, but critics say that these penalties are less severe than those that many state laws mandate for similar crimes. The act was strengthened in 2002, but the first known trial and conviction for violating the law, involving Kevin Kjonaas and five other members of the U.S. branch of the British organization Stop Huntingdon Animal Cruelty (SHAC-USA), did not occur until 2006.

ANIMAL ENTERPRISE TERRORISM ACT (PL 102-346, 2006)

Responding to stepped-up activity by extremist animal rights groups such as the Animal Liberation Front (ALF) and SHAC (Stop Huntingdon Animal Cruelty)-USA, which often targeted individuals and companies whose connection with animal experimentation was tenuous at best, Congress passed a second and stronger law against such activities, the Animal Enterprise Terrorism Act, in late 2006. President George W. Bush signed the act into law on November 27. The new law's purpose was "to provide the Department of Justice the necessary authority to apprehend, prosecute, and convict individuals committing animal enterprise terror." It expanded the definition of "animal enterprise" and "economic damage" from those used in the 1992 Animal Enterprise Protection Act and raised penalties for those who traveled in interstate commerce to cause, or threaten to cause, economic or personal damage to individuals or businesses connected directly or indirectly with animal enterprises. Under this law, the penalty for causing "major" economic damage or disruption, which was defined as exceeding $100,000, could include a prison term of up to 10 years. The law amended Section 43 of Title 18 of the U.S. Code.

State Laws Against Cruelty to Animals

The first clear legal statement of a responsibility toward animals in themselves, rather than as someone's property, was part of the "Body of Liberties," a set of 100 rules of conduct which the Reverend Nathaniel Ward drew up for the Pilgrims' Massachusetts Bay Colony in 1641. Liberty 92 stated that "No man shall exercise any tirranny or crueltie towards any bruite creature which are usuallie kept for man's use."[3]

This statement was far ahead of its time. No other American colonies wrote laws or rulings forbidding animal abuse, nor did the new states of the fledgling United States, until Maine passed one in 1821. This law, like the better-known one that wealthy ex-diplomat Henry Bergh wrote and persuaded the New York legislature to pass in 1867, focused chiefly on horses and cattle. The more expansive New York law, however, forbade beating, overworking, torturing, or killing "any living creature," depriving animals of sustenance (neglect), or abandoning old, maimed, or sick horses or mules.

All states of the United States had laws against cruelty to animals by 1921, and all still do today. These laws differ in their level of detail and specific requirements, but, according to Jordan Curnutt's *Animals and the Law*, all specify to some degree the kinds of animals protected, the actions prohibited, the mental state required to establish liability, and the uses of animals that are exempted.

Many state anticruelty laws apply to "any animal," but others cover only mammals or mammals and birds. "Cruel" actions forbidden usually include killing, maiming, torturing, mutilating, and tormenting—terms which may or may not be defined and are often qualified by the adjectives *unnecessary, needless,* or *unjustifiable,* leaving it up to judges to decide when killing, injuring, or causing pain is necessary or justifiable. Neglect, including deprivation of food and water and, sometimes, shelter or veterinary care, is also usually included, and abandonment is illegal in three-fourths of the states. Most anticruelty laws require that cruel acts be done "knowingly" or with some similar type of guilty mental state, which is often hard to prove. People are almost always exempted from animal cruelty laws if they harm an animal in defense of themselves or others or for purposes of euthanasia to end suffering. Some states also exempt particular types of activities, including research, agricultural, or veterinary practices that are "generally accepted," hunting done in compliance with state law, and sometimes forms of entertainment such as rodeos and circuses.

Until recently, convictions under state animal cruelty laws were few and sentences usually light because the laws considered animal cruelty to be merely a misdemeanor crime against "public order" or "public morals." In the last 10 or 20 years, however, thanks in part to the activities of animal protection groups, this situation has been changing. By April 2006, 43 states, the District of Columbia, Puerto Rico, and the U.S. Virgin Islands classified severe animal abuse as a felony.

COURT CASES

A number of court cases, including some that reached the Supreme Court, have affected judicial views of animal welfare and animal rights. Some were

Animal Rights

criminal cases involving alleged cruelty to animals, while others addressed more basic legal issues such as the requirements an animal protection or environmental organization must meet in order to have the right ("standing") to bring a civil suit against a government agency. The remainder of this chapter discusses some key cases in this field.

TENNESSEE VALLEY AUTHORITY V. HILL
437 U.S. 153 (1978)

Background

The Tennessee Valley Authority (TVA), a corporation wholly owned by the U.S. federal government, began constructing the Tellico Dam and Reservoir Project in the area of the Little Tennessee River in 1967. The project, which included a proposed dam on the river that would create a 30-mile-long reservoir, was intended to stimulate shoreline development, generate electricity for 20,000 homes, provide flatwater recreation and flood control, and improve economic conditions in a depressed area.

Several environmental groups, chiefly the Environmental Defense Fund (now Environmental Defense), and some local citizens opposed the Tellico Dam because it would obliterate what the Supreme Court later described as "clear, free-flowing waters [moving] through an area of great natural beauty . . . much of which represents valuable and productive farmland." They filed lawsuits claiming that the project violated the National Environmental Policy Act of 1969 and obtained a temporary injunction from a district court that stopped work on the dam for almost two years (1972–1973). After TVA provided an improved environmental impact statement in late 1973, however, the court allowed the project to proceed.

In August 1973, a few months before the dam building started again, a University of Tennessee biologist discovered a previously unknown type of perch, a three-inch-long tan fish that became known as the snail darter (*Percina imostoma tonasi*). This new species appeared to live only in the Little Tennessee River, although about 130 other species of darters were found elsewhere.

Four months after the snail darter was identified, the Endangered Species Act (ESA) became law. In January 1975, the biologist who had found the new fish and the groups who had been trying to stop the Tellico Dam petitioned the secretary of the interior to classify the snail darter as an endangered species, and it was so classified in November. The secretary also designated the stretch of river that would be flooded by the dam as critical habitat for the fish and stated, "The proposed impoundment of water behind the proposed Tellico Dam would result in total destruction of the snail darter's habitat."

94

Working with the FWS, the TVA attempted to relocate a number of snail darters to the nearby Hiwassee River, but the agency said that more than a decade might be needed to determine whether the transplantation "took" to the extent of producing a breeding population. In April 1975, even before the darter was listed as endangered, TVA representatives also told a congressional subcommittee that they did not believe that the ESA prohibited (or at least should prohibit) completion of a project that was more than half finished by the time the law was passed. The committee agreed and approved additional funding for the project. By the time the snail darter was classified as endangered, the dam was 80 percent completed.

In February 1976, the groups who opposed the Tellico Dam, including a local citizen named Hiram Hill, filed a new lawsuit, claiming that completion of the dam would violate section 7 of the ESA (16 U.S.C. 1536), which requires all federal agencies to "tak[e] . . . action necessary to insure that actions authorized, funded, or carried out by them do not jeopardize the continued existence of . . . endangered . . . and threatened species or result in the destruction or modification of habitat of such species which is determined by the Secretary . . . to be critical." At the end of April, the district court agreed that the dam would probably cause the extinction of the snail darter but nonetheless refused to grant the injunction the groups had requested because, if the dam were scrapped permanently, "some $53 million [of the $78 million spent on the project to date] would be lost in nonrecoverable obligations," which the court considered an "absurd result" of applying the law— one that Congress surely had never intended. (The environmental groups later claimed, based on a General Accounting Office study, that the loss in fact might be considerably less.) The court pointed out that Congress had continued to grant funds for the project even after its likely effect on the endangered fish had been brought up, which suggested that it had not meant the ESA to apply in this case.

The environmentalists appealed the case, and on January 31, 1977, the Sixth Circuit Court of Appeals reversed the lower court's decision. The appeals court granted a permanent injunction to keep the dam from closing until Congress passed legislation to specifically exempt it from the ESA, the snail darter was no longer classified as endangered, or the fish's critical habitat had been substantially redefined. Neither the dam's stage of completion nor Congress's granting of funds for it was relevant, the judges ruled.

Even after this decision, Congress continued to approve funds for the dam. In June 1977, the House Appropriations Committee stated, "It is the Committee's view that the Endangered Species Act was not intended to halt projects such as these in their advanced stage of completion." The equivalent Senate committee agreed. Meanwhile, the TVA appealed the legal case to the Supreme Court, which agreed to review it.

Legal Issues

One issue before the court was whether the ESA required cancellation of a project that was mostly finished before the law was passed and, by the time of the court's decision, was "virtually completed and . . . essentially ready for operation." A second question was whether Congress had intended the needs of endangered species to outweigh all other considerations, including the irrecoverable loss of millions of dollars in public funds. TVA attorneys contended that, on the contrary, Congress had by implication repealed the relevant portion of the ESA as applied to the Tellico Dam by continuing to grant funds for the dam project after the snail darter had been classified as endangered.

Decision

On June 15, 1978, the Supreme Court voted to uphold the appeals court's decision and its injunction. Chief Justice Warren Burger wrote the court's majority opinion.

Burger stated that "one would be hard pressed to find a statutory provision whose terms were any plainer than those in Section 7 of the Endangered Species Act." The requirement for government agencies to ensure that their actions did not jeopardize or destroy the habitat of endangered species "admits of no exception," he wrote. Furthermore, he claimed, "examination of the language, history and structure of the legislation under review here indicates beyond doubt that Congress intended endangered species to be afforded the highest of priorities." He cited examples to prove that Congress foresaw and accepted the possibility that section 7 might require agencies to alter or halt ongoing projects. It was not the court's job, he wrote, to weigh the monetary loss of stopping a project, no matter how great, against the value of an endangered species, which Congress had called "incalculable."

Burger denied that Congress's continued granting of funds for the Tellico Dam amounted to an "implied repeal" of Section 7 as it applied to that project. For one thing, he wrote, it was court policy to find "implied repeal" only when an old law was completely incompatible with a newly passed one, which he did not believe was true in this case. Furthermore, the statements maintaining that the ESA did not require halting the dam came only from subcommittees, not from the whole Congress, and therefore did not override the plain language of the ESA itself.

Having found that there was "an irreconcilable conflict between operation of the Tellico Dam and the explicit provisions of Section 7 of the Endangered Species Act," Burger went on to consider whether an injunction against the dam's completion was an appropriate remedy. The TVA had asked the court to view the ESA "reasonably" and choose a remedy for the legal conflict "that accords with some modicum of commonsense and the public weal." However, Burger felt that defining such a settlement was both beyond the court's expertise and an overstepping of its authority relative to Congress. "Once the meaning of an enactment is discerned and its constitutionality determined, the judicial process comes to an end," he wrote. Since the court had found that completion of the dam would violate the ESA, he concluded that the dam should be stopped.

Justices Lewis F. Powell, Jr. and Harry A. Blackmun filed a dissent, written by Justice Powell. Powell claimed that "this decision casts a long shadow over the operation of even the most important [government] projects, serving vital needs of society and national defense." He held that Congress had not intended Section 7 of the ESA to apply to projects that were completed or nearly so and that using the law in this way essentially made it retroactive. He disagreed with Burger about the "plainness" of Section 7's language, holding that "actions" in the law referred only to actions an agency is deciding whether to perform—that is, actions not yet accomplished. He also interpreted the ESA's and the dam project's legislative history differently, finding Congress's continued voting of funds for the dam more significant than Burger had. He labeled Burger's decision "an extreme example of a literalist construction, not required by the language of the Act and adopted without regard to its manifest purpose." Justice Rehnquist also dissented, saying that the district court was right not to issue an injunction against the dam because of the very unclearness of Congress's intention, as evidenced by the other justices' differing interpretations.

Impact

Congress's first response to the Supreme Court's decision was to develop a process through which federal agencies could seek an exemption from Section 7 of the ESA. It put this procedure into law as an ESA amendment in late 1978. The amendment stated that an "Endangered Species Committee," chaired by the secretary of the interior, would decide whether an exemption would be granted.

Not surprisingly, the first agency to ask for an exemption was TVA. What perhaps *was* surprising was that the committee unanimously rejected the request. Not daunted, Congress then passed a bill specifically ordering completion of the Tellico Dam and waiving any federal laws that might oppose it. The dam went into operation in November 1979.

Although the environmentalists (and animal protectionists who shared their interest in saving the snail darter) lost the battle to stop the Tellico

Animal Rights

Dam, *TVA v. Hill* took them a step forward in the overall war to protect endangered species. Congress might have opened a loophole to allow federal agencies—with some difficulty—to avoid the ESA in selected cases, but the Supreme Court's statement of the primacy of preserving endangered species over economic or other considerations nonetheless still stood overall.

The snail darter also survived. A year after the Tellico Dam closed its gates, the biologist who had discovered the species found another population of the fish in South Chickamauga Creek, which was unaffected by the dam. Additional groups were found in other waterways during the next several years. In 1984, the Fish and Wildlife Service reclassified the snail darter as merely threatened rather than endangered, a classification it still holds.

INTERNATIONAL PRIMATE PROTECTION LEAGUE V. INSTITUTE FOR BEHAVIORAL RESEARCH 799 F.2D 934 (1986)

Background

In May 1981, Alex Pacheco, who had recently joined Ingrid Newkirk in founding People for the Ethical Treatment of Animals (PETA), decided to personally investigate the conditions under which laboratory animals were kept. Pacheco, then an undergraduate student at George Washington University, chose the laboratory of Edward Taub, chief of the Behavioral Biology Center of the Institute for Behavioral Research in Silver Spring, Maryland, because it was near his home.

In an effort to discover whether regrowth of nerves and perhaps restoration of function was possible following injuries or strokes, Taub had cut nerves leading from the spinal cords to the arms of macaque monkeys so that the animals could no longer feel pain or other sensations in the operated limbs. He then tried to force the monkeys to use the numbed arms (over which they still had muscle control) to see whether such use would stimulate regrowth in the cut nerves. After a certain length of time he planned to euthanize the monkeys and examine their spinal cords to check for regrowth. His work was funded by the National Institutes of Health (NIH)—in other words, by the federal government.

Taub signed Pacheco on as a volunteer and immediately allowed him to work with the monkeys in spite of Pacheco's admitted lack of experience in caring for laboratory animals. Pacheco discovered to his horror that the creatures were kept in small cages under filthy conditions—despite the fact that, as required by the Animal Welfare Act (AWA), the laboratory had been inspected by representatives of the U.S. Department of Agriculture (USDA) and found to be in compliance with the law. Furthermore, the

98

monkeys apparently no longer recognized the treated limbs as part of their bodies and had viciously bitten and chewed them, producing wounds that often became infected and were left untreated.

Working alone in the laboratory at night, Pacheco filmed the animals and their miserable surroundings. He also brought in several primate experts to witness the conditions. He then took his film, notes, and witnesses' sworn statements to local police. On September 11, the police searched the laboratory, confiscated 17 monkeys, and charged Taub with 17 counts of animal cruelty, one for each monkey. The seized monkeys were sent to a facility run by the NIH.

Legal Issues

What came to be known as "the Silver Spring monkey case" marked the first time a federally funded researcher had been charged under a state animal cruelty law or raided by police. Most anticruelty laws specifically exempted scientific researchers or at least were never enforced in regard to them. Maryland's law, however, contained no such exemption.

The case took on even greater legal importance because of several civil suits filed in connection with it. In early 1982, PETA and the Humane Society of the United States sued the USDA to demand that it enforce the AWA, provisions of which they claimed that Taub had violated. This lawsuit was the first time that animal protection groups had tried this approach, which environmentalist organizations had already attempted in regard to the Endangered Species Act. As the environmental groups had done in cases such as *Sierra Club v. Morton*, the animal rightists faced the stiff legal challenge of convincing the courts that they had standing to sue.

Two other suits, one filed by the Fund for Animals in 1982 and another by the International Primate Protection League (IPPL) and PETA in 1984, brought up the same problem. The first suit attempted to stop the NIH from returning the monkeys to Taub and the Institute for Behavioral Research on the grounds that the scientists had violated the AWA, and the second suit asked for legal guardianship of the monkeys and claimed that the groups' members would suffer financial and other injuries if the research organization was allowed to reacquire the monkeys.

Decision

In December 1981, the District Court for Montgomery County convicted Edward Taub of six counts of cruelty for failing to provide adequate veterinary care for his monkeys, but it acquitted him on the other 11 counts. Taub appealed the conviction, swearing that no one else in the laboratory had observed the mistreatment Pacheco had alleged. A jury in a local circuit court overturned five of the six convictions after a new trial, and a state appeals court reversed the remaining one in 1983. The courts ruled that the monkeys' suffering was not "unnecessary or unjustifiable," as the Maryland anticruelty law required, but rather was part of the "purely incidental and unavoidable pain" that can occur during research, which, they concluded, state legislators had not meant the law to cover. The appeals court also ruled that the state law did not apply to research done with federal funding.

All the civil suits were dismissed. In the 1982 suits, the courts ruled that the USDA was entitled to decide when and how to enforce the AWA and that nothing in the AWA obliged the NIH to do what the Fund for Animals asked. In March 1985, a federal district court denied PETA and the IPPL standing to sue in the guardianship case. The animal rights groups appealed the decision, but the Fourth Circuit Court of Appeals upheld the lower court's ruling in September 1986. As the Supreme Court had done in *Sierra Club v. Morton*, the appeals court held that an organization's general interest in a problem was not enough to constitute an "injury in fact." Furthermore, Judge Wilkinson wrote in his majority opinion,

> to imply a cause of action in [i.e., to grant standing to] these plaintiffs . . .
> might open the use of animals in biomedical research to the hazards and vicissitudes of courtroom litigation. . . . It might unleash a spate of private lawsuits that would impede advances made by medical science in the alleviation of human suffering. To risk consequences of this magnitude in the absence of clear direction from the Congress would be ill-advised.

In addition to denying standing, Wilkinson pointed out that, unlike the Endangered Species Act, the AWA contains no provision for private individuals to sue for enforcement of the law, and he claimed that Congress had not wanted it to have any such provision. Citizen monitoring of the AWA as it applied to laboratories was expected to occur only through the Institutional Animal Care and Use Committees authorized by the 1985 amendments to the AWA. Most important, Wilkinson said the AWA was not intended to allow citizens or courts to pass judgment on the conduct of medical research. He quoted a congressional statement that under the AWA "the research scientist still holds the key to the laboratory door."

Impact

Supporters of animal research such as Adrian Morrison have claimed that Edward Taub's eventual acquittal on all charges of animal cruelty showed that Alex Pacheco's accusations were false. Animal rightists, for their part, say that Taub was freed merely on a technicality. In any case, the publicity surrounding Taub's trials made his monkeys what Jordan Curnutt calls "perhaps the most famous lab animals in the history of science."[4] Public horror at the conditions in Taub's laboratory, as Pacheco described them, helped to pressure Congress to strengthen the AWA considerably in 1985. Maryland lawmakers also revised the state anticruelty law in 1992 to explicitly cover "all animals . . . [used in] federally funded scientific medical activities."

The failure of the animal rights groups' civil suits showed that the difficulties in obtaining standing to sue that had hamstrung environmental groups in cases such as *Sierra Club v. Morton* applied to animal protection groups as well. Supporters of animal research were heartened by the dismissal of the rightists' suits. Nonetheless, PETA, the Animal Legal Defense Fund, and others continued to attempt to use lawsuits against what they saw as the USDA's inadequate enforcement of the AWA, and in a later case (*Animal Legal Defense Fund v. Glickman*) they were successful at least in obtaining standing as regards the AWA's application to animal exhibitors.

The legal battles over Taub's monkeys, which continued throughout the 1980s, allowed most of the animals to live far longer than Taub had originally planned. When several of the surviving monkeys were finally returned to Taub and killed in 1990 and 1991—more than 10 years after their original operations—autopsies showed that many of their cut nerve fibers had in fact regrown. This discovery suggested that Taub's research, whatever its moral or other drawbacks, did have potential medical value.

THE BOBBY BEROSINI ORANGUTAN CASE

Background

Entertainer Bobby Berosini used five orangutans in a comedy act at the Stardust Hotel and Casino in Las Vegas, Nevada, in the 1980s. Ottavio Gesmundo, a dancer working at the Stardust, made a videotape that appeared to show Berosini striking the animals with a rod or baton backstage before several performances in July 1989. As part of an ongoing campaign to end the use of animals in entertainment, the animal rights groups People for the Ethical Treatment of Animals (PETA) and the Performing Animal Welfare Society (PAWS) distributed the tape and publicly accused Berosini of animal abuse. PETA also said that Berosini violated the Animal Welfare Act by keeping the orangutans "in refrigerator-sized metal containers" on a bus between shows.[5]

In August 1989, soon after the tape was made public, Berosini sued PETA and other animal rights activists in a Clark County district court for defamation of character and invasion of privacy. He claimed that Gesmundo and others had deliberately made noises that upset the orangutans, forcing Berosini to use the rod to quiet them, and that the backstage tape had been edited to produce a false effect. The USDA had just inspected the animals' housing, he said, and found no signs of abuse. PETA filed a countersuit, requesting custody of the orangutans.

Legal Issues

The Berosini case brought into question the degree of proof an animal rights group needs to have in order to publicly call someone an animal abuser. It also spotlighted possible remedies that either an accused person or institution or an animal rightist accuser might find in the courts. Finally, the case and comments about it illustrate how opposing biases can cause different people to perceive the same actions differently.

Decision

In August 1990, after a five-week trial that included a court appearance by Berosini's orangutans, a jury in the district court ruled against the animal rightists and ordered them to pay a total of $3.1 million in damages to Berosini. PETA appealed the case, however, and in January 1994 and again in May 1995 the Nevada State Supreme Court unanimously reversed the decision. According to PETA, the judges wrote:

> *All of the members of the court have viewed the tape; and what is shown on the tape is clear and unequivocal; Berosini is shown, immediately before going on stage, grabbing, slapping, punching and shaking the animals while several handlers hold the animals in position.*[6]

The court ordered Berosini to pay PETA's court costs (although part of this requirement was waived in 1995). According to a PETA news release, Berosini gave the organization $340,230 in May 2000.

Impact

The state supreme court ruling ended the significant legal issues in the Berosini case, though the war between Berosini and PETA over the court costs has continued. In the most recent battle, according to a PETA press release, the U.S. Court of Appeals for the Ninth Circuit ruled on February 9, 2007 (for the fourth time, PETA said), that Berosini had to pay the organization more than $250,000 in ongoing costs, most of which were incurred in the process of uncovering assets that Berosini and his wife had hidden in an attempt to avoid previous judgments.

The court records may not tell the whole story, however. In an article published in *Harper's Magazine* in 1993, animal trainer Vicki Hearne described spending a week with Berosini (whom she had not previously known) and seeing his act a dozen times in an attempt to ascertain the truth of

PETA's accusations. She saw no signs of abuse; she pointed out, for instance, that the orangutans were unconfined during their stage performances and could have attempted to escape if they had felt threatened. On the contrary, she perceived the relationship between Berosini and the apes as close and loving, supporting his claim that the animals were "comedians" like himself and developed the act collaboratively with him. Ward Clark, a strong critic of animal rights groups, reported similar experiences in his 2001 book, *Misplaced Compassion*. On a visit to the Berosini home, he wrote, he found all the orangutans "obviously happy, content, loved and well cared for."[7]

Who had the true picture of the way Bobby Berosini treated his coperformers? Only the orangutans really knew. In any case, their relationship is over: A press release issued by PETA in February 2007 stated that Berosini no longer owned orangutans.

BABBITT V. SWEET HOME CHAPTER OF COMMUNITIES FOR A GREAT OREGON 515 U.S. 687 (1995)

Background

As the Supreme Court's decision in *TVA v. Hill* showed, the Endangered Species Act (ESA) could be read very broadly, and the court interpreted its requirements as overriding economic or other considerations under almost all circumstances. Groups who suffered economic losses as a result of the act, however, continued trying to persuade the courts to set limits on it.

In the late 1980s, several logging projects on private land were halted because their continuation was expected to damage the habitats of the endangered red cockaded woodpecker and the threatened northern spotted owl to an extent that would result in injury or death of members of these species. In response, a group of logging companies and individuals who supported or earned their living from forest products industries in the Pacific Northwest and Southeast, calling themselves the Sweet Home Chapter of Communities for a Great Oregon, sued the secretary of the interior, Bruce Babbitt, and the director of the Fish and Wildlife Service (FWS), John F. Turner, in the federal district court for the District of Columbia in 1992. Halting logging to preserve endangered species habitat, they said, had injured them economically.

Legal Issues

Section 9(a)(1) of the Endangered Species Act forbids anyone in the United States to take endangered species, and section 3(19) further defines *take* as "to harass, harm, pursue, hunt, shoot, wound, kill, trap, capture, or collect, or to attempt to engage in any such conduct." The act itself does not further define *harm*. However, a 1975 Fish and Wildlife Service (FWS) regulation defines *harm* as

> *an act which actually kills or injures wildlife. Such act may include significant habitat modification or degradation where it actually kills or injures wildlife by significantly impairing essential behavioral patterns, including breeding, feeding, or sheltering.*

The logging group challenged the validity of the 1975 regulation "on its face," rather than as applied to any particular situation, claiming that the regulation's definition of *harm* as including significant habitat modification went further than Congress had intended. It offered three arguments to support its position:

1. that the Senate had deleted from its version of the ESA language that would have defined *take* to include "destruction, modification, or curtailment of [the] habitat or range" of endangered wildlife;
2. that Congress intended habitat to be preserved only by government purchase of relevant private land, as provided for in section 5 of the act; and
3. that because the Senate had added *harm* to the definition of *take* without debate, it should not be given much weight.

The district court rejected all three arguments and ruled that a definition of *take* that included habitat modification was a reasonable interpretation of the ESA. When the Sweet Home group appealed the case, a divided panel of the District of Columbia Court of Appeals initially agreed with the district court, but on rehearing, a majority of the court reversed the decision. Based on the meanings of the words around *harm* in the ESA's definition of *take*, the court read *harm* as requiring "the perpetrator's direct application of force against the animal taken." They also claimed that the inclusion of habitat modification in the definition of *harm* was not supported by the legislative history of the ESA and its amendments.

The appeals court's decision was in conflict with a decision by the Ninth Circuit Court of Appeals in a 1988 case, *Palila v. Hawaii Department of Land and Natural Resources (Palila II)*. In that case (one of the rare examples in which a species of animal was named as a plaintiff, in this case an endangered species of Hawaiian bird), the appeals court had concluded that inclusion of habitat modification that might endanger a species in the future in the ESA's definition of *harm* was appropriate. The Supreme Court agreed to hear the Sweet Home case in order to resolve this conflict.

The Law and Animal Rights

Decision

The high court rendered its decision on June 29, 1995, reversing the appeals court by a 6-3 vote. Justice John Paul Stevens wrote the court's majority opinion. In supporting the idea that the meaning of *harm* could include habitat modification, as the 1975 regulation stated, Stevens first maintained that the dictionary definition of *harm* supported the interpretation that the word could include indirect and unintended as well as direct and willful damage. Furthermore, he said, if the word did not include indirect damage, there would have been no reason to add it to the definition of *take*.

Next, Stevens reiterated the court's conclusion in *TVA v. Hill* that "the plain intent of Congress in enacting . . . [the ESA] was to halt and reverse the trend toward species extinction, whatever the cost." This understanding of the ESA's broad scope made inclusion of habitat modification in the definition of *harm* reasonable, whether the modification came from a federal agency, as in *TVA v. Hill*, or private industry. Third, Stevens wrote, the fact that Congress had added an amendment to the ESA in 1982 that allowed groups to obtain permits for taking that the ESA would otherwise forbid "if such taking is incidental to . . . the carrying out of an otherwise lawful activity" suggested that "taking" had been meant to include indirect actions—otherwise there would have been no need for the amendment, since permits for direct, deliberate destruction of members of a threatened or endangered species were hardly likely to be requested or granted.

Stevens went on to cite several more general reasons for disagreeing with the appeals court. First, he wrote, buying land might be the best method for preserving habitat under some circumstances, but Stevens believed that Congress did not intend it to be the only method available. Second, drawing by analogy on the court's ruling in a previous key case, *Chevron U.S.A., Inc., v. Natural Resources Defense Council,* Stevens stated that the authority that Congress had granted to the secretary of the interior for enforcing and interpreting the ESA, as well as the secretary's regulatory expertise, was great enough that the court should accept the secretary's interpretations unless they were shown to be obviously unreasonable, which he did not believe they were in this case. Finally, he maintained that the legislative history of the ESA and its amendments supported the belief that Congress intended *take* to encompass indirect as well as direct actions.

Justice Antonin Scalia wrote a dissenting opinion (in which Chief Justice William H. Rehnquist and Justice Clarence Thomas concurred) in which he offered several reasons for believing that the 1975 regulation should be declared invalid because it was far broader than Congress had intended the ESA to be. Justice Sandra Day O'Connor wrote a concurring opinion in which, among other things, she claimed that *Palila II* had been wrongly decided because the harm to the palila resulting from destruction of plant seedlings by sheep and goats was speculative rather than actual.

Impact

The Supreme Court's decision carried even further the tendency it had shown in *TVA v. Hill* to interpret Congress's intention in passing the ESA as being to preserve endangered species literally "at any cost." Shelli Lyn Iovino, writing in the *Villanova Environmental Law Journal* in 1996, maintained that the decision "is consistent with jurisdictional trends." She claimed that most jurisdictions have recognized that some degree of destructive habitat modification can reasonably be included under the "harm" provision in Section 9 of the ESA.

The court's decision removed the inconsistency between the appeals court ruling in this case and that in *Palila II*, providing "a clear and concise interpretation of the section 9 taking provision" for future courts. It emphasized the discretion of government agencies to establish reasonable regulations and, above all, strengthened and expanded the power of the ESA. Environmentalists and animal rights groups would be expected to regard the decision as a victory, while those whose businesses brought them into potential conflict with the ESA no doubt viewed it with dismay. Such businesses include not only logging companies and other large corporations but builders of low-income housing and certain other projects of potential social benefit.

ANIMAL LEGAL DEFENSE FUND V. GLICKMAN
154 F.3D 426 (1998) 204 F.3D 229 (2000)

Background

Marc Jurnove, a member of several animal protection organizations who was "very familiar with the needs of and proper treatment of wildlife," paid frequent visits to (among others) the Long Island Game Park Farm and Zoo during 1995 and early 1996. There he saw apes and monkeys living under conditions that distressed him because he believed that the conditions were inhumane. For instance, a chimpanzee and a Japanese snow macaque (a type of monkey) were kept in cages out of sight of other primates, which Jurnove knew was likely to make the animals unhappy because primates are social animals and like to be with others of their kind. The only object in the cage with the macaque was a swing, which the animal did not use. In another cage, squirrel monkeys were kept near a cage that contained bears. The bears could not actually harm the monkeys, but the smell of them upset the smaller creatures.

In Jurnove's opinion, these arrangements were violations of the Animal Welfare Act (AWA), which specifies the minimum conditions under which animals in exhibitions such as the Long Island zoo must be kept. Amendments to the AWA passed in 1985 state that exhibitors must establish programs to promote "the psychological well-being of primates," and AWA regulations recommended (but did not require) housing primates together, providing enrichment objects in their enclosures, and keeping them separate from predator animals. Beginning on the day after his first visit to the Long Island zoo in 1995, Jurnove complained repeatedly to the U.S. Department of Agriculture (USDA), which administers and enforces the AWA. In response, the USDA sent inspectors to the zoo four times, but they found no significant AWA violations. As far as the USDA was concerned, the zoo animals' housing was perfectly legal.

In June 1996, Jurnove, the Animal Legal Defense Fund (ALDF), and several other plaintiffs sued Daniel Glickman, the secretary of agriculture, in a federal district court. They claimed that Glickman had not fulfilled the AWA's requirement to "promulgate standards to govern the humane handling, care, treatment, and transportation of animals by dealers, research facilities, and exhibitors" because the USDA's regulations allowed the regulated institutions to design their own programs for primate well-being rather than specifying such programs in detail.

Jurnove, in particular, alleged that seeing the primates kept as they were in the zoo caused him "extreme aesthetic harm and emotional and physical distress" and would continue to do so unless the conditions changed. He explicitly stated that he planned to "return to the [Long Island Game] Farm in the next several weeks" and to "continue visiting the Farm to see the animals there" in the future. He claimed that the conditions that distressed him would not be legal if the USDA issued and implemented regulations detailed enough to meet the AWA requirements, so improvements in the regulations would end his injury.

Legal Issues

As in *Sierra Club v. Morton* and numerous other lawsuits filed by environmental and animal rights groups, the first hurdle the plaintiffs had to leap was establishment of standing to sue. In cases such as *Lujan v. Defenders of Wildlife* (1992), the Supreme Court had elaborated on the requirements for gaining standing in a particular case. Plaintiffs, they stated, had to prove that they suffered from an "injury in fact," that the injury is "fairly traceable" to the defendants' conduct, and that a court ruling in the plaintiffs' favor would be likely to "redress" the injury—repair it or stop it from continuing. Plaintiffs also had to fulfill "prudential" requirements for standing, which meant that their "grievance must arguably fall within the zone of interests protected or regulated by the statutory provision or constitutional guarantee invoked in the suit." At the time Jurnove and the other plaintiffs filed their suit, no individual or group had succeeded in establishing standing to sue for a violation of the AWA.

If standing to sue could be established, the case would then be tried on its merits. Such a trial would produce a ruling on whether the USDA had violated Congress's intention in passing the AWA in the way the agency wrote and, perhaps, enforced the regulations that implemented the act.

Decision

In October 1996, District Court Judge Charles R. Richey granted the plaintiffs standing to sue and ruled in their favor, holding that the USDA's lack of detailed regulations regarding promotion of primate well-being violated the Administrative Procedure Act (APA), a 1946 law establishing procedural requirements for rule making by federal agencies, as well as the AWA. The agriculture department's lawyers appealed, however, and in March 1997, two judges out of a three-judge panel from the District of Columbia Circuit Court of Appeals reversed the decision, saying that the plaintiffs did not have standing to sue because they failed to meet the requirements of cause and redressability.

The ALDF demanded a rehearing by all 11 judges of the circuit court, claiming that the appeals panel's majority opinion not only went against previous court rulings but set such high standards for proving causation and redressability that this decision essentially made it impossible for third parties to sue a government agency for failing to comply with legislation's requirement to issue appropriate regulations. If allowed to stand, the ruling, therefore, "would virtually end judicial review of agency action."[8] The rehearing was granted and occurred on May 13, 1998. On September 1, the full appeals court granted Marc Jurnove standing to sue by a 7-4 vote. Once one plaintiff was granted standing, the court did not need to rule on the others.

Judge Patricia Wald, who had cast a dissenting vote in the previous appeals court ruling, wrote the court's majority opinion. She said Jurnove had established that he had been injured "in a personal and individual way . . . by seeing with his own eyes the particular animals whose condition caused him aesthetic injury." He had thus suffered the required "injury in fact." She also held that Jurnove had satisfactorily demonstrated that the lack of specificity in USDA regulations concerning primate housing had caused his injury because the conditions that distressed him were legal under the present regulations but (the plaintiffs alleged) would not have been so if the regulations had been as specific as the AWA required. Finally, Wald wrote, Jurnove had satisfied the redressibility requirement of standing because he had described specific plans to visit the zoo in the future and had claimed that more stringent USDA regulations would be likely to prevent future aesthetic injury by improving the conditions he witnessed.

Jurnove also met the prudential requirements for standing, Wald wrote, because Supreme Court decisions in *Sierra Club v. Morton* and other cases had established that aesthetic interest, including an interest in "view[ing] animals free from . . . 'inhumane treatment,'" was a protected interest. Wald held that it was specifically an interest protected by the AWA, since "the very purpose of animal exhibitions is . . . to entertain and educate people." She pointed out that the legislative history of the AWA also indicated that Congress had expected and desired that "humane societies and their members" would monitor animal exhibitions "to ensure that the purposes of the Act were honored."

Judge Sentelle wrote a dissenting opinion for the en banc hearing, in which Judges Silberman, Ginsburg, and Henderson joined. Sentelle wrote that by allowing Jurnove standing to sue, the majority "significantly weakens existing requirements of constitutional standing." He claimed that aesthetic injury regarding animals so far had been accepted only for circumstances in which the numbers of a species were reduced, not for conditions under which individual animals were viewed. Expanding the doctrine, he said, "opens an expanse of standing bounded only by what a given plaintiff finds to be aesthetically pleasing." There is no precise, objective definition for "humane treatment," he noted, and exactly what Jurnove would require in this line was unknown.

Sentelle was not convinced that Jurnove had satisfied the causation requirement, either, because the actions that produced his alleged injury were those of a third party (the zoo), not the USDA. "I find frightening at a constitutional level the majority's assumption that the government causes everything that it does not prevent," he wrote. Finally, because the conditions that would satisfy Jurnove's definition of humaneness were unknown, Sentelle stated that there was no real reason for thinking that a judicial order requiring the USDA to write new regulations would be likely to redress his injury.

The USDA appealed the case to the U.S. Supreme Court, but the high court declined to hear it in 1999, thereby allowing the appeals court ruling to stand. Obtaining standing to sue proved to be insufficient for Jurnove and the ALDF to achieve their aims, however. District Court Judge Richey again ruled in their favor when he reheard the case on its merits, but the case was appealed, and in February 2000 another three-judge panel from the D.C. appeals court (including Sentelle but not Wald) ruled by a split vote (2-1) that the USDA regulations about primates did not violate either the AWA or the APA. Neither the USDA nor the zoo, therefore, had done anything illegal, so the suit was dismissed.

In the majority opinion for the 2000 appeals court hearing, Judge Williams wrote that regulations, including the USDA's regulations for implementing the AWA, normally contain one or both of two types of rules: engineering standards, which "dictate the required means to achieve a result," and performance standards, which "state the desired outcomes, leaving to the facility the choice of means." According to Williams, Jurnove and the other plaintiffs claimed that the USDA had issued no engineering standards for furthering the psychological well-being of primates. The USDA's response, which Williams supported, was that it had in fact issued such standards, for instance by requiring specific cage sizes and placing limits on the use of restraint devices.

Williams believed that the USDA had made most other requirements less specific because designing detailed regulations that would work well for all of the several hundred diverse species of primates was almost impossible. Even experts in the field disagreed about what the best social arrangements for captive primates should be, for instance. Because of such disagreement, Williams said, the vagueness of the USDA's regulations was not "arbitrary and capricious," as the district court had held.

Impact

The en banc appeals court decision in *ALDF v. Glickman* I in 1998 marked the first time that standing to sue had been granted for an alleged USDA violation of the AWA. Naturally, animal protection groups were delighted with the ruling. ALDF senior staff attorney Valerie Stanley called it "a landmark decision for anyone concerned about promoting humane treatment for animals."[9] Rob Roy Smith, a student at the Northwestern School of Law of Lewis and Clark College, wrote in 1999 that it "la[id] a foundation for animal welfare litigation to follow" and potentially would "spark a legal and political revolution in animal law."[10] On the other hand, Judge Santelle in his dissent expressed a fear that "allowing unrestricted taxpayer or citizen standing would significantly alter the allocation of power at the national level, with a shift away from a democratic form of government" because it would "increase federal judicial power at the expense of that of the political [legislative and executive] branches."

The ability to establish standing to sue in an AWA case probably does, as Smith wrote, "open a door to judicial review previously closed to animal welfare plaintiffs" and "provide a roadmap for future plaintiffs to follow."[11] However, the fact that the case was rejected on its merits shows that the door has hardly swung wide, and the road has more than a few bumpy places. Clearly, obtaining standing to sue is not enough to make the courts demand improvement in AWA regulations. Also, unlike the Endangered Species Act, the AWA lacks a "citizen suit" provision, so trying to sue for enforcement of parts of the AWA itself, as opposed to using the grounds of the USDA's failure to promulgate adequate rules (the legal theory the courts accepted in *ALDF v. Glickman*), may still be difficult. It is also unclear whether it will be as easy to establish standing in regard to laboratories, which are not normally open to the public, as for animal exhibitions, although one student laboratory worker was granted standing in a later (2000) AWA case.

TEXAS BEEF GROUP V. WINFREY
201 F.3D 680 (2000)

Background

In the mid-1990s, a mysterious brain ailment called variant Creutzfeldt-Jakob disease killed 10 young people in Britain. A British Ministry of Health announcement in March 1996 linked this illness to a similar brain disease in cattle called bovine spongiform encephalopathy (BSE), or "mad cow disease," which had been common in British cattle since the late 1980s. Ministry scientists raised the terrifying possibility that the disease's human victims might have contracted it by eating beef from cattle with BSE, just as BSE itself appeared to have spread through cattle feed that contained the remains of cattle with BSE and sheep that had a similar disease called scrapie. Mad cow disease had never been reported in the United States, but some ranchers did feed cattle material that contained animal remains, and some people speculated that an outbreak of BSE and perhaps variant Creutzfeldt-Jakob disease could occur in this country as well.

One person who thought this might happen was Howard Lyman, a Montana rancher who had become an ardent vegetarian and believed that a diet high in animal foods caused numerous health problems. Famous talk show host Oprah Winfrey interviewed Lyman, among others, on an episode of her show called "Dangerous Food," broadcast on April 16, 1996. On the air, Lyman said that an epidemic of human brain disease spread by tainted beef could "make AIDS look like the common cold" by comparison. Winfrey exclaimed that his words had "stopped [her] cold from eating another burger."

Other guests on Winfrey's show gave reasons for thinking that eating American beef was safe, but in the weeks following the broadcast the nationwide price of cattle plummeted to its lowest level in four decades. Several Texas cattle ranchers sued Winfrey, Lyman, and the producers and distributors of Winfrey's show in May 1996, claiming that they had violated the Texas False Disparagement of Perishable Food Products Act. This 1995 law, which stated that "a person may be held liable for damages sustained by the producer of a perishable food product if that person knowingly disseminates false information to the public stating or implying that the producer's product is not safe for public consumption," was one of the food disparagement, or "veggie libel," laws that 13 states had passed after a 1989 media scare about a chemical sprayed on apples had caused a catastrophic drop in apple prices. The ranchers also sued for business disparagement, defamation, and negligence.

Legal Issues

This case was one of the first to be brought under the Texas food disparagement law, and both supporters and opponents of such laws hoped that the Winfrey suit could be used as a test case to determine the laws' constitutionality. However, Mary Lou Robinson, the judge of the federal district court to which the trial was moved, dismissed the food disparagement claim. The law applied only to perishable food products, which it defined as "food product[s] of agriculture or aquaculture that [are] sold or distributed in a form that will perish or decay beyond marketability within a limited period of time," and Robinson ruled that live cattle did not meet this definition. When she gave the case to a jury, she told the jurors that their only job was to rule on whether a business disparagement had occurred. She instructed them to find the defendants guilty only if they believed that the defendants had knowingly or recklessly published false, disparaging statements "of and concerning" the plaintiffs' cattle and that such statements had "played a substantial and direct part in inducing specific damage to the business interest of the Plaintiff[s]."

Decision

The jury found the defendants not guilty in February 1998. They and the judge agreed that Lyman's statements were based on "reasonable and reliable scientific inquiry, facts, [and] data." Furthermore, although those who edited the program for airing had removed some material from other interviewees that might have presented American beef in a better light (describing, for instance, some of the steps that government authorities were taking to prevent BSE's appearance in the United States and the fact that ranchers had agreed to a voluntary ban on feeding ruminant parts to cattle), their work also did not produce a result that was actually false.

The Texas Beef Group appealed the case, and a three-judge panel of the Fifth Circuit Court of Appeals gave its opinion in February 2000. The appeals court did not rule on the issue of whether cattle should be considered "perishable" for purposes of the food disparagement law, although one, Edith L. Jones, wrote in a concurring opinion that she believed that cattle should so qualify. The circuit court judges agreed with the district court that the defendants had not knowingly made false statements about the safety of eating American beef, and they therefore upheld the lower court's acquittal on the business disparagement charge. Some of Lyman's statements might have been overdramatic and exaggerated, the judges wrote, but they cited a ruling in another case that "exaggeration does not equal defamation." Similarly, they stated, "so long as the factual underpinnings remained accurate, as they did here, the editing did not give rise to an inference that knowingly false information was being disseminated."

Impact

The *Winfrey* case did not provide a ruling on the constitutionality of food disparagement laws, not only because the district court ruled that cattle were not perishable products but also because, as the appeals court wrote, "the insufficiency of the cattlemen's evidence . . . render[ed] unnecessary a complete inquiry into the [Texas] Act's scope." However, Winfrey and Lyman's victory, like that of the animal rightist defendants in a similar case in England involving hamburger giant McDonald's, the so-called McLibel case, showed that animal rights groups or others were entitled to criticize animal agriculture publicly as long as their statements were based on sound information.

The publicity surrounding Lyman's and Winfrey's statements may also have played a role in the fact that in August 1997, the U.S. Food and Drug Administration made the ban on the use of most animal products in food for cattle and other ruminants mandatory. Some people were sure to have recalled the case, too, in 2003, when mad cow disease was diagnosed for the first time in cattle from Canada (May) and the United States (December)— and hoped that Lyman's words were not prophetic.

THE TRIAL OF THE "SHAC SEVEN" (2006)
Background

SHAC-USA is the U.S. arm of a British animal rights group, Stop Huntingdon Animal Cruelty (SHAC). SHAC was formed in 1999 with the aim of shutting down Huntingdon Life Sciences (HLS), Europe's largest contract animal testing laboratory, after People for the Ethical Treatment of Animals (PETA) and others accused HLS employees of abusing animals in their facility. When SHAC published the names of Huntingdon shareholders, leading to the harassment of some, HLS moved its financial center to the United States (under the name of Life Sciences Research) because U.S. securities laws allowed greater anonymity of shareholders. SHAC, in turn, set up its own U.S. branch.

SHAC and SHAC-USA were frequently accused of causing, or encouraging others to cause, property damage and threats of severe bodily harm to individuals connected in any way with HLS. Kevin Kjonaas (sometimes spelled Jonas), the first president of SHAC-USA, said in 2002 that "when push comes to shove, we're ready to push, kick, shove, bite, do whatever to win."[12]

Animal Rights

On May 27, 2004, Kjonaas and six other members of the organization were indicted on charges of violating the Animal Enterprise Protection Act and other federal laws by using the Internet to terrorize employees and business associates of HLS and Life Sciences Research. According to the indictment, the SHAC-USA web site had published contact information for HLS employees and executives, including their home addresses and telephone numbers and, in some cases, the names, ages, and schools of their children. The site encouraged people to engage in "direct action . . . outside the confines of the legal system" and posted a list of "top 20 terror tactics," including threats and numerous forms of personal assault, property destruction, and vandalism.[13]

Legal Issues

Although the Animal Enterprise Protection Act had been passed in 1992 and strengthened in 2002, it had never been used in a successful prosecution of animal rights groups. In addition to the applicability of this law, a second question was whether SHAC-USA's Internet postings constituted "true threats" as defined by the Ninth Circuit Court of Appeals in two recent cases. In *Planned Parenthood of Columbia/Willamette, Inc. v. American Coalition of Life Activists*, an abortion-protest case decided in 2002, the court defined a "true threat" as a statement that a "reasonable person would foresee . . . would be interpreted by those to whom the maker communicates the statement as a serious expression of intent to harm."[14] In a 2005 case, a panel from the appeals court added the requirement that the defendant be shown to have intended the speech as a threat.

If the animal rights group's postings were not found to be true threats, the postings would probably be protected as free speech under the First Amendment. In *Brandenburg v. Ohio*, a 1969 case, the U.S. Supreme Court had ruled that political speech, even when inflammatory, is legal unless a defendant has told specific individuals to commit specific and imminent acts of violence.

Decision

The trial of the "SHAC Seven," as supporters called them, took place in a federal district court in Trenton, New Jersey, in February 2006. After hearing testimony from HLS employees describing numerous acts of intimidation and vandalism following SHAC-USA's postings, a jury rejected the defendants' free speech argument and, after three days of deliberation, found six of the seven guilty of some or all of the charges against them on March 2. On September 12, 2006, three of the six, including Kjonaas, were sentenced to jail terms of up to six years. SHAC-USA, as a corporation, was placed on five years' probation and ordered to pay a million-dollar restitution fine.

The Law and Animal Rights

Impact

This trial, the first conviction under the Animal Enterprise Protection Act, was widely considered to represent an increasing determination to "get tough" with those that the Bush administration and animal enterprise groups considered to be terrorists. U.S. attorney Christopher J. Christie called the verdict a "trial victory of national importance" and referred to the SHAC-USA members as "thugs."[15] The trial also drew attention to the technique of using the Internet to intimidate people and distribute information that would help others attack them.

In September 2006, just a few days before the SHAC Seven were sentenced, a new and stronger bill against animal rights and environmental "terrorism," the Animal Enterprise Terrorism Act, was introduced into Congress. The bill passed both houses during the next few months and was signed into law on November 27, 2006.

ALSEA VALLEY ALLIANCE V. EVANS 161 F. SUPP. 2D 1154 (D. OR. 2001) *ALSEA VALLEY ALLIANCE V. OREGON NATURAL RESOURCES* 01-36071 (2004)

Background

The Klamath River, which flows through southern Oregon and northern California, was once the third-largest producer of salmon on the West Coast and is still considered prime habitat for king (Chinook) and coho (silver) salmon and steelhead and rainbow trout. However, according to the Pacific Coast Federation of Fishermen's Associations, the combination of six dams, constructed for hydroelectric power between 1908 and 1962, and diversion of water from Upper Klamath Lake to provide irrigation for farms in the arid upper Klamath valley left water remaining in the river so reduced in volume, hot, and laced with harmful chemicals from agricultural runoff that it was often fatal to the fish, cutting salmon runs to less than 10 percent of their former size.

Numbers of naturally spawned coho salmon in the Klamath became so low that the National Marine Fisheries Service (NMFS) classified the Oregon Coast coho salmon as threatened in 1998, placing that group of fish under the protection of the Endangered Species Act (ESA). In doing so it followed the "hatchery policy" that it had set forth in 1993, which stated that salmon spawned in hatcheries would be counted along with wild-spawned fish to determine population size only "sparingly," when the hatchery-spawned fish were considered "essential to recovery" of the species. NMFS felt that this was not true of hatchery-spawned coho salmon, which made up the bulk of salmon in the Klamath, so it did not count them in making its determination to list the Oregon Coast coho.

During the next several years, a number of actions in the Klamath valley, including federal timber sales, road building, and diversion of irrigation water from Upper Klamath Lake, were halted at least in part to protect the Oregon Coast coho as required by the ESA, greatly angering the landowners and businesspeople affected by the changes. In 2001, therefore, a local property rights group, the Alsea Valley Alliance, sued in the U.S. District Court of Oregon to challenge the validity of the listing of the Oregon Valley coho under the ESA. By contrast, environmental and animal welfare groups, local American Indians, and fishermen who depended on the salmon for their living supported the NMFS's action and the continued protection of the Oregon Coast coho.

Legal Issues

In their suit, *Alsea Valley Alliance v. Evans*, the plaintiffs pointed out that the National Marine Fisheries Service had earlier ruled that wild-spawned and hatchery-spawned coho in the Klamath belonged to the same Evolutionarily Significant Unit (ESU), a term the agency had introduced in 1991 to substitute for "distinct population segment" (undefined by Congress), the smallest group that the Endangered Species Act allows to be given separate consideration for listing as threatened or endangered. If the two salmon groups were part of the same ESU, the alliance's attorneys said, NMFS's decision to count one and not the other was "arbitrary and capricious" as defined by the Administrative Procedures Act, and the listing of the Oregon Coast coho as threatened was therefore invalid.

Decision

On September 10, 2001, U.S. District Court Judge Michael Hogan accepted the alliance's reasoning and ruled in its favor. "The NMFS listing decision creates the unusual circumstance of two genetically identical coho salmon swimming side-by-side in the same stream, but only one receives ESA protection while the other does not," Hogan wrote. "The distinction is arbitrary." The listing of the Oregon Coast coho was also unlawful, he said, because the ESA does not permit distinctions below that of distinct population segment, or, as the NMFS chose to call it, evolutionarily significant unit. Hogan therefore set aside the 1998 listing of the Oregon Coast coho salmon and returned the matter to NMFS for further consideration.

The NMFS received its first petition to have the Oregon Coast coho delisted before September ended, and projects previously halted because of the coho's protected status resumed. The George W. Bush administration announced on November 9, 2001, that NMFS would not appeal Hogan's decision; rather, it would conduct a review of 23 of its 25 salmon and steelhead listings, in which hatchery-bred fish had not been counted.

Meanwhile, fisheries and environmental groups filed an appeal of their own. On December 14, 2001, the Ninth Circuit Court of Appeals ordered Hogan's order, and all actions stemming from it, stayed until the court could rule on the appeal, thus returning at least temporary protection to the salmon.

When the higher court issued its ruling on February 24, 2004, it denied the appeal because, the three-judge panel said, Hogan's ruling was not a "final order" and therefore could be appealed only by NMFS. The judges pointed out that NMFS's review process allowed for public comment, and they said that the groups who had appealed could have their say by that means. The appeals court opinion included no comments about the merits of Hogan's decision, but the court's rejection of the environmentalists' appeal automatically reinstated that decision and thus, in effect, mandated the delisting of the Oregon Coast coho salmon.

Impact

A summary of the case written by Kristen M. Fletcher for the Mississippi-Alabama Sea Grant Legal Program at the end of 2001 stated that 20 out of 26 West Coast salmon species or groups could be delisted as a result of Hogan's ruling, "even though the wild population may be on the brink of extinction."[16] According to Fletcher, government biologists felt that because of behavioral differences between wild and hatchery fish, which existed in spite of the genetic sameness of the two groups, delisting would "threaten the long-term survival of West Coast salmon."[17] Similarly, Brian J. Perron, writing in the Summer 2003 issue of *Environmental Law*, expressed fear that the coho delisting, which he called "misguided," would profoundly impact salmon recovery efforts in the Northwest.[18]

On the other hand, Russell C. Brooks, managing attorney for the Northwest Center of the Pacific Legal Foundation, a property-oriented legal group that had provided attorneys for the Alsea Valley Alliance, praised Hogan's ruling and called it "the most groundbreaking environmental decision of the last decade." In a press release issued by the foundation, Brooks said that because of Hogan's decision, "this attempt to control private land use in the name of species protection has been successfully shut down."[19]

Perhaps the least arguable description of the decision came from Erik Robinson, writing in *The Columbian* on October 4, 2001. Hogan's ruling, Robinson said, "complicates an already-complex issue."[20] In 2007, that issue is still far from settled.

Animal Rights

[1] Jordan Curnutt, *Animals and the Law: A Sourcebook*. Santa Barbara, Calif.: ABC-CLIO, 2001, p. 448.

[2] *Tennessee Valley Authority v. Hill*, 437 U.S. 153 (1978).

[3] Nathaniel Ward, quoted in Curnutt, *Animals and the Law*, p. 70.

[4] Curnutt, *Animals and the Law*, p. 50.

[5] "Orangutan Beater Pays PETA $340,320." People for the Ethical Treatment of Animals. Available online. URL: http://www.peta-online.org/news/500/500berov.html. Posted May 4, 2000.

[6] Nevada Supreme Court opinion, quoted in "Orangutan Beater Pays PETA $340,320."

[7] Ward Clark, *Misplaced Compassion: The Animal Rights Movement Exposed*. San Jose, Calif.: Writers Club Press, 2001, pp. 219–220.

[8] Animal Legal Defense Fund, quoted in Rob Roy Smith, "Standing on Their Own Four Legs," *Environmental Law*, vol. 29, Winter 1999, pp. 989 ff.

[9] Valerie Stanley, quoted in Rob Roy Smith, "Standing on Their Own Four Legs," pp. 989 ff.

[10] Rob Roy Smith, "Standing on Their Own Four Legs," pp. 989 ff.

[11] Rob Roy Smith, "Standing on Their Own Four Legs," pp. 989 ff.

[12] Kevin Kjonaas, quoted in Catherine E. Smith, "Radical Animal Rights Activists Set the Stage for a First Amendment Showdown," *Southern Poverty Law Center Intelligence Report*, Summer 2005, n.p.

[13] SHAC-USA web site, quoted in Catherine E. Smith, "Radical Animal Rights Activists Set the Stage for a First Amendment Showdown," n.p.

[14] *Planned Parenthood of Columbia/Willamette, Inc. v. American Coalition of Life Activists*, 290 F.3d (9th Cir. 2002) at 1074, 1088, quoted in Catherine E. Smith, "Radical Animal Rights Activists Set the Stage for a First Amendment Showdown," n.p.

[15] Christopher J. Christie, quoted in "Militant Animal Rights Group, Six Members Convicted in Campaign to Terrorize Company, Employees and Others." United States Attorney's Office, District of New Jersey. Available online. URL: http://www.usdoj.gov/usao/nj/press/files/shac0302_r.htm. Posted on March 2, 2006.

[16] Kristen M. Fletcher, "Status of Endangered Salmon Challenged in Northwest." Mississippi-Alabama Sea Grant Legal Program. URL: http://www.olemiss.edu/orgs/SGLC/MS-AL/Water%20Log/21.4salmon.htm. Accessed on January 30, 2007.

[17] ———, "Status of Endangered Salmon Challenged in Northwest."

[18] Brian J. Perron, "Just Another Goldfish down the Toilet? The Fate of Pacific Salmon after *Alsea Valley* and the de Facto Rescission of the 4(d) Rule," *Environmental Law*, vol. 33, Summer 2003, p. 548.

[19] Russell C. Brooks, "Oregon Coast Salmon Listing Invalidated: Ninth Circuit Dismisses Appeal of Landmark Alsea Case." Pacific Legal Foundation. Available online. URL: http://www.pacificlegal.org/?mvcTask=pressReleases&id=451&PHPSESSID=043633008b9b0e7a39f65f64589cc0de. Posted on February 24, 2004.

[20] Erik Robinson, quoted in Kristen M. Fletcher, "Status of Endangered Salmon Challenged in Northwest."

CHAPTER 3

CHRONOLOGY

This chapter presents a chronology of important events that have affected development of attitudes and laws concerning animal welfare and animal rights. The focus is on events in the United States and Britain, although important events in some other countries are also mentioned.

circa 450 B.C.

- Alcmeon of Croton performs the first recorded act of vivisection by cutting the optic nerve of a dog and showing that the dog becomes blind as a result.

1200s

- Christian philosopher Thomas Aquinas states that animals deserve no consideration in themselves because they lack reason. They should be treated kindly, however, because being cruel to animals may lead one to be cruel to human beings.

early 1600s

- French philosopher René Descartes maintains that animals are mere machines that cannot really suffer because they lack reason, soul, and feeling.

1628

- British physician William Harvey publishes a groundbreaking book, *On the Movement of the Heart and Blood in Animals*, describing the circulation of the blood accurately for the first time. It is based on his dissections of dead and living animals.

Animal Rights

1641

■ Reverend Nathaniel Ward draws up the "Body of Liberties" to govern the Massachusetts Bay Colony, including Liberty 92, the first known Western law against cruelty to animals.

1789

■ British utilitarian philosopher Jeremy Bentham states that even if animals cannot reason, they can suffer, and their right to avoid suffering should be respected.

1809

■ The Liverpool Society for Preventing Wanton Cruelty to Brute Animals, the world's oldest known animal protection society, is founded.

1821

■ Maine passes the first U.S. state law against animal cruelty, forbidding the beating of horses or cattle.

1822

■ Britain passes the Martin Act, the first national law against animal cruelty; it outlaws cruelty to horses and cattle.

1824

■ Arthur Broome founds the Society for the Prevention of Cruelty to Animals (later the Royal Society for the Prevention of Cruelty to Animals, or RSPCA), the world's first national animal protection society, in England.

1835

■ The Martin Act is expanded to cover all domestic animals, thereby making bullbaiting and cockfighting illegal in Britain.

1866

■ Henry Bergh, a wealthy New York diplomat, founds the American Society for the Prevention of Cruelty to Animals.

1867

■ Bergh persuades the New York legislature to pass a law against cruelty to animals that becomes the model for most later anticruelty laws.

Chronology

1873

- U.S. Congress passes the Twenty-eight-Hour Act, which requires rest and access to food and water every 28 hours for mammalian livestock being transported by rail or ship.

1875

- Publication of a description of vivisection in the laboratory of French physiologist Claude Bernard arouses British sentiment against the practice.

1876

- Britain passes Cruelty to Animals Act, the world's first law to regulate the use of animals in scientific research.

1896

- U.S. Supreme Court rules in *Geer v. Connecticut* that states have the right to regulate actions that affect wild animals, even if the actions involve interstate commerce.

1900

- U.S. Congress passes the Lacey Act, which forbids interstate transportation of birds or other animals killed in violation of state laws.

1911

- The United States, Britain (for Canada), Japan, and Russia sign the Fur Seal Treaty, which forbids hunting of fur seals on the open ocean; this is the first international agreement aimed at conservation of wildlife that involves the United States.

1914

- The last passenger pigeons and Carolina parakeets die in zoos, rendered extinct by excessive hunting.

1918

- U.S. Congress passes the Migratory Bird Treaty Act, which implements a treaty that the United States and Canada had agreed to in 1913. This is the first U.S. law that implements that country's share of an international treaty concerning animal protection.

Animal Rights

1924

- The League Against Cruel Sports is founded to work toward outlawing fox hunting in Britain.

1927

- The LD50 ("lethal dose for 50 percent") test, a commonly used but controversial animal test for acute toxicity, is invented in Britain.

1928

- Basing its decision on the Constitution's property clause, the U.S. Supreme Court rules in *Hunt v. United States* that the federal government can regulate activity on federal lands such as national forests, even if such regulations contradict state hunting and wildlife laws.

late 1940s

- In response to a growing need for animals to be used in biomedical research, some states and cities pass laws that force pounds and shelters to release homeless dogs and cats to researchers on demand.
- The practice of intensive farming, which involves keeping large numbers of animals indoors, develops in response to growing demand for meat.
- U.S. Food and Drug Administration researcher John Draize invents tests for eye and skin irritation using rabbits that later become commonly used on cosmetics and household products.

early 1950s

- Groups such as the Animal Welfare Institute (1951) and the Humane Society of the United States (1954) spin off from the American Humane Association because of what they see as the Humane Association's weak stand on vivisection.
- Heini Hediger, director of the Basel Zoo in Switzerland, recommends that zoos create habitats for their animals that allow the animals to engage in as many of their natural behaviors as possible.

1958

- U.S. Congress passes the Humane Slaughter Act, which requires all livestock except birds to be rendered unconscious before being slaughtered.

Chronology

1959

■ British scientists W. M. S. Russell and Rex Burch publish *The Principles of Humane Experimental Technique*, which describes the "three Rs" (reducing, replacing, and refining) of developing alternatives for research and testing on animals.

1964

■ Ruth Harrison's book *Animal Machines* makes the British public aware of animal abuses involved in what she calls factory farming.
■ The Hunt Saboteurs Association splits off from the League Against Cruel Sports because it believes that direct action in the field is necessary to stop fox hunting in Britain.

1965

■ The Brambell Committee, established by the British Parliament after publication of Ruth Harrison's book, recommends standards for treatment of farm animals and urges that such standards be made legally binding.
■ *July:* Publicity following a Pennsylvania family's discovery that their lost dog has been sold to a research laboratory produces a demand for federal legislation to regulate animal dealers and laboratories that use animals.

1966

■ U.S. Congress passes the Fur Seal Act, implementing the Fur Seal Treaty of 1911 and later sealing treaties.
■ The Tennessee Valley Authority, a federal agency, begins building the Tellico Dam on the Little Tennessee River.
■ U.S. Congress passes the Endangered Species Preservation Act, the first federal law aimed at protecting endangered species as such.
■ *February 4:* *Life* magazine publishes an article that describes miserable conditions in the kennels of a dealer who sells animals to laboratories, producing many letters to Congress.
■ *August:* President Lyndon Johnson signs into law the Laboratory Animal Welfare Act, which chiefly regulates the way cats and dogs used in medical research are bought and sold.

1968

■ British Parliament passes the Agriculture (Miscellaneous Provisions) Act, which establishes standards for housing and treatment of livestock on intensive farms.

123

Animal Rights

1970

- Animal rights philosopher Richard Ryder coins the term *speciesism*, which Peter Singer later adopts and makes famous.
- U.S. Congress passes the Animal Welfare Act (AWA), which revises and expands the Laboratory Animal Welfare Act to cover more kinds of animals and regulate animals used in exhibitions as well as laboratories.
- U.S. Congress passes the Horse Protection Act, which outlaws soring, a practice in which horses' feet are deliberately made sore in order to produce a gait valued in shows.

1970s

- Landscape architect Grant Jones creates the first "landscape immersion" habitat for the Woodland Park Zoo in Seattle, Washington.
- Animal protection groups that run shelters for homeless dogs and cats begin promoting the idea that pet owners should spay and neuter their pets to prevent overpopulation.
- Animal rights groups begin campaigns against the wearing of fur.
- Animal rights activist Henry Spira establishes the Coalition to Abolish the Draize Test.
- American scientists develop the Porcine Zona Pellucida (PZP) vaccine, an animal contraceptive that can be injected by dart and thus can be used on wildlife.
- The Band of Mercy breaks off from the Hunt Saboteurs Association and begins using violence, primarily property damage, in attempts to stop fox hunting in Britain; this group later becomes the Animal Liberation Front.

1972

- U.S. Department of Agriculture issues regulations implementing the Animal Welfare Act, including the stipulation that the act will not cover mice, rats, and birds.
- U.S. Supreme Court rules in *Sierra Club v. Morton* that the club has no standing to sue to stop development of a wilderness area because it has not proved that the development would cause an "injury in fact" to its members.

1973

- **March:** Representatives of 80 countries establish the Convention on International Trade in Endangered Species of Wild Fauna and Flora (CITES), the chief international agreement that regulates or bans trade in endangered species or materials made from them.

- *August:* A biologist discovers a new species of fish, the snail darter, in the Little Tennessee River, site of the Tellico Dam and Reservoir Project.
- *December:* President Richard Nixon signs into law the Endangered Species Act, the chief U.S. law protecting endangered and threatened species.

1974

- U.S. Supreme Court affirms in *Jones v. Butz* that the Humane Slaughter Act's exemptions for kosher and halal slaughter do not violate the Constitution's prohibition against making laws concerning religion.

1975

- Australian philosopher Peter Singer's *Animal Liberation,* called "the Bible of the animal rights movement," is published; this event is often considered to be the start of the modern crusade for animal rights.
- U.S. Fish and Wildlife Service issues regulations implementing the Endangered Species Act, one of which states that the term *harm* in the act can include "significant habitat modification or degradation."
- *November:* The snail darter is listed as endangered.

1976

- U.S. Congress passes the Animal Fighting Venture Prohibition Act, an amendment to the Animal Welfare Act, which prohibits all animal fighting (except cockfighting in states where it is legal).
- U.S. Supreme Court rules in *Kleppe v. New Mexico* that the federal government can regulate disposition of wildlife on public lands, even when doing so contradicts state laws.

1978

- U.S. Congress revises and expands the Humane Slaughter Act (1958) and the Meat Inspection Act (1906) to produce the Humane Methods of Slaughter Act, which specifies stunning and slaughter methods for mammalian livestock (but not birds).
- U.S. Supreme Court rules in *Tennessee Valley Authority v. Hill* that the almost-completed Tellico Dam violates the Endangered Species Act because closing the dam would destroy the critical habitat of the endangered snail darter. The court issues a permanent injunction to stop building on the dam.

1979

- *November:* After Congress passes a bill specifically exempting the Tellico Dam from the Endangered Species Act, the dam goes into operation.

1980

- Henry Spira launches a campaign against cosmetics giant Revlon, criticizing its use of the painful Draize rabbit eye irritancy test.
- Ingrid Newkirk, Alex Pacheco, and others found People for the Ethical Treatment of Animals (PETA).

1981

- *May:* Alex Pacheco begins work at Edward Taub's laboratory in Silver Spring, Maryland, where federally funded research on monkeys is taking place.
- *September 11:* After seeing videotapes made by Pacheco and statements from witnesses about conditions in Taub's laboratory, local police charge Taub with 17 counts of animal cruelty—the first time a research scientist has been so charged.
- *December:* A district court convicts Taub of six counts of animal cruelty.

1982

- Congress amends the Endangered Species Act to permit habitat conservation plans, in which landowners may be granted a permit to harm or kill a limited number of members of an endangered species (incidental take) or destroy a limited amount of habitat in exchange for other actions that mitigate the damage and result in better conservation of the habitat as a whole. Other amendments include the No Surprises rule, which states that once a developer has produced an acceptable habitat conservation plan and received an incidental take permit from the Fish and Wildlife Service, the developer is not liable for any additional expenditure that might later be found necessary to conserve endangered species on the land.

1983

- On appeal, Edward Taub is acquitted of all charges.

1984

- American philosopher Tom Regan publishes *The Case for Animal Rights*, which says that all human uses of animals that cause animal suffering are morally wrong and should be abolished.

Chronology

- PETA circulates a documentary made from videotapes stolen from the University of Pennsylvania's Head Injury Clinical Research Laboratory, showing researchers making fun of injured baboons.

1985

- Congress makes substantial revisions to the Animal Welfare Act, including establishment of Institutional Animal Care and Use Committees (IACUCs) to oversee experiments using animals and addition of a requirement for programs to promote the psychological well-being of primates.

late 1980s

- Cosmetics giants Revlon and Avon, responding to campaigns by animal rights groups, agree to stop testing their products on animals.
- "No-kill" animal shelters begin to be established.

1986

- Britain passes the Animals (Scientific Procedures) Act, an extremely comprehensive set of regulations governing experiments on animals, and West Germany passes a similarly rigorous law.
- The European Union passes a directive that provides a legal framework for the regulation of experiments on animals in member countries.
- The Fourth Circuit Court of Appeals denies standing to PETA in a suit in which that group asks for guardianship of the Silver Spring monkeys. The court claims that granting standing could unleash a spate of lawsuits that would impede medical research.
- "Mad cow disease" (bovine spongiform encephalopathy) appears in Britain, probably spread by the intensive-farming practice of using cattle feed that contains ground-up remains of other cattle and sheep.
- The International Whaling Commission imposes a moratorium on commercial whaling.

1988

- In *Palila v. Hawaii Department of Land and Natural Resources*, the Ninth Circuit Court of Appeals grants the palila, an endangered species of Hawaiian bird, standing to sue under the Endangered Species Act.
- California passes a law requiring that students who have moral objections to performing dissections in biology classes be given alternative assignments.

Animal Rights

1989

- Bobby Berosini, a Las Vegas entertainer, sues PETA and other animal rights groups for defamation of character after they distribute a videotape appearing to show him abusing the orangutans in his nightclub act before a performance.
- Under CITES (the Convention on International Trade in Endangered Species of Wild Fauna and Flora), international trade in ivory from elephants is banned because such trade endangers the species.

1990

- U.S. Congress passes the Pet Protection Act, an amendment to the Animal Welfare Act that requires pounds and shelters to hold animals for at least five days before selling them to dealers.
- *August:* A jury awards Bobby Berosini damages against PETA and other groups for defamation of character.

1991

- The American Society for the Prevention of Cruelty to Animals, the Humane Society of the United States, and more than 100 other animal protection groups publish a joint resolution in the *New York Times* stating that they oppose use of threats or violence against people or property.
- The European Union establishes the European Centre for Validation of Alternative Methods (ECVAM) to develop and validate nonanimal alternatives to tests and experimental methods using animals.
- The National Marine Fisheries Service introduces the term evolutionarily significant unit (ESU) to substitute for "distinct population segment," the smallest unit that Congress permits to be considered separately for threatened or endangered status under the Endangered Species Act.

1992

- In its ruling on *Lujan v. Defenders of Wildlife*, the U.S. Supreme Court lists three criteria that plaintiffs, including environmental and animal rights organizations, must fulfill in order to have standing to sue.
- U.S. Congress passes the Animal Enterprise Protection Act, which makes physical disruption of animal production and research facilities a federal crime.

1993

- U.S. Congress passes the NIH Revitalization Act, which, among other things, orders the director of the National Institutes of Health to develop, validate, and promote nonanimal alternatives to animal tests and experiments.

■ The National Marine Fisheries Service establishes its "hatchery policy," which states that salmon spawned in hatcheries will be counted along with wild-spawned fish to determine population size (for the purpose of deciding whether to list a species or subspecies as threatened or endangered under the Endangered Species Act) only "sparingly" and when the hatchery-spawned fish are considered "essential to recovery" of the species.

1994

■ U.S. Congress passes the Recreational Hunting Safety and Preservation Act, which makes it illegal to "engage in any physical conduct that hinders a lawful hunt."

■ U.S. Congress modernizes the Twenty-eight-Hour Act and expands it to include animals transported by truck.

■ The National Institutes of Health (NIH) establishes the Interagency Coordinating Committee on the Validation of Alternative Methods (ICCVAM) as an ad hoc (temporary) committee to carry out the requirements of the NIH Revitalization Act concerning establishment, validation, and promotion of nonanimal tests.

■ The Nevada Supreme Court reverses a lower court's decision in the Bobby Berosini case, ruling that PETA's videotape did show that Berosini abused his orangutans. It orders Berosini to pay a substantial sum to cover PETA's court costs.

1995

■ Massive protests at British ports attempt to halt the export of live animals, which animal rights groups claim often occurs under cruel conditions.

■ *June 29:* U.S. Supreme Court rules in *Babbitt v. Sweet Home Chapter of Communities for a Great Oregon* that environmental degradation can be included in the definition of *harm* in the Endangered Species Act.

1996

■ Britain bans biomedical research on great apes.

■ *March:* The British government announces that 10 people have died of a brain disease similar to "mad cow disease," by then widespread among British cattle, and may have contracted the disease from infected beef.

■ *May:* Texas cattlemen sue prominent television host Oprah Winfrey under a state food disparagement law after a guest on her program warns that the practice of giving American cattle feed that contains the ground-up bodies of other animals, linked to the spread of mad cow disease and possible infection of humans in Britain, could lead to a devastating outbreak of human brain disease in the United States.

1997

- Gillette Corporation agrees to stop testing its products on animals.
- U.S. Supreme Court rules that landowners as well as animal and environmental protection groups can use the citizen suit provision of the Endangered Species Act.
- *August:* The United States and Canada ban use of cattle feed containing ground-up animal parts, which can spread mad cow disease (bovine spongiform encephalopathy).

1998

- A Wisconsin judge sentences a man to 12 years in prison for severe animal abuse, probably the longest sentence ever given for such a crime.
- After seven years of litigation, a British judge rules against McDonald's in the "McLibel" case, holding that London animal rights activists did not libel the fast food giant because some of the conditions they described in their pamphlets could in fact be considered cruel.
- The National Marine Fisheries Service classifies the Oregon Coast coho salmon as threatened, placing that "evolutionarily significant unit" (a category below subspecies) of salmon under the protection of the Endangered Species Act.
- The Environmental Protection Agency asks companies to provide health and safety test information for 2,800 high-production-volume chemicals.
- *February:* A Texas judge acquits Oprah Winfrey, Howard Lyman, and other defendants of violating the state food disparagement law.
- *September 1:* In *Animal Legal Defense Fund v. Glickman* I, the District of Columbia Circuit Court rules that Marc Jurnove has standing to sue the USDA for not making specific regulations under the Animal Welfare Act that promote the psychological well-being of primates—the first time an individual has been granted standing to sue for a violation of the AWA.

1999

- New Zealand passes a law that essentially bans research on great apes.
- The law schools of Harvard and Georgetown Universities begin offering courses in animal law.

Chronology

- Writer Jan Pottker files suit against Ringling Bros. and Barnum & Bailey Circus and its owner, Ken Feld, claiming that Feld hired people to harass and spy on her after she published an article critical of the circus and the Feld family.
- Mary Kay Cosmetics and Procter & Gamble agree to stop testing their products on animals.
- The Animal Liberation Front in Britain kidnaps documentary filmmaker Graham Hall and burns the group's initials into his back.
- The European Union agrees to phase out battery cages for laying hens in all member nations by 2012.
- Responding to criticism from animal rights groups, the Environmental Protection Agency and the Clinton administration agree to modify the EPA's planned testing program for high-production-volume chemicals so that it will use fewer animals.
- Sow gestation stalls are banned in Britain.
- Giant fast-food chain McDonald's announces that it will no longer buy eggs from producers who do not follow its animal care guidelines.
- *October:* The Justice Department, an extremist animal rights group, mails razor blades and threats to 87 American scientists who do research on primates.
- *November:* In Britain, Greg Avery and Heather James form Stop Huntingdon Animal Cruelty (SHAC), an animal rights organization dedicated to putting Huntingdon Life Sciences (HLS), Europe's largest contract animal testing laboratory, out of business because the company allegedly abuses animals.

2000

- A PETA campaign featuring a picture of then New York mayor Rudolph Giuliani, who had recently been found to have prostate cancer, in an attempt to link a diet high in dairy products with the disease draws widespread criticism for exploiting Giuliani's illness and is withdrawn. Mothers Against Drunk Driving criticizes a second PETA antimilk campaign, which claims that beer is more healthful than milk, and forces its withdrawal as well.
- *February:* Following a minor traffic accident, a man in San Jose, California, throws a small dog belonging to the woman who hit him into traffic, where the dog is killed. Animal rights groups and an outraged public establish a $120,000 reward for the man's identification and arrest.
- *February:* The Fifth Circuit Court of Appeals upholds a district court's acquittal of Oprah Winfrey and others in a food disparagement case.

Animal Rights

- *February:* Hearing Marc Jurnove's case against the USDA for violation of the Animal Welfare Act *(ALDF v. Glickman* II*)* on its merits, a three-judge panel from the District of Columbia Court of Appeals reverses a lower court's decision and finds that the department's regulations for promoting the psychological well-being of primates meet the AWA's requirements.
- *June:* A committee set up by the British Parliament releases the Burns Report, which says that hunting with dogs is an important feature of social life in rural Britain and is no more cruel to foxes than other common methods of exterminating them.
- *August:* Following a PETA campaign accusing it of animal cruelty, fast-food giant McDonald's agrees to make changes in its requirements for meat suppliers' treatment of animals.
- *September:* A district court grants standing to sue to a plaintiff in a suit against the U.S. Department of Agriculture (USDA) that is aimed at making the USDA remove its controversial exclusion of mice, rats, and birds from the Animal Welfare Act. Within days, the USDA settles the suit out of court by promising to remove the exemption.
- *October:* United Egg Producers, a large industry trade group, issues new guidelines that promise to gradually increase the size of cages in which laying hens are kept and make other improvements to their care.
- *November:* Britain passes the Fur Farming (Prohibition) Act, which essentially outlaws breeding animals for their fur.
- *December:* U.S. Congress makes the Interagency Coordinating Committee for the Validation of Alternative Methods (ICCVAM) a permanent standing body.
- *December:* U.S. Congress passes the Chimpanzee Health Improvement, Maintenance, and Protection (CHIMP) Act, which authorizes establishment of a system of sanctuaries to which chimpanzees no longer needed for medical research can be "retired."

2001

- PETA sues Kenneth Feld, head of the Ringling Bros. and Barnum & Bailey Circus, and some of his employees, alleging that they carried out covert operations against and infiltration of the animal rights group between 1988 and 1998.
- *February:* British animal rights protesters attack Brian Cass, managing director of Huntingdon Life Sciences, breaking one of his ribs and inflicting a head wound that requires 10 stitches.
- *May:* A jury in Washington, D.C., awards $500,000 to Shan Sparshott, a former employee of the Ringling Bros. and Barnum & Bailey Circus,

because a former executive vice president of the circus had Sparshott's telephone illegally wiretapped.

- *June:* Following PETA campaigns, Wendy's and Burger King issue revised guidelines for their suppliers' treatment of animals, similar to those that McDonald's issued the previous year.
- *June:* Andrew Burnett, identified as the man who threw a small dog into traffic in a road rage incident in February 2000, causing its death, is convicted of felony animal abuse and sentenced to three years in prison.
- *September 10:* U.S. District Court Judge Michael Hogan rules in *Alsea Valley Alliance v. Evans,* an Oregon case, that the National Marine Fisheries Service's 1998 decision to count wild-spawned but not hatchery-spawned fish in determining that the Oregon Coast coho salmon should be classified as threatened under the Endangered Species Act was "arbitrary and capricious." Hogan's decision, which invalidates the listing, has major implications for several industries in the Klamath River valley and for preservation of other West Coast salmon species and groups.
- *November 9:* The National Marine Fisheries Service (NMFS) and the George W. Bush administration announce that they will not appeal Judge Hogan's decision. Instead, a review of 23 of 25 NMFS salmon and steelhead trout listings under the Endangered Species Act will be conducted.
- *December:* After less than two hours of deliberation, a jury in San Jose, California, acquits Ringling Bros. and Barnum & Bailey Circus animal trainer Mark Gebel of abusing an elephant.
- *December 14:* Following fisheries' and environmental groups' appeal of Judge Michael Hogan's September 10 decision in *Alsea Valley Alliance v. Evans,* the Ninth Circuit Court of Appeals stays all changes resulting from Hogan's ruling until it can determine the validity of the appeal. The higher court's ruling effectively reinstates protection for the Oregon Coast coho salmon under the Endangered Species Act.

2002

- The Food Marketing Institute and the National Council of Chain Restaurants release new guidelines for food suppliers' treatment of animals, including such requirements as increased confinement space for pregnant sows.
- *February:* The American Horse Slaughter Prevention Act, which if passed would forbid the slaughter of horses for human consumption, is introduced into the House of Representatives.
- *March:* Scotland passes a bill prohibiting hunting of mammals with hounds.
- *May:* Congress permanently blocks the USDA from expanding Animal Welfare Act regulations to cover rats, mice, and birds.

Animal Rights

- *May 6:* Pim Fortuyn, a popular Dutch politician who had expressed support for fur farming, is shot to death in Amsterdam. Animal rights activist Volkert van der Graaf is accused of his murder.
- *May 23:* Congress strengthens the Animal Enterprise Protection Act as part of the Public Health Security and Bioterrorism Preparedness and Response Act.
- *June:* Germany becomes the first country in the European Union to guarantee protection of animals in its constitution.
- *November:* Florida passes an amendment to the state constitution banning sow gestation crates, a move that animal rights groups support. This is the first U.S. legislation to limit means of confining farm animals.
- *December:* A compromise bill that would regulate hunting rather than banning it is introduced into the British Parliament.

2003

- *January:* The European Union votes to ban all cosmetics testing on animals and most sales of cosmetics tested on animals elsewhere in the world by 2009.
- *spring:* The European Parliament and the Council of Ministers pass the seventh amendment to the European Union's Cosmetics Directive, banning the testing of cosmetic products and ingredients on animals when workable alternative testing methods exist. It also forbids the sale of cosmetics tested in ways that violate the law. This agreement, which is less stringent than a similar proposal accepted by the parliament in June 2002, is scheduled to go into force in 2009.
- *April 16:* Volkert van der Graaf, who had confessed to the murder of Dutch politician Pim Fortuyn, is sentenced to 18 years in prison.
- *May:* A cow with mad cow disease (bovine spongiform encephalopathy) is discovered in Alberta, Canada, the first report of the disease in North America.
- *May 14:* A U.S. law making it illegal to knowingly sell, buy, transport, deliver, or receive a cock or other bird in interstate commerce for purposes of participation in a fighting venture takes effect.
- *June 30:* British Parliament's House of Commons votes by 362 to 154 to ban foxhunting.
- *July 7:* People for the Ethical Treatment of Animals files a lawsuit in California Superior Court in Los Angeles to stop what it alleges are deceptive statements on fast food chain Kentucky Fried Chicken's web site and customer hotline. PETA claims that the company misleads people about the treatment of the chickens whose meat they sell.

Chronology

- **August 28:** A group calling itself Revolutionary Cells sets off two pipe bombs at California-based Chiron Corporation, a biotechnology company that pays Huntingdon Life Sciences to test Chiron's new drugs on animals. No one is injured, but the group's use of explosives marks an escalation in violence in support of animal rights in the United States.
- **September 2:** People for the Ethical Treatment of Animals drops its lawsuit against Kentucky Fried Chicken after the company agrees to change allegedly false statements on its website and customer hotline.
- **October 21:** British Parliament's House of Lords votes by 261 to 49 to allow regulated hunting to continue.
- **October 29:** The European Commission (EC) adopts a proposal for the new European Union (EU) regulatory framework for chemicals, REACH (Registration, Evaluation and Authorisation of Chemicals). This concerns animal welfare groups because the program potentially would require a huge number of laboratory animals to test the safety of chemicals.
- **late 2003:** As the Endangered Species Act's 30th anniversary nears, Congress considers revising it in ways that would limit its powers.
- **December 19:** The Captive Wildlife Safety Act, an amendment to the Lacey Act (1900), becomes law. It bans interstate transport of big cats and other large predators for private use as pets.
- **December 22:** A Holstein cow in Washington state, slaughtered for meat on December 9, is discovered to have had mad cow disease, the first case of this illness reported in the United States. The USDA recalls 10,000 pounds of meat that the meat factory that processed the sick cow handled on the same day. Several Asian countries immediately ban beef imports from the United States; within a week, the ban includes 30 countries that make up 90 percent of the U.S. beef export market.
- **December 30:** Agriculture Secretary Ann Veneman proposes new regulations aimed at controlling the possible spread of mad cow disease and easing the fears of consumers, including a ban on slaughtering of "downer" cattle—those too sick or lame to stand and walk on their own—for use as meat.

2004

- Britain's Oxford University begins building a laboratory for research on animals, drawing immediate protest from animal rights organizations.
- The 30th anniversary of the Endangered Species Act brings numerous evaluations of the law's performance and calls for its revision.
- A law is passed that exempts lands owned by the military from requirements of the Endangered Species Act regarding critical habitat. The law also requires the Fish and Wildlife Service to consider impacts on

national security when making designations of critical habitat that might affect military activities.

- **January 27:** Cambridge University cancels plans to build a primate research center under pressure from animal rights protesters.
- **February 24:** The U.S. Ninth Circuit Court of Appeals rejects an appeal by fisheries and environmental groups (*Alsea Valley Alliance v. Oregon Natural Resources*), thereby affirming a lower court's ruling that the National Marine Fisheries Service acted illegally by counting wild-spawned but not hatchery-spawned salmon in determining the numbers, and therefore the protection status, of the Oregon Coast coho salmon under the Endangered Species Act. This decision confirms that the listing of this population of salmon is invalid.
- **May:** The British government opens the National Centre for the Replacement, Refinement and Reduction of Animals in Research (NC3Rs).
- **May 27:** Kevin Kjonaas and six other members of SHAC-USA, an extremist animal rights group, are indicted on charges of violating the Animal Enterprise Protection Act and other federal laws by posting contact information for employees and families of a targeted animal testing laboratory, along with a list of "terror tactics."
- **July:** Montpellier PLC, the major contractor scheduled to build Oxford University's animal research center, withdraws from the project after animal rights protesters harass and threaten its stockholders.
- **September 16:** The British Parliament votes to outlaw hunting of foxes or other mammals with dogs.
- **October:** Animal rights protesters steal the remains of Gladys Hammond from a grave in Yoxall, England. They offer to return the body if Christopher Hall, Hammond's son-in-law, and Hall's brother David will close Darley Oaks, their Newchurch farm, which raises guinea pigs for use in medical research.
- **November 22:** The European Council adopts a directive providing new rules for transporting livestock.
- **November 24:** An amendment to the Serious Organised Crime and Police Act is proposed in Britain's Parliament. The amendment would make it a criminal offense to use intimidation campaigns to cause economic or other damage to individuals or companies indirectly associated with research on animals.
- **November 30:** People for the Ethical Treatment of Animals (PETA) releases "If This Is Kosher . . . ," a video that the group says it filmed secretly in 2004 at Agriprocessors Inc., the world's largest kosher slaughterhouse. The video appears to show brutal treatment of cattle during slaughter.

Chronology

2005

- **February 18:** The Hunting Act, which bans hunting of foxes or other mammals with dogs, goes into effect in England and Wales.
- **April:** As part of an agreement with People for the Ethical Treatment of Animals (PETA), the pet store chain PETCO announces that it will no longer sell large birds such as parrots in its stores. The agreement ends a campaign against PETCO by PETA, which claims that large birds suffer in captivity.
- **May 25:** The World Organisation for Animal Health issues the first worldwide standards for animal welfare. The standards, agreed upon by representatives of 167 member countries, cover live transport of animals by land and sea and slaughter of animals for food or disease control.
- **June:** The U.S. Department of Agriculture announces that a cow born and raised in Texas has died of bovine spongiform encephalopathy, or "mad cow disease"—the first native case of the disease reported in the United States.
- **July:** After a comprehensive review, McDonald's Corporation concludes that the standard practice of using electricity to stun poultry prior to slaughter and the alternative technique of controlled atmosphere stunning, which animal rights groups such as the Humane Society of the United States (HSUS) and People for the Ethical Treatment of Animals (PETA) say is more humane, are equally acceptable for its suppliers.
- **July 1:** New amendments to Britain's Serious Organised Crime and Police Act, which give police increased powers to prosecute animal-rights groups and other activists who use or threaten violence against companies or individuals associated with research on animals, become law.
- **July 26:** The Inhumane Trapping Prevention Act, a bill that would ban steel-jawed leghold traps nationwide, is introduced into the House of Representatives.
- **August:** Succumbing to harassment by an animal rights protest group, Christopher and David Hall close Darley Oaks, the British farm on which they raised guinea pigs for medical research.
- **August 26:** Vandals cover the exterior of the Manhasset Bay Yacht Club, in Port Washington, New York, with red paint and animal rights slogans. The Animal Liberation Front takes responsibility for the attack and says that it occurred because the club's members include two executives of Carr Securities, a stock trading firm that has sold shares of Life Sciences Research, the United States arm of animal rights target Huntingdon Life Sciences.
- **September:** The U.S. Department of Agriculture confirms that the Humane Methods of Slaughter Act does not apply to chickens or other birds.

137

- **September 7:** The New York Stock Exchange postpones the listing of Life Sciences Research, the United States arm of Huntingdon Life Sciences (HLS). Although the stock exchange gives no official reason for its action, the postponement is widely held to have been the result of threats and harassment from animal rights groups that oppose HLS because of its allegedly abusive experiments on animals.
- **September 19:** Richard Pombo, a rancher and Republican representative from Tracy, California, introduces the Threatened and Endangered Species Recovery Act (HR 3824), a revision of the Endangered Species Act, into the House of Representatives. Pombo's bill, which offers additional incentives for private property owners to cooperate with the ESA, is strongly criticized by environmental and animal rights groups, who say that it weakens the ESA significantly.
- **September 29:** The House of Representatives passes the Threatened and Endangered Species Recovery Act (HR 3824) by a vote of 229 to 193.
- **October 13:** The Animal Welfare Bill, which Margaret Beckett, Britain's Secretary of State for Environment, Food and Rural Affairs (DEFRA) calls the greatest reform in laws governing animal welfare in a hundred years, is introduced into the British Parliament.
- **November:** Construction resumes on Oxford University's animal research laboratory.
- **December:** The Humane Society of the United States and others sue the U.S. Department of Agriculture to have poultry included in the 1978 Humane Methods of Slaughter Act, which currently excludes birds.

2006

- **January 23:** The European Commission approves the 2006–2010 Animal Welfare Action Plan, which would tighten current minimum welfare standards for livestock and other domestic animals. Individual member states of the European Union and the European Parliament must still approve the plan before it goes into effect.
- **March 2:** A jury in a federal district court convicts six members of Stop Huntingdon Animal Cruelty (SHAC)-USA of violating antiterrorism laws, including the Animal Enterprise Protection Act.
- **March 15:** A jury in Fairfax County, Virginia, clears Kenneth Feld, head of the Ringling Bros. and Barnum & Bailey Circus, of charges that he was responsible for wiretapping of phones and theft of documents from the animal rights group People for the Ethical Treatment of Animals (PETA).
- **April 27:** Chicago passes a citywide ban on selling foie gras (goose liver) because its production is considered cruel.

Chronology

- **May:** British Animal Health Minister Ben Bradshaw announces new rules governing the transportation of vertebrate animals in the European Union. The rules will take effect in 2007 and 2008.
- **May:** British police recover the body of Gladys Hammond, stolen by animal rights protesters in October 2004 with the aim of forcing Hammond's son-in-law and his brother to close their farm, which raised guinea pigs for use in animal research.
- **May 11:** Three animal rights activists are sentenced to 12 years in prison for stealing the corpse of Gladys Hammond and harassing Christopher and David Hall.
- **June:** Agriculture ministers from eight European Union states block adoption of a measure that would support the EU's ambitious Community Action Plan on the Protection and Welfare of Animals, which, if implemented, would cause major changes in the way farm animals are treated.
- **September 7:** The U.S. House of Representatives passes HR 503, the American Horse Slaughter Prevention Act.
- **September 12:** A judge in Trenton, New Jersey, sentences six members of SHAC-USA, convicted in March 2006 of violating the Animal Enterprise Protection Act and other laws, to prison terms ranging from one to six years.
- **September 30:** The U.S. Senate passes the Animal Enterprise Terrorism Act.
- **November:** At the urging of the Humane Society of the United States, the U.S. Department of Agriculture confirms that the Twenty-eight Hour Law applies to animals transported by truck.
- **November 7:** California Representative Richard Pombo (R-Tracy), whose revision of the Endangered Species Act (the Threatened and Endangered Species Recovery Act) was passed by the House of Representatives in September 2005, loses his seat in the House of Representatives to Democrat Jerry McNerny. Environmental and animal rights groups applaud Pombo's defeat because they believe that his bill would greatly weaken the ESA.
- **November 7:** Voters in Arizona pass a law that will ban gestation crates for sows, beginning in 2013.
- **November 8:** The Animal Welfare Act, a sweeping reform of British animal welfare laws, takes effect. The law applies to pets and farm animals but not to animals used in scientific procedures.
- **November 13:** The U.S. House of Representatives passes the Animal Enterprise Terrorism Act.
- **November 27:** President George W. Bush signs the Animal Enterprise Terrorism Act into law.

Animal Rights

2007

- *January:* New European Union regulations governing treatment of farm animals during transport go into effect.
- *February 9:* The U.S. Court of Appeals for the Ninth Circuit affirms a lower court ruling that Bobby Berosini, accused by People for the Ethical Treatment of Animals (PETA) of abusing orangutans in his Las Vegas nightclub act in 1989, must pay PETA more than $250,000 to reimburse attorneys' fees that the organization incurred, partly through efforts to uncover assets held by Berosini and his wife that the couple had hidden in an attempt to avoid earlier court judgments against them.
- *April 25:* A Senate committee approves the American Horse Slaughter Prevention Act.
- *May:* More than 30 people are arrested and documents, cash, computers, and other equipment are seized in a Europe-wide police crackdown on animal rights extremists.
- *June 5:* Citing the cost of caring for the animals, the National Institutes of Health's National Center for Research Resources announces that it will no longer breed chimpanzees for research. This ruling makes permanent a breeding moratorium established in 1995.
- *July 17:* A federal grand jury indicts Atlanta Falcons quarterback and National Football League star Michael Vick and three others on charges of raising pit bulls for dog fighting and running a dog fighting ring. National outrage stirred by the high-profile case was said to be greater than that aroused by many human murders.
- *August 27:* Michael Vick accepts a guilty plea and awaits sentencing.

CHAPTER 4

BIOGRAPHICAL LISTING

This chapter offers brief biographical information on people who have played major roles in development of crusades for animal welfare and animal rights. Most of these people were or are active in the United States or Britain, but some important figures from other countries are also included.

Alcmeon of Croton, ancient Greek physiologist. Around 450 B.C., he performed the first recorded act of vivisection by cutting the optic nerve of a dog and showing that the dog became blind as a result.

Thomas Aquinas, 13th-century Christian theologian and philosopher. Aquinas stated that animals deserve no consideration in themselves because they lack reason. He professed that they should be treated kindly only because cruelty to animals may lead to cruelty to human beings.

Richard Avanzino, current president of Maddie's Fund and former head of the San Francisco SPCA. He is a strong advocate of no-kill animal shelters.

Greg Avery, animal rights activist. In November 1999, after hearing about alleged abuse of animals at Huntingdon Life Sciences (HLS), Europe's largest contract animal testing laboratory, he and fellow activist Heather James founded Stop Huntingdon Animal Cruelty (SHAC). The aim of this organization, they said, was to close HLS permanently. SHAC later became known for threats, vandalism, and even physical violence aimed not only at HLS employees but at anyone connected with HLS in any way, no matter how indirect.

Jeremy Bentham, British philosopher. In 1789, he opposed cruelty to animals on the grounds that animals could suffer, even though they might not possess reason or language, and inflicting such suffering was in itself an immoral act. He also speculated that eventually animals, as sentient beings, might be granted certain legal rights.

Henry Bergh, 19th-century American diplomat. Upset by abuse to animals, especially horses, that he had seen during his diplomatic career and inspired by the work of the Royal Society for the Prevention of Cruelty

141

to Animals in Britain, Bergh, a wealthy New Yorker, founded the American Society for the Prevention of Cruelty to Animals in 1866 and, a year later, persuaded New York legislators to pass one of the first state laws against animal cruelty.

Claude Bernard, French physiologist. Bernard stated that he saw nothing wrong with performing painful or fatal experiments on animals if the experiments seemed likely to benefit humans. A scientist's account of the suffering caused by Bernard's innumerable operations stirred strong opposition to vivisection in Britain in the late 1870s.

Bobby Berosini, Las Vegas entertainer. Berosini, who used orangutans in his act, sued People for the Ethical Treatment of Animals (PETA) and other groups for defamation of character in 1989 after they accused him of abusing the animals. A lower court supported Berosini in 1990, but in 1994 the Nevada Supreme Court reversed that decision and ordered Berosini to pay a large sum to the animal rights groups. In 2007, Berosini was still engaged in (and losing) court battles with PETA over costs. He no longer owned orangutans.

Steven Best, associate professor in the philosophy department of the University of Texas, El Paso, and cofounder (with Jerry Vlasak) of the North American Animal Liberation Press Office. The press office gives out information about actions of the Animal Liberation Front, which Vlasek and Best support. In August 2005, Best's strong animal rights stance led the British government to forbid him to enter the country because it believed that he would foment acts of terrorism there.

Arthur Broome, British minister. He founded the Society for the Prevention of Cruelty to Animals, the first national animal welfare society, in 1824.

Rex Burch, British scientist. With W. M. S. Russell, he codeveloped the concept of the "three Rs" of alternatives to animal research: *replace* animal tests with nonanimal ones whenever possible, *reduce* the number of animals needed per test, and *refine* tests so that they cause less pain and stress to animals. Russell and Burch first described the three Rs in *The Principles of Humane Experimental Technique,* published in 1959.

Andrew Burnett, California man convicted of animal cruelty in a highly publicized case. Following a minor traffic accident in the city of San Jose in February 2000, Burnett seized Leo, a small dog riding with the woman whose car had bumped his, and threw him into passing traffic, where the dog was killed. Burnett, whose identity was unknown at the time, then left the scene. Donations from the public and animal rights groups established a $120,000 reward for his identification and capture. In June 2001, he was convicted of felony cruelty to animals and sentenced to three years in prison.

Biographical Listing

Brian Cass, managing director of Huntingdon Life Sciences, a large animal testing firm in Britain. Animal rightists attacked Cass with baseball bats in front of his home in February 2001, breaking one of his ribs and inflicting a head injury that required 10 stitches.

Frances Power Cobbe, British animal welfare activist and antivivisectionist. She cofounded the Victoria Street Society for the Protection of Animals from Vivisection in 1875. She drew an explicit parallel between abuse of animals and mistreatment of women.

J. M. Coetzee, a well-known author who has made the issue of human cruelty to animals central to several of his works. The title character in his novel *Elizabeth Costello* (2003) gives a series of lectures offering philosophical perspectives on this subject. In another novel, *The Lives of Animals,* Coetzee discusses the contradictions in humans' attitudes toward other species.

Rodney Coronado, Animal Liberation Front activist convicted of a firebombing at Michigan State University in the early 1990s. People for the Ethical Treatment of Animals (PETA) helped to pay for his defense.

Neda DeMayo, American wildlife conservationist. She has devoted her career to preserving communities of wild horses (mustangs) in the United States. She also uses the horses as a symbol in efforts to teach people the importance of preserving wildlife and wilderness in general.

René Descartes, 17th-century French philosopher. He maintained that animals cannot really suffer because they lack reason, a soul, and feeling.

John Draize, researcher with the U.S. Food and Drug Administration. In the 1940s, he developed two tests using rabbits that became standard for discovering whether cosmetics, household products, or other substances could irritate eyes and skin.

Kenneth Feld, owner of the Ringling Bros. and Barnum & Bailey Circus. Feld takes an aggressive stand against animal rights groups who say that the circus is cruel to its animals. Several people have accused him of spying on and harassing those who disagree with him. On March 15, 2006, a jury in Fairfax County, Virginia, cleared Feld of charges that he was responsible for wiretapping of phones and theft of documents from the animal rights group People for the Ethical Treatment of Animals (PETA). A suit against Feld by writer Jan Pottker was still pending in 2007.

Pim Fortuyn, Dutch politician. Fortuyn, a popular leader who had expressed support for the fur industry, was shot to death in Amsterdam on May 6, 2002. Animal rights activist Volkert van der Graaf was convicted of the murder and sentenced to 18 years in prison in April 2003.

Michael Fox, a veterinarian and bioethicist. He is famous for radical animal rights statements such as: "The life of an ant and the life of my child should be granted equal consideration." Fox has been scientific director

Animal Rights

(1980–1987), vice president for bioethics and farm animal protection (1988–1997), and senior scholar in bioethics (1997–2002) for the Humane Society of the United States. In 2007 he was the chief consultant and veterinarian for the India Project for Animals and Nature.

Gary Francione, law and philosophy professor at Rutgers University. He is a leading advocate of the idea that chimpanzees and bonobos, and perhaps some other animals, should have legal rights.

Mark Gebel, animal trainer with Ringling Bros. and Barnum & Bailey Circus. Two animal rightists claimed that they saw Gebel strike an elephant with an ankus, or bullhook, during a parade in San Jose, California, in August 2001, and he was brought to trial on charges of abusing an elephant. The witnesses admitted under cross-examination that they had actually only seen Gebel lunge at the animal, and a veterinarian testified that he had found no injuries on the elephant. The jury deliberated less than two hours before acquitting Gebel.

Jane Goodall, British primatologist. Goodall's long-running studies of chimpanzees in the wild in Tanzania showed that the animals exhibit many humanlike behaviors, including the making of tools. Goodall now works for numerous environmental and animal welfare causes, including efforts to end medical research on great apes.

Frederick Goodwin, former director of the National Institute of Mental Health, part of the National Institutes of Health. Goodwin is a major supporter of the use of animals in biomedical research.

Volkert van der Graaf, Dutch animal rights activist. Van der Graaf, founder of a group called Environmental Offensive, which opposed animal agriculture, was charged with the murder of popular Dutch politician Pim Fortuyn on May 6, 2002. He confessed and was sentenced to 18 years in prison on April 16, 2003.

Temple Grandin, American expert on treatment and slaughter of livestock. She has invented simple, inexpensive improvements in the design of slaughterhouses and other animal handling facilities that greatly reduce stress on the animals.

Christopher and David Hall, British farmers who ran Darley Oaks, a facility in Newchurch, England, that raised guinea pigs for use in medical research. The brothers became targets of harassment from an animal rights group, Save the Newchurch Guinea Pigs, which stole the remains of Gladys Hammond, Christopher Hall's deceased mother-in-law, in October 2004. The group said that it would return Hammond's body if the brothers would close their farm, and the Halls did so in August 2005. Three members of the group were arrested, convicted of the theft, and given substantial prison sentences in May 2006.

Biographical Listing

Graham Hall, British documentary filmmaker. After Hall made a film about the British arm of the Animal Liberation Front, the group kidnapped him and branded the organization's initials on his back.

David Hancocks, director of the Open Range Zoo in Victoria, Australia. Hancocks criticizes conventional zoos' animal environments and educational benefits and says that zoos do not present an accurate picture of the complexity of nature.

Ruth Harrison, British author. Her book *Animal Machines,* published in 1964, drew the British public's attention to abuses of animals involved in what she called "factory farming," a term she probably coined.

William Harvey, British physician. In 1628, he published a groundbreaking book describing the heart and circulation of the blood, based on discoveries he had made by dissecting dead and living animals. Harvey's work is one of many major medical breakthroughs that supporters of research on animals cite.

Heini Hediger, director of the Basel Zoo in Switzerland. In the 1950s, Hediger suggested that zoo environments should be designed to allow animals to carry out as many of their normal behaviors as possible. His ideas influenced zoo designers to create more naturalistic habitats.

Michael Hogan, judge of the U.S. District Court for Oregon. On September 10, 2001, Hogan ruled in *Alsea Valley Alliance v. Evans* that the National Marine Fisheries Service's 1998 decision to count wild-spawned but not hatchery-spawned fish in determining that the Oregon Coast coho salmon should be listed as threatened under the Endangered Species Act was "arbitrary and capricious." Hogan's ruling, which invalidated the listing, was later upheld by a higher court. It had major implications for industries in the Klamath River valley and for the preservation of West Coast salmon in general.

George Hoggan, British scientist. His account of experiences in the laboratory of French physiologist Claude Bernard, who experimented extensively on living animals, stirred British opposition to vivisection in 1875.

Hubert Humphrey, Democratic senator from Minnesota, vice president from 1965 to 1969. Humphrey's support was important in achieving passage of the Humane Slaughter Act, which was intended to reduce the suffering of livestock in slaughterhouses, in 1958.

Heather James, animal rights activist. In November 1999, after hearing about alleged abuse of animals at Huntingdon Life Sciences (HLS), Europe's largest contract animal testing laboratory, she and fellow activist Greg Avery founded Stop Huntingdon Animal Cruelty (SHAC). The aim of this organization, they said, was to close HLS permanently. SHAC

145

later became known for threats, vandalism, and even physical violence aimed not only at HLS employees but at anyone connected with HLS in any way, no matter how indirect.

Grant Jones, landscape designer. In the mid-1970s, he designed a new type of habitat for the Woodland Zoo in Seattle, Washington, that he called "landscape immersion." It was intended to make visitors feel surrounded by a natural landscape and experience its grandeur, while at the same time providing features that allow the habitat's animal occupants to carry out normal behaviors. Other zoos soon adapted his ideas.

Marc Jurnove, plaintiff in a landmark 1998 legal case *(ALDF v. Glickman)*. He gained standing to sue the Department of Agriculture for not establishing adequate regulations for promoting the psychological well-being of primates as mandated by the Animal Welfare Act, leading to conditions in a Long Island zoo that caused Jurnove aesthetic distress during his frequent visits there.

Kevin Kjonaas (Kevin Jonas), former president of SHAC-USA. This group is the U.S. branch of a British animal rights organization, Stop Huntingdon Animal Cruelty (SHAC), which was formed to close down Huntingdon Life Sciences, a British contract animal testing laboratory that is the largest such facility in Europe. On May 27, 2004, Kjonaas and six other members of his organization were indicted on charges of conspiracy to violate the Animal Enterprise Protection Act by harassing employees of companies that did business with Huntingdon. They were convicted on March 2, 2006. On September 12, 2006, Kjonaas was sentenced to six years in prison.

Markos Kyprianou, the European Union's Health and Consumer Protection Commissioner. Kyprianou favors raising minimum standards for the welfare of farm animals throughout the EU and supports the regulations in the 2006–2010 Animal Welfare Action Plan, which he presented to EU ministers on January 23, 2006. The European Commission approved the plan on that date, but as of mid-2007, the European Parliament had not yet accepted it.

John Lewis, deputy assistant director for counterterrorism in the Federal Bureau of Investigation (FBI). Lewis has frequently warned of dangers presented by extremist animal rights groups such as the Animal Liberation Front. In May 2005 he stated that these groups were the greatest domestic terror threat to the United States.

Howard Lyman, Montana rancher turned ardent vegetarian. Lyman's prediction on a 1996 Oprah Winfrey talk show that contaminated American beef might cause an outbreak of "mad cow disease," a deadly human brain disease, resulted in his being sued under a Texas food disparagement law. He was acquitted in 1998.

Biographical Listing

Richard Martin, Irish Minister of Parliament. In 1822, he introduced a bill prohibiting mistreatment of horses and cattle into the British Parliament that, when passed, became the first national law against mistreatment of animals.

Sara McBurnett, a Lake Tahoe realtor. Her small dog, Leo, was thrown into traffic by an enraged motorist whose car she had bumped in San Jose, California, in February 2000. The man, later identified as Andrew Burnett, was convicted of felony cruelty to animals and sentenced to three years in prison in June 2001.

Adrian Morrison, American researcher and defender of biomedical research on animals. Morrison, a veterinarian, is the former director of the Office of Animal Research Issues at the Substance Abuse and Mental Health Services Administration, part of the U.S. Department of Health and Human Services. He now does research on the brain's function during sleep at the University of Pennsylvania's School of Veterinary Medicine. Animal rightists have criticized both his own experiments, which use animals, and his defense of other researchers such as Edward Taub. Morrison, in turn, is highly critical of the animal rights movement.

Ingrid Newkirk, American animal rights activist. In 1980, she and four friends, including Alex Pacheco, founded People for the Ethical Treatment of Animals (PETA), described in 2001 as "the world's largest and most controversial animal rights organization." Newkirk, president of PETA, has become famous for such attention-getting statements as "A rat is a pig is a dog is a boy."

Wayne Pacelle, chief executive officer of the Humane Society of the United States (HSUS) since June 2004. Pacelle has focused the organization's activities on improving the welfare of animals raised for food, and opponents of his policies allege that his ultimate aim is to end meat eating.

Alex Pacheco, cofounder of PETA with Ingrid Newkirk and three of Newkirk's other friends. After obtaining volunteer employment in 1981 in the laboratory of Edward Taub, a researcher in Silver Spring, Maryland, Pacheco secretly filmed monkeys being kept there under filthy conditions. His exposé of these conditions led to Taub's arrest, several court cases, and considerable publicity supporting animal rights groups' claim that animals in laboratories were mistreated.

Lewis Petrinovich, emeritus professor of psychology at the University of California, Riverside. Petrinovich maintains that a desire to put the interests of one's own species over those of others, which Peter Singer calls speciesism, is built into humans (and all other animals) by evolution.

Richard Pombo, a rancher and former Republican representative from Tracy, California. He was chair of the powerful House Resources Committee. He drew criticism from environmental and animal rights organizations because he supported oil exploration in the Arctic National Wildlife Refuge and elsewhere and sponsored the Threatened and Endangered Species Recovery Act, a revision of the 1973 Endangered Species Act that made the act more acceptable to private landowners. The House of Representatives passed Pombo's bill on September 29, 2005, but the bill was not taken up by the Senate. Pombo lost his House seat to Democrat Jerry McNerny in the elections of November 7, 2006.

Carl Pope, executive director of the Sierra Club since 1992. Pope has sought to mend rifts with hunting groups and others who have often felt themselves at odds with the environmental movement but share some of its goals, such as preservation of wildlife. Pope himself is a hunter.

Janice Pottker, American writer. In a 1999 suit against Ringling Bros. and Barnum & Bailey Circus, Pottker claimed that the circus's owner, Ken Feld, had hired people to spy on her, harass her, and derail her career after she published an article critical of the circus and the Feld family. Pottker's suit is still pending in 2007.

Tom Regan, North Carolina State University philosopher. Regan's 1984 book, *The Case for Animal Rights*, provides the philosophical rationale for the more radical wing of the animal rights movement. He claims that animals have basic rights, such as the right to life and bodily integrity, that must be respected, and he demands an end to essentially all human uses of animals.

Andrew N. Rowan, senior vice president for research, education, and international issues at the Humane Society of the United States. He is also an adjunct professor at Tufts University and a faculty member of the Johns Hopkins University Center for Alternatives to Animal Testing. He writes frequently about animal welfare issues.

W. M. S. Russell, British scientist. With Rex Burch, he codeveloped the concept of the "three Rs" of alternatives to animal research: *replace* animal tests with nonanimal ones whenever possible, *reduce* the number of animals needed per test, and *refine* tests so that they cause less pain and stress to animals. Russell and Burch first described the three Rs in *The Principles of Humane Experimental Technique*, published in 1959.

Richard Ryder, British philosopher and bioethicist. He is credited with coining the term *speciesism*, later adopted by Peter Singer, in 1970. He is a former chairman of the Royal Society for Prevention of Cruelty to Animals and currently directs animal welfare studies for the International Fund for Animal Welfare. He has been called "the Moses of the animal rights movement" and "the stormy petrel of the RSPCA."

Matthew Scully, a former speechwriter for President George W. Bush. Scully is an avowed conservative but also a strong critic of the treatment of animals in intensive farming. He does not believe that animals have rights, but he feels that humans have a moral obligation to treat them with respect and kindness.

Peter Singer, Australian philosopher, now at Princeton University. Singer's book *Animal Liberation,* first published in 1975, has frequently been called the Bible of the animal rights movement, and its publication is often held to mark the start of that movement. Singer, a utilitarian, believes that human uses of animals may be permissible if they do more good than harm overall. However, he says that animals deserve as much consideration as other sentient beings that can feel pain but cannot reason, such as human babies.

Henry Spira, American animal rights leader. Spira, a veteran of many social movements, founded Animal Rights International in 1976. He introduced tactics that had been effective in other movements into the fledgling animal rights movement and helped to establish dialogues among the new groups, traditional animal welfare societies, and the industries that animal rights groups opposed. In the early 1980s, he led a campaign that persuaded cosmetics giant Revlon to stop using the painful Draize irritancy tests on rabbits.

Edward Taub, American researcher. While conducting federally funded studies of nerve regrowth after injury at the Institute for Behavioral Research in Silver Spring, Maryland, in 1981, Taub allowed his experimental subjects, 17 rhesus monkeys, to be kept under substandard conditions that were secretly documented by animal rights activist Alex Pacheco. When Pacheco took his films to the police, Taub was arrested and charged with cruelty to animals. Taub was convicted of six counts of animal abuse, but the convictions were overturned on appeal in 1982 and 1983.

Frankie Trull, president of the National Association for Biomedical Research and the Foundation for Biomedical Research. These associations, based in Washington, D.C., are lobbying groups that work to protect the interests of scientists who experiment on animals.

Queen Victoria (Victoria I), 19th-century British monarch. In 1840, she lent her patronage to the Society for the Prevention of Cruelty to Animals, allowing it to add "Royal" to its name. She also appointed a royal commission to investigate vivisection in the early 1870s.

Jerry Vlasak, California heart surgeon and cofounder (with Steven Best) of the North American Animal Liberation Press Office. The press office, which Vlasak currently heads, gives out information about the Animal Liberation Front, which Vlasak and Best support. Vlasak was banned from traveling to Britain in 2004 because the British government considered him a terrorism risk.

Nathaniel Ward, English Puritan minister and lawyer. In 1641, Ward drew up a set of laws for the Massachusetts Bay Colony called the "Body of

Liberties," which included (as Liberty 92) the first known specific statute against cruelty to animals.

Caroline White, 19th-century animal activist. White cofounded the Pennsylvania Society for the Prevention of Cruelty to Animals (SPCA) in 1868. In 1870, she helped establish the first animal shelter, which was intended to provide more humane living conditions and more painless deaths for stray animals than were available at pounds. White also cofounded the American Anti-Vivisection Society in 1883.

Oprah Winfrey, American talk show host. After a 1996 program in which Winfrey supported an interviewee (Howard Lyman) who predicted that the practice of giving beef cattle food that contained animal remains might lead to an outbreak in the United States of "mad cow disease" and an equivalent illness in humans, a group of Texas cattlemen sued her and others involved with the show for violating a state food disparagement law. Winfrey and the others were acquitted in 1998.

Steven Wise, professor of law at Harvard and several other universities. Wise maintains that chimpanzees and bonobos, and perhaps some other animals, should be entitled to legal personhood because of their intellectual and emotional similarities to humans, and he works toward this end with groups such as the Great Ape Project. He has written several books to explain his ideas, including *Rattling the Cage* and *Drawing the Line.* Wise is also a former president of the Animal Legal Defense Fund and the president and founder of the Center for the Expansion of Fundamental Rights.

Clive D. L. Wynne, associate professor in the Department of Psychology at the University of Florida, Gainesville. Wynne is among those who say that behavioral studies of great apes do not necessarily prove that the animals possess such humanlike abilities as self-awareness and the power to understand and use language.

CHAPTER 5

GLOSSARY

Discussions about animal welfare and animal rights draw on their own specialized vocabulary as well as those of science, agriculture, philosophy, law, medicine, and other fields. This chapter presents some of the terms that the general reader is likely to encounter while researching these subjects.

American Horse Slaughter Prevention Act (HR 503 and S 1915)   This bill seeks to ban the slaughter of horses for human consumption in the United States. Animal rights and animal welfare organizations such as the Humane Society of the United States support it. The House of Representatives passed its version of the bill on September 7, 2006.

Animal and Plant Health Inspection Service (APHIS)   The agency of the U.S. Department of Agriculture that implements and enforces the Animal Welfare Act.

Animal Enterprise Protection Act   A U.S. law, passed in 1992, that makes physical disruption of animal production and research facilities a federal crime.

Animal Enterprise Terrorism Act   This bill, passed by the Senate in September 2006 and the House of Representatives in November, became law when President George W. Bush signed it on November 27, 2006. It increases the ability of the Justice Department to prosecute violent acts committed by animal rights activists against individuals and businesses involved in, or associated with other businesses involved in, animal enterprises such as raising of animals for research or fur.

animal law   The body of law covering human actions that affect animals.

"animal on a chip"   A silicon or plastic chip containing cells from different organs of a single animal species. It can be used instead of whole animals for some kinds of drug tests.

animal protection organizations   A term often used to encompass both animal welfare and animal rights organizations.

151

animal rights movement   A social movement dedicated to the idea that nonhuman animals possess, or should possess, at least some of the moral and legal rights granted to humans, including the right not to be killed, injured, or held captive. Some organizations in the animal rights movement see all human use of animals as inherently cruel and work to abolish it.

Animal Welfare Act   This act, which provides stringent regulation of the way individuals in England and Wales treat vertebrate animals, became law in Britain on November 8, 2006. It replaces the 1911 Protection of Animals Act and covers both pets and farmed animals but not animals used in scientific procedures.

Animal Welfare Act (AWA)   A U.S. law, passed in 1970, that regulates the housing and care of animals in laboratories and most types of animal exhibitions.

animal welfare organizations   Organizations holding that humans should harm animals as little as possible but accepting the morality of human uses of animals. The American and Royal (British) Societies for the Prevention of Cruelty to Animals are examples.

anthropomorphism   Attribution of human emotions and thoughts to animals.

bag limit   A limit on the number of animals of a certain type that a hunter may kill.

battery cage   A wire cage in which three to six laying hens are kept in intensive farming. The cages are stacked in rows and tiers to form "batteries" that may contain thousands of birds.

body-gripping trap   A type of trap, also called the Conibear trap, which is intended to kill an animal by snapping shut on its neck and breaking it. Animal rightists say the traps are cruel because they may close on an animal's chest or hips instead, producing a slow death from shock and suffocation.

bonobo   A great ape formerly called a pygmy chimpanzee but now considered a separate species *(Pan paniscus)*.

bovine growth hormone (BGH)   A hormone sometimes given to dairy cattle to increase milk production. Animal rights groups often object to use of this hormone, and some countries and the European Union have outlawed it.

bovine spongiform encephalopathy (BSE)   A brain-destroying disease of cattle, popularly called "mad cow disease," that is transmitted by feeding cattle the remains of other ruminants that have died of the disease. It may be transmissible to humans who eat meat from cattle with the disease. The human form of the illness is called variant Creutzfeldt-Jakob disease.

broiler chickens   Chickens reared for meat rather than eggs.

Glossary

buncher   A person who collects animals from random sources for an animal dealer to sell. Animal rightists say that some bunchers obtain pet cats and dogs under false pretenses or even steal them.

cage-free eggs   Eggs from hens that are not kept in cages, as they are in many intensive farms.

canned hunt   Derogatory term for a hunt in which a hunter pays a private game preserve for the chance to hunt an animal, often an exotic species, on the preserve. A kill and a trophy (head or skin) are often guaranteed.

Captive Wildlife Safety Act   An amendment to the Lacey Act (1900) that forbids interstate transport of big cats and other large predators for private use as pets. It became law on December 19, 2003.

Chimpanzee Health Improvement, Maintenance, and Protection Act (CHIMP Act)   A U.S. law, passed in 2000, that authorizes the establishment of sanctuaries to which chimpanzees formerly used in medical research may be "retired" when they are no longer needed.

class A dealer   As defined in the U.S. Animal Welfare Act, a dealer who breeds animals specifically for the purpose of selling them.

class B dealer   As defined in the U.S. Animal Welfare Act, a dealer who obtains animals from random sources and then sells them. These sources are often shelters, pounds, and animal auctions, but they may also include "bunchers" who, animal rightists allege, steal or fraudulently obtain family pets.

closed season   The time of year during which a particular type of game animal may not be hunted.

companion animal   Animal rights and some animal welfare organizations prefer this term for what is commonly known as a pet.

controlled atmosphere stunning   A technique that uses a mixture of gases to deprive poultry of oxygen, thereby rendering them unconscious before they are shackled to a conveyor belt for slaughter. Several animal rights organizations say that this method is more humane than the electrical stunning currently in use, but McDonald's and the World Organisation for Animal Health concluded after comparing the two techniques that both are equally acceptable.

Convention on International Trade in Endangered Species of Wild Flora and Fauna (CITES)   An international agreement, established by representatives of 80 countries in 1973, that limits or bans trade in endangered plant and animal species or any material made from them.

critical habitat   As defined in the Endangered Species Act, the geographic areas "on which are found those physical or biological features essential to the conservation of [an endangered] species and which may require special management considerations or protection."

distinct population segment   The smallest unit that Congress permits to be considered separately for listing as threatened or endangered under the Endangered Species Act. Congress did not define this term precisely, but it covers a population smaller than a subspecies. See also **evolutionarily significant unit**.

DNA chip   Also called DNA microarray. Each "chip" contains hundreds or even thousands of short strands of DNA that act as probes for different genes. DNA chips may replace animals in some toxicity tests.

"downer cattle"   Animals too sick or lame to walk to slaughter. Until December 2003 in the United States they could be carried to the slaughterhouse, killed, and used as meat, a practice animal rightists called cruel as well as a threat to the human-food supply. The U.S. Secretary of Agriculture banned their use after a case of mad cow disease was discovered in that country.

Draize tests   Tests commonly used to determine whether a cosmetic or other product is likely to irritate skin or eyes. The tests, which usually use rabbits, were invented by John Draize, a scientist working for the U.S. Food and Drug Administration, in the 1940s. Animal rightists oppose the tests because they are painful to the animals involved.

duck stamp   Informal name for the Migratory Bird Hunting Stamp, which a federal law passed in 1934 requires adult waterfowl hunters to purchase each year in addition to hunting licenses. The U.S. Fish and Wildlife Service uses the resulting money to buy or lease land for waterfowl habitat.

endangered species   As defined in the Endangered Species Act, a species that is "in danger of extinction throughout all or a significant portion of its range."

Endangered Species Act   A U.S. law, passed in 1973, that protects species classified as endangered or threatened, along with their "critical habitat."

evolutionarily significant unit (ESU)   A term substituted by the National Marine Fisheries Service in 1991 for the term *distinct population segment* in the Endangered Species Act. See also **distinct population segment**.

factory farming   A derogatory term (probably coined by British author Ruth Harrison in a 1964 book) often used by animal rights activists to describe what is more neutrally called intensive farming.

farrowing crate   A tight enclosure in which a sow is kept while she is nursing her piglets. The crate's purpose is to keep the sow from lying on and crushing the piglets, but animal rightists say it is excessively confining.

Fish and Wildlife Service   The agency of the U.S. Department of the Interior that implements and enforces the Endangered Species Act.

Glossary

five freedoms Originally defined by the European Union's Farm Animal Welfare Council as being required for farm animals, these "freedoms" are guaranteed to all vertebrate animals in England and Wales by Britain's Animal Welfare Act, which became law on November 8, 2006: freedom from hunger and thirst; freedom from discomfort; freedom from pain, injury, and disease; freedom from fear and distress; and freedom to express normal behavior.

foie gras A gourmet food made from the livers of geese or ducks that have been force-fed to make their livers enlarge and become fatty; some animal rights groups seek to ban this food because they consider its method of production to be cruel.

food disparagement law A type of law that forbids intentional dissemination of false information claiming that a food product is unsafe for consumption. Sometimes called "veggie libel law."

Food Safety and Inspection Service (FSIS) The agency of the U.S. Department of Agriculture that inspects slaughterhouses and meatpacking plants in the United States and other countries that import meat to the United States to ensure that (among other things) the Humane Methods of Slaughter Act is followed.

forced molting The practice, often used with laying hens in intensive farming, of forcing all the hens to molt (lose their feathers) at once, usually by temporarily depriving them of food and sometimes water and light.

Fur Seal Act A U.S. law, passed in 1966, that implements international agreements limiting hunting of fur seals that the United States signed in 1911 and 1957.

gestation stall A small enclosure in which a sow is kept while she is pregnant. Many animal rights groups object to gestation stalls.

great apes Primates belonging to the family *Pongidae*, including chimpanzees, bonobos, gorillas, and orangutans.

habitat conservation plan (HCP) A document authorized under 1982 amendments to the Endangered Species Act that permits landowners to harm or kill a limited number of members of an endangered species (incidental take) or destroy a limited amount of habitat in exchange for other actions that mitigate the damage and result in better conservation of the habitat as a whole. The habitat conservation plan, which is prepared by the landowner and must be approved by the Fish and Wildlife Service before the service grants the landowner's incidental take permit, sets forth both the predicted damage and the proposed mitigation.

halal slaughter Slaughter of meat animals carried out in accordance with the dietary practices of the Muslim religion, which, like Jewish kosher slaughter, requires animals to be conscious at the time of death. The

Humane Methods of Slaughter Act exempts halal slaughter from its requirement that livestock be stunned before it is killed.

hatchery policy A policy set forth by the National Marine Fisheries Service in 1993 that stated that salmon spawned in hatcheries would be counted along with wild-spawned fish to determine population size (for the purpose of deciding whether to list a species or subspecies as threatened or endangered under the Endangered Species Act) only "sparingly" and when the hatchery-spawned fish were considered "essential to recovery" of the species. This policy was invalidated following a federal district court ruling in 2001.

high-production-volume chemicals (HPV chemicals) Chemicals manufactured at the rate of 1 million pounds or more per year. In 1998, the U.S. Environmental Protection Agency began a program requiring additional safety testing data for these chemicals, which animal rightists objected to because they said it would cost the lives of more than 1 million animals.

Horse Protection Act A U.S. law, passed in 1970, which bans soring of horses.

Humane Methods of Slaughter Act A U.S. law, passed in 1978, that establishes rules for treatment of livestock (except for birds) in and around slaughterhouses, including a requirement that the animals be rendered unconscious before being killed unless they are being killed according to kosher or halal slaughter.

Hunting Act A law, passed by the British Parliament on September 16, 2004, which bans the hunting of foxes or other mammals with dogs, a prohibition long sought by antihunting and animal rights groups. The ban went into effect on February 17, 2005.

Huntingdon Life Sciences (HLS) A British firm that is Europe's largest contract animal testing laboratory. In 1999, after seeing videos of alleged animal abuse that PETA had filmed at Huntingdon, British animal rights activists Greg Avery and Heather James founded Stop Huntingdon Life Sciences (SHAC) with the aim of forcing Huntingdon to close. Huntingdon, its U.S. arm (Life Sciences Research), and individuals or businesses connected with it have been primary targets of SHAC, the Animal Liberation Front (ALF), and other animal rights organizations ever since.

incidental take permit A permit, obtained from the U.S. Fish and Wildlife Service, that allows developers to unintentionally harm or kill a limited number of protected species members during a project without penalty, in exchange for preparing and following a habitat conservation plan that includes mitigating activities to conserve habitat and protect species elsewhere. The issuing of incidental take permits was authorized by amendments to the Endangered Species Act passed by Congress in 1982.

Glossary

inherent value   Value that is inseparable or inborn, not determined by how a living thing is used or what experiences it has had.

Institutional Animal Care and Use Committee (IACUC)   A committee charged with ensuring the proper care and minimal harm of experimental animals, which every scientific institution that uses animals must establish, according to the 1985 revision of the Animal Welfare Act.

intensive farming   Farming in which hundreds or thousands of animals are kept together indoors in close quarters for part or all of their lives and usually fed and watered automatically. Animal rightists disapprove of this type of farming, which they call factory farming.

kosher slaughter   Slaughter of meat animals carried out according to the dietary rules of the Jewish religion, which, among other things, requires animals to be conscious and standing when they are killed. The Humane Methods of Slaughter Act exempts kosher slaughter from its requirement that livestock be stunned before it is killed.

Lacey Act   A U.S. law, passed in 1900, that forbids movement of protected birds or their body parts across state lines.

landscape immersion   A style of zoo habitat first developed by landscape architect Grant Jones for Seattle's Woodland Park Zoo in the mid-1970s. It is intended to make both resident animals and human visitors feel immersed in a natural landscape and to allow the animals to carry out natural behaviors.

LD50 test ("lethal dose for 50 percent" test)   A widely used test for acute toxicity, developed in Britain in 1927, in which groups of about 100 animals (usually rats) are given (usually by force feeding) varying doses of the test substance until half of one group dies. Animal rightists call this test crude as well as cruel.

legal personhood   The status of possessing certain legal rights, including the right to be a plaintiff in a lawsuit. All humans are considered legal persons, whether or not they can understand or take an active part in legal proceedings; so, by convention, are certain other entities, such as corporations and ships. Some animal rightists believe that legal personhood should be extended to great apes and, perhaps, certain other animals.

legal standing   The quality of being recognized by law as having value and dignity in one's own right, rather than simply because of one's usefulness to others. Animals do not have legal standing at present, but some animal rightists believe that they should.

Live-Shot.com   A Texas-based web site that allows paying customers to use their computers to shoot captive wild animals by remote control, an Internet version of the "canned hunt." It is no longer available. See also **canned hunt.**

mad cow disease   Popular name for bovine spongiform encephalopathy. See **bovine spongiform encephalopathy** and **Variant Creutzfeldt-Jakob disease**.

Martin Act   The name sometimes given to the Ill Treatment of Horses and Cattle Bill, which the British Parliament passed in 1822. Aimed at preventing cruelty to horses, cattle, and other livestock, it was the first national animal protection law.

mastitis   A painful inflammation of the udder that dairy cows often suffer, particularly in intensive farms.

Migratory Bird Treaty Act   A U.S. law, passed in 1918, that implemented an agreement the government had made with Canada in 1913 to protect nongame migratory birds and limit the hunting of game birds. It was the first U.S. law that implemented that country's share of an international treaty concerning animal protection.

no-kill shelter   A shelter in which animals are kept until they are adopted, no matter how long this takes.

"No Surprises" rule   A policy established by amendments to the Endangered Species Act in 1982, stating that once a developer has produced an acceptable habitat conservation plan and received an incidental take permit from the Fish and Wildlife Service, the developer is not liable for expenditure beyond that agreed upon in the permit that might later be found necessary to conserve species. See also **habitat conservation plan; incidental take permit.**

open season   The time of year during which hunters may legally kill a particular type of animal.

orangutan   A type of great ape, now endangered, indigenous to Indonesia.

Pet Protection Act   An amendment to the Animal Welfare Act, passed in 1990, that requires pounds and shelters to hold animals for a minimum of five days before selling them to dealers.

pound   A facility for holding stray dogs or (sometimes) other animals, usually run by a city or other municipality, as opposed to a shelter, which is generally operated by a private organization.

pound seizure laws   Laws that some U.S. states passed in the late 1940s and 1950s that required pounds and shelters to surrender animals to research laboratories on demand. Also called pound procurement laws.

primate   Any member of the order of animals that includes lemurs, monkeys, apes, and humans.

puppy mill   A large dog-breeding facility that keeps its animals in substandard conditions, thereby making them likely to have health problems.

PZP vaccine (porcine zona pellucida vaccine)   A form of animal contraceptive, invented in the 1970s, that can be injected with a dart and, therefore, can be used on wildlife such as deer.

Glossary

REACH (Registration, Evaluation, and Authorisation of Chemicals) A European Union–wide program for chemical testing, adopted by the European Commission in 2003 and scheduled to begin in 2007, which concerns animal welfare groups because it may require the use of millions of animals.

Recreational Hunting Safety and Preservation Act A U.S. law, passed in 1994, that makes it a federal crime to physically interfere with a lawful hunt.

sentient being A living thing capable of feeling pleasure and pain.

Serious Organised Crime and Police Act An amendment to this act, which became law in Britain in July 2005, gives police increased power to act against violent animal rights groups and other extremist protesters who cause economic or other harm to companies or individuals linked to research on animals.

shelter A facility that takes in unwanted or homeless animals, chiefly cats and dogs, and usually tries to find homes for them. Unlike pounds, shelters are generally operated by private organizations.

Silver Spring monkey case A case of alleged abuse of monkeys in the laboratory of Edward Taub in Silver Spring, Maryland, in the early 1980s, revealed by film shot by PETA cofounder Alex Pacheco. Taub was initially convicted of six counts of animal abuse, but the convictions were reversed on appeal.

snail darter A three-inch-long fish whose designation as endangered in 1975 almost stopped the building of the Tellico Dam in Tennessee because the dam would destroy the fish's critical habitat, thus violating the Endangered Species Act.

snare A trap in which a wire loop, which may or may not be coated, tightens around an animal's leg or neck.

soring A practice of deliberately injuring and irritating a horse's front legs to make it perform a type of high-stepping gait valued in shows. The Horse Protection Act (1970) makes soring illegal.

speciesism Term, coined by Richard Ryder and made popular by Peter Singer's use of it in *Animal Liberation*, defined as automatically placing the interests of one's own species ahead of those of other species.

standing to sue The right to be a plaintiff in a particular lawsuit. Justice Antonin Scalia spelled out the requirements for having standing to sue in a 1992 Supreme Court case, *Lujan v. Defenders of Wildlife*.

steel-jawed leghold trap A commonly used type of trap that animal rightists say is particularly cruel and causes extensive tissue damage.

tertiary targeting The tactic, employed by certain extremist animal rights groups beginning in the late 1990s, of attacking individuals or businesses that are connected with an allegedly abusive company in any way, no

159

matter how indirect; for example, businesses (and the employees of businesses) that buy or sell stock in the company or provide services for its employees.

Threatened and Endangered Species Recovery Act   A bill (HR 3824) sponsored by former California Representative Richard Pombo (R-Tracy) that was intended to make the Endangered Species Act more acceptable to private landowners. The House of Representatives passed the bill on September 29, 2005, but the Senate did not take it up.

threatened species   As defined in the Endangered Species Act, a species that is "likely to become endangered . . . in the foreseeable future."

three Rs   The approach to reducing the use of animals in science first described by British scientists W. M. S. Russell and Rex Burch in 1959. Russell and Burch said that scientists should *replace* tests that use animals with nonanimal tests wherever possible, *reduce* the number of animals used in each test, and *refine* tests and experiments to make them cause less pain and distress to animals.

tort   A wrongful injury to a person or property that is grounds for a civil lawsuit.

transgenic animal   An animal that has been engineered to carry genes from another species.

Twenty-eight-Hour Act   A U.S. law, passed in 1873, that requires animals being transported over long distances to be given rest, food, and water every 28 hours.

utilitarianism   A school of philosophy, founded by British philosopher Jeremy Bentham, that states that the most moral choice of action is the one that produces the best outcome (greatest amount of pleasure) for all those involved in a situation.

variant Creutzfeldt-Jakob disease   A mysterious and deadly human brain-destroying ailment that may be transmitted by eating beef from cattle infected with bovine spongiform encephalopathy, popularly called "mad cow disease."

vegan   A person whose diet contains no meat or animal products.

vegetarian   A person who eats no meat but may eat animal products such as milk and cheese.

veggie libel law   Slang term for a food disparagement law.

vivisection   Performing surgery on a living animal for experimental purposes; sometimes, performing any painful or stressful experiment on an animal.

PART II

GUIDE TO FURTHER RESEARCH

CHAPTER 6

HOW TO RESEARCH
ANIMAL RIGHTS ISSUES

The subject of animal welfare and animal rights has generated a considerable amount of information in recent years. This chapter presents a selection of resources, techniques, and research suggestions for investigating issues related to human treatment and uses of animals.

Although students, teachers, journalists, and other investigators may ultimately have different objectives, all are likely to begin with the same basic steps. The following general approach should be suitable for most purposes:

- Gain a general orientation by reading the first part of this book. Chapter 1 can be read as a narrative, while Chapters 2–5 are best skimmed to get an idea of what is covered. They can then be used as a reference source for helping make sense of the events and issues encountered in subsequent reading.

- Skim some of the general books listed in the first section of the bibliography (Chapter 7). Neutral overviews and books that provide pro and con essays on various issues in the field are particularly recommended.

- Browse the many web sites provided by organizations involved in animal welfare and animal rights (see Chapter 8), including those of groups that support industries that animal rightists criticize. Their pages are rich in news, articles and links to other organizations, as well as describing particular cases and discussing the pros and cons of various practices involving animals.

- Use the relevant sections of Chapter 7 to find more books, articles, and online publications on particular topics of interest.

- Find more (and more recent) materials by using the bibliographic tools such as the library catalogs and periodical indexes discussed later.

- To keep up with current events and breaking news, check back periodically with media and organization web sites and periodically search the catalogs and indexes for recent material.

The rest of this chapter is organized according to types of resources and tools. The three major categories are online resources, print resources, and the special area of law, legislation, and legal research.

ONLINE RESOURCES

With the increasing amount of information being made available online, turning to the World Wide Web is a logical way to begin any research project. It is easy to drown in the sea of information the Web reveals, but starting with a few well-organized, resource-rich sites and then applying selective Web searching can provide a logical thread through the labyrinth.

GENERAL SITES ON ANIMAL WELFARE ISSUES

As Chapter 8 shows, dozens of groups present information or take stands on various animal-related issues. The following major sites (listed in alphabetical order) are recommended as good starting places for research. They offer well-organized overviews of issues, provide numerous resources and links, and answer frequently asked questions. As described in the annotations for the sites, some favor animal rights, some explicitly oppose animal rights, and others are neutral or advocate animal welfare but not necessarily animal rights.

Animal Information Network
URL: http://www.animal-info.net
This site provides links related to a variety of subjects, including animal welfare, animal legislation, animal rights, companion animals, conservation, research, and shelters.

has many articles on animal rights philosophy, speciesism, the morality of the animal rights position, the biology of animals, animal testing and research, positions of different religions on animal rights, animal rights and the law, and other subjects.

Animal Liberation Front
URL: http://www.animal liberationfront.com
This site, sponsored by one of the most radical animal rights groups,

Animal Protection Institute
URL: http://www.api4 animals.org/a_campaigns.php
The Campaigns and Programs page of this animal welfare organization's

web site contains many reports on abuse of animals and other resources. It includes sections on animals in entertainment, animals in research, companion animals, and more.

Animal Welfare Institute
URL: http://www.awionline.org
Includes extensive collection of articles and other material on animal-related topics. Supports animal welfare but not necessarily animal rights.

Envirolink
URL: http://www.envirolink.org
Large web site devoted to environmental issues; includes links to some material that covers animal welfare/animal rights issues, such as wildlife preservation and animals in agriculture.

The Humane Society of the United States
URL: http://www.hsus.org
Provides numerous reports and news stories from an animal welfare/animal rights point of view on animals in research, pets/companion animals, farm animals, marine mammals, and wildlife.

Man in Nature
URL: http://www.maninnature.com
Provides access to an assortment of articles that oppose animal rights and support hunting and other uses of animals.

National Animal Interest Alliance (NAIA)
URL: http://www.naiaonline.org
The site of this animal industry trade association, which supports "responsible animal use" by humans as well as animal welfare, provides news articles, including archived ones, on topics including animals and the law and what the NAIA views as animal rights extremism.

U.S. Department of Agriculture Animal Welfare Information Center
URL: http://awic.nal.usda.gov/
Extensive government web site with many links is devoted primarily to care and use of animals in science but also includes material on animals in agriculture, animals in entertainment, and companion animals.

World Animal Net Directory
URL: http://worldanimalnet.org
Claims to be the world's largest database of animal protection societies (grouped by categories and regions as well as searchable individually), with listings for more than 17,000 international animal rights and welfare organizations. Resources include material on animal protection laws in various countries.

Animal Rights

SITES ON SPECIFIC ANIMAL TOPICS

The following sites feature material on the specific areas of animal use discussed in Chapter 1. As with the general sites, some of the specific sites are neutral, while others support or oppose particular human uses of animals.

Companion Animals

International Society for Animal Rights
URL: http://www.isaronline.org
Provides reports on such subjects as pet overpopulation, spay/neuter, and puppy mills.

National Council on Pet Population Study and Policy
URL: http://www.petpopulation.org
Provides abstracts of academic studies on companion animals and shelters, chiefly studies examining why people give up their pets.

Animals in Agriculture

Compassion in World Farming
URL: http://www.ciwf.org.uk
British animal rights organization has detailed reports and videos on allegedly harmful conditions on intensive farms, as well as on such subjects as genetic engineering of farm animals and the effect of World Trade Organization rules on animal welfare.

European Union (Europa site)
URL: http://ec.europa.eu/food/animal/welfare/index_en.htm
This page from the European Union's subsite, "Food Safety—From the Farm to the Fork," includes links to information on EU policies regarding farm animal welfare (and, to some extent, animal welfare in general), including welfare on the farm, during transport, and at slaughter.

Feedstuffs Foodlink
URL: http://www.feedstuffsfood link.com/ME2/dirsect.asp?sid =9F171E31AEE34017A92834 AE077CAB91&nm=Animal+ Welfare
The animal welfare page of this agricultural trade magazine's resource web site provides links to information on sow gestation crates, horse slaughter, caged egg production, and foie gras.

U.S. Department of Agriculture, National Agricultural Statistics Service (NASS)
URL: http://www.nass.usda.gov
Includes information on the numbers and different types of animals in U.S. agriculture.

Animals in Research, Testing, and Education

Altweb: Alternatives to Animal Testing
URL: http://altweb.jhsph.edu
Sponsored by Johns Hopkins University, this site provides miscella-

neous news, conference proceedings, and more on development of alternatives to tests on animals.

Americans for Medical Progress
URL: http://www.ampef.org
Offers news stories and other information supporting the use of animals in research and criticizing animal rights groups.

Animal Protection Information Service (APIS)
URL: http://www.hennet.org/apis/index.php
Sponsored by the Humane Education Network, this site contains summaries of books, articles, and other documents related to the use and care of and alternatives to animals in laboratories, education, entertainment, farming, and fur. The group urges reform and minimization of animal use.

National Centre for the Replacement, Refinement and Reduction of Animals in Research (NC3Rs) Information Portal
URL: http://www.nc3rs.org.uk/landing.asp?id=38

This page, from the site of a British government–sponsored institution, provides annotated links to online databases, web sites, journal articles, legislation, and other publications about many issues related to the "three Rs" as well as information on humane handling of particular species used in research.

National Institutes of Health (NIH), Office of Laboratory Animal Welfare
URL: http://www.grants.nih.gov/grants/olaw/olaw.htm
Government site includes policies and laws, guidance in meeting regulations, general information, and Public Health Service and NIH policies and laws for care of laboratory animals.

Norwegian Inventory of Alternatives (NORINA)
URL: http://oslovet.veths.no/ fag.aspx?fag=57&mnu=databases_1
Provided by the Norwegian Reference Centre for Laboratory Animal Science & Alternatives, this database lists audiovisual alternatives or supplements to use of animals in education.

Animals in Entertainment

Performing Animal Welfare Society
URL: http://www.pawsweb.org
Gives news stories on alleged abuses of elephants and other performing animals and on refuges for rescued performing animals.

Ringling Bros. and Barnum & Bailey Circus
URL: http://www.ringling.com/animals
Includes material on training and care of animals in this famous circus as well as descriptions of particular types of animals such as elephants and big cats.

Animal Rights

Wildlife

Convention on International Trade in Endangered Species of Wild Fauna and Flora (CITES)
URL: http://www.cites.org
Contains material describing and related to CITES, the chief international agreement for preservation and limitation of trade in endangered species.

Defenders of Wildlife
URL: http://www.defenders. org
Includes publications regarding the Endangered Species Act and preservation of wildlife.

New Mexico School of Law Institute of Public Law Center for Wildlife Law
URL: http://ipl.unm.edu/cwl
Includes handbooks of federal and state wildlife laws and reports on biodiversity and on the Endangered Species Act arranged by state.

U.S. Fish and Wildlife Service Endangered Species Program
URL: http://www.fws.gov/ endangered
Provides information about the Endangered Species Act and the program designed to implement it, as well as news, information on the state of particular species, and other features.

MEDIA SITES

News (wire) services, most newspapers, and many magazines have web sites that include breaking news stories and links to additional information. The following media sites have substantial listings for stories on animal rights and animal welfare:

- Cable News Network (CNN)
  URL: http://www.cnn.com
- Reuters
  URL: http://www.reuters.com/
- *New York Times*
  URL: http://www.nytimes.com
- *Time* magazine
  URL: http://www.time.com/time

Yahoo! maintains a large set of links to many newspapers that have web sites or online editions: http://dir.yahoo.com/News_and_Media/Newspapers/Web_ Directories

FINDING MORE ON THE WEB

Although the resource sites mentioned earlier provide a convenient way to view a wide variety of information, the researcher will eventually want to seek additional data or views elsewhere. The two main approaches to Web research are the portal (guide or index) and the search engine.

Web Portals

A web guide or index is a site that offers a structured, hierarchical outline of subject areas. This format enables the researcher to zero in on a particular aspect of a subject and find links to web sites for further exploration. The links are constantly being compiled and updated by a staff of researchers.

The best known (and largest) web index is Yahoo! (http://www.yahoo.com). Its home page gives a top-level list of topics, which researchers simply click to find more specific areas. Alternatively, there is a search box into which researchers can type one or more keywords and receive a list of matching categories and sites.

Web indexes such as Yahoo! have two major advantages over undirected "web surfing." First, the structured hierarchy of topics makes it easy to find a particular topic or subtopic and then explore its links. Second, Yahoo! does not make an attempt to compile every link on the Internet (a task that is virtually impossible, given the size of the Web). Instead, Yahoo!'s indexers evaluate sites for usefulness and quality, giving the researcher a better chance of finding more substantial and accurate information. The disadvantage of web indexes is the flip side of their selectivity: researchers are dependent on the indexer's judgment for determining what sites are worth exploring.

To research animal rights via Yahoo!, call up the directory site at http://dir.yahoo.com, leave "the directory" checked, and type "animal rights" into the search box. At the time of writing, the following topics appeared under Animal Rights in the directory:

- Animal Abuse
- Animal Experimentation
- Bear Farming Issues
- Bullfighting Views
- Cat Declawing
- Circus Animals
- Dog Ear Cropping

Animal Rights

- Dog Meat
- Dog Tail Docking
- Endangered Animals
- Factory Farming
- Fishing Views
- Fur
- Humane and Rescue Societies
- Hunting Views
- Illegal Wildlife Trade and Poaching
- Magazines
- Opposing Views
- Organizations
- Petitions
- Puppy Mill Issues
- Shahtoosh Ban
- Vegetarianism
- Zoos

A variety of sites selected by the editors are available for browsing. Several other subtopics under "Animals, Insects, and Pets" are also worth examining, including "Animal Abuse," "Organizations," "Pets," "Wildlife," and "Zoos." *Animal welfare* does not have its own subdirectory, but typing these words into the Yahoo! search engine will pull up some relevant web sites and news stories. The two topics, of course, also overlap to a moderate extent. In any case, there is clearly no shortage of links that can be explored using Yahoo! as a starting point.

About.com, run by About, formerly The Mining Company (http://www. about.com), now owned by the New York Times Company, is rather similar to Yahoo! but emphasizes overviews or guides prepared by self-declared experts in various topics. The site does a good job of creating a guide page "on the fly" when a keyword or phrase is entered in the search box. The About listing provides many pages both within the About network itself and on the Web in general. Note that About generates special URLs that keep pages "tied" to the About site, so for bookmarking purposes it is probably a good idea when visiting a linked site to reload it under its own URL.

New guide and index sites are constantly being developed, and capabilities are improving as the Web matures.

Search Engines

Search engines take a very different approach to finding materials on the Web. Instead of organizing topically in a "top down" fashion, search engines work their way "from the bottom up," scanning through web documents and indexing them. There are hundreds of search engines, but some of the most widely used include:

- AltaVista: http://www.altavista.com
- Excite: http://www.excite.com
- Google: http://www.google.com
- Hotbot: http://www.hotbot.com
- Lycos: http://www.lycos.com

To search with a search engine, one can employ the same sorts of keywords that work in library catalogs. There are a variety of Web search tutorials available online (try entering "web search tutorial" in a search engine to find some). One good one is published by Bright Planet at http://www.brightplanet.com/resources/details/searching.html.

Here are a few basic rules for using search engines:

- When looking for something specific, use the most specific term or phrase. For example, when looking for information about slaughterhouses, use that specific term.
- Phrases should be surrounded by quotation marks if you want them to be matched as phrases rather than as individual words. Examples include "animal rights movement," "Draize test," and "battery cages."
- When looking for a general topic that might be expressed using several different words or phrases, use several descriptive words (nouns are more reliable than verbs), such as *circus animal training*. Most engines will automatically put pages that match all terms first on the results list.
- Use "wildcards" when a desired word may have more than one ending. For example, *animal** will include results containing both "animal" and "animals."
- Most search engines support Boolean *(and, or, not)* operators, which can be used to broaden or narrow a search.
- Use AND to narrow a search. For example, *circuses* **and** *zoos* will match only pages that have both terms.
- Use OR to broaden a search: *"companion animals"* **or** *pets* will match any page that has *either* term, and since these terms are often used interchangeably, this type of search is necessary to retrieve the widest range of results.

• Use NOT to exclude unwanted results: *horses* **not** *racing* finds articles about horses but not horse racing.

Since each search engine indexes somewhat differently and offers somewhat different ways of searching, it is a good idea to use several search engines, especially for a general query. Some "metasearch" programs, such as Metacrawler (http://www.metacrawler.com), WebCrawler (http://www.webcrawler.com), and SurfWax (http://www. surfwax.com), automate the process of submitting a query to multiple search engines. Metasearch engines may overwhelm you with results (and insufficiently prune duplicates), however, and they often do not use some of the more popular search engines, such as Google.

There are also search utilities that can be run from the researcher's own computer rather than through a web site. A good example is Copernic (http://www.copernic.com).

Finding Organizations and People

Chapter 8 of this book provides a list of organizations involved with research, advocacy, or opposition to animal rights. New organizations continue to emerge, however. The resource sites and Web portals mentioned earlier are good places to look for information and links to organizations. If the name of an unfamiliar organization turns up during reading or browsing, the name can be entered in a search engine. For best results, the complete name should be put in quotation marks (for instance, "San Francisco Society for the Prevention of Cruelty to Animals"), although some search engines, such as Google, do not require this. If omitting the quotation marks, also omit common words such as *the* and *of*; for instance, type *San francisco society prevention cruelty animals* rather than the organization's complete name. Including these words will confuse the search engine.

Another approach is to take a guess at the organization's likely Web address. For example, People for the Ethical Treatment of Animals is commonly known by the acronym PETA, so it is not a surprise that the organization's web site is at http://www.peta.org. (Note that noncommercial organization sites normally use the *.org* suffix, government agencies use *.gov*, educational institutions have *.edu*, and businesses use *.com*.) This technique can save time, but it does not always work. In particular, watch out for "spoof" sites that mimic or parody organizational sites. For instance, an animal rights opponent named Michael Doughney originally reserved the domain name www.peta.org for a site on which the acronym was used to stand for "People Eating Tasty Animals." (PETA sued him for trademark infringement, and he was forced to give up the domain name.) Of course, parody sites may be of interest in themselves as forms of criticism or dissent.

When reading materials by an unfamiliar author, it is often useful to learn about that person's affiliation, credentials, and other achievements. There are several ways to find a person on the Internet:

- Put the person's name (in quotes) in a search engine, which may lead you to that person's home page or a biographical sketch listed by the institution for which the person works.

- Contact the person's employer (such as a university for an academic or a corporation for a technical professional). Most such organizations have web pages that include a searchable faculty or employee directory.

- Try a people-finder service, such as Yahoo! People Search (http://people. yahoo.com) or BigFoot (http://www.bigfoot.com). These services may yield contact information, including an e-mail address, regular address, and/or phone number.

PRINT SOURCES

As useful as the Web is for quickly finding information and the latest news, in-depth research can still require trips to the library or bookstore. Getting the most out of the library, in turn, requires the use of bibliographic tools and resources. *Bibliographic resources* is a general term for catalogs, indexes, bibliographies, and other guides that identify the books, periodical articles, and other printed materials that deal with a particular subject. They are essential tools for researchers.

LIBRARY CATALOGS

Most readers are probably familiar with the basics of using a library catalog, but they may not know that many catalogs besides that of their local library can be searched online. The largest library catalog, that of the Library of Congress, can be accessed at http://catalog.loc.gov, a page that includes a guide to using the catalog as well as both basic and advanced catalog searches. Yahoo! offers a categorized listing of libraries at http://dir. yahoo. com/Reference/Libraries. WorldCat (http://www.worldcat.org) allows searches of more than 10,000 libraries worldwide.

Most catalogs can be searched in at least the following ways:

- An author search is most useful if researchers know or suspect that a person has written a number of works of interest. However, it may fail if they do not know the person's exact name. (Cross-references are intended to deal with this problem, but they cannot cover all possible variations.)

- A title search is best if a researcher knows the exact title of a book and just wants to know if a particular library has it. Generally, researchers need only use the first few words of the title, excluding initial articles (*a, an,* or *the*). This search will fail if a researcher does not have the exact title.

- A keyword search will match words found anywhere in the title. It is thus broader and more flexible than a title search, although it may still fail if all keywords are not present.

- A subject search will find all works to which a library has assigned that subject heading. The advantage of a subject search is that it does not depend on certain words being in a book's title. However, using this kind of search can require knowing the appropriate Library of Congress subject headings for a topic. These can be obtained from the Library of Congress catalog site (http://catalog.loc.gov) by clicking on Basic Search, then selecting Subject Browse and typing in a term such as *animal rights.*

Once the record for a book or other item is found, it is a good idea to see what additional subject headings and name headings have been assigned to that item. These, in turn, can be used for further searching. For instance, in addition to *animal rights,* researchers will probably also want to check out *animal welfare* and *animal rights activists.*

BOOKSTORE CATALOGS

Many people have discovered that online bookstores such as Amazon.com (http://www.amazon.com) and Barnes & Noble (http://www.barnesandnoble. com) provide convenient ways to shop for books. A less-known benefit of online bookstore catalogs is that they often include publisher information, book reviews, and reader comments about a given title. They can thus serve as a form of annotated bibliography. Out-of-print or highly specialized materials may not appear in such catalogs, however.

BIBLIOGRAPHIES, INDEXES, AND DATABASES

Printed or online bibliographies provide a convenient way to find books, periodical articles, and other materials. Some bibliographies include abstracts (brief summaries of content), while others provide only citations. Some bibliographies and indexes are available online (at least for recent years), but researchers may be able to access them only through a library where they hold a card. (When searching on a college campus, researchers can ask a university reference librarian for help.) However, UnCover Web (http://www. ingentaconnect.com) contains brief descriptions of about 13 million documents from about 27,000 journals in almost every subject area. Copies of complete documents can be ordered with a credit card, or they may be obtained free at a local library.

PERIODICAL INDEXES

Most public libraries subscribe to database services such as InfoTrac or EBSCOhost, which index articles from hundreds of general-interest periodicals (and some moderately specialized ones). This kind of database can be searched by author or by words in the title, subject headings, and sometimes words found anywhere in the article text. Depending on the database used, "hits" can produce just a bibliographical citation (author, title, pages, periodical name, issue date, and other information), a citation and abstract, or the full text of the article. Before using such an index, it is a good idea to view the list of newspapers and magazines covered and determine the years of coverage.

Many libraries provide dial-in, Internet, or telnet access to their periodical databases as an option in their catalog menu. However, licensing restrictions usually mean that only researchers who have a library card for that particular library can access the database (by typing in their name and card number). Check with local public or school libraries to see what databases are available.

For periodicals not indexed by InfoTrac or another index (or for which only abstracts rather than complete text is available), check to see whether the publication has its own web site (most now do). Some scholarly publications are putting most or all of their articles online. Popular publications tend to offer only a limited selection. Some publications of both types offer archives of several years' back issues that can be searched by author or keyword.

Nearly all newspapers now have web sites with current news and features. Generally a newspaper offers recent articles (perhaps from the last 30 days) for free online access. Earlier material can often be found in an archive section. A citation and, perhaps, an abstract is frequently available for free, but a fee of a few dollars may be charged for the complete article. One can sometimes buy a "pack" of articles at a discount as long as the articles are retrieved within a specified time. Of course, back issues of newspapers and magazines may also be available in hard copy, bound, or on microfilm at local libraries.

LEGAL RESEARCH

As with all complex and controversial topics, animal welfare and animal rights have been the subject of intense litigation in the courts. Animal rights groups

175

have often used lawsuits in attempts to pressure government agencies to enforce animal protection laws such as the Animal Welfare Act and the Endangered Species Act, and these groups in turn have been sued by some of the individuals and businesses they have attacked. Although one can find news coverage of some important cases in the general media, many researchers will need to find specific court opinions or the text of existing or pending legislation.

Because of the specialized terminology of the law, legal research can be more difficult to master than bibliographical or general research tools. Fortunately, the Internet has also come to the rescue in this area, offering a variety of ways to look up laws and court cases without having to pore through huge bound volumes in law libraries (which may not be easily accessible to the general public, anyway.) To begin with, simply entering the name of a law, bill, or court case into a search engine will often lead the researcher directly to both text and commentary.

Finding Laws

Federal legislation is compiled into the massive U.S. Code. The U.S. Code can be searched online in several locations, but the easiest site to use is probably that of Cornell Law School: http://www4.law.cornell.edu/uscode. The fastest way to retrieve a law is by its title and section citation (listed for all laws discussed in Chapter 2), but popular names (Animal Welfare Act, Endangered Species Act, and so on) and keywords can also be used.

Many state agencies have home pages that can be accessed through the FindLaw state resources website (http://findlaw.com/11stategov). This site also has links to state law codes. These links may or may not provide access to the text of specific regulations, however.

Keeping Up with Legislative Developments

Pending legislation is often tracked by advocacy groups, both national and those based in particular states. See Chapter 8, "Organizations and Agencies," for contact information for particular groups.

The Library of Congress Thomas web site (http://thomas.loc.gov) includes files summarizing legislation by the number of the Congress (each two-year session of Congress has a consecutive number; for example, the 110th Congress was in session in 2007 and 2008). Legislation can be searched for by the name of its sponsor(s), the bill number, or by topical keywords. (Laws that have been passed can be looked up under their Public Law number.) For instance, selecting the 109th Congress and typing the phrase "animal protection" into the search box at the time of writing retrieved 23 bills containing that phrase. Further details retrievable by clicking on the bill number and then the link to the bill summary and status file include sponsors, committee action, and amendments.

A second extremely useful site is maintained by the Government Printing Office (http://www.gpoaccess.gov/index.html). This site has links to the Code of Federal Regulations (which contains federal regulations that have been finalized), the Federal Register (which contains announcements of new federal agency regulations), the Congressional Record, the U.S. Code, congressional bills, a catalog of U.S. government publications, and other databases. It also provides links to individual agencies, grouped under government branch (legislative, executive, judicial), and to regulatory agencies, administrative decisions, core documents of U.S. democracy such as the Constitution, and web sites hosted by the federal government.

Finding Court Decisions

Legislation is only part of the story, of course. The Supreme Court and state courts make important decisions every year that determine how laws are interpreted. Like laws, legal decisions are organized using a system of citations. The general form is: *Party1* v. *Party2 volume reporter* [optional start page] *(court, year).* Here are some examples:

Sierra Club v. Morton, 405 U.S. 727 (1972)

Here the parties are Sierra Club and Morton (the first listed is the plaintiff or appellant, the second the defendant). The case is in volume 405 of the *U.S. Supreme Court Reports,* beginning on page 727, and the case was decided in 1972. (For the U.S. Supreme Court, the name of the court is omitted).

The following case was decided by the 3rd U.S. Circuit Court of Appeals in 1998:

Animal Legal Defense Fund v. Glickman, 154 F.3d 426 (1998)

A state court decision can generally be identified because it includes the state's name. For example, in *Texas Beef Group v. Winfrey,* 11 F. Supp. 2d 858 (N.D. Tex. 1998), *F. Supp. 2d* refers to the federal district court to which the case was transferred, but *N.D. Tex.* refers to the Texas state court where it was first heard.

Once the jurisdiction for a case has been determined, a researcher can then go to a number of places on the Internet to find cases by citation and sometimes by the names of the parties or by subject keywords. Some of the most useful sites are:

The Legal Information Institute (http://supct.law.cornell.edu/supct/index.html) supplies all Supreme Court decisions since 1990, plus 610 of "the most important historic" decisions.

Animal Rights

Washlaw Web (http://www.washlaw.edu) lists a variety of courts (including state courts and courts of other countries) and legal topics, making it a good jumping-off place for many sorts of legal research. However, the actual accessibility of state court opinions (and the formats they are provided in) varies widely.

Lexis and Westlaw

Lexis and Westlaw are commercial legal databases that have extensive information, including an elaborate system of notes, legal subject headings, and ways to show relationships among cases. Unfortunately, these services are too expensive for most individual researchers to use unless they can access the services through a university or corporate library.

Sites Specific to Animal Law

Several animal welfare/animal rights sites feature access to the text of major laws and court cases specific to animal law. Some of the best are the following:

- **Animal Legal and Historical Web Center**
  URL: http://www.animallaw.info
  This site, sponsored by Michigan State University College of Law, provides links to laws and cases sorted by state, topic (for instance, animal rights, dog fighting), subject (for instance, anticruelty, constitutional law), species, and country, as well as to pleadings and briefs, comments and opinions, journals and articles, and historical materials.

- **International Institute for Animal Law**
  URL: http://www.animallaw.com
  This site's extensive database allows searching for legislation/laws (by state and subject category). It also has a bibliography, divided by topic and type of material (books, magazine articles, government documents, law journal articles, and more). The items are not annotated, however, and some appear to be quite old.

More Help on Legal Research

For more information on conducting legal research, see the "Legal Research FAQ" at http://www.faqs.org/faqs/law/research. After a certain point, however, the researcher who lacks formal legal training may need to consult with or rely on the efforts of professional researchers or academics in the field.

A WORD OF CAUTION

Thanks to the Web, there is more information from more sources available than ever before. There is also a greater diversity of voices since any person or group with a computer and Internet service can put up a web site—in some cases a site that looks as polished and professional as that of an "established" group. One benefit of this situation is that dissenting views can be found in abundance, including even sites maintained by more-radical groups such as the Animal Liberation Front or their supporters.

However, the other side of the coin is that the researcher—whether journalist, analyst, teacher, or student—must take extra care to try to verify facts and to understand the possible biases of each source. Some good questions to ask include:

- Who is responsible for this web site?
- What is the background or reputation of the person or group?
- Does the person or group have a stated objective or agenda?
- What biases might this person or group have?
- Do a number of high-quality sites link to this one?
- What is the source given for a particular fact? Does that source actually say what or whom is quoted? Where did *they* get the information?

In a sense, in the age of the Internet each person must be his or her own journalist, verifying sources and evaluating the extent to which they can be relied upon.

CHAPTER 7

ANNOTATED BIBLIOGRAPHY

Hundreds of books, articles, and Internet documents related to animal protection and animal rights have appeared in recent years, as this issue has attracted increasing attention in the United States, Britain, and other industrialized countries. This bibliography lists a representative sample of serious nonfiction sources dealing with various aspects of this subject. Sources have been selected for clarity and usefulness to the general reader, recent publication (mostly from 2004 or later), and variety of points of view.

Listings are grouped in the following subject categories:

- general and historical works on animal protection and human relationships with animals
- the philosophy of animal rights
- animals and the law
- the animal rights movement, its opponents, and their tactics
- companion animals and animal shelters
- animals in agriculture
- animals in research, testing, and education
- animals in entertainment
- wildlife

Items are listed only once, under what appears to be their most important category, even though they might also fit under other categories.

Within each category, items are listed by type (books, articles, and web documents). Newspaper articles have not been included because magazines usually cover the same material and back issues of magazines are easier to obtain than those of most newspapers. Magazine articles available on the Internet are listed as articles, not as Internet documents.

Annotated Bibliography

GENERAL AND HISTORICAL WORKS ON ANIMAL PROTECTION AND HUMAN RELATIONSHIPS WITH ANIMALS

BOOKS

Aftandilian, David, Marian W. Copeland, and David Scofield Wilson, eds. *What Are the Animals to Us?: Approaches from Science, Religion, Folklore, Literature, and Art.* Knoxville: University of Tennessee Press, 2006. The authors of these essays survey meanings given to animals and cultural products about animals from a wide range of disciplines and points of view.

Animal Studies Group. *Killing Animals.* Urbana: University of Illinois Press, 2006. This book provides a range of scholarly opinions on human killing of animals—by far the most common form of human-animal interaction, it claims. It reveals the complexity of the killing phenomenon by showing the diversity of killing practices and meanings attached to them in societies from the 17th century to the present.

Bayvel, A. C. D., S. A. Rahman, and A. Gavinelli, eds. *Animal Welfare: Global Issues, Trends and Challenges.* Paris: World Organisation for Animal Health (OIE), 2005. This book recounts deliberations by the OIE on such subjects as the transport of animals, slaughter of animals for human consumption, and the killing of animals to control disease.

Bekoff, Marc, ed. *Animal Passions and Beastly Virtues: Reflections on Redecorating Nature.* Philadelphia, Pa.: Temple University Press, 2006. Bekoff's anthology presents scientific papers and articles on animal behavior, especially that of dogs, and on the ways that humans "redecorate" nature by using animals for their own purposes.

———, and Carron A. Meaney, eds. *Encyclopedia of Animal Rights and Animal Welfare.* Westport, Conn.: Greenwood Press, 1998. This collection focuses more on animal rights than animal welfare, especially on the animal rights movement's impact on medical research. It covers a variety of viewpoints and includes short biographies (only of deceased persons), philosophical essays, and discussions of scientific topics such as genetic engineering.

Bulliet, Richard W. *Hunters, Herders, and Hamburgers: The Past and Future of Human-Animal Relationships.* New York: Columbia University Press, 2005. Bulliet compares humans' past and current relationships with animals. He claims that humans today live in an era of "postdomesticity," in which they are separated physically and psychologically from the animals they rely upon for food and clothing.

Animal Rights

Carroll, Jamuna, ed. *At Issue: Do Animals Have Rights?* Farmington Hills, Mich.: Greenhaven Press, 2005. This anthology considers several controversies related to animal rights, including animal cloning, organ transplants between species, farm animal slaughtering methods, and legal rights for animals.

Council of Europe Publishing. *Ethical Eye: Animal Welfare.* Strasbourg, France: Council of Europe, 2006. This book examines ethical issues, religious viewpoints, and attitudes of different European countries toward animal welfare. It also covers Council of Europe conventions and other European instruments that attempt to regulate animal welfare on an international level.

Crossley, Ceri. *Consumable Metaphors: Attitudes Towards Animals and Vegetarianism in Nineteenth-Century France.* New York: Peter Lang Publishing, 2005. This work considers different definitions of animal nature provided by key thinkers and writers of the period. It shows how thinking about animals offered a way to conceptualize power relationships in human society as well as human fears and wishes in general.

Dolins, Francine L. *Attitudes to Animals.* New York: Cambridge University Press, 2006. This book reviews current philosophical, behavioral, and neurophysiological work related to the question of animal consciousness and self-awareness.

Drummond, William H. *The Rights of Animals and Man's Obligation to Treat Them with Humanity* (1838), edited by Rod Preece and Chien-Hui Li. Lewiston, N.Y.: Edwin Mellen Press, 2005. This is one of several early 19th-century books that urges concern for the well-being of animals. The editors place the work in its historical and literary setting.

Dudley, William. *Introducing Issues with Opposing Viewpoints: Animal Rights.* Farmington Hills, Mich.: Greenhaven Press, 2006. This anthology provides diverse views on such topics as research on animals, pet ownership, vegetarianism, zoos, and animal cloning.

Evans, Kim Masters. *Animal Rights 2005: Information Series on Current Topics.* Farmington Hills, Mich.: Thomson Gale, 2005. This book surveys current thinking on animal rights.

Favre, David, ed. *Proceedings from International Animal Welfare Conference.* East Lansing, Mich.: Animal Legal and Historical Web Center, 2004. This collection includes most of the papers presented at the first international conference on animal welfare by experts from around the world.

Fisanick, Nick, and Nick Treanor. *The History of Issues—Animal Rights.* San Diego, Calif.: Greenhaven Press, 2004. This book discusses the historical and philosophical roots of the animal rights movement, the controversial tactics used by some animal rights advocates, and specific issues such as the use of animals in science.

Franklin, Adrian. *Animal Nation: The True Story of Animals and Australia.* Sydney, Australia: University of New South Wales Press, 2006. This book traces the complicated relationships between animals and humans in Australia, beginning with the colonial period. It shows how attitudes toward native species have changed over time and explains why animals have been the focus of intense political and social conflict.

Fudge, Erica, ed. *Renaissance Beasts: Of Animals, Humans, and Other Wonderful Creatures.* Urbana: University of Illinois Press, 2004. Fudge considers the ways that animals were used and thought about in Renaissance culture and uses the animal-human relationship as a springboard for viewing many types of texts and social issues from the period.

Gaughen, Shasta, ed. *Contemporary Issues Companion: Animal Rights.* San Diego, Calif.: Greenhaven Press, 2005. Issues discussed in this anthology include the philosophical basis of animal rights, the degree to which animals should have legal protection, and the ethics of using animals for food and research.

Kean, Hilda. *Animal Rights: Political and Social Change in Britain since 1800.* London: Reaktion Books, 1998. Kean describes 200 years of controversy over vivisection, zoos, and hunting in Britain.

Kistler, John M., ed. *Animals Are the Issue: Library Resources on Animal Issues.* Binghamton, N.Y.: Haworth Information Press, 2004. This guide lists books, journals, and web sites on animal treatment in modern and historic times, including animals as companions, in sports and entertainment, in religion, in science and education, in industry, and in hunting.

Knight, John, ed. *Animals in Person: Cultural Perspectives on Human-Animal Intimacies.* Oxford, England: Berg Publishers, 2005. This book draws on case studies to consider humans' complex and contradictory relationships with animals, which include projection of human thoughts and emotions onto them.

Mason, Jennifer. *Civilized Creatures: Urban Animals, Sentimental Culture, and American Literature, 1850–1900.* Baltimore, Md.: The Johns Hopkins University Press, 2005. Mason claims that the most important influence on U.S. writers' attitudes toward animals in this period was their feelings about the "civilized" animals they encountered in their daily lives, not their views of farm animals or wildlife. She provides cultural histories of equestrianism, petkeeping, and the animal welfare movement.

Mason, Jim. *An Unnatural Order: Uncovering the Roots of Our Domination of Nature and Each Other,* rev. ed. New York: Lantern Books, 2005. The author claims that "dominationism"—the belief that humans are separate from animals and have the right to control and use them—is related to similar beliefs holding that some human groups are superior to and have the right to dominate others (sexism, racism, colonialism). He calls for a total rethinking of humans' relationships with the animal world.

Masson, Jeffrey Moussaieff, and Susan McCarthy. *When Elephants Weep: The Emotional Lives of Animals.* New York: Delacorte Press, 1995. The authors argue that many animals possess an emotional sensibility and, possibly, a consciousness similar to that of humans.

McGrew, William. *The Cultured Chimpanzee: Reflections on Cultural Primatology*. New York: Cambridge University Press, 2004. Defining culture broadly as "the way we do things," McGrew builds a case for believing that culture exists in chimpanzee society.

Ojeda, Auriana, ed. *Current Controversies: The Rights of Animals*. San Diego, Calif.: Greenhaven Press, 2004. Authors in this anthology discuss whether animals should be accorded the same rights that humans are granted. Issues examined include laboratory experimentation and animals raised for human consumption.

Pflugfelder, Gregory M., and Brett L. Walker, eds. *JAPANimals: History and Culture in Japan's Animal Life*. Ann Arbor: University of Michigan, Center for Japanese Studies, 2005. Nine essays, each on a different species, consider the roles of animals in the cultural and political life of Japan throughout the country's history.

Pluskowski, Aleksander, ed. *Breaking and Shaping Beastly Bodies: Animals as Material Culture in the Middle Ages*. Oxford, England: Oxbow Books, 2006. The authors in this essay collection draw on zoological, artistic, economic, and anthropological perspectives to examine animals in the context of the medieval world.

Pollock, Mary Sanders, and Catherine Rainwater, eds. *Figuring Animals: Essays on Animal Images in Art, Literature, Philosophy, and Modern Culture*. New York: Palgrave Macmillan, 2005. Fifteen essays consider the representation of animals in the visual arts, literaure, philosophy, and cultural practice.

Preece, Rod. *Brute Souls, Happy Beasts, and Evolution: The Historical Status of Animals*. Vancouver, B.C., Canada: University of British Columbia Press, 2005. This book investigates the status of animals in human society from the fifth century B.C. to the present. It shows that, contrary to common belief, ethical consideration of animals is by no means a recent phenomenon.

Rivera, Michelle A. *Canines in the Classroom: Raising Humane Children Through Interactions with Animals*. New York: Lantern Books, 2004. This book provides guidance for people in homes, classrooms, churches, organizations, and communities who wish to teach children to respect all living things. The author maintains that humane education reduces not only violence against animals but violence against humans as well.

Salem, Deborah J., Andrew N. Rowan, and Humane Society of the United States. *The State of the Animals III: 2005*. Washington, D.C.: Humane Society Press, 2005. This book focuses on dogs and cats but also discusses animal law, competition between marine animals and fisheries, and chimpanzees in research.

Scigliano, Eric. *Love, War, and Circuses: The Age-Old Relationship Between Elephants and Humans*. London: Bloomsbury Publishing, 2004. Scigliano surveys the range of attitudes, from adoration to abuse, that people of different cultures and periods have had toward elephants, especially Asian elephants. He claims that humans may have more in common with elephants than with any other species except apes.

Solisti, Kate, and Michael Tobias, eds. *Kinship with Animals*, rev. ed. San Francisco: Council Oak Books, 2006. In this book, authors including scientists, artists, and spiritual leaders share personal experiences with animals and consider the meaning of human-animal relationships. The revised edition contains new scientific findings and new contributors.

Sunstein, Cass R., and Martha C. Nussbaum, eds. *Animal Rights: Current Debates and New Directions*, rev. ed. New York: Oxford University Press, 2004. This essay collection provides a range of perspectives on legal, political, and ethical/philosophical issues related to animal rights. Reviewers cite its material on animals and the law as being particularly valuable.

Turner, Jacky, and Joyce D'Silva, eds. *Animals, Ethics and Trade: The Challenge of Animal Sentience*. London: Earthscan, 2006. The first part of this book offers scientific and ethical perspectives on the consciousness, mental powers, and emotions of animals. The second part discusses how human activities in such areas as farming and food production, science, law, and trade respect or ignore animals' sentience and welfare and considers possible changes in such activities.

Webster, John. *Animal Welfare: Limping Towards Eden*, 2nd ed. Malden, Mass.: Blackwell, 2005. The author critically reviews areas of development in animal welfare and recommends future improvements, including an ethical framework that balances animal and human needs and provides "five freedoms" for animals.

Wolloch, Nathaniel. *Subjugated Animals: Animals and Anthropocentrism in Early Modern European Culture*. Amherst, N.Y.: Humanity Books, 2006. This study of attitudes toward animals in early modern Western culture emphasizes the influence of anthropocentrism and links historical trends to modern discussions of animal rights and ecology.

ARTICLES

Bekoff, Marc, and Jan Nystrom. "The Other Side of Silence: Rachel Carson's Views of Animals." *Zygon*, vol. 39, December 2004, pp. 861–884. The authors examine famed ecologist Rachel Carson's attitude toward animals, as shown in *Silent Spring* and other writings. They conclude that she was primarily an animal welfarist, focusing on ecosystems and species, rather than an animal rights activist who concentrated on individuals.

Bittel, Carla. "Science, Suffrage, and Experimentation: Mary Putnam Jacobi and the Controversy over Vivisection in Late Nineteenth-Century America." *Bulletin of the History of Medicine*, vol. 79, Winter 2005, pp. 664–694.

Animal Rights

This article uses renowned pioneer woman physician Mary Putnam Jacobi's medical activism, including public defense of experimentation on animals, to illustrate problems of gender and science in regard to medicine, suffrage, and experimentation during this crucial historical period.

Brower, Charles H., II. "The Lives of Animals, the Lives of Prisoners, and the Revelations of Abu Ghraib." *Vanderbilt Journal of Transnational Law*, vol. 37, November 2004, pp. 1353–1388. The author identifies animals and prisoners as two groups who have been denied the protections of legal personhood and describes chilling similarities between the treatment of animals and the treatment of prisoners in Iraq. He offers three potential lessons from this similarity.

Clayton, Liz. "Animal Welfare Societies." *History Magazine*, vol. 6, October–November 2004, pp. 44–47. This article surveys animal welfare societies and laws in Europe and the United States in the 19th century.

Cowen, Tyler. "Market Failure for the Treatment of Animals." *Society*, vol. 43, January–February 2006, pp. 39–44. Policies regarding treatment of animals must be thought through carefully in order to avoid unexpected and damaging economic effects.

Farrell, Stephen. "Richard Martin, 'Humanity Dick' (1754–1834)." *History Today*, vol. 54, June 2004, p. 60. Farrell briefly profiles eccentric Irish parliamentarian Richard Martin, whose concern for animals resulted in the first British animal welfare law.

Fuentes, Augustín. "The Humanity of Animals and the Animality of Humans." *American Anthropologist*, vol. 108, March 2006, pp. 124–132. Inspired by the discussion of human cruelty to animals in J. M. Coetzee's novel *Elizabeth Costello*, Fuentes uses anthropological data to investigate constructed notions of "human cruelty" and "human nature." He also discusses the animal rights movement and cultural variation in humans' use of animals.

Gray, John. "The Best Hope for Animal Liberation Is That Humans Kill Each Other in Wars." *New Statesman*, vol. 133, February 9, 2004, pp. 29–31. Human research on animals, especially apes, is morally unsupportable, but it is only one of the damaging effects that "homo rapiens," as the author terms humanity, inflicts on other species. Fortunately for the rest of the Earth, Gray believes, resource wars in the coming century will reduce human populations.

Heleski, C. R., A. G. Mertig, and A. J. Zanella. "Assessing Attitudes Toward Farm Animal Welfare: A National Survey of Animal Science Faculty Members." *Journal of Animal Science*, vol. 82, September 2004, pp. 2806–2814. This survey of animal science teachers in the United States found that more than 90 percent of those surveyed supported general principles of animal welfare, but only 32 percent were concerned about specific practices thought to produce distress, such as castration without anesthetic.

Annotated Bibliography

Kendall, Holli A., Linda M. Lobao, and Jeff S. Sharp. "Public Concern with Animal Well-Being: Place, Social Structural Location, and Individual Experience." *Rural Sociology,* vol. 71, September 2006, pp. 399–428. A survey of more than 4,000 Ohio residents, conducted in 2002, found that childhood experience had the greatest effect on attitudes toward animal well-being, but social structural factors were also important.

Pattnaik, Jyotsna. "On Behalf of Their Animal Friends: Involving Children in Animal Advocacy." *Childhood Education,* vol. 81, Winter 2004, pp. 95–100. The author argues that children should be prepared in school to be caring, compassionate, and eco-friendly individuals.

Sager, Gene C. "Captive Royals and Meat Machines: The Contradictions in How We Treat Animals." *Natural Life,* March–April 2006, pp. 22–25. Most modern, urbanized people have a double standard regarding treatment of animals: They spend ridiculous amounts of money to pamper their pets, yet they are indifferent to the sufferings of mere "livestock" on factory farms.

Smith, Barbara Herrnstein. "Animal Relatives, Difficult Relations." *Differences: A Journal of Feminist Cultural Studies,* vol. 15, Spring 2004, pp. 1–23. Ideas about the degree of relatedness between humans and animals are inevitably numerous and affected by many cultural factors.

Sztybel, David. "Can the Treatment of Animals Be Compared to the Holocaust?" *Ethics and the Environment,* vol. 11, Spring 2006, 97–132. The author finds 39 points of similarity between treatment of animals and the Holocaust. He reviews and dismisses four objections to the comparison.

WEB DOCUMENTS

"Animal Health and Welfare Strategy for Great Britain." Department of Environment, Food and Rural Affairs (DEFRA). Available online. URL: http://www.defra.gov.uk/animalh/ahws/strategy/ahws.pdf. Posted in 2004. This report, from a British government agency, describes the government's plans for improving the welfare of animals, including farmed animals, companion animals, fish and other animals in aquaculture, game animals, and wildlife, over the next 10 years.

Commission of the European Communities. "Commission Working Document on a Community Action Plan on the Protection and Welfare of Animals 2006–2010: Strategic Basis for the Proposed Actions." Europa. Available online. URL: http://ec.europa.eu/food/animal/welfare/work_doc_strategic_basis230106_en.pdf. Posted on January 23, 2006. This document describes the Community Action Plan on the Protection and Welfare of Animals, which was adopted by the European Commission on January 23, 2006.

"The State of Animal Welfare in the UK 2005." Royal Society for the Prevention of Cruelty to Animals. Available online. URL: http://www.rspca.org.

uk/servlet/Blobserver?blobtable=RSPCABlob&blobcol=urlblob&blobkey
=id&blobwhere=1158755034097&blobheader=application/pdf. Posted in
2005. This report provides statistics on animals in general, research animals, wildlife, farm animals, and pets in Britain, assessing their welfare in
terms of 25 indicators.

THE PHILOSOPHY OF ANIMAL RIGHTS

BOOKS

Acampora, Ralph R. *Corporal Compassion: Animal Ethics and Philosophy of
Body*. Pittsburgh, Pa.: University of Pittsburgh Press, 2006. Acampora
says that humans' compassion for other animals does not have to depend
on animals' mental capacities or sentience, but rather should arise from
the fact that both humans and animals are "bodily beings" with similar
vulnerabilities and experiences.

Agamben, Giorgio. *The Open: Man and Animal*. Stanford, Calif.: Stanford
University Press, 2004. Agamben, a contemporary Italian philosopher,
examines supposed distinctions between humans and other animals and
concludes that these concepts have been manufactured by the presupposi-
tions of Western thought.

Bernstein, Mark H. *Without a Tear: Our Tragic Relationship with Animals*.
Urbana: University of Illinois Press, 2004. Bernstein argues that if it is
wrong to intentionally harm an innocent being, most of humans' common practices regarding nonhuman animals must be considered immoral.
He claims that among popular religions, Judaism presents the best resources for grounding moral obligations to animals.

Boulogne, Jack. *Animals Don't Have Rights*. Victoria, B.C., Canada: Trafford
Publishing, 2006. This book by a philosopher attacks the animal rights
movement's reasoning in language suitable for a general audience.

Calarco, Matthew, and Peter Atterton, eds. *Animal Philosophy: Ethics and
Identity*. New York: Continuum, 2004. This anthology considers the place
and treatment of animals in Continental thought. Each primary-source
reading is followed by comment and analysis from a leading contemporary thinker.

Cavalieri, Paola, tr. Catherine Woollard. *The Animal Question: Why Nonhuman Animals Deserve Human Rights*, rev. ed. New York: Oxford University
Press, 2004. Cavalieri claims that the logic of universal human rights
theory can be extended to nonhuman animals.

Cohen, Carl, and Tom Regan. *The Animal Rights Debate*. Lanham, Md.:
Rowman and Littlefield, 2001. Two philosophy professors argue opposite
sides of the animal rights issue.

188

Annotated Bibliography

Dunayer, Joan. *Speciesism.* Deerwood, Md.: Ryce Pub., 2004. Dunayer claims that many writings inside as well as outside the animal rights movement perpetuate speciesism, "a failure . . . to accord any nonhuman being equal consideration and respect" as compared to humans. Even respected animal rights thinkers such as Peter Singer and Tom Regan are "new speciesists," she says, because they espouse rights for only some animal species. She calls for a "species equality" view that would grant basic legal rights to virtually all animals, including insects, spiders, and snails.

Francione, Gary. *Introduction to Animal Rights: Your Child or the Dog?* Philadelphia, Pa.: Temple University Press, 2000. A leading animal rights lawyer discusses dilemmas in animal ethics and the "moral schizophrenia" with which Western society views animals.

Franklin, Julian H. *Animal Rights and Moral Philosophy.* New York: Columbia University Press, 2005. Franklin examines the major arguments for animal rights proposed so far, including positions of utilitarianism, ecofeminism, and rationalism. He concludes that Kant's categorical imperative can be expanded to become the basis for an ethical system that includes all sentient beings.

Fudge, Erica. *Brutal Reasoning: Animals, Rationality, and Humanity in Early Modern England.* Ithaca, N.Y.: Cornell University Press, 2006. Examining a variety of texts, Fudge emphasizes the role of reason in this period's conceptions of human and animal nature and of the differences between humans and animals.

Garner, Robert. *Animal Ethics.* Cambridge, England: Polity Press, 2005. The author examines different positions regarding human relationships with animals and considers the implications of each position for the ethics of particular actions affecting animals. He concludes that animals should not be granted the same moral status as humans but should be given a higher status than that provided in the standard animal welfare position.

———. *Animals, Politics and Morality,* 2nd ed. Manchester, England: Manchester University Press, 2004. This book examines the "second generation" of animal ethics literature from the perspectives of both philosophy and politics. The second edition covers the latest developments in controversial areas such as genetic engineering and hunting.

———. *The Political Theory of Animal Rights.* Manchester, England: Manchester University Press, 2005. In this book, Garner examines the effect that regarding animals as morally important beings can have on political thinking. He concludes that liberalism, despite some weaknesses, is the best ideological position for protecting animals' interests.

Gray, John. *Straw Dogs: Thoughts on Humans and Other Animals,* rev. ed. New York: Granta Books, 2003. Gray, a British philosopher, states that from the standpoint of evolution, humanity—a species he calls "homo rapiens"—is neither different from nor superior to other animal species.

Linzey, Andrew, and Paul Barry Clarke, eds. *Animal Rights: A Historical Anthology*. New York: Columbia University Press, 2005. This anthology, which includes writings from ancient Greece to the present, examines the complex evolution of moral, religious, political, and philosophical thought regarding animals.

Loftus-Hills, Alison. *Do Animals Have Rights?* Thriplow, England: Icon Books, 2005. Hills defends a practical style of ethics regarding treatment of animals, saying that animals are the equal of humans in some ways but not others.

Machan, Tibor. *Putting Humans First: Why We Are Nature's Favorite*. Lanham, Md.: Rowman & Littlefield, 2004. Machan argues that only humans can have rights because they are the only beings with the capacity for moral choice. Animals are mere property, which humans can treat as they please.

McKenna, Erin, and Andrew Light, eds. *Animal Pragmatism: Rethinking Human-Nonhuman Relationships*. Bloomington: Indiana University Press, 2004. This collection presents thoughts on animal welfare from American pragmatists, including consideration of issues such as animal experimentation and treatment of farm animals.

Newmyer, Stephen. *Animals, Rights and Reason in Plutarch and Modern Ethics*. New York: Routledge, 2005. Unlike almost all other classical authors, Plutarch argues that animals are sentient and rational and that humans must recognize their interests. Newmyer points out that some of Plutarch's arguments strikingly prefigure those of popular animal rights philosophers such as Peter Singer and Tom Regan.

Nordenfelt, Lennart. *Animal and Human Health and Welfare: A Comparative Philosophical Analysis*. Cambridge, Mass.: CABI Publishing, 2006. This book compares theories of human health and welfare with those on the health and welfare of animals. Nordenfelt provides a holistic framework that encompasses both types of theory by focusing on the individual's ability to achieve its vital goals.

Nussbaum, Martha C. *Frontiers of Justice: Disability, Nationality, Species Membership*. Cambridge, Mass.: Belknap Press, 2006. Nussbaum reveals serious problems with using social contract theory for modeling liberal ideas of inclusiveness and equal respect, pointing out that this theory neglects several important groups, including nonhuman animals. She recommends applying a capabilities approach instead.

Orlans, F. Barbara, et al., eds. *The Human Use of Animals: Case Studies in Ethical Choice*. New York: Oxford University Press, 1998. This anthology presents case studies that show the complexity of moral issues related to animal welfare and human use of animals, with an emphasis on use of animals in research.

Annotated Bibliography

Phelps, Norm. *The Great Compassion: Buddhism and Animal Rights.* New York: Lantern Books, 2004. The author examines the position of different strains of Buddhism on treatment of animals, especially on the question of whether eating meat is permitted.

Preece, Rod, ed. *Immortal Animal Souls.* Lewiston, N.Y.: Edwin Mellen Press, 2005. This book reprints several important 19th-century works on the question of whether animals possess immortal souls, which caused great controversy in the Victorian period. Preece's introduction places these writings in the context of earlier and later thought and shows how they reflect Victorian patterns of thinking about human-animal relationships.

Regan, Tom. *Defending Animal Rights.* Urbana: University of Illinois Press, 2001. Regan is considered the chief philosopher of the more radical wing of the animal rights movement. This volume of short essays written during the 1990s elaborates his thinking on animal rights issues.

———. *Empty Cages: Facing the Challenge of Animal Rights,* rev. ed. Lanham, Md.: Rowman & Littlefield, 2004. Regan, one of the founders of the animal rights movement, states in this popular book that "being kind to animals" is not enough; all exploitation of animals should be forbidden because, like humans, animals (at least mammals, birds, and possibly fish) care what happens to them and are therefore "subjects-of-a-life."

Rollin, Bernard E. *Animal Rights and Human Morality,* 3rd ed. Amherst, N.Y.: Prometheus Books, 2006. Rollin, who has been called "the father of veterinary ethics," argues that society must raise the moral status of animals and be more active in protecting their rights. The third edition of his book includes a new chapter on animal agriculture as well as additional discussions of topics such as animal law and genetic engineering.

Rosen, Steven. *Holy Cow: The Hare Krishna Contribution to Vegetarianism and Animal Rights.* New York: Lantern Books, 2004. Rosen shows the link between the contemporary Hare Krishna movement, founded in the 1960s, and the ancient worship of the Hindu god Vishnu. He explains how both have expressed support for vegetarianism and animal rights.

Scruton, Roger. *Animal Rights and Wrongs,* rev. ed. London: Continuum, 2006. Scruton presents practical arguments on animal rights and human duties to animals, contradicting both the extreme animal rights position and the "weak welfarism" of those who think that being kind to their pets is sufficient to make them humane to animals. The revised edition provides new ideas about livestock and fishing.

Scully, Matthew. *Dominion: The Power of Man, the Suffering of Animals, and the Call to Mercy.* New York: St. Martin's Press, 2002. Conservative Christian Scully criticizes the idea that animals are morally equal to humans but says that treating animals with respect and kindness is a moral imperative.

Sharpe, Lynne. *Creatures Like Us?* Exeter, England: Imprint Academic, 2005. Sharpe claims that many philosophers have viewed animals from an excessively narrow, even bizarre, perspective that does not reflect experience with actual animals. They put too much stress on thought and language, not only in discussion of animals, but in consideration of human life.

Singer, Peter. *Animal Liberation: A New Ethics for Our Treatment of Animals*, rev. ed. New York: HarperCollins/Ecco Press, 2001. This is a revised and expanded edition of the seminal 1975 book by controversial Australian philosopher Singer (now teaching at Princeton University), which has frequently been called "the Bible of the animal rights movement." In this work, which is both a philosophy treatise and a practical call to action, Singer, a utilitarian, says that animals deserve respect because they are sentient, or able to feel pleasure and pain.

Steiner, Gary. *Anthropocentrism and Its Discontents: The Moral Status of Animals in the History of Western Philosophy*. Pittsburgh, Pa.: University of Pittsburgh Press, 2005. This book comprehensively examines views of animals in the history of Western philosophy from ancient Greece to the present. The author concludes with an attempt to balance the need to preserve a sense of the uniqueness and dignity of humans with the need to recognize indebtedness to and kinship with nonhuman animals.

Taylor, Angus. *Magpies, Monkeys, and Morals: What Philosophers Say about Animal Liberation*. Orchard Park, N.Y.: Broadview Press, 1999. Offers a thorough and balanced description of views on the subject, including historical background. The author teaches philosophy at the University of Victoria in British Columbia, Canada.

ARTICLES

Anchustegui, A. T. "Biocentric Ethics and Animal Prosperity." *International Journal of Applied Philosophy*, vol. 19, Spring 2005, pp. 105–119. Anchustegui holds that although mental properties may be sufficient for moral standing, they are not necessary. Instead, the author presents a theory of biocentric individualism that holds all species to be basically equal. Although this theory recognizes that human needs must outweigh the needs of nonhumans in some cases, it requires an end to harmful animal experimentation, factory farming, and killing for sport.

Bernstein, Mark. "On the Dogma of Hierarchical Value." *American Philosophical Quarterly*, vol. 43, July 2006, pp. 207–220. Hierarchism claims that human lives have more intrinsic value than nonhuman lives. Bernstein maintains that the reasoning that underlies this philosophy is false.

Donovan, Josephine. "Feminism and the Treatment of Animals: From Care to Dialogue." *Signs*, vol. 31, Winter 2006, pp. 305–329. Donovan argues that humans should do more than care for animals as mothers care for their infants; they should pay attention to what the animals communicate about their own needs and emotional state. She recommends extending feminist standpoint theory to animals.

Mameli, M., and L. Bortolotti. "Animal Rights, Animal Minds, and Human Mindreading." *Journal of Medical Ethics*, vol. 32, February 2006, pp. 84–89. Humans engage in mindreading, or ascribing mental states to other organisms, but their ability to do this with nonhuman animals is very limited, these authors maintain. This failure makes it difficult to determine what rights, if any, nonhuman animals should be given.

Markie, Peter J. "Respect for People and Animals." *The Journal of Value Inquiry*, vol. 38, March 2004, pp. 33–47. Markie says that respect is not something to which someone has a right, but rather is a form of duty. This duty varies across the positions that other moral subjects, including animals, occupy relative to fully sentient humans, which means that the limits of appropriate treatment for people are not the same as those for treatment of animals.

WEB DOCUMENTS

"Universal Declaration of Animal Rights." Uncaged. Available online. URL: http://www.uncaged.co.uk/declarat.htm. Accessed December 25, 2006. Modeled on the Universal Declaration of Human Rights, signed by the United Nations General Assembly in 1948, this declaration calls for rights to life, liberty, and natural enjoyment for all sentient creatures.

ANIMALS AND THE LAW

BOOKS

Favre, David, ed. *Federal Wildlife Laws*. East Lansing, Mich.: Michigan State University Animal Legal and Historical Web Center, 2004. This book gathers and explains the most common federal laws that affect wildlife, including the Endangered Species Act.

Francione, Gary. *Animals, Property, and the Law*. Philadelphia, Pa.: Temple University Press, 1995. Francione, a law professor at Rutgers University, is a leading proponent of the idea that animals should have legal rights. He claims that the law has failed to protect animals because they are viewed as property.

Hauser, Marc D., Fiery Cushman, and Matthew Kamen, eds. *People, Property, or Pets?* Lafayette, Ind.: Purdue University Press, 2006. The essays in this collection consider (but do not all support) the idea that the law should treat companion animals as it treats children. From this stand-point, people would be legal guardians of the animals, responsible by law for their care, but would not own them as inanimate objects are owned.

Matlack, Carolyn B. *We've Got Feelings Too! Presenting the Sentient Property Solution.* Davidson, N.C.: Log Cabin Press, 2006. The author introduces a new legal concept that would place animals somewhere between hu-mans and inanimate property, for instance by allowing people to claim damages for loss of a pet that go beyond the animal's market value in recognition of its emotional significance.

Otto, Stephan. *Animal Protection Laws of the United States of America*, 2nd ed. Petaluma, Calif.: Animal Legal Defense Fund, 2005. This comprehensive collection of animal protection laws covers all 50 states and the District of Columbia.

Waisman, Sonia S., Pamela D. Frasch, and Bruce A. Wagman. *Animal Law: Cases and Materials*, 3rd edition. Durham, N.C.: Carolina Academic Press, 2006. This textbook covers the rapidly developing field of animal law, defined as statutory and decisional law in which the nature of nonhuman animals is an important factor. The new edition includes a chapter on commercial use of animals, including animals in entertainment, agricul-ture, and scientific research.

Wise, Steven M. *Drawing the Line: Science and the Case for Animal Rights.* Cambridge, Mass.: Perseus Publishing, 2002. Wise, a Harvard law pro-fessor, is one of the chief advocates of the belief that animals should have legal rights. Here he offers evidence from scientific studies to bolster his claim that certain animal species, especially chimpanzees and bonobos, meet the criteria for legal personhood.

ARTICLES

Allen, Mahalley D. "Laying Down the Law?" *Policy Studies Journal*, vol. 33, August 2005, pp. 443–457. This article shows that the Humane Society of the United States, although not one of the traditional insider groups that usually shapes policymaking, has played a significant part in develop-ment and diffusion of state laws against animal cruelty.

Bronstad, Amanda. "Pet Set Finds Champion in Attorney Who Handles the Beastliest Cases." *Los Angeles Business Journal*, vol. 26, June 21, 2004, pp. 3–4. This article profiles Los Angeles attorney Sandra Toye, who special-izes in animal law.

Clarke, Jeremy. "Animals Don't Have Human Rights." *Spectator*, vol. 297, January 22, 2005, pp. 12–13. Clarke claims that Britain's Animal Welfare Bill, which later (in November 2006) became law, puts too much power in the hands of the Royal Society for the Prevention of Cruelty to Animals and excessively restricts the behavior of pet owners, pet businesses, and participants in country sports such as fishing and pheasant shooting.

Hamilton, Anita. "Woof, Woof, Your Honor." *Time*, vol. 164, December 13, 2004, p. 46. Animal law is gaining respect among lawyers, law schools, and legal scholars, Hamilton says. In court, meanwhile, the number and range of animal-related lawsuits are growing, and penalties for mistreatment of animals are increasing.

Norman, Emma R., and Norma Contreras Hernandez. "'Like Butter Scraped Over Too Much Bread': Animal Protection Policy in Mexico." *Review of Policy Research*, vol. 22, January 2005, pp. 59–76. Mexico has an impressive-looking collection of laws and agreements that claim to protect animal welfare, but the laws are seldom implemented effectively. The authors explore the reasons for this failure and recommend ways to improve the situation.

WEB DOCUMENTS

British Parliament. "Animal Welfare Act 2006." Office of Public Sector Information. Available online. URL: http://www.opsi.gov.uk/acts/acts2006/ukpga_20060045_en.pdf. Posted November 2006. This act, which became law on November 8, 2006, provides stringent regulation of the way individuals in England and Wales treat vertebrate animals. It covers both pets and farmed animals but not animals used in scientific procedures.

"Facing the Facts: Behind the Scenes of Ten Animal Welfare Areas." Royal Society for the Prevention of Cruelty to Animals. Available online. URL: http://www.rspca.org.uk/servlet/Satellite?blobcol=urlblob&blobheader=application%2Fpdf&blobkey=id&blobtable=RSPCABlob&blobwhere=1116592354796&ssbinary=true&Content-Type=application/pdf. Accessed December 27, 2006. This report surveys the legal protection given to animals in Britain and the European Union in 10 key areas, including animals in circuses and use of primates and other animals in research and testing. It concludes that even when animal protection laws exist, they are not always effective.

Otto, Stephan K. "Model Animal Protection Laws." Animal Legal Defense Fund. Available online. URL: http://www.aldf.org/assets/62_aldfmodellawsv133.pdf. Posted on January 1, 2006. This collection defines key terms in animal protection laws and sets forth prohibitions that the Animal Legal Defense Fund believes should be included in such laws, including prohibitions against abuse, neglect, animal fighting, and sexual assault of an animal. It also discusses defenses, preconviction provisions, post-conviction provisions, and other provisions.

THE ANIMAL RIGHTS MOVEMENT, ITS OPPONENTS, AND THEIR TACTICS

BOOKS

Beers, Diane L. *For the Prevention of Cruelty: The History and Legacy of Animal Rights Activism in the United States.* Athens, Ohio: Swallow Press, 2006. This book surveys the animal advocacy movement in the United States, beginning with the founding of the American Society for the Prevention of Cruelty to Animals in 1866. It shows that early efforts to improve animal welfare were more successful and had a greater impact than has generally been recognized.

Best, Steven, and Anthony J. Nocello II, eds. *Terrorists or Freedom Fighters? Reflections on the Liberation of Animals.* New York: Lantern Books, 2004. This anthology, which includes contributions from both academics and activists, examines the history, ethics, tactics, and politics of the Animal Liberation Front, one of the most extreme animal rights groups. It places the group in the historical context of civil disobedience and sabotage and shows different perspectives from which its activities may be viewed.

Clark, Ward M. *Misplaced Compassion: The Animal Rights Movement Exposed.* San Jose, Calif.: Writers Club Press, 2001. Clark, a supporter of hunting and other activities that use animals for human benefit, provides a highly critical description of the philosophy and tactics of the animal rights movement.

Currie-McGhee, Leanne. *Overview: Animal Rights.* San Diego, Calif.: Lucent Books, 2004. This book surveys the animal rights movement and explains how it has affected activities such as farming, hunting, and scientific research.

Finsen, Lawrence, and Susan Finsen. *The Animal Rights Movement in America: From Compassion to Respect.* New York: Twayne Publishers, 1994. The Finsens describe the history, tactics, issues, and philosophies of the movement, which they call the quintessential movement for social justice; they also discuss the movement's opponents and related movements, such as environmentalism.

Grant, Catherine. *The No-Nonsense Guide to Animal Rights.* Oxford, England: New Internationalist, 2006. This book outlines the growth of the animal rights movement, describes the key issues on which it focuses, surveys laws that protect the welfare of animals, and offers practical steps that individuals can take to minimize animal exploitation.

Guither, Harold D. *Animal Rights: History and Scope of a Radical Social Movement.* Carbondale: Southern Illinois University Press, 1998. Guither presents a neutral overview of the animal rights movement, its history and philosophy, and different uses of animals with which it is concerned, including research and entertainment.

Hall, Lee. *Capers in the Churchyard: Animal Rights Advocacy in the Age of Terror.* Darien, Conn.: Friends of Animals/Nectar Bat Press, 2006. This book discusses recent trends in animal advocacy tactics in North America, Britain, and Australia, focusing on animal rights groups' attacks on Huntingdon Life Sciences, the largest contract animal testing laboratory in Europe.

Kistler, John M. *People Promoting and People Opposing Animal Rights: In Their Own Words.* Westport, Conn.: Greenwood Press, 2002. This collection of profiles is written by and about people actively involved in supporting or opposing the animal rights and animal welfare movements.

Liddick, Donald R. *Eco-Terrorism: Radical Environmental and Animal Liberation Movements.* Westport, Conn.: Praeger Publishers, 2006. Liddick exposes the activities of radical environmental and animal rights groups, providing a clear portrait of who these groups are, what they do, and how to respond to them.

Munro, Lyle. *Confronting Cruelty: Moral Orthodoxy and the Challenge of the Animal Rights Movement.* Boston: Brill Academic Publishers, 2005. Munro examines why and how people campaign on behalf of other species and discusses the animal rights movement in terms of social movement theory.

Newkirk, Ingrid. *Free the Animals: The Story of the Animal Liberation Front.* New York: Lantern Books, 2000. Newkirk, founder of People for the Ethical Treatment of Animals (PETA), describes the Animal Liberation Front (ALF), known for its violent tactics, and portrays its leader, "Valerie" (a pseudonym), in a sympathetic light.

Singer, Peter. *Ethics into Action: Henry Spira and the Animal Rights Movement.* Lanham, Md.: Rowman and Littlefield, 2000. Premier animal rights philosopher Singer describes one of the former leaders of the movement, known both for his successful publicity campaigns and his willingness to treat opponents with respect even while working relentlessly to end their abusive actions. Singer shows how other activists can adapt Spira's approach.

———, ed. *In Defense of Animals: The Second Wave*, 2nd ed. Malden, Mass.: Blackwell, 2006. This anthology highlights key stories and campaigns from the animal protection movement, such as the affair of the Silver Spring laboratory monkeys.

Tobias, Michael. *Voices from the Underground: For the Love of Animals.* Pasadena, Calif.: New Paradigm Books, 1999. This book profiles people who have founded well-known animal rights or animal welfare organizations such as PETA or in other ways have devoted their lives to stopping cruelty to animals.

Animal Rights

Unti, Bernard Oreste. *Protecting All Animals: A Fifty-Year History of the Humane Society of the United States.* Washington, D.C.: Humane Society Press, 2004. Unti shows how this group, founded by a handful of visionaries in 1954, grew into the largest animal protection organization in the United States and a leader in the modern animal welfare movement.

Warner, Randy N. *To Look Within: Showing the Need for Change in the Animal Protection Movement.* Frederick, Md.: PublishAmerica, 2006. Warner claims that humane education—persuading individuals to become involved in the animal protection movement—is the best, indeed only, way to guarantee animal welfare.

Workman, Dave P. *PETA Files: The Dark Side of the Animal Rights Movement.* Bellevue, Wash.: Merril Press, 2003. This outdoor writer criticizes alleged extremism and tendencies toward violence in the animal rights organization People for the Ethical Treatment of Animals (PETA).

ARTICLES

Agres, Ted. "Fighting Back Against Terror." *The Scientist,* vol. 19, September 12, 2005, p. 44. Companies threatened by animal rights extremists are increasingly both able and willing to use the law to protect themselves.

"Animal Rights Jeopardise Fair Portrayal of Farming Practices." *Farmers Guardian,* January 20, 2006, p. 16. This brief article describes techniques used by British animal rights activists against farmers, including violence.

Bird, Maryann. "Animal Passions." *Time International,* vol. 162, December 15, 2003, p. 50. Animal rights activists in Britain increasingly demonstrate against use of animals in scientific research and testing. A proposed new primate research facility at Cambridge University is a recent target.

Blum, Debra. "Animal-Rights Lobbyist Is Selected to Be Top Dog at Humane Society." *Chronicle of Philanthropy,* vol. 16, June 24, 2004, n.p. This article presents an interview with Wayne P. Pacelle, who took over the leadership of the Humane Society of the United States in mid-2004. Pacelle says he plans to focus the society's political efforts on improving the welfare of animals raised for meat.

Brown, Heidi. "Beware of People." *Forbes Global,* vol. 7, July 26, 2004, p. 28. Some animal rights groups are becoming more violent and targeting individuals and companies with only tenuous connections to research on animals.

Clark, Ross. "The Terror War We Can Win." *Spectator,* vol. 295, July 31, 2004, pp. 12–13. The British government has done little to protect the victims of animal rights extremists, which often include people whose connection with animal experimentation is minimal.

Annotated Bibliography

Fazackerley, Anna. "Extremists Are Winning War of Words." *Times Higher Education Supplement*, July 9, 2004, pp. 18–19. Universities that sponsor research on animals or in other controversial fields need to respond publicly to complaints from extremists, rather than leaving individual faculty members to defend themselves without institutional support.

———. "UK Terror Tourists Hit Europe's Animal Labs." *Times Higher Education Supplement*, January 13, 2006, pp. 1–2. Animal rights extremist "terror tourists" are traveling across Europe, causing an international rise in attacks on testing laboratories and other facilities, according to Britain's national policing unit for domestic extremism. The United Kingdom suffered more attacks than any other country.

Fodor, Kate. "When the Protesters Are Shareholders." *The Scientist*, vol. 19, May 23, 2005, pp. 38–39. Animal rights groups such as People for the Ethical Treatment of Animals (PETA) are acquiring stock in companies they target and using shareholders' resolutions to pressure the companies into opening dialogues with them.

"Good News for Humans: Animal Rights." *The Economist*, July 29, 2006, p. 31. Public sympathy for the animal rights movement is dropping because the well-publicized violence of a few groups has tainted the image of the entire movement.

Leiby, Richard. "Send in the Clowns." *Washington Post*, November 20, 2005, p. D01. Update on the lawsuit of writer Jan Pottker, who accused Kenneth Feld, head of Ringling Bros. and Barnum & Bailey Circus, and his employees of having carried out a program of covert surveillance and other actions against her in the 1990s because she criticized the Feld family and the circus.

Maag, Chris. "America's #1 Threat." *Mother Jones*, vol. 31, January–February 2006, pp. 18–19. Maag provides a sympathetic portrait of Kevin Kjonaas (Jonas), former president of SHAC-USA, the U.S. branch of the British animal rights organization Stop Huntingdon Animal Cruelty. The article describes the arrest of Kjonaas and six other SHAC members in 2004 for harassing U.S. employees of Huntingdon Life Sciences, an animal testing firm based in Britain, in violation of the Animal Enterprise Protection Act.

Miller, John J. "In the Name of the Animals: America Faces a New Kind of Terrorism." *National Review*, vol. 58, July 3, 2006, p. 38. Terrorist acts by animal rights extremists are a serious threat. These groups often target companies and individuals who have only indirect connections to animal experimentation.

Owen, Ed. "The Dangers of Cuddly Extremism." *New Statesman*, September 12, 2005, pp. 20–21. Only a small number of people support animal rights extremists who break the law, but public opinion may be more swayed by law-abiding groups who express their opposition to the use of animals in research equally strongly.

Pace, Lesli. "Image Events and PETA's Anti-Fur Campaign." *Women and Language*, vol. 28, Fall 2005, pp. 33–41. Pace analyzes the antifur campaign sponsored by People for the Ethical Treatment of Animals (PETA), which ended in 2000, in order to discover the implications of an environmental campaign consisting primarily of images that feature women's bodies. She concludes that, rather than objectifying women, these images represent continuation of a tradition in which women use their bodies to create social change.

"Senators Clash over Terrorist Priorities." *Issues in Science and Technology*, vol. 21, June 22, 2005, pp. 21–22. This article describes arguments among senators at a hearing on May 18, 2005, before the Senate Committee on Environment and Public Works concerning the potential terrorist threat of the Animal Liberation Front and the Earth Liberation Front.

Smallwood, Scott. "Speaking for the Animals, or the Terrorists?" *The Chronicle of Higher Education*, vol. 51, August 5, 2005, n.p. This article profiles University of Texas (El Paso) professor Steven Best, who describes himself as a "philosopher in action" but has been called a "spokesman for terrorists" because the North American Animal Liberation Press Office, which he cofounded, posts information about and defends the controversial Animal Liberation Front.

WEB DOCUMENTS

"Animal Welfare—Human Rights: Protecting People from Animal Rights Extremists." Home Office (British government). Available online. URL: http://police.homeoffice.gov.uk/news-and-publications/publication/operational-policing/humanrights.pdf?view=Binary. Posted July 2004. This document sets out the British government's strategy for countering animal rights extremism, especially attacks on companies and individuals associated with medical research on animals.

Cowles-Hamar, David. "The Manual of Animal Rights." Animal Liberation Front. Available online. URL: http://animalliberationfront.com/ALFront/FAQs/Manual%20of%20Animal%20Rights.htm. Accessed December 26, 2006. This document outlines the animal rights position and replies to statements of critics on such issues as eating meat and animals in circuses.

"History of the Animal Liberation Movement." North American Animal Liberation Press Office. Available online. URL: http://www.animalliberationpressoffice.org/history.htm. Accessed December 24, 2006. This document, published by an organization that supports the Animal Liberation Front and similar radical animal rights groups, includes coverage of the movement's philosophy, history, and liberation guidelines.

"The Humane Society Crosses the Line." North American Animal Liberation Press Office. Available online. URL: http://www.animalliberationpressoffice.org/Writings_Speeches/HSUS%20Crosses%20the%20Line.htm. Posted September 2005. This position paper criticizes the Humane Society of the United States (HSUS) for its attempts to distance itself from the Animal Liberation Front, which go so far as supporting police attacks on the ALF. The Press Office claims that this stance is divisive to the animal rights movement and is intended to protect HSUS from federal prosecution and possible loss of membership and funding.

"An Interview with Animal Liberation Prisoner Peter Young." North American Animal Liberation Press Office. Available online. URL: http://www.animalliberationpressoffice.org/Writings_Speeches/2006-08-04_peteryoung_interview.htm. Posted August 4, 2006. Peter Young pled guilty on September 2, 2005, to two counts of violating the Animal Enterprise Protection Act, relating to the release of more than 8,000 mink from fur farms. On November 8, he was sentenced to two years in prison. This interview discusses support of Young, the relationship of animal liberation to other movements such as the environmental defense movement, and advice for people arrested for animal defense actions.

Lewis, John E. "Congressional Testimony Before the Senate Judiciary Committee." Federal Bureau of Investigation. Available online. URL: http://www.fbi.gov/congress/congress04/lewis051804.htm. Posted May 18, 2004. The testimony of Lewis, then deputy assistant director of the FBI's Counterterrorism Division, explains why the agency considers certain extreme animal rights and "ecoterrorist" groups to be major domestic terrorist threats.

"Serious Organised Crime and Police Bill." Parliament (Britain). Available online. URL: http://www.publications.parliament.uk/pa/cm200405/cmbills/044/2005044.htm. Posted January 24, 2005. An amended version of this law, which went into effect on July 1, 2005, includes sections that give British police increased power to prosecute animal rights activists who harass or harm companies or individuals associated with experimentation on animals.

"Showtrials and Scarecrows: 'Ecoterrorism' and the War on Dissent." North American Animal Liberation Press Office. Available online. URL: http://www.animalliberationpressoffice.org/Writings_Speeches/showtrials_and_scarecrows.htm. Accessed December 24, 2006. This article responds to the Senate Environment and Public Works Committee's hearing on ecoterrorism, held on May 18, 2005. It defends the actions of the Animal Liberation Front, Stop Huntingdon Animal Cruelty, and similar organizations.

Vlasak, Jerry. "Statement by Dr. Jerry Vlasak to the Senate Sub-Committee on Public Works and the Environment, Hearings on Eco-Terrorism and Animal Rights, SHAC and the Anti-HLS Campaign." North American Animal Liberation Press Office. Available online. URL: http://www.animalliberationpressoffice.org/Writings_Speeches/2005-10_Vlasak_testimony_USSenate.htm. Posted October 26, 2005. Vlasak, cofounder of the North American Animal Liberation Press Office and a supporter of the Animal Liberation Front and similar radical animal rights groups, defends the action of one such group against Huntingdon Life Sciences, the largest contract animal testing laboratory in Europe and a major target of animal rights organizations. Vlasak also provides background information on the philosophy and actions of the animal rights movement and addresses the question of violence in movement actions.

"Your Kids, PETA's Pawns." Center for Consumer Freedom. Available online. URL: http://www.consumerfreedom.com/downloads/reference/docs/040817_petakids.pdf. Accessed December 19, 2006. This pamphlet describes campaigns in which People for the Ethical Treatment of Animals (PETA), the well-known animal rights group, attempts to recruit children and teenagers and indoctrinate them with its philosophy.

COMPANION ANIMALS AND ANIMAL SHELTERS

BOOKS

Arluke, Arnold. *Brute Force: Animal Police and the Challenge of Cruelty*. West Lafayette, Ind.: Purdue University Press, 2004. The author reports on a year spent with humane law enforcement officers and dispatchers, who see animal abuse and its effects firsthand every day.

———. *Just a Dog: Understanding Animal Cruelty and Ourselves*. Philadelphia, Pa.: Temple University Press, 2006. Drawing on interviews with more than 250 people, including both those who witness the results of animal cruelty on a regular basis, such as humane society agents and shelter workers, and those who admit to having committed acts of cruelty, Arluke shows how a deeper understanding of cruelty to animals can illuminate the complexity of humans' overall relationship to other species.

Ascione, Frank R. *Children and Animals: Exploring the Roots of Kindness and Cruelty*. West Lafayette, Ind.: Purdue University Press, 2005. Ascione presents the current scientific and professional consensus about the relationship between cruelty to animals and cruelty to other human beings, especially children.

Annotated Bibliography

Bryant, John. *Fettered Kingdoms.* Washington, D.C.: People for the Ethical Treatment of Animals, 1982. Bryant maintains that pet animals are "slaves and prisoners" and that pet ownership should be phased out.

Carlisle-Frank, Pamela, and Tom Flanagan. *Silent Victims: Recognizing and Stopping Abuse of the Family Pet.* Lanham, Md.: University Press of America, 2006. This book presents scientific and anecdotal findings about the causes and effects of animal cruelty in a family context and examines commonly used strategies for recognizing and addressing animal abuse cases.

Figley, Charles R., and Robert G. Roop. *Compassion Fatigue in the Animal-Care Community.* Washington, D.C.: Humane Society Press, 2006. The authors examine the causes of compassion fatigue—exhaustion caused by the demands of helping those who are suffering—in shelter workers and others who care for animals. They offer help to those who experience such fatigue.

Fine, Aubrey H., ed. *Handbook on Animal-Assisted Therapy: Theoretical Foundations and Guidelines for Practice,* 2nd ed. San Diego, Calif.: Academic Press, 2006. This book provides an in-depth overview of ways that animals can help human therapists. It shows how to design an animal-assisted therapy program and select appropriate animals for particular environments.

Gaita, Raymond. *The Philosopher's Dog: Friendships with Animals.* New York: Random House, 2004. Gaita, a professor of moral philosophy at King's College, London, explores what (if anything) animals know, sense, and feel and examines what humans can learn from their relationships with companion animals about both the animals and themselves.

Glen, Samantha. *Best Friends: The True Story of the World's Most Beloved Animal Sanctuary.* New York: Kensington Publishing Corporation, 2001. Glen describes the formation of the sanctuary in Angel Canyon (formerly Kanab), Utah, which houses several thousand animals (cats, dogs, rabbits, birds, and farm animals), many of which have special needs.

Grier, Katherine C. *Pets in America: A History.* Chapel Hill: University of North Carolina Press, 2006. Drawing on a variety of sources, Grier describes the changing roles that pets have played in U.S. culture from colonial times to the present.

Gunter, Barrie. *Pets and People: The Psychology of Pet Ownership.* Hoboken, N.J.: Wiley, 2005. This book examines the phenomenon of pet ownership, the importance of this human-animal relationship in modern society, and the psychological benefits that involvement with a companion animal can bring.

Harbolt, Tami L. *Bridging the Bond: The Cultural Construction of the Shelter Pet.* West Lafayette, Ind.: Purdue University Press, 2003. This scholarly study of humane societies, animal shelters, and rescue leagues from sociological and cultural perspectives is enriched by in-depth interviews with people who work at such institutions and the author's own experience with them.

Irvine, Leslie. *If You Tame Me: Understanding Our Connection with Animals.* Philadelphia, Pa.: Temple University Press, 2004. Irvine builds a case for believing that dogs and cats have a sense of self. She also looks closely at the connections that humans form with these companion animals.

Leigh, Diane, and Marilee Geyer. *One at a Time: A Week in an American Animal Shelter.* Santa Cruz, Calif.: No Voice Unheard, 2005. This book chronicles the stories of 75 animals who passed through a Northern California animal shelter in a single week, creating a vivid portrait of the tragedy of homeless animals in the United States.

Podberscek, Anthony L., Elizabeth S. Paul, and James A. Serpell, eds. *Companion Animals and Us: Exploring the Relationships Between People and Pets,* rev. ed. New York: Cambridge University Press, 2005. This collection brings together research from a variety of disciplines on human relationships with companion animals.

Rogers, Katharine M. *First Friend: A History of Dogs and Humans.* New York: St. Martin's, 2005. Rogers surveys the roles that dogs have played in human society from ancient times to the present. She points out that until the 19th century, dogs were kept primarily for their usefulness rather than their companionship.

ARTICLES

Barker, Randolph T. "On the Edge or Not?" *Journal of Business Communication,* vol. 42, July 2005, pp. 299–315. The presence of companion animals has been shown to improve physical and mental health and social interaction in many settings, and it may do so in the workplace as well.

Fischman, Josh. "The Pet Prescription." *U.S. News & World Report,* December 12, 2005, pp. 72–74. Studies indicate that animal-assisted therapy and pet ownership often convey significant physical as well as emotional health benefits, and more health-care facilities are using animals.

Frank, Joshua. "An Interactive Model of Human and Companion Animal Dynamics." *Human Ecology: An Interdisciplinary Journal,* vol. 32, February 2004, pp. 107–130. Applying a model he developed, Frank concludes that a society in which dog overpopulation is not countered by killing unwanted animals is achievable at an acceptable human cost. Spay/neuter programs are likely to be the most effective technique for reaching this goal, he says, but increasing adoptions is also useful, particularly when these two approaches are used together.

Annotated Bibliography

Haden, Sara C., and Angela Scarpa. "Childhood Animal Cruelty: A Review of Research, Assessment, and Therapeutic Issues." *The Forensic Examiner,* vol. 14, June 22, 2005, pp. 23–32. Professionals who treat abuse within families should pay attention to animal abuse committed by children in such families, partly because such abuse may be linked with later criminal behavior.

Lucich, Jennifer. "Thou Shalt Not Kill: Non-lethal Shelters Are the New 'Humane Societies.'" *E,* vol. 16, May 1, 2005, pp. 14–16. About 5 million dogs and cats are killed in the United States each year because animal shelters do not have enough space to house them. A small but growing number of shelters is trying to find other solutions to the pet overpopulation problem.

Lutwack-Bloom, Patricia, Rohan Wijewickrama, and Betsy Smith. "Effects of Pets Versus People Visits with Nursing Home Residents." *Journal of Gerontological Social Work,* vol. 44, January–February 2005, pp. 137–159. Nursing home residents who received visits from volunteers with a dog showed a significant improvement in mood over a six-month period, whereas no such change occurred in similar residents who received visits that did not include a dog.

McIlwain, Doris. "Therapists with Fur." *Meanjin,* vol. 63, December 2004, pp. 167–171. Animals make good "therapists" because they lack human failings such as projection and dishonesty, this author maintains.

McNicholas, June, et al. "Education and Human Health." *British Medical Journal,* vol. 331, November 26, 2005, pp. 1252–1255. The authors conclude that the emotional bond between a companion animal and its owner can convey psychological benefits similar to those from a close bond with another human.

Pugh, Abigail. "Harnessing the Benefits of Animal-Assisted Therapy." *CrossCurrent, the Journal of Addiction and Mental Health,* vol. 8, December 22, 2004, pp. 5 ff. Animal-assisted therapy (AAT) programs are being used increasingly, especially in mental health settings, to harness the many psychosocial benefits of relationships with companion animals. Pugh defines AAT as a goal-directed intervention in which an animal that meets specific criteria becomes an integral part of treatment facilitated by a health care professional.

Reeve, Charlie L., et al. "The Caring-Killing Paradox." *Journal of Applied Social Psychology,* vol. 35, January 2005, pp. 119–143. Shelter employees who must euthanize healthy animals experience significant stress related to this activity. This stress not only lowers their job satisfaction but also increases the likelihood of their suffering family conflicts, substance abuse, and complaints of physical illness.

Risley-Curtiss, Christina, et al. "'She Was Family': Women of Color and Animal-Human Connections." *Affilia Journal of Women and Social Work,* vol. 21, Winter 2006, pp. 433–447. A study exploring beliefs about and experiences with companion animals revealed the reciprocity that exists in women's relationships with their animals.

Sarmicanic, Lisa. "Goffman, Pets, and People: An Analysis of Humans and Their Companion Animals." *ReVision*, vol. 27, Fall 2004, pp. 42–47. Pets not only assist in the "performances" we use to present ourselves to others; they also reflect back to us our past and present selves.

Staats, Sara, Kelli Sears, and Loretta Pierfelice. "Teachers' Pets and Why They Have Them: An Investigation of the Human-Animal Bond." *Journal of Applied Social Psychology*, vol. 36, August 2006, pp. 1881–1891. Although this survey showed that most of the pet-owning university faculty members sampled believed that pet ownership improves human health, their own pet ownership did not correlate with self-reported health status, happiness, or quality of work life. Of five possible reasons for owning a pet, women were more likely than men to choose reasons related to social support from the pet, whereas men chose more pragmatic reasons.

Tallichet, Suzanne E., and Christopher Henley. "Exploring the Link Between Recurrent Acts of Childhood and Adolescent Animal Cruelty and Subsequent Violent Crime." *Criminal Justice Review*, vol. 29, Autumn 2004, pp. 304–316. In a survey of 261 prison inmates who admitted to past acts of animal abuse, respondents who had more siblings and who had committed repeated (as opposed to single) acts of animal cruelty were more likely to have carried out recurrent acts of violence to other humans.

Wood, Lisa, Billie Giles-Corti, and Max Bulsara. "The Pet Connection: Pets as a Conduit for Social Capital?" *Social Science and Medicine*, vol. 61, September 15, 2005, pp. 1159–1173. This study suggests that pet ownership provides potential opportunities for friendly interactions between neighbors, thus increasing civic engagement and "social capital." This increase may be one of the mechanisms by which pets influence human health.

WEB DOCUMENTS

"Bringing Feral Cat Populations Under Control: Targeted TNR." Alley Cat Allies. Available online. URL: http://www.alleycat.org/pdf/targeted.pdf. Posted October 2006. This article explains targeted TNR (trap-neuter-release), an organized feral cat trapping plan executed in "hot spots"—the locations from which animal control officers take in the most cats. Targeted TNR enables feral cat groups to achieve specific goals for reducing cat populations and provides measurable evidence that TNR is effective.

"The Case Against Random Source Dog and Cat Dealers." Animal Welfare Institute. Available online. URL: http://www.awionline.org/pubs/online_pub/casebdealers/bdealers.html. Accessed December 26, 2006. These dealers are often accused of stealing or fraudulently obtaining family pets and selling them to animal research laboratories. In addition to examining such charges, this report discusses these dealers' deficiencies in the areas of animal welfare, recordkeeping, and adherence to applicable laws.

"A Life Sentence: The Sad and Dangerous Realities of Exotic Animals in Private Hands in the U.S." Animal Protection Institute. Available online. URL: http://www.api4animals.org/downloads/pdf/Exotic_Pets_Report. pdf. Accessed December 26, 2006. This report of an investigation into private ownership of exotic animals reveals that the practice produces threats to public safety, threats to public health, and threats to animal welfare. It discusses laws pertaining to ownership of exotic animals, including the Animal Welfare Act, and presents case studies and recommendations.

"Little Shop of Sorrows: An Undercover Investigation into California Pet Shops." Animal Protection Institute. Available online. URL: http://www. api4animals.org/downloads/pdf/PetShops_Report.pdf. Posted 2005. This animal welfare institute's investigation in spring 2005 revealed abuses including illness, injury, overcrowding, unsanitary conditions, and psychological distress of animals. The report also discusses the legal status of pet shops and makes recommendations for state legislators, law enforcement officers, and consumers.

"The Price of a Pedigree: Dog Breed Standards and Breed-Related Illness." Advocates for Animals. Available online. URL: http://www.advocatesforanimals.org.uk/pdf/Thepriceofapedigree.pdf. Posted 2006. This report by an animal rights group explains how overbreeding of dogs to maintain "purity" of breed lines leads to an increase in breed-related (genetic) illnesses such as hip dysplasia and thus is damaging to the welfare of dogs.

ANIMALS IN AGRICULTURE

BOOKS

Benson, G. John, and Bernard E. Rollin. *The Well-Being of Farm Animals: Challenges and Solutions*. Malden, Mass.: Blackwell, 2004. This book offers both theoretical underpinnings, including the ethical and economic importance of farm animal well-being, and practical methods for enhancing farm animals' comfort and reducing their pain.

Centner, Terence J. *Empty Pastures: Confined Animals and the Transformation of the Rural Landscape*. Urbana: University of Illinois Press, 2004. Centner ex-

207

amines the troubling social, political, economic, and environmental impacts of the rise of intensive ("factory") farming, including effects on animal welfare, and proposes practical reforms and regulations to halt the damage.

Davis, Karen. *The Holocaust and the Henmaid's Tale: A Case for Comparing Atrocities.* New York: Lantern Books, 2005. Davis, president of United Poultry Concerns, offers reasons for saying that a significant comparison can—and must—be drawn between the Holocaust and the abuse and deaths of billions of animals on "factory farms."

Eisnitz, Gail A. *Slaughterhouse: The Shocking Story of Greed, Neglect, and Inhumane Treatment Inside the U.S. Meat Industry,* rev. ed. Amherst, N.Y.: Prometheus Books, 2007. This book explores the impact of unprecedented changes in the meat-packing industry during the last 25 years, including the most recent developments, revelations of abuses, and attempts at reform.

Herren, Ray V. *The Science of Animal Agriculture,* 3rd ed. Clifton Park, N.Y.: Thomson Delmar Learning, 2007. Animal welfare/animal rights and consumer concerns about the animal agriculture industry are among the issues considered by this textbook.

Kallen, Stuart A., ed. *At Issue: Is Factory Farming Harming America?* Farmington Hills, Mich.: Greenhaven Press, 2006. This anthology offers essays and articles from different points of view on several aspects of intensive farming, including farm animal welfare.

Marcus, Eric. *Meat Market: Animals, Ethics, and Money.* Boston: Brio Press, 2005. Marcus aims to reduce the exaggeration in claims made by both the meat industry and its opponents regarding the welfare of animals raised for meat. He illuminates cruelties in intensive agriculture and their social costs, but he also highlights shortcomings of the animal protection movement and recommends strategies for improvement.

Perry, G. C., ed. *Welfare of the Laying Hen.* Cambridge, Mass.: CABI Publishing, 2004. Papers from a 2003 symposium consider all aspects of hens' welfare, including such controversial subjects as battery cages, space requirements, and "free-range" eggs.

Sapontzis, Steve F., ed. *Food for Thought: The Debate over Eating Meat.* Amherst, N.Y.: Prometheus, 2004. This collection offers essays from many points of view, including those of several religions, on the ethics of killing animals for food.

Vidal, John. *McLibel: Burger Culture on Trial.* New York: New Press, 1997. This book describes the trial—the longest in British history—that resulted when fast-food giant McDonald's sued two members of London Greenpeace for libel for distributing a flyer that accused the company of cruelty to animals and other "crimes," forcing the two to prove the truth of all the flyer's allegations.

Annotated Bibliography

Volpe, Tina. *The Fast Food Craze: Wreaking Havoc on Our Bodies and Our Animals*. Kagel Canyon, Calif.: Canyon Publishing, 2005. Volpe shows how "fast food" both harms human health and encourages abuse of the animals raised on the "factory farms" that provide meat for fast food chains.

Weeks, C. A., and A. Butterworth, eds. *Measuring and Auditing Broiler Welfare*. Cambridge, Mass.: CABI Publishing, 2004. This collection presents international experts' recommendations for measuring and auditing the welfare of broiler chickens on the farm, in transit, and before slaughter.

ARTICLES

Arnot, Charlie, and Cliff Gauldin. "'People Factor' Major Part of Housing Issue." *Feedstuffs*, vol. 78, September 18, 2006, pp. 16–17. Group pens and individual sow gestation stalls each have advantages and disadvantages in terms of the pigs' welfare, two scientists conclude. They say that the behavior of the people managing the animals is at least as important in determining sows' welfare as the way in which the animals are housed.

———. "Transport Law Under Scrutiny." *Feedstuffs*, vol. 78, November 6, 2006, p. 33. The U.S. Department of Agriculture has acknowledged that the 130-year-old Twenty-eight Hour Law applies to the transport of livestock by truck as well as by rail. The meat industry is considering the implications of this ruling.

———. "Welfare: Can Industry Handle Moral Issues?" *Feedstuffs*, vol. 78, July 24, 2006, pp. 14–15. American pork producers need to find better arguments to counter the complaints of animal rights protesters, because complying with the activists' demands could be very expensive.

Cohen, Nick. "God's Own Chosen Meat." *New Statesman*, vol. 133, July 5, 2004, pp. 22–24. Cohen maintains that orthodox Jewish and Muslim ritual slaughter of meat animals, which requires that the animals be killed while they are conscious, is cruel and is demanded by only a small proportion of people of those faiths. This form of slaughter should be banned, Cohen says.

Dawkins, Marian Stamp, Christi A. Donnelly, and Tracey A. Jones. "Chicken Welfare Is Influenced More by Housing Conditions than by Stocking Density." *Nature*, vol. 427, January 22, 2004, pp. 342–344. This article describes present conditions of the broiler chicken industry in the European Union. Although it focuses on housing conditions, it also recommends limiting maximum stocking density.

Gross, Aaron. "When Kosher Isn't Kosher." *Tikkun*, vol. 20, March–April 2005, pp. 52–55. Undercover videotapes made by members of People for the Ethical Treatment of Animals (PETA) at Agriprocessors Inc., the largest kosher slaughterhouse in the world, reveal inhumane slaughter methods that violate the moral underpinnings of Jewish dietary law.

Klinkenborg, Verlyn. "What Do Animals Think?" *Discover*, vol. 26, May 2005, pp. 46–53. Livestock behavior expert Temple Grandin, herself autistic, says that animals and autistic people view the world in similar ways, for example thinking in pictures rather than words and focusing on small details that "normal" humans tune out.

Lobo, Philip. "HSUS Agenda: A Threat to Animal Agriculture." *Feedstuffs*, vol. 78, October 30, 2006, p. 9. The Humane Society of the United States supports measures that, in the author's opinion, damage not only animal agriculture but animal welfare.

Marohasy, Jennifer. "Campaigning Against Our Cultural Heritage." *Review—Institute of Public Affairs*, vol. 57, March 31, 2005, pp. 16–17. Marohasy maintains that animal liberation campaigns, such as those against several aspects of the wool industry, challenge key historical assumptions about Australia's national character and make rural and regional Australia feel under seige.

Mitchell, Richard. "Handle with [Greater] Care." *National Provisioner*, vol. 218, July 2004, pp. 32–35. Many companies that raise animals for slaughter are improving their animal handling practices for economic as well as ethical reasons: Consumers and end-user companies are increasingly demanding such improvement.

Mohr, Paula. "Handle with Care: Rough Treatment of Cattle Causes Animal Stress and Avoidance and Lowers Production." *Dairy Today*, vol. 20, April 1, 2004, p. 11. Dairy cattle fear rough treatment, and when they are stressed and afraid, they produce less milk.

Petrak, Lynn. "Temple Grandin's Best Practices." *National Provisioner*, vol. 220, August 2006, pp. 20–21. Animal handling expert Temple Grandin has seen many improvements in the way animals are treated in slaughterhouses, she says, but further improvements could be made with relatively simple and inexpensive steps.

Porcher, Jocelyne, Florence Cousson-Gelie, and Robert Dantzer. "Affective Components of the Human-Animal Relationship in Animal Husbandry." *Psychological Reports*, vol. 95, August 2004, pp. 275–290. The authors developed a questionnaire to identify the main dimensions of the human-animal relationship in animal husbandry. The factors that varied most significantly among farmers were friendship and power.

Rollin, B. E. "Annual Meeting Keynote Address: Animal Agriculture and Emerging Social Ethics for Animals." *Journal of Animal Science*, vol. 82, March 2004, pp. 955–965. Treatment of animals in various areas of human use has emerged as a major social ethical issue in the past several decades. This speech cites five major reasons for this new concern and considers its meaning for animal agriculture.

Scully, Matthew. "Fear Factories: The Case for Compassionate Conservatism—for Animals." *The American Conservative*, May 23, 2005, n.p. According to Scully, intensive farming involves abuses of animals that represent a serious moral problem.

Smith, Rod. "Costs of Cageless Shown." *Feedstuffs*, vol. 77, August 1, 2005, p. 8. United Egg Producers, a trade organization, shows what it would cost the United States egg industry to abandon battery cages for hens, as some animal rights groups have demanded.

———. "Welfare Depends on Management." *Feedstuffs*, vol. 78, October 16, 2006, p. 8. Smith claims that the welfare of laying hens depends more on the human management of the system in which they live than on the type of housing (caged or cage-free) that they occupy.

Wilkie, Rhoda. "Sentient Commodities and Productive Paradoxes." *Journal of Rural Studies*, vol. 21, April 2005, pp. 213–230. In both commercial and hobby livestock production in northeast Scotland, producers have contradictory roles as empathetic "carers" for animals and as producers of "sentient commodities" valued chiefly in economic terms.

WEB DOCUMENTS

"Animal Handling and Welfare in Meat Plants." American Meat Institute. Available online. URL: http://www.meatami.com/Template.cfm?Section=Animal_Welfare1&CONTENTID=4480&TEMPLATE=/ContentManagement/ContentDisplay.cfm. Posted March 2006. This fact sheet put out by the meat trade association discusses the background of the issue, government oversight, voluntary effort and audits, and the economic benefits of humane handling. It claims that animal handling has improved considerably in recent years.

"Animal Suffering in the Broiler Industry." Compassion Over Killing. Available online. URL: http://www.cok.net/images/pdf/COKBroilerReport.pdf. Accessed December 28, 2006. This report concludes that selective breeding, confinement, transport, and slaughter practices in the broiler industry cause chickens to experience both acute and chronic pain.

"Animal Suffering in the Egg Industry." Compassion Over Killing. Available online. URL: http://www.cok.net/images/pdf/COKLayerReport.pdf. Accessed December 28, 2006. This report describes pain and other problems experienced by laying hens confined in battery cages.

"Animal Suffering in the Turkey Industry." Compassion Over Killing. Available online. URL: http://www.cok.net/images/pdf/COKTurkeyReport.pdf. Accessed December 28, 2006. This report details animal health problems arising from breeding and drugs that make turkeys grow so heavy and so fast that their skeletons cannot keep up. Crowded housing conditions and inhumane slaughter practices also threaten the birds' welfare.

"Best Food Nation: A Celebration of Our Safe, Abundant, Affordable Food System." National Council for Chain Restaurants. Available online. URL: http://www.bestfoodnation.com/index.asp. Accessed December 24, 2006. This booklet, which defends the U.S. food system, includes a discussion of the welfare of animals used for meat.

"The Case Against Cages." Royal Society for the Prevention of Cruelty to Animals. Available online. URL: http://www.rspca.org.uk/servlet/Satellite ?blobcol=urlblob&blobheader=application%2Fpdf&blobkey=id&blobtable =RSPCABlob&blobwhere=1126511568395&ssbinary=true&Content-Type=application/pdf. Accessed December 28, 2006. This report claims that "enriched" cages provide minimal additional space for hens than conventional cages and calls for the banning of all battery cages. It offers alternatives to this allegedly cruel confinement and explains why barn and free-range systems improve the welfare of laying hens.

"Driving Pain: The State of Farmed-Animal Transport in the U.S. and across Our Borders." Animal Protection Institute. Available online. URL: http://www.api4animals.org/a6a_transport.php. Accessed December 26, 2006. This series of linked web pages describes inhumane aspects of animal transport as revealed by a 2005 investigation sponsored by the Animal Protection Institute and Compassion in World Farming. The document also makes recommendations for improvement.

"Enriched Cages." Farm Animal Welfare Network. Available online. URL: http://www.fawn.me.uk. Accessed December 28, 2006. This report critiques the so-called enriched cage, a supposed improvement on battery cages for egg-laying hens. The Farm Animal Welfare Network believes that these cages offer little real improvement in the hens' welfare and contends that hens should not be kept in cages at all.

"Everyone's a Winner." Royal Society for the Prevention of Cruelty to Animals. Available online. URL: http://www.rspca.org.uk/servlet/Satellite ?blobcol=urlblob&blobheader=application%2Fpdf&blobkey=id&blobtable =RSPCABlob&blobwhere=1158755016591&ssbinary=true&Content-Type=application/pdf. Posted September 2006. This report provides evidence that meat chickens reared in accordance with higher welfare standards are significantly healthier than those raised in worse conditions. It argues that improving broiler chickens' welfare benefits producers, retailers, and consumers as well as the animals themselves.

"Factory Farming." Humane Farming Association. Available online. URL: http://www.hfa.org/factory/index.html. Accessed December 29, 2006. This report describes the "true costs" of large-scale farming, including the costs in animal suffering.

Annotated Bibliography

"Farm Animal Welfare: An Assessment of Product Labeling Claims, Industry Quality Assurance Guidelines and Third Party Certification Standards." Farm Sanctuary. Available online. URL: http://www.farmsanctuary. org/campaign/FAWS_Report.pdf. Accessed December 29, 2006. This book-length report concludes that most claims of "humane" treatment or standards leave much to be desired. They permit some types of treatment that Farm Sanctuary considers abusive, or they are vague, subjective, or only sporadically enforced. Most also affect only a tiny percentage of animals raised for food.

"Fur Farming in North America." Fur Commission USA. Available online. URL: http://www.furcommission.com/farming/index.html. Accessed December 29, 2006. This web page presents details of fur farming from a point of view favorable to the industry.

McDonald's Corporation Corporate Responsibility Committee. "Report of the Corporate Responsibility Committee of the Board of Directors of McDonald's Corporation Regarding the Feasibility of Implementing Controlled Atmosphere Stunning for Broilers." McDonald's. Available online. URL: http://www.mcdonalds.com/corp/invest/gov/mcd_cr062905. RowPar.0001.ContentPar.0001.ColumnPar.0002.DownloadFiles.0001. File.tmp/CORPORATE_RESPONSIBILITY_STATEMENT_ AND_CAS_REPORT.pdf. Posted June 29, 2005. This report compares controlled atmosphere stunning as a way of rendering chickens unconscious before slaughter, a method favored by animal rights groups, against electrical stunning, the currently used method. It concludes that both techniques are equally acceptable.

"National Chicken Council Animal Welfare Guidelines and Audit Checklist." National Chicken Council. Available online. URL: http://www.national chickencouncil.com/files/AnimalWelfare2005.pdf. Posted April 2005. This checklist presents guidelines for practices that promote good health and welfare of broiler chickens.

Pickett, Heather. "The Way Forward for Europe's Egg Industry: Keeping the Ban on Battery Cages in 2012." Compassion in World Farming. Available online. URL: http://www.ciwf.org.uk/publications/reports/Battery_ Cages2006.pdf. Posted 2006. This report explains how keeping laying hens in battery cages restricts natural behaviors such as perching, foraging, and dust-bathing. It also discusses the economic aspects of discontinuing battery cages. It concludes with a strategy for adhering to the ban on battery cages while safeguarding the economic well-being of E.U. egg producers.

"Report on Welfare Labeling." Farm Animal Welfare Council. Available online. URL: http://www.fawc.org.uk/reports/welfarelabel-0606.pdf. Posted June 2006. This report from a British animal welfare group offers a case for labeling all food products in the European Union with a single, mandatory label, backed by international standards, that describes the conditions under which the animals that produced the products were raised. It discusses conditions and types of welfare labeling, effectiveness of labeling, benefits of labeling, and practical issues.

Royal Society for the Prevention of Cruelty to Animals, Eurogroup for Animal Welfare, and World Society for the Protection of Animals. "Animals and People First." Eurogroup for Animal Welfare. Available online. URL: http://www.eurogroupforanimals.org/documents/pdf/animalsand-peoplefirst_2005.pdf. Posted 2005. This pamphlet explains why improving the welfare of farmed animals is important for feeding people, for trade, and for the future. It concludes that World Trade Organization (WTO) stakeholders need better understanding of animal welfare, farmers should be given financial help to meet costs of improving animal welfare, and labeling programs should be improved to give consumers more information about their food.

"Sentient Beings: A Summary of the Scientific Evidence Establishing Sentience in Farmed Animals." Farm Sanctuary. Available online. URL: http://www.sentientbeings.org/SB_report_web.pdf. Accessed December 29, 2006. This report provides evidence that cattle, sheep, chickens, and other animals raised for food experience consciousness and a variety of emotions. This sentience should be taken into account in determining how the animals are treated.

"Teacher Resource Guide to Farm Animal Care and Use Issues." Animal Agriculture Alliance. Available online. URL: http://www.animalagalliance. org/images/ag_insert/TeachersResource.pdf. Accessed December 28, 2006. This resource guide, which covers prekindergarten through college, provides a directory of educational curricula and other materials that address animal use, production, welfare, food, fiber, nutrition, food safety and environmental issues, and the importance of animals in society.

Vernelli, Toni. "The Dark Side of Dairy." Vegetarians International Voice for Animals. Available online. URL: http://www.milkmyths.org.uk/pdfs/ dairy_report.pdf. Posted November 2005. Vernelli provides evidence that mental and physical suffering is inflicted on millions of dairy cows and their calves.

ANIMALS IN RESEARCH, TESTING, AND EDUCATION

BOOKS

Akins, Chana K., Sangeeta Panicker, and Christopher L. Cunningham, eds. *Laboratory Animals in Research and Teaching: Ethics, Care, and Methods.*

Annotated Bibliography

Washington, D.C.: American Psychological Association, 2005. These essays consider scientists' role in balancing scientific, ethical, and practical concerns related to experimenting on animals.

Carbone, Larry. *What Animals Want: Expertise and Advocacy in Laboratory Animal Welfare Policy.* New York: Oxford University Press, 2004. Carbone discusses laboratory animal welfare from the point of view of a veterinarian whose job is to care for such animals. Among issues he considers are the philosophical debate about the use of animals in research and testing, the laws that affect such use, and the recent explosion in research on genetically altered mice.

Eila, Kaliste. *The Welfare of Laboratory Animals.* New York: Springer, 2004. The first part of this book describes general principles for maintaining laboratory animals and using them in experiments. The second half considers requirements for the welfare of particular species.

Hamilton, Susan, ed. *Animal Welfare and Anti-Vivisection 1870–1910.* New York: Routledge, 2004. This book brings together numerous documents from the vivisection controversy in the 19th century, focusing on pro-vivisection writings (two earlier volumes covered anti-vivisection material).

Hartinger, Werner. *The Animals Are Our Brothers and Sisters: Why Animal Experiments Are Misleading and Wrong.* Herndon, Va.: Temple Lodge Publishing, 2006. The author provides scientific reasons for thinking that research on animals does not provide results that are useful in human medicine, as well as spiritual reasons for thinking that such research is morally wrong.

Haugen, Dave, ed. *Opposing Viewpoints: Animal Experimentation.* Farmington Hills, Mich.: Greenhaven Press, 2007. This anthology provides different points of view on questions related to use of animals in scientific research and testing, including military testing and animal-to-human transplants. The introduction provides a brief history of the animal rights movement and its reactions to experimentation on animals.

Institute for Laboratory Animal Research. *Science, Medicine, and Animals.* Washington, D.C.: National Academies Press, 2004. This book explains animals' role in biomedical research and discusses ways in which scientists, governments, and citizens have tried to balance the need for use of animals in science with concerns for the animals' welfare.

Mur, Cindy, ed. At Issue Series: *Animal Experimentation.* San Diego, Calif.: Greenhaven Press, 2004. This anthology provides different views on the scientific and ethical value of experimenting on animals.

Rudacille, Deborah. *The Scalpel and the Butterfly: The Conflict between Animal Research and Animal Protection.* Berkeley: University of California Press, 2000. Rudacille provides a neutral history of the conflict between animal research and the animal protection and animal rights

215

movements and considers the issue from both ethical and scientific standpoints.

Silverman, Jerald, Mark A. Suckow, and Sreekant Murthy, eds. *The IACUC Handbook*, 2nd. ed. Boca Raton, Fla.: CRC, 2006. This is a reference book for those heading or serving on Institutional Animal Care and Use Committees (IACUCs) as well as for researchers who must deal with these committees, which are mandated by the Animal Welfare Act.

Wolfensohn, Sarah, and Paul Honess. *Handbook of Primate Husbandry and Welfare*. Malden, Mass.: Blackwell, 2005. This practical book covers all aspects of primate care in laboratories and zoos. It also considers definitions of welfare for primates and the ethics of keeping nonhuman primates in captivity.

Yarri, Donna. *The Ethics of Animal Experimentation: A Critical Analysis and Constructive Christian Proposal*. New York: Oxford University Press, 2005. Yarri gives ethical, philosophical, and religious reasons for significantly limiting experimentation on animals. She also provides a model of benign experimentation and a burden-benefit analysis that can be used to decide when an experiment is justified.

ARTICLES

Aaltola, Elisa. "The Politics and Ethics of Animal Experimentation." *International Journal of Biotechnology*, vol. 7, August 21, 2005, p. 234. This paper analyzes the ethics of experimentation on animals through different perspectives and considers political elements that have affected the ethical debate.

Archibald, Kathy. "Animal Testing: Science or Fiction?" *The Ecologist*, vol. 35, May 2005, pp. 14–16. Assurance of the safety and efficacy of new drugs rests on results of testing the drugs on animals, but a number of studies claim that animal testing procedures are flawed.

Balcombe, J. P. "Laboratory Environments and Rodents' Behavioral Needs: A Review." *Laboratory Animals*, vol. 40, 2006, pp. 217–235. After reviewing published studies, the author concludes that laboratory housing conditions have significant physiological and psychological effects on rodents, raising both scientific and humane concerns. Adding environmental "enrichments" to small cages reduces but does not eliminate these problems; more substantial changes are needed.

———, N. D. Barnard, and C. Sandusky. "Laboratory Routines Cause Animal Stress." *Contemporary Topics in Laboratory Animal Science*, vol. 43, November 2004, pp. 42–51. After examining changes in several physiological measurements caused by routine, noninvasive handling of laboratory animals, the authors conclude that animals do not become accustomed to such handling and that it causes significant fear and stress.

Barley, Jas. "Balancing the Needs of Animals and Science." *Schools Science Review*, vol. 87, December 2005, pp. 105–106. This study shows that good human-animal relationships as well as good environment and other husbandry conditions are important in maintaining research animals' health and normal behavior.

Bateson, Patrick. "Using Animals in Research." *Psychology Review*, vol. 11 February 2005, pp. 2–6. Bateson presents a "decision cube" for determining the costs (in terms of animal suffering) versus the benefits of experiments in behavioral psychology that use animals, which can help scientists decide whether the experiments should proceed. Suffering is assessed by comparing the animals' behavior under experimental conditions with their behavior in their natural environment.

Borrego, Anne Marie. "Politics, Culture, and the Lab." *Chronicle of Higher Education*, vol. 51, March 11, 2005, n.p. Experiments on animals cause more concern in Britain than in the United States, whereas the opposite is true of research on embryonic stem cells. Variations in history and religion may explain this difference.

Brainerd, Jeffrey. "Undercover among the Cages." *Chronicle of Higher Education*, vol. 52, March 3, 2006, n.p. Moles from People for the Ethical Treatment of Animals (PETA) filmed alleged mistreatment of mice and rats at a laboratory on the University of North Carolina's Chapel Hill campus. Later inspections by the National Institutes of Health also found violations, but the NIH refused to censure the university and thereby drew criticism from animal rights groups.

Epstein, Alex. "Animal Rights Movement Is Cruelty to Humans." *San Diego Business Journal*, vol. 26, August 22, 2005, pp. 46–47. Epstein claims that campaigns such as that of People for the Ethical Treatment of Animals (PETA) against Covance, an animal research laboratory in Princeton, New Jersey, harm humans by blocking potentially lifesaving medical advances.

Fiester, Autumn. "Creating Fido's Twin: Can Pet Cloning Be Ethically Justified?" *Hastings Center Report*, vol. 35, July–August 2005, pp. 34–39. Pet cloning may seem frivolous at best, but it may be useful in raising the moral status of companion animals in the public eye, because it demonstrates the trouble and expense that some people are willing to endure in an attempt to preserve their pets.

"Four Legs Good, Two Legs Bad: Animal Rights Extremists." *The Economist*, vol. 376, August 27, 2005, p. 45. The author states that if animal rights extremists really want to reduce animal suffering, they have chosen a poor target by attacking research companies that use animals, because research on animals is already highly regulated in Britain.

Animal Rights

Goldberg, Alan M., and Thomas Hartung. "Protecting More Than Animals." *Scientific American*, vol. 294, January 2006, pp. 84–90. New techniques involving statistics, noninvasive imaging, and cell and tissue cultures are reducing both the need for and the suffering involved in animal testing.

Goldberg, Alan M., and Paul A. Locke. "To 3R Is Humane." *The Environmental Forum*, vol. 21, July/August 2004, pp. 19–26. The authors claim that new techniques in toxicology make reduction, replacement, and refinement in testing of environmental toxins on animals more practical than ever before.

"Guidelines for the Treatment of Animals in Behavioral Research and Teaching." *Animal Behaviour*, vol. 71, January 2006, pp. 245–253. Topics covered in the guidelines include legislation, nonanimal alternatives, procedures, obtaining and transporting animals, and housing and care.

Kempner, Joanna, Clifford S. Perlis, and Jon F. Merz. "Forbidden Knowledge." *Science*, vol. 307, February 11, 2005, p. 854. This paper states that some scientists avoid certain types of research because such research might trigger attacks by animal rights activists.

MacNeil, Jane Salodof. "Improving the Lives of Laboratory Animals: No Easy Task for Mice or Men." *The Scientist*, vol. 18, April 26, 2004, p. 43 ff. This article explains why pain management and environmental enrichment for laboratory animals can be difficult to measure and achieve.

Newman, Carol. "Replacement of Animal Experiments Is the Ultimate Aim." *School Science Review*, vol. 87, December 2005, pp. 115–120. This article supplies details of in vitro (test-tube) technologies and computer models that can replace animals in some kinds of research.

Ortiz, Sara Elizabeth Gavrell. "Beyond Welfare: Animal Integrity, Animal Dignity, and Genetic Engineering." *Ethics and the Environment*, vol. 9, January 2004, p. 94 ff. Respect for an animal's dignity forbids genetic alteration that would inhibit development of functions that an animal of that species would normally perform, even if such modification would improve the animal's welfare. An example of such alteration is the creation of "animal microencephalic lumps"—animals, intended for food or other human uses, that have brains too small to feel pain or have interests.

Pocha, Jehangir. "Animal Tester." *Forbes Global*, vol. 2, October 30, 2006, p. 24. A U.S. venture company called Bridge helps pharmaceutical businesses outsource controversial animal experiments to China, where animal rights groups have less influence than they do in North America and Europe.

Pound, Pandora, et al. "Where Is the Evidence that Animal Research Benefits Humans?" *British Medical Journal*, vol. 328, February 28, 2004, pp. 514–517. Systematic reviews of six medical research projects on animals showed that the results of animal tests were regarded as irrelevant to later human clinical trials and were also poorly designed, casting doubt on claims that such tests are essential to the advancement of human medicine.

Robinson, Vicky. "Finding Alternatives: An Overview of the 3Rs and the Use of Animals in Research." *School Science Review*, vol. 87, December 2005, pp. 111–114. Robinson presents methods and advantages of replacing, refining, and reducing use of animals in research laboratories. She also considers future challenges to the "3Rs."

Schuppli, Catherine A., and Michael McDonald. "Contrasting Modes of Governance for the Protection of Humans and Animals in Canada." *Health Law Review*, vol. 13, March 22, 2005, pp. 97–106. The authors argue that, in some ways, research on animals is more stringently regulated than is research on human subjects in both Canada and the United States.

"Testing Times." *The Economist*, vol. 379, June 10, 2006, p. 82. New methods of testing chemicals without using animals are being developed, but other trends, especially in basic genetic research, may increase the use of animals.

Thomas, D. "Laboratory Animals and the Art of Empathy." *Journal of Medical Ethics*, vol. 31, April 2005, pp. 197–202. Thomas says that by the standard of empathy—putting oneself in the place of a potential victim—research on animals is no more ethical than nonconsensual research on human beings.

Weiss, Peter. "Frankenstein's Chips." *Science News*, vol. 167, January 8, 2005, p. 24, p. 26. "Animals-on-a-chip"—silicon or plastic wafers containing cells from different organs, connected by fluid "blood"—could reduce the need for testing new drugs on animals as well as saving money for drug developers.

WEB DOCUMENTS

"The Animal Care Program and the U.S. Department of Agriculture's Authority Under the Animal Welfare Act: Basic Questions and Answers." U.S. Department of Agriculture Animal and Plant Health Inspection Service (APHIS). Available online. URL: http://www.aphis.usda.gov/lpa/pubs/fsheet_faq_notice/faq_awusda.html. Posted July 2005. This fact sheet answers frequently asked questions about the Animal Welfare Act and its enforcement.

"Bad Science: Using Primates Kills People." SPEAK. Available online. URL: http://www.speakcampaigns.org/badscience.php. Accessed December 25, 2006. This opinion piece claims that testing drugs on nonhuman primates or other animals produces results that are not valid for human beings. It recommends nonanimal test procedures that it says are more accurate and effective.

"Enrichment for Nonhuman Primates." National Institutes of Health Office of Laboratory Animal Welfare. Available online. URL: http://grants. nih.gov/grants/olaw/Enrichment_for_Nonhuman_Primates.pdf. Posted 2005. This series of six booklets covers baboons, capuchins, chimpanzees, macaques, marmosets, tamarins, and squirrel monkeys.

European Partnership for Alternative Approaches to Animal Testing. "Action Programme." Europa. Available online. URL: http://ec.europa.eu/ enterprise/epaa/ap.htm. Accessed December 23, 2006. The objective of this program, formulated by a collaboration between the European Commission and major companies from seven industry sectors, is to promote and support the development, validation, and acceptance of alternative approaches to refine, reduce, and replace animal use for safety testing within those sectors. This summary describes the plan's objectives, approach, areas of action, and activities.

"FELASA Statement on EU White Paper REACH (Registration, Evaluation and Authorisation of Chemicals)." Federation of European Laboratory Animal Science Associations. Available online. URL: http://www. felasa.eu/Documents/Policy_statements/PositionPaperREACH 20041124.doc. Posted November 2004. FELASA comments on the REACH program, a proposed new regulatory framework for evaluation of chemicals adopted by the European Commission on October 29, 2003, which might require a huge number of laboratory animals. FELASA recommends that animal experiments be performed in conjunction with validated alternative methods and that risk evaluations be carried out before planning experiments on animals.

FELASA Working Group on Ethical Evaluation of Animal Experiments. "Principles and Practice in Ethical Review of Animal Experiments Across Europe." Federation of European Laboratory Animal Science Associations. Available online. URL: http://www.lal.org.uk/pdffiles/FELASA_ ethics_FULL_Report.pdf. Posted December 2005. This report describes the results of a survey designed to find out how each of the 20 countries represented in FELASA conducts ethical reviews of laboratory animal use. It presents the emerging consensus on the key elements that such a review should include and provides recommendations for conducting reviews.

"Fifty Deadly Consequences of Lab Animal Experiments." Americans for Medical Advancement. Available online. URL: http://www.curedisease. com/Harms.html. Accessed December 29, 2006. This document briefly describes 50 cases in which animal tests did not correctly predict human reactions to drugs or other substances.

Goldberg, Alan M. "Animals and Alternatives: Societal Expectations and Scientific Need." Johns Hopkins University Center for Alternatives to

Animal Testing. Available online. URL: http://caat.jhsph.edu/publications/ articles/FRAME2004.pdf. Posted October 6, 2004. This lecture discusses the "3 Rs" (replace, reduce, refine) of product testing on animals and their relationship to societal demands for improved animal welfare and animal rights. Goldberg concludes that "humane science is the best science," the point where societal expectations and scientific needs converge.

Greek, Ray. "The History of Medical Progress." In Defense of Animals. Available online. URL: http://www.idausa.org/ir/reports/medprogess. html. Accessed December 27, 2006. This report contradicts claims that research on animals has benefited human medicine.

Hepple, Bob, et al. "Ethics of Research Involving Animals." Nuffield Council on Bioethics. Available online. URL: http://www.nuffieldbioethics. org/go/browseablepublications/ethicsofresearchanimals/report_230. html. Posted May 25, 2005. This report by a respected British bioethical institute surveys the use of animals in different types of research and makes recommendations for future policy and practice regarding scientific employment of animals. It urges scientists and the British government to provide more information to citizens about the way research on animals is conducted, the implications of such research for animal welfare, and its benefits to humans.

"The Humane Care and Treatment of Laboratory Animals." National Association for Biomedical Research. Available online. URL: http://www. nabr.org/pdf/orange.pdf. Accessed December 30, 2006. This pamphlet describes how scientists care for laboratory animals and why good animal care is essential to good science.

Langley, Chris. "Designer Mice: A BUAV Special Report into the Use of Mice in Genetic Experiments." European Coalition to End Animal Experiments. Available online. URL: http://www.eceae.org/pdf/Designer-Mice.pdf. Accessed December 23, 2006. This report from a group opposed to animal research discusses the "making" of genetically engineered mice, the nature of experiments on them, and animal welfare concerns that these experiments raise.

Langley, Gill. "Chemical Safety and Animal Testing: A Regulatory Smoke-screen?" British Union for the Abolition of Vivisection and European Coalition to End Animal Experiments. Available online. URL: http:// www.buav.org/pdf/Smokescreen.pdf. Accessed December 19, 2006. Citing case studies, this report claims that excessive reliance on data from animal tests is a major barrier to effective regulation of potentially toxic chemicals. It offers alternatives to testing such chemicals on animals.

———. "Next of Kin: A Report on the Use of Primates in Experiments." British Union for the Abolition of Vivisection and European Coalition to

End Animal Experiments. Available online. URL: http://www.eceae.org/ english/documents/NoKReport.pdf. Posted June 2006. Langley calls for laws to prohibit all experiments on nonhuman primates in Britain and Europe. She claims that nonhuman primates are inaccurate models for human beings and that regulation is inadequate to stop the suffering of primates in medical experiments.

"Pet Cloning: Separating Facts from Fluff." American Anti-Vivisection Society. Available online. URL: http://www.nopetcloning.org/images/ report21605.pdf. Posted February 16, 2005. This report stresses dangers and concerns surrounding pet cloning, including effects on animal welfare.

"Regulation of Biomedical Research Using Animals." National Association for Biomedical Research. Available online. URL: http://www.nabr.org/ pdf/green.pdf. Accessed December 30, 2006. This pamphlet describes the Animal Welfare Act and other U.S. laws and regulations that govern the care of animals used in scientific research.

Reinhardt, Viktor, and Annie Reinhardt. "Variables, Refinement and Environmental Enrichment for Rodents and Rabbits Kept in Research Institutions." Animal Welfare Institute. Available online. URL: http://www. awionline.org/pubs/rabrodent/rodrab.html. Posted January 10, 2006. This book-length report discusses issues such as necessities and enrichment in cage furnishings, restraints, noise, relationships with other animals, and stress reduction.

Ritskes-Hoitinga, Merel, Line Bjoerndal Gravesen, and Inger Marie Jegstrup. "Refinement Benefits Animal Welfare and Quality of Science." National Centre for the Replacement, Refinement and Reduction of Animals in Research. Available online. URL: http://www.nc3rs.org.uk/ news.asp?id=212. Posted March 2006. The authors present examples showing how refinement of laboratory procedures and experimental design can both improve the welfare of laboratory animals and provide better quality in experimental results.

Roberts, Ian. "Testing Treatments on Animals: Relevance to Humans." University of Birmingham. Available online. URL: http://www.pcpoh.bham. ac.uk/publichealth/nccrm/PDFs%20and%20documents/Publications/ JH18_Final_Report_May_2006.pdf. Posted May 2006. The author used systematic review methodology to compare results from animal experiments and later trials on humans in six examples of drug treatment for specific medical conditions. He considers reasons why the results from the two types of experiments often did not match and makes recommendations for increasing concordance between human and animal experiments.

Smith, Jane A., and Maggy Jennings, eds. "Categorising the Severity of Scientific Procedures on Animals." The Boyd Group. Available online. URL: http://www.boyd-group.demon.co.uk/severity_report.pdf. Posted July 2004.

This document, issued on behalf of the Boyd Group and the Royal Society for the Prevention of Cruelty to Animals, summarizes three round-table discussions held in 2004. It discusses difficulties with the current system for evaluating severity and suggests practical solutions to these problems.

Weatherall, David. "The Use of Non-Human Primates in Research." Academy of Medical Sciences. Available online. URL: http://www.acmedsci.ac. uk/images/project/nhpdownl.pdf. Posted December 2006. Weatherall concludes that there is a strong scientific case for maintaining research on nonhuman primates for carefully selected research problems in many, but not all, of the medical areas studied. He states that cases should be judged individually in terms of welfare costs to the animals involved, potential scientific or medical benefit of the work, and availability of other approaches.

Young, Robert W. "Audit Report: APHIS Animal Care Program Inspection and Enforcement Activities." U.S. Department of Agriculture, Office of Inspector General. Available online. URL: http://www.usda.gov/oig/ webdocs/33002-03-SF.pdf. Posted September 2005. This report states that wealthy universities frequently violate federal rules for the care of research animals, as specified in the Animal Welfare Act, but are given only relatively small fines by the USDA's Animal Care Program, part of the Animal and Plant Health Inspection Service (APHIS).

ANIMALS IN ENTERTAINMENT

BOOKS

Baratay, Eric, and Elisabeth Hardouin-Fugier. Zoo: A History of Zoological Gardens in the West. London: Reaktion Books, 2004. This heavily illustrated book presents a social history of zoos, showing how the way people look at wild animals has changed over time.

Bonner, Jeffrey P. Sailing with Noah: Stories from the World of Zoos. Columbia: University of Missouri Press, 2006. Bonner, president and CEO of the St. Louis (Missouri) Zoo, tells entertaining tales of a zoo director's complicated life. He also stresses zoos' new role as conservators of endangered species, both in the wild and in captivity.

Donahue, Jesse, and Erik Trump. The Politics of Zoos: Exotic Animals and Their Protectors. Dekalb: Northern Illinois University Press, 2006. This book provides a political biography of the American Association of Zoological Parks and Aquariums (AZA), an organization formed partly to help zoos and aquariums fend off attacks from animal rights groups. It shows how AZA members crafted a new mission to assist with conservation of wild species, ensure the welfare of captive animals, and offer environmental education to the public.

Hancocks, David. *A Different Nature: The Paradoxical World of Zoos and Their Uncertain Future.* Berkeley: University of California Press, 2001. Hancocks, director of the Open Range Zoo in Werribee, Australia, offers criticism of conventional zoos, although he praises certain model institutions such as the Bronx Zoo. He recommends that the zoo be reshaped into "a new type of institution . . . that . . . engenders respect for all animals and . . . interprets a holistic view of nature."

Hanson, Elizabeth. *Animal Attractions: Nature on Display in American Zoos,* rev. ed. Princeton, N.J.: Princeton University Press, 2004. This history of American zoos illuminates tensions in the meaning of nature in the city (for instance between wildness and civilization) by showing changes in the ways zoos have collected and displayed animals.

Hediger, Heini. *Wild Animals in Captivity.* New York: Dover Publications, 1964. This seminal book views zoo design from the perspective of ethology, the study of animal behavior in the wild. It maintains that zoo habitats should be made to look as natural as possible to the animals that live in them and to allow as many of the animals' natural behaviors as possible.

Heller, Bill. *After the Finish Line: The Race to End Horse Slaughter in America.* Irvine, Calif.: BowTie Press, 2005. If retired racehorses are unsuccessful at stud, they are often killed in slaughterhouses and sent to other countries as meat. Heller attacks that practice and urges passage of the Horse Slaughter Prevention Act, which would stop it.

Lee, Keekok. *Zoos: A Philosophical Tour.* New York: Palgrave Macmillan, 2005. Lee considers zoos from the standpoint of a philosopher, discussing what it is that zoos really conserve and what their moral duties are toward the animals they care for.

Ogorzaly, Michael A. *When Bulls Cry: The Case Against Bullfighting.* Bloomington, Ind.: AuthorHouse, 2006. Ogorzaly describes the history of bullfighting from an animal protection perspective, laying bare what he sees as its extreme cruelty.

Rothfels, Nigel. *Savages and Beasts: The Birth of the Modern Zoo.* Baltimore, Md.: Johns Hopkins University Press, 2002. This book profiles Carl Hagenbeck, who initiated the idea of modern, naturalistic zoos in Germany in the mid-19th century.

ARTICLES

Chaudhuri, Una. "Animal Acts for Changing Times." *American Theatre,* vol. 21, October 2004, pp. 36–40. In theater, as in other arts, use of animals as mirrors or metaphors of humanity is being replaced by a concern for animals in themselves. Humans gain a deeper understanding of both themselves and their relationship with alien-seeming "others" as a result.

Cohn, Jeffrey P. "Do Elephants Belong in Zoos?" *Bioscience,* vol. 56, September 2006, pp. 714–717. This article describes the differing perspectives of zoos and animal welfare advocates on the question of how elephants fare in captivity.

Harkinson, Josh. "The Killing Floor." *E*, vol. 17, June 30, 2006, pp. 32–39. Horse lovers and animal rights groups are trying to close horse slaughterhouses in the United States, but some fear that shutting down these operations will consign unwanted horses to an even worse fate.

Horwitch, Lauren. "Snakes on a Set: How the American Humane Association Protects Animals and Human Actors." *Back Stage West*, vol. 13, August 3, 2006, p. 5. Actors must learn how to interact with nonhuman costars in ways that promote safety for both parties.

Knipe, Tim. "Zoos Take Paws Before Going Wild." *Amusement Business*, vol. 117, June 2005, pp. 14–15. Driven by needs to increase revenue and compete with theme parks, zoos are balancing attempts to entertain visitors against animal welfare requirements.

Lloyd, Natalie. "'Among Birds and Beasts': Environmental Reform, Racial Preservation and Australian Progressives at the Zoological Gardens." *Journal of Australian Studies*, vol. 84, January 1, 2005, pp. 43–55. Lloyd describes the role of zoos in Australian cultural and environmental history and shows how changes in these institutions reflect changes in Australian society and in human-animal relationships.

Lubrano, Alfred. "Horse Racing Is Still Saddled by Cruelty Issue." *Philadelphia Inquirer*, May 27, 2006, n.p. Little evidence exists to show whether or not racing as a whole is cruel to horses.

Motavalli, Jim. "The High-Stakes Battle over Horse Slaughter." *E*, vol. 17, June 30, 2006, p. 38 ff. Animal rights organizations and others are trying to close the three remaining horse slaughterhouses in the United States, but they face an uphill battle.

Rees, Paul A. "The EC Zoos Directive: A Lost Opportunity to Implement the Convention on Biological Diversity." *Journal of International Wildlife Law and Policy*, vol. 8, January 1, 2005, pp. 51–62. This article considers the effectiveness of the European Commission's Zoos Directive in implementing the obligation, agreed upon by the international Convention on Biological Diversity in 1992, to protect biodiversity in the wild.

Stevenson, Miranda, and Daniel Turner. "Zoos: The Debate." *The Ecologist*, vol. 34, February 2004, pp. 20–23. Stevenson, director of the Federation of Zoos of Great Britain and Ireland, defends zoos' role in conservation, while Turner, coordinator of the Born Free Foundation, maintains that artificial environments are no substitute for preservation of animals in their native habitats.

WEB DOCUMENTS

Ahern, James J., et al. "The Unintended Consequences of a Ban on the Humane Slaughter (Processing) of Horses in the United States." Na-

tional Animal Interest Alliance. Available online. URL: http://www.naia
online.org/pdfs/AWC_UnintendedConsequences_5%5B1%5D.16.06.
pdf. Posted May 15, 2006. This report, prepared for the Animal Welfare
Council, claims that a ban on horse slaughter would result in accumula-
tion of unwanted horses which might then be neglected or abused because of lack of money to maintain them. Other negative economic
consequences would also ensue.

"Animals in Travelling Circuses: The Science on Suffering." Animal Defenders International. Available online. URL: http://www.ad-interna-
tional.org/admin/downloads/circuses_science_awb_lords_(low_res).pdf.
Posted May 17, 2006. This report discusses the effects of traveling, close
confinement, training and performance, inappropriate social groupings,
and isolation on both domestic and exotic species in circuses. It urges
prohibition of the use of animals in traveling circuses.

Berry, Christine. "The Slaughter of America's Horses—An American Tragedy." Equine Protection Network. Available online. URL: http://www.
equineprotectionnetwork.com/saveamericashorses/index.html. Accessed
December 30, 2006. Berry makes a personal plea for Congress to pass the
American Horse Slaughter Prevention Act, a law that would ban the
slaughter of unwanted horses for food.

Casamitjana, Jordi. "Aquatic Zoos (2): A Critical Study of Scottish Public
Aquaria in the Year 2004." Advocates for Animals. Available online. URL:
http://www.advocatesforanimals.org.uk/pdf/aquaticzoos2.pdf. Posted
2004. This animal rights group's report considers aquaria's effects on
animal welfare, conservation, education, and scientific research. It also
discusses exhibit design and interactions between visitors and animals. It
concludes by questioning the usefulness of public aquaria from an animal
welfare point of view.

"Everything You Need to Know About the Use of Animals in Circuses."
Animal Defenders International. Available online. URL: http://www.ad-
international.org/animals_in_entertainment/go.php?id=249&ssi=10.
Posted January 13, 2006. This series of linked pages presents reports,
videos, and still pictures showing the suffering of animals in traveling
circuses, which this animal welfare group says is inevitable even if the
circuses attempt to treat their animals well.

"Report on the Implementation of the EU Zoo Directive." Eurogroup for
Animals. Available online. URL: http://www.eurogroupforanimals.org/
policy/pdf/zooreportmar2006.pdf. Posted n March 2006. This report
examines member countries' implementation of the European Union's
1999 directive to maintain animals in zoos in ways that encourage preservation of wild species and respect the welfare of the captive animals. The
group's survey found that implementation of the directive is weak.

Annotated Bibliography

Rushton, Bruce. "Video Reveals Rodeo Abuse." Showing Animals Respect and Kindness. Available online. URL: http://www.sharkonline.org/?P=0000000536. Posted October 1, 2006. This article, which originally appeared in the Illinois *State Journal-Register*, reports that videos taken by an animal rights group appear to confirm cruelty to bulls during the National High School Finals Rodeo in Springfield in summer 2006.

"Solving the Problem of Unwanted Horses in America." Equine Protection Network. Available online. URL: http://www.equineprotectionnetwork.com/presentations/UnwantedHorseMay2005.pdf. Posted May 2005. This white paper from a horse protection organization recommends steps that horse owners and the horse industry can take to reduce the population of unwanted horses by means other than slaughter.

WILDLIFE

BOOKS

Adams, Clark E., Kieran J. Lindsey, and Sara J. Ash. *Urban Wildlife Management*. Washington, D.C.: CRC Press, 2006. This book considers human-wildlife interactions in cities and strategies for managing them from ecological, political, economic, and societal viewpoints.

Asa, Cheryl S., and Ingrid J. Porton, eds. *Wildlife Contraception: Issues, Methods, and Applications*. Baltimore, Md.: Johns Hopkins University Press, 2005. This book considers issues related to contraception in managing wildlife population size, including problems related to unrestricted population growth, the ethics of wildlife contraception, and issues affecting zoos and animal rights organizations.

Baron, David. *Beast in the Garden: A Modern Parable of Man and Nature*. New York: Norton, 2004. This book uses the environmentally conscious city of Boulder, Colorado, as a microcosm of the conflict between humans and mountain lions, which has increased as people move into lion habitats and endangers both species.

Belozerskaya, Marina. *The Medici Giraffe*. New York: Little, Brown and Co., 2006. The author uses exotic animals and different cultures' obsession with collecting them as a jumping-off point for examining the societies themselves.

Biel, Alice Wondrak. *Do (Not) Feed the Bears: The Fitful History of Wildlife and Tourists in Yellowstone*. Lawrence: University of Kansas Press, 2006. Biel uses the history of bears in Yellowstone National Park to illuminate the park's changing wildlife policies and ideologies and the way tourists and others have reacted to those changes.

Buchanan, Molly. *Safari: The Romance and the Reality*. Washington, D.C.: National Geographic, 2003. Buchanan considers the relationships among professional hunting, poaching, and ecotourism in attempts to preserve the wildlife of Africa, highlighting the difficulties of balancing human economics and animal needs.

Bulbeck, Chilla. *Facing the Wild: Ecotourism, Conservation and Animal Encounters*. London: Earthscan, 2005. Bulbeck considers why people seek out animals in their natural environment and whether viewing such animals actually changes their environmental perspectives and behavior.

CITES Handbook. Geneva, Switzerland: Convention on International Trade in Endangered Species of Wild Fauna and Flora, 2004. This handbook provides the most essential texts for implementation of this important international convention, including decisions made at the 13th conference of the parties to CITES in Bangkok in 2004.

Clayton, Michael. *Endangered Species: Foxhunting: The History, the Passion and the Fight for Survival*. Wykey, England: Country Books Direct, 2004. Clayton provides a history of British foxhunting in the 20th century from a pro-hunting point of view, criticizing groups who oppose the sport. He says that hunt supporters feel they are defending not merely an enjoyable activity but a way of life and view of the world.

Davies, Ben. *Black Market: Inside the Endangered Species Trade in Asia*. San Rafael, Calif.: Earth Aware Editions, 2005. Describing a grisly trade in detail, Davies issues an urgent call to save species in Asia that are threatened by poaching driven by a growing demand for animal parts used in traditional Asian medicine.

Dizard, Jan E. *Mortal Stakes: Hunters and Hunting in Contemporary America*. Amherst: University of Massachusetts Press, 2003. Hunting was once accepted without question as part of American life, but this is no longer the case. Dizard considers why this is so. He examines the role of hunting in the United States today, focusing on hunters' own views, through interviews, opinion surveys, and demographic statistics.

Fox, Camilla F., and Christopher F. Papouchis, eds. *Cull of the Wild: A Contemporary Analysis of Wildlife Trapping in the United States*. Animal Protection Institute, Sacramento, Calif.: 2004. This report presents the history of trapping in the United States, types of traps, state and international trapping standards, trapping in national wildlife refuges and other public lands, and how to target trapping through public policy.

Franke, Mary Ann. *To Save the Wild Bison: Life on the Edge in Yellowstone*. Norman: University of Oklahoma Press, 2005. Franke presents a history of the controversy over maintenance of wild bison in Yellowstone National Park, which involves the competing interests of environmentalists, property owners, and cattle ranchers as well as the animals themselves. She sees no easy solutions to the problem and feels that keeping the animals in natural conditions is almost impossible.

Annotated Bibliography

Frye, Bob. *Deer Wars: Science, Tradition, and the Battle over Managing White-tails in Pennsylvania*. University Park: Pennsylvania State University Press, 2006. The story of deer management in Pennsylvania in the 20th century is both complex and controversial, Frye explains. He shows the effects of deer management on the state's citizens and discusses the possibility of compromise on this contentious issue.

Ghrist, Tommy. *Fox Hunting: The Good Debate*. Murray, Iowa: Hillock House Press, 2004. This book focuses on the debate about fox hunting in Britain but also considers fox hunting in North America. It strongly supports traditional hunting and denounces the antihunting lobby.

Goble, Dale D., J. Michael Scott, and Frank W. Davis, eds. *The Endangered Species Act at Thirty: Vol. 1, Renewing the Conservation Promise*. Washington, D.C.: Island Press, 2006. The first of two volumes surveying issues surrounding the Endangered Species Act provides background on the act, its implementation, and the consequences thereof, and changes it has undergone and might benefit from undergoing in the future.

Great Ape Project Census. Seattle, Wash.: Great Ape Project, 2004. This book documents the living conditions of thousands of great apes in the United States. It also includes biographies of representative apes and essays by ape experts such as Jane Goodall.

Gunter, Michael M., Jr. *Building the Next Ark: How NGOs Work to Protect Biodiversity*. Hanover, N.H.: Dartmouth College Press, 2006. Gunter concludes that nongovernmental organizations (NGOs) offer the best hope for negotiating the powerful assortment of political and economic interests involved in species loss and preservation. He offers a detailed prescription for improving these organizations' effectiveness.

Herda-Rapp, Ann, and Theresa L. Goedeke, eds. *Mad About Wildlife: Looking at Social Conflict over Wildlife*. Boston: Brill Academic Publishers, 2005. Qualitative case studies show how social groups create opposing symbolic meanings for nature and explore the ways that these meanings affect ordinary citizens, wildlife management professionals, and wildlife itself.

Jones, Robert F., ed. *On Killing: Meditations on the Chase*. Guilford, Conn.: Lyons Press, 2005. Most of these short writings and excerpts favor or have mixed feelings about hunting for food or to eliminate pests; they often oppose recreational hunting, but not from an animal rights point of view.

Lapinski, Mike. *Grizzlies and Grizzled Old Men: A Tribute to Those Who Fought to Save the Great Bear*. Guilford, Conn., Falcon Publishing, 2006. This book profiles eight men and one woman who fought to change the belief, inherited from the 19th century, that grizzly bears should be exterminated. It also includes information about current grizzly conservationists and their efforts.

Manore, Jean L., and Dale G. Miner, eds. *The Culture of Hunting in Canada*. Vancouver, B.C., Canada: University of British Columbia Press, 2006.

This anthology presents different points of view on the history of hunting, hunting as a contemporary issue, and the social, political, and economic context of hunting in Canada.

Mauro, Anthony P., Sr. *The New Age Hunter*. New York: iUniverse, 2004. Mauro provides evidence to support his claim that hunters are essential guardians of healthy and balanced wildlife populations in the 21st century.

Medin, Douglas L., Norbert O. Ross, and Douglas G. Cox. *Culture and Resource Conflict: Why Meanings Matter*. New York: Russell Sage Foundation Publications, 2006. The authors show how the conflict between whites and Menominee Indians over hunting and fishing reveals both similarities and differences in the groups' attitudes about these activities. They use this conflict as an example of the way that misunderstandings, stereotyping, and mistrust contribute to culture clashes.

Osofsky, Steven A., et al., eds. *Conservation and Development Interventions at the Wildlife/Livestock Interface: Implications for Wildlife, Livestock and Human Health*. Gland, Switzerland: IUCN, 2005. African experts provide innovative suggestions for handling the conflicts between conservation, economic development, and human and animal health that beset that continent.

Posewitz, James. *Rifle in Hand: How Wild America Was Saved*. Helena, Mont.: Riverbend Publishing, 2004. Posewitz shows how certain hunters, such as Theodore Roosevelt and Aldo Leopold, played key roles in establishing the framework of wildlife conservation in the United States.

Scott, Michael J., Dale D. Goble, and Frank W. Davis, eds. *The Endangered Species Act at Thirty, vol. 2: Conserving Biodiversity in Human-Dominated Landscapes*. Washington, D.C.: Island Press, 2006. This book revisits basic questions in conservation and examines key policy tools available for protecting biodiversity in the United States.

Shogren, James F. *Species at Risk: Using Economic Incentives to Shelter Endangered Species on Private Lands*. Austin: University of Texas Press, 2005. This book discusses economic and other aspects of incentive programs designed by governments to motivate private landowners to protect endangered species on their land. It considers how to make such programs both more socially acceptable and more cost effective.

Silvius, Kirsten M., Richard E. Bodmer, and José M. Fragoso, eds. *People in Nature: Wildlife Conservation in South and Central America*. New York: Columbia University Press, 2004. This book describes both the historical development and the current state of unique South and Central American approaches to wildlife conservation.

Whisker, James B. *Hunting in the Western Tradition. Vol. 1: The Western Hunting Tradition*. Lewiston, N.Y.: Edwin Mellen Press, 2004. This book is the first of a four-volume series on the origin of American hunting rights. The author believes that the right to hunt is one of humankind's most substantial and ancient rights.

Annotated Bibliography

Wijnstekers, Willem. *The Evolution of CITES*, 8th ed. Lanham, Md.: Bernan Press, 2004. This books provides an accessible overview of the provisions of the Convention on International Trade in Endangered Species of Wild Fauna and Flora and related resolutions and decisions.

Wildlife Conservation Society. *State of the Wild: A Global Portrait of Wildlife, Wildlands, and the Oceans.* Washington, D.C.: Island Press, 2005. Including vital statistics from around the world and discussion of ways to assess the state of wildlife and wilderness, this volume, the first of a planned annual series, focuses on the impacts of hunting and the wildlife trade.

Woodroffe, Rosie, Simon Thirgood, and Alan Rabinowitz, eds. *People and Wildlife: Conflict or Coexistence?* New York: Cambridge University Press, 2005. This book presents a variety of solutions to the growing number of conflicts between humans and wildlife.

ARTICLES

Bean, Michael J. "The Endangered Species Act Under Threat." *BioScience*, vol. 56, February 2006, p. 98. Amendments to the Endangered Species Act passed by the House of Representatives in 2005 would limit the federal government's ability to protect endangered species on private land.

Blundell, Arthur G., and Michael B. Mascia. "Discrepancies in Reported Levels of International Wildlife Trade." *Conservation Biology*, vol. 19, December 2005, pp. 2020–2025. The authors say that discrepancies between U.S. customs data and data from CITES (the Convention on International Trade in Endangered Species of Wild Fauna and Flora) suggest that the risk of wildlife exploitation may be distorted.

Bosse, Sherry L. "Defenders of Wildlife vs. EPA: Testing the Boundaries of Federal Agency Power Under the ESA." *Environmental Law*, vol. 36, Summer 2006, pp. 1025–1063. This paper examines a decision made by the Ninth Circuit Court of Appeals in August 2005, which gave government agencies very broad authority to protect species under the Endangered Species Act.

Botello-Samson, Darren. "You Say Takings, and I Say Takings: The History and Potential of Regulatory Takings Challenges to the Endangered Species Act." *Duke Environmental Law and Policy Forum*, vol. 16, Spring 2006, pp. 293–343. Regulatory takings challenges, one of a number of tactics used by groups seeking judicial limitation of the Endangered Species Act, may increase in popularity because of shifts in the political environment.

Bulte, Ervin H., and Daniel Rondeau. "Why Compensating Wildlife Damages May Be Bad for Conservation." *Journal of Wildlife Management*, vol. 69, January 2005, pp. 14–16. Programs that compensate farmers and herders for damage done by wildlife have been promoted as ways to reduce conflict between humans and wild animals and promote conservation of large animals, but such programs may lead to wildlife overpopulation by reducing hunting pressure.

Burke, Marcilynn A. "Klamath Farmers and Cappucino Cowboys: The Rhetoric of the Endangered Species Act and Why It (Still) Matters." *Duke Environmental Law and Policy Forum*, vol. 14, Spring 2004, pp. 441–521. This article shows how political rhetoric has undermined the Endangered Species Act by claiming problems that do not really exist and proposing ill-advised solutions that protect property at the expense of endangered species. Defenders of the act need to recognize and counter such rhetoric.

Cooper, Mary H. "Endangered Species Act: The Issues." *CQ Researcher*, vol. 15, June 3, 2005, pp. 495–502. Issues examined include the question of whether the ESA has done enough to save endangered plants and animals and an evaluation of the scientific basis for the ESA's species listing and recovery plans.

Davidson, Steve. "Sustainable Use of Native Animals: A Great Debate." *Ecos*, vol. 123, January–March 2005, p. 34. Two recent reports from the Australian government show increasing support for sustainable use, as opposed to complete protection, of native species.

Doremus, Holly. "The Purposes, Effects, and Future of the Endangered Species Act's Best Available Science Mandate." *Environmental Law*, vol. 34, Spring 2004, pp. 397–450. The Endangered Species Act's mandate to use the "best available science" in making decisions about endangered species provides a useful case study of the role of science in environmental policy. Doremus discusses proposals to change the way scientific information is evaluated and used under the ESA.

"Endangered Species Act: Bush Policy." *CQ Researcher*, vol. 15, June 3, 2005, pp. 508–510. This article claims that several policies adopted or proposed by President George W. Bush and passed by Congress weaken key environmental protection laws and put additional pressure on struggling species.

"Endangered Species Act: Controversies." *CQ Researcher*, vol. 15, June 3, 2005, pp. 505–506. Legal protection of listed species' habitat under the Endangered Species Act has often led to heated arguments between environmentalists and advocates of property rights because habitat protection may restrict the use of landowners' property.

"Endangered Species Act: Has the Endangered Species Act Lived up to Its Mandate?" *CQ Researcher*, vol. 15, June 3, 2005, p. 509. This article presents a debate on whether the ESA has complied with its mandate to protect endangered and threatened species.

"Endangered Species Act: Species Status." *CQ Researcher*, vol. 15, June 3, 2005, pp. 507–508. Efforts to protect listed species over the past three decades have produced mixed results: the recovery of some species and loss of others.

Annotated Bibliography

Evans, Lloyd. "The Unspeakable in Pursuit of the Unspeakable." *Spectator*, vol. 299, November 26, 2005, pp. 22–23. Evans's experiences on a hunt convince him that the foxhunting ban in Britain has removed most action from legal hunts and left hunt supporters as embittered and marginalized as hunt saboteurs.

"Farmers Will Protect Endangered Species." *Western Farm Press*, July 28, 2005, n.p. This article provides an example that shows farmers cooperating in efforts to preserve a rare species, but the author says that the farmers' actions would have been prevented if the species had been listed under the Endangered Species Act. The author favors former California representative Richard Pombo's (R-Tracy) reform of the act, which was later passed by the House of Representatives, but stalled in the Senate.

Fischman, Robert L. "Predictions and Prescriptions for the Endangered Species Act." *Environmental Law*, vol. 34, Spring 2004, pp. 451–481. Fischman considers the ESA as an indicator of environmental law trends, presents three alternative views of the act's performance so far, and offers prescriptions for ESA reform in the areas of funding, limits to technology's ability to control habitat degradation, and preventive health care for biodiversity.

Glick, Daniel. "Back from the Brink." *Smithsonian*, vol. 36, September 2005, pp. 54–62. Glick profiles a number of endangered or threatened species that have made a comeback since the U.S. government and citizens began protecting species at the start of the 20th century.

Hart, David. "The Need to Hunt: Is Hunting Still a Relevant Tool for Wildlife Managers?" *Hunting*, vol. 33, February–March 2005, pp. 10–12. Populations of certain kinds of large wild animals are increasing, and so are dangerous encounters with humans and other problems. Controlled hunting seasons may be the best way to manage this increase.

Heffer, Simon. "Gunning for Game-Shooting." *Spectator*, vol. 298, August 27, 2005, pp. 14–15. Having banned foxhunting with dogs in Britain in 2004, animal rights activists now hope to stop the shooting of grouse and other game birds, or at least to end the breeding of such birds for hunting—and the Labour government, despite its protests to the contrary, may go along with them.

Hillgren, Sonja. "Endangered Species Act." *Farm Journal*, October 30, 2005, n.p. This article supports the efforts of former California Representative Richard Pombo (R-Tracy) and others to reform the Endangered Species Act, which limits the rights of farmers and others to develop private lands as they see fit.

"I'm Gonna Need to See Your DNA." *OnEarth*, vol. 27, Summer 2005, pp. 42–44. Genetic analysis is being used to remove federal protections from endangered species by showing that potentially endangered animals are too genetically similar to nonendangered ones elsewhere to be considered separate subspecies; however, this may not be a valid approach.

Kirkwood, Scott. "Too Much of a Good Thing?" *National Parks*, vol. 80, Fall 2006, pp. 8–10. Observers agree that the elk herd in Colorado's Rocky Mountain National Park is too large for the land to support, but deciding what to do about the problem is difficult.

Langpap, Christian, and JunJue Wu. "Voluntary Conservation of Endangered Species: When Does No Regulatory Assurance Mean No Conservation?" *Journal of Environmental Economics and Management*, vol. 47, May 2004, pp. 235–257. The authors analyze voluntary conservation agreements, which are becoming increasingly important in implementing the Endangered Species Act on private land. They conclude that the likelihood of establishing an effective agreement depends on the threat of regulation, the cost advantage offered by such agreements, and the availability of assurances that future regulation will not change the agreement.

Larson, Christina. "The Emerging Environmental Majority." *Washington Monthly*, vol. 38, May 2006, pp. 21–26. Hunters and environmentalists may be becoming more friendly because of shared concerns about global warming and other issues. The groups often united in environmental activities before the late 1970s, when animal rights groups began to oppose hunting.

Low, Bobbi S. "Human Behavior and Conservation." *Endangered Species Update*, vol. 21, January 1, 2004, pp. 14–22. Low considers strategies for overcoming the human conflicts of interest that hamper attempts to protect endangered species.

Marshall, Robert. "The Conservamentalists: Can the Sports and the Greens Find Common Ground?" *Field and Stream*, vol. 109, November 1, 2004, p. 28. The first American environmentalists were hunters. Mutual distrust developed between environmentalists and lovers of outdoor sports beginning in the 1960s, but today the two groups are cautiously approaching the idea of working together to protect wildlife and its habitat.

Maruca, Mary. "Room at the Table: Voices of NGOs." *Endangered Species Bulletin*, vol. 30, September 2005, pp. 20–21. Maruca interviews representatives of three nongovernmental organizations that have participated in deliberations concerning the Convention on International Trade in Endangered Species of Wild Fauna and Flora (CITES): Safari Club International, the Humane Society of the United States, and the World Wildlife Fund.

Mills, Christopher S. "Incentives and the ESA: Can Conservation Banking Live up to Its Potential?" *Duke Environmental Law and Policy Forum*, vol. 14, Spring 2004, pp. 523–561. Mills examines the evolution of habitat conservation plans and the "no surprises policy," amendments to the Endangered Species Act made in 1982, which provide incentives for landowners to cooperate in conserving endangered species on their land. He compares these policies with a new incentive approach, conservation banking.

Mukherjee, Pablo. "Nimrods: Hunting, Authority, Identity." *Modern Language Review*, vol. 100, October 1, 2005, 923–940. Mukherjee traces the roots of the passionate feelings aroused by the current controversy about foxhunting in Britain back to the 19th century, when a similar controversy occurred in an imperial context.

"Neda DeMayo (1960–)." *Biography Today*, vol. 15, April 2006, pp. 23–31. This article describes the life and career of Neda DeMayo, a U.S. wildlife conservationist whose specialty is preserving wild horse (mustang) communities.

Norris, Scott. "Only 30: A Portrait of the Endangered Species Act as a Young Law." *BioScience*, vol. 54, April 2004, pp. 288–294. This article evaluates the successes and failures of the Endangered Species Act and makes suggestions for improving the act's effectiveness and making it less divisive.

Nowicki, Brian. "Delays in Endangered Species Act Protections Lead to Extinctions." *Earth Island Journal*, vol. 19, Autumn 2004, pp. S6–7. According to a report by the Center for Biological Diversity, 49 plants and animals in the United States went extinct while the federal government delayed classifying them as endangered under the Endangered Species Act, thus denying them legal protection. The report claims that in many cases the neglect was intentional.

Plater, Zygmunt J. B. "Endangered Species Act Lessons over 30 Years, and the Legacy of the Snail Darter, a Small Fish in a Pork Barrel." *Environmental Law*, vol. 34, Spring 2004, pp. 289–308. The Endangered Species Act has become more complex and politicized in 30 years, but industrial foes of regulation still use it and the pivotal 1970s court case that pitted the snail darter against the Tellico Dam as a way to misrepresent and trivialize environmental laws in general.

Raloff, Janet. "A Galling Business: The Inhumane Exploitation of Bears for Traditional Asian Medicine." *Science News*, vol. 168, October 15, 2005, pp. 250–252. Bear gall and gallbladders are popular in Asian medicine, but obtaining the gall causes great suffering for farmed bears in Asia as well as a thriving market in parts from killed bears in the United States.

Raymond, Leigh. "Cooperation Without Trust: Overcoming Collective Action Barriers to Endangered Species Protection." *Policy Studies Journal*, vol. 34, February 2006, pp. 37–57. A study of habitat conservation plans, a method of implementing the Endangered Species Act that often requires cooperation among hostile groups, suggests that trust among those involved in the plans is less important to the plans' success than targeted economic incentives for cooperation and political leadership's assumption of some of the initial costs of cooperation.

Schlickeisen, Roger. "The Endangered Species Act at 30." *Earth Island Journal*, vol. 19, Autumn 2004, pp. S2–3. For the benefit of the president's special-interest supporters, the George W. Bush administration has made unprecedentedly relentless and all-encompassing attacks on the Endangered Species Act.

Animal Rights

Simmons, Daniel R., and Randy T. Simmons. "The Endangered Species Act Turns 30." *Regulation*, vol. 26, Winter 2003, pp. 6–8. The authors decry the ESA's limitation of private landowners' rights, which they say does a disservice to the species the act is supposed to protect because landowners often preemptively destroy habitat or kill animals in order to avoid the law's onerous regulations.

Stanley, Denise L. "Local Perception of Public Goods: Recent Assessments of Willingness-to-Pay for Endangered Species." *Contemporary Economic Policy*, vol. 23, April 2005, pp. 165–179. Stanley compares the results of a 2001 survey in Orange County, California, with national surveys and concludes that, although the public says it is willing to pay to preserve endangered species and biodiversity, the amounts of money specified probably would not be large enough to pay for acquisition of necessary habitat.

Taylor, Martin F. J., Kieran F. Suckling, and Jeffrey J. Rachlinski. "The Effectiveness of the Endangered Species Act: A Quantitative Analysis." *BioScience*, vol. 55, April 2005, pp. 360–367. Early listing, designation of critical habitat, and dedicated recovery plans (especially those aimed at a single species rather than multiple species) all improve the chances of survival for endangered and threatened species. Results of the analysis show that the Endangered Species Act can be effective in protecting species, and the authors recommend increased funding for earlier listing of species and prompt provision of critical habitat and recovery plans.

Tisdell, C., C. Wilson, and H. Swarna Nantha. "Public Choice of Species for the 'Ark': Phylogenetic Similarity and Preferred Wildlife Species for Survival." *Journal for Nature Conservation*, vol. 54, July 2006, n.p. This article reports results of a survey of 204 Australians, who were asked to choose native animal species for saving in a hypothetical "ark." Species most similar to humans—that is, mammals—were overrepresented in the respondents' choices, but reptiles and birds were also supported.

Van Norman, Tim. "Fact or Fiction: CITES and the ESA." *Endangered Species Update*, vol. 23, January 1, 2006, pp. S8–9. The chief of the Branch of Permits in the U.S. Fish and Wildlife Service's Division of International Affairs clears up misconceptions about the respective roles of CITES (the Convention on International Trade in Endangered Species of Wild Fauna and Flora) and the Endangered Species Act in regulating actions involving movement of endangered species between the United States and other countries.

Woodard, Colin. "Can Whaling Be Sustainable?" *E*, vol. 15, April 30, 2004 p. 10. Anti-whaling organizations contend that whale hunting is a barbaric practice, but whalers in Iceland and Norway argue that harvesting relatively abundant minke whales is more humane and environmentally sound than factory farming. Woodard discusses several concerns and implications of the issue.

WEB DOCUMENTS

"Caught in the Web: Wildlife Trade on the Internet." International Fund for Animal Welfare. Available online. URL: http://www.caughtintheweb. co.uk/atf/cf/{9FDE63D6-73CA-4D8C-BB39-D60BCCC83E28}/Intern et%20Trade%20Report%20FINAL.pdf. Posted July 2005. This report describes a three-month investigation of five categories of animals and animal products: live primates, ivory items, turtle and tortoise products, bags and fashion items made from endangered reptiles, and wild cats. It states that Internet trade is a major threat to endangered species.

"Conservation Profiles: Landowners Help Imperiled Wildlife." U.S. Fish and Wildlife Service. Available online. URL: http://www.fws.gov/ endangered/pubs/Safe%20Harbor/SafeHarbor.pdf. Accessed December 31, 2006. This brochure describes landowners who are using Safe Harbor Agreements and Candidate Conservation Agreements with Assurances, two amendments to the Endangered Species Act designed to encourage landowners to conserve species while protecting their own interests.

"The Fur Trade." World Animal Net. Available online. URL: http://world-animal.net/fur-trade.html. Accessed December 28, 2006. This report describes the overall structure of the industry (which the sponsoring group opposes), trapping of wild animals for their fur, fur farming, and uses of fur.

Greenwald, D. Noah, and Kieran F. Suckling. "Progress or Extinction? A Systematic Review of the U.S. Fish and Wildlife Service's Endangered Species Act Listing Program 1974–2004." Center for Biological Diversity. Available online. URL: http://www.biologicaldiversity.org/swcbd/ press/ESAreport-revised.pdf. Posted May 2005. This paper details negligence of the U.S. Fish and Wildlife Service in preserving endangered species during the George W. Bush administration, as compared with previous administrations.

Hindi, Steve. "What's the Matter with Government Deer Culls?" Showing Animals Respect and Kindness. Available online. URL: http://www.shar-konline.org/?P=0000000428. Accessed December 31, 2006. Using the example of an incident in Lake County, Illinois, during the winter of 2000, this animal advocacy group claims that deer management programs, far from being efficient and humane ways to control overpopulation, are simply "mass slaughters."

Hood, Laura C. "Frayed Safety Nets: Conservation Planning Under the Endangered Species Act." Defenders of Wildlife. Available online. URL: http://www.defenders.org/pubs/hcp01.html. Accessed December 31,

2006. This report exhaustively examines a representative sample of Habitat Conservation Plans, authorized under Section 10 of the Endangered Species Act and promoted by the Clinton administration as a solution to the problem of saving endangered species on private property. It identifies aspects of the plans that should be emulated or avoided in the future.

"How CITES Works." Convention on International Trade in Endangered Species of Wild Fauna and Flora. Available online. URL: http://www.cites.org/eng/disc/how.shtml. Accessed December 31, 2006. CITES works by subjecting international trade in specimens of selected species to certain controls. The species covered by CITES are listed in three appendices to the convention, according to the degree of protection they need. This paper describes the CITES licensing system and the management and scientific authorities who administer it, as well as explaining the classification of endangered species in the convention's appendices.

"How Ducks Unlimited Conserves." Ducks Unlimited. Available online. URL: http://www.ducks.org/Conservation/HowWeConserve/1598/How WeConserveHome.html. Accessed December 31, 2006. This web page explains how the hunting group preserves habitat and protects duck species.

"The Killing Game: Out of Control Predator Control." League Against Cruel Sports. Available online. URL: http://league.org.uk/uploads/documents/doc_297.pdf. Accessed December 31, 2006. This report describes types of snares and traps and the snaring of foxes and birds of prey in different parts of Britain. It calls for a ban on snaring.

"The Killing Game 2: Bred to Be Wasted." League Against Cruel Sports. Available online. URL: http://league.org.uk/uploads/documents/doc_298.pdf. Accessed December 31, 2006. An undercover investigation by the league revealed cruelty, cannibalism, and overcrowding inside British gamebird rearing estates.

Lerner, Jeff, Bobby Cochran, and Julia Michalak. "Conservation Across the Landscape: A Review of the State Wildlife Action Plans." Defenders of Wildlife. Available online. URL: http://www.defenders.org/statewildlife-plans/report.pdf. Posted March 2006. This paper reviews state wildlife action plans, an important part of the State Wildlife Grants Program, which Congress created in 2000. The authors conclude that the plans vary widely in their approaches, in their effectiveness in guiding strategic action for wildlife conservation, and their likelihood of being implemented successfully. They do not yet add up to a national strategy for conservation.

"On the Front Foot: A New Way Forward for Shooting." Countryside Alliance. Available online. URL: http://www.countryside-alliance.org.uk/images/stories/pdf/c_s_on_the_front_foot.pdf. Accessed December 22,

2006. This position paper suggests public relations and advertising campaigns to defend and preserve game shooting.

"Protected Species: International Convention and U.S. Laws Protect Wildlife Differently." General Accounting Office. Available online. URL: http://www.gao.gov/new.items/d04964.pdf. Posted September 2004. This government agency's report discusses changes in implementation of the Convention on International Trade in Endangered Species of Wild Fauna and Flora (CITES) and U.S. funding and other resources spent on activities related to the convention. It also compares CITES and the Endangered Species Act.

Roberts, Adam M. "Shackled or Shot: Global Threats to Elephants and Conservation Strategies to Save Them." Born Free USA. Available online. URL: http://www.bornfreeusa.org/pdf/shackled-or-shot.pdf. Posted fall 2005. This article makes recommendations for a long-term, integrated global strategy to conserve elephants and counter the increased killing of elephants by farmers and other landowners with whom the animals come in conflict.

"The Silent Killer: Can the Code of Practice Stop Cruelty?" League Against Cruel Sports. Available online. URL: http://www.league.org.uk/uploads/documents/doc_403.pdf. Posted 2006. This group, which opposes hunting, trapping, and related activities, investigated commercial shooting estates using snares in England, Scotland, and Wales in 2006. It found that 78 percent of the estates were "blatantly ignoring" the code of conduct for snare use published by the British government's Department for Environment, Food and Rural Affairs (DEFRA). It claims, therefore, that codes of conduct such as DEFRA's are not enforceable and that snares should be banned completely.

Snape, William II, Michael Senatore, and John M. Carter II. "Sabotaging the Endangered Species Act: How the Bush Administration Uses the Judicial System to Undermine Wildlife Protections." Defenders of Wildlife. URL: http://www.defenders.org/wildlife/esa/report/report.pdf. Posted fall 2003. This third report of the Defenders of Wildlife Judicial Accountability Project continues the project's critical examination of the George W. Bush administration's environmental record by focusing on the administration's arguments in federal court cases dealing with the Endangered Species Act.

"Trapping Facts." National Trappers Association. Available online. URL: http://www.nationaltrappers.com/facts.html. Accessed December 31, 2006. On this web page, a group that supports trapping refutes statements by the Humane Society of the United States, which opposes the activity.

CHAPTER 8

ORGANIZATIONS AND AGENCIES

Many organizations and groups handle various aspects of animal protectionism and uses of animals. The following entries include general-purpose animal welfare and animal rights organizations and also organizations related to animals and animal use in particular areas: companion animals, animals in agriculture, animals in science, animals in entertainment, and wildlife. These latter organizations, which include advocacy groups, trade organizations, and government agencies, may favor or oppose animal use to varying degrees or hold a neutral position on the subject. Most organizations described in this chapter are located in the United States, but some groups in Britain, Canada, and other countries are also listed. In keeping with the widespread use of the Internet and e-mail, the web site address (URL) and e-mail address of each organization are given first (when available), followed by the phone number, postal address, and a brief description of the organization's work or position. When calling an organization in another country, please locate and use the appropriate country code, which is not included. These codes may vary depending on which country one is calling from.

GENERAL-PURPOSE ANIMAL ORGANIZATIONS

Advocates for Animals
URL: http://www.
  advocatesforanimals.org.uk
E-mail: info@
  advocatesforanimals.org
Phone: (0) 131-225-6039
10 Queensferry Street
Edinburgh EH2 4PG, Scotland
Moderate animal rights group that encourages rational discussion by people on both sides of issues such as the use of animals in research.

American Society for the Prevention of Cruelty to Animals
URL: http://www.aspca.org/
E-mail: information@aspca.org
Phone: (212) 876-7700
424 East 92nd Street
New York, NY 10128-6804

Exists to promote humane principles, prevent cruelty, and alleviate fear, pain, and suffering in animals. Protests cruelty to animals in entertainment and distributes educational materials on treatment of companion animals.

Animal Aid
URL: http://www.animalaid.org.uk
E-mail: info@animalaid.org.uk
Phone: (0) 173-236-4546
The Old Chapel
Bradford Street
Tonbridge, Kent TN9 1AW, UK
Britain's largest animal rights group. Campaigns against all forms of animal abuse, including factory farming, vivisection, and hunting, and promotes a cruelty-free lifestyle.

Animal Alliance of Canada
URL: http://www.animalalliance.ca
E-mail: info@animalalliance.ca
Phone: (416) 462-9541
221 Broadview Avenue
Suite 101
Toronto, Ontario
Canada M4M 2G3
Organization of professionals in animal protection. Works on local, national, and international educational and legislative advocacy initiatives to protect animals and the environment. Opposes killing, eating, wearing, experimenting on, and exploiting animals.

Animal Defenders International
URL: http://www.ad-international.org/home

Phone: (415) 876-2344
953 Mission Street
Suite 201
San Francisco, CA 94103
This group is associated with the National Anti-Vivisection Society (Britain). Issues it covers include animals in entertainment (especially circuses), research on animals (with a focus on research on primates), animal rescues, farm animals, fur, and conservation.

Animal Legal Defense Fund
URL: http://www.aldf.org
E-mail: info@aldf.org
Phone: (707) 795-2533
170 East Cotati Avenue
Cotati, CA 94931
Uses litigation and legal advocacy both to defend the interests of particular animals or groups of animals and to reform the field of animal law. Particular aims are to ensure that anticruelty statutes are enforced and strengthened and to end animals' legal status as property.

Animal Liberation Front
URL: http://www.animalliberationfront.com
E-mail: annxtberlin@gmail.com
Carries out direct action against those it classifies as animal abusers, including rescuing animals and destroying property. Advocates illegal (but nonviolent) actions when necessary to force exploitative companies out of business. Consists of small, autonomous, anonymous groups worldwide.

Animal Protection Institute
URL: http://www.api4animals.
org
E-mail: info@api4animals.org
Phone: (916) 447-3085
1122 S Street
Sacramento, CA 95814
P.O. Box 22505
Sacramento, CA 95822
Campaigns for protection of wild-
life, companion animals, and ani-
mals in agriculture, entertainment,
science, and education.

Animals and Society Institute
URL: http://www.animalsand
society.org
E-mail: office@animalsand
society.org
Phone: (734) 677-9240
2512 Carpenter Road
Suite 201-A2
Ann Arbor, MI 48108
The Institute for Animals and Soci-
ety merged with the Society and
Animals Forum to form this think
tank that focuses on institutional
change.

Animals Australia
URL: http://www.
animalsaustralia.org
E-mail: enquiries@
animalsaustralia.org
37 O'Connell Street
North Melbourne, Victoria,
Australia 3051
The Australian arm of the Australian
and New Zealand Federation of Animal Societies, Inc. (ANZFAS). It
presents the point of view of approximately 40 animal protection

groups in Australia and New Zealand on a variety of animal welfare
issues to government, the media,
animal users, and the general public.

Animal Welfare Institute
URL: http://www.awionline.org
E-mail: awi@awionline.org
Phone: (703) 836-4300
P.O. Box 3650
Washington, DC 20027
Does not oppose human uses of
animals but works to see that those
uses are carried out in ways that
cause as little pain and fear to the
animals as possible. Issues include
animals in science, endangered species and trade in wildlife, and animals in agriculture. Incorporated
the Society for Animal Protective
Legislation in 2003.

**Canadian Federation of
Humane Societies**
URL: http://cfhs.ca
E-mail: info@cfhs.ca
Phone: (613) 224-8072
102-30 Concourse Gate
Ottawa, Ontario
Canada K2E 7V7
National voice on animal welfare
issues that represents more than
100 member societies. Works to
end suffering of companion ani-
mals, wildlife, and animals in enter-
tainment, farming, and research.

**Department for Environment,
Food, and Rural Affairs
(DEFRA)**
URL: http://www.defra.gov.uk
E-mail: helpline@defra.gsi.gov.uk
Phone: (0) 845-933-5577

Customer Contact Unit
Eastbury House
30-34 Albert Embankment
London SE1 7TL, UK
DEFRA, a department of the British government, regulates (among other things) the welfare of farm animals and the hunting and trapping of wildlife. Its goal is sustainable development.

Eurogroup for Animals
URL: http://www.
  eurogroupforanimals.org
E-mail: info@
  eurogroupforanimals.org
Phone: (2) 740-0820
6 rue des Patriotes
B-1000 Brussels, Belgium
Aims to influence and promote introduction, implementation, and enforcement of animal protection legislation in the European Union.

Friends of Animals
URL: http://www.
  friendsofanimals.org
E-mail: info@ friendsofanimals.
  org
Phone: (203) 656-1522
777 Post Road, Suite 205
Darien, CT 06820
Works to preserve animals and their habitats around the world and protect them from abuse and institutionalized exploitation. Campaign issues include spay/neuter, antifur, antihunting, vegetarianism, wildlife protection, and circus animals.

Great Ape Project
URL: http://www.
  greatapeproject.org

E-mail: info@greatapeproject.
  org
Phone: (206) 579-5975
806A NW 51st Street
Seattle, WA 98107
Seeks to locate, identify, and tell the stories of individual nonhuman great apes. Works to extend legal rights to great apes.

The Humane Society of the
  United States
URL: http://www.hsus.org
Phone: (202) 452-1100
2100 L Street, NW
Washington, DC 20037
Encourages a strong human-animal bond but wants human relationships with animals to be guided by compassion. Issues of interest include pets, wildlife, animals in research, farm animals, animals in circuses, the fur trade, and the connection between animal abuse and human violence.

Humane USA Political Action
  Committee
URL: http://www.humaneusa.
  org
E-mail: humaneusa@humane
  usa.org
P.O. Box 19224
Washington, DC 20036
Nation's first major political action committee devoted to election of humane-minded candidates at federal and state levels. Represents numerous animal protection organizations. Issues of concern include treatment of companion animals, farm animals, and wildlife.

In Defense of Animals
URL: http://www.idausa.org
E-mail: idainfo@idausa.org
Phone: (415) 388-9641
3010 Kerner Boulevard
San Rafael, CA 94901
Campaign issues include animals in sport, animals in experimentation, dissection, circuses, marine mammals, and puppy mills.

The International Institute for Animal Law
URL: http://www.
    animallawintl.org
E-mail: info@AnimalLawIntl. org
Phone: (312) 917-8850
30 North LaSalle Street
Suite 2900
Chicago, IL 60602
Encourages development of legal scholarship and advocacy skills on behalf of animals internationally. Works to enhance development of laws that promote animal welfare, particularly regarding companion animals and animals in laboratories.

Jane Goodall Institute
URL: http://www.janegoodall.org
Phone: (703) 682-9220
4245 North Fairfax Drive
Suite 600
Arlington, VA 22203
Educates people to improve the environment of all living things. Issues of concern include primate habitat conservation, promoting the welfare of chimpanzees and other primates, and encouragement of noninvasive research programs on primates.

National Animal Interest Alliance
URL: http://www.naiaonline.org
E-mail: ideas@naiaonline.org
Phone: (503) 761-1139
P.O. Box 66579
Portland, OR 97266
Association of business, agricultural, scientific, and recreational interests working to present a moderate alternative to animal rights groups and correct animal rights misinformation.

National Center for Animal Law
URL: http://www.lclark.edu/
    org/ ncal
E-mail: ncal@lclark.edu
Phone: (503) 768-6849
Lewis and Clark Law School
10015 Southwest Terwilliger
    Boulevard
Portland, OR 97219
Promotes legal education for animal advocacy, furthers the field of animal law, and promotes animal rights.

North American Animal Liberation Press Office
URL: http://www.animal
    liberationpressoffice.org
E-mail: press@animalliberation
    pressoffice.org
Phone: (818) 227-5022
6320 Canoga Avenue
Suite 1500
Woodland Hills, CA 91306
This small organization communicates the actions, strategies, and philosophy of the animal liberation movement, especially that of radical

groups such as the Animal Liberation Front, to the public and the media.

**People for the Ethical
    Treatment of Animals**
URL: http://www.peta.org
Phone: (757) 622-7382
501 Front Street
Norfolk, VA 23510
Believes that animals are not for humans to eat, wear, experiment on, or use for entertainment. Conducts numerous campaigns to educate policy makers and the public about animal abuse.

Protecting Animals in Democracy
URL: http://www.vote4animals.
    org.uk
E-mail: pad@vote4animals.org.uk
Phone: (0) 114-272-2220
9 Bailey Lane
Sheffield S1 4EG, UK
This group, established by the animal rights organization Uncaged, urges citizens to pressure their representatives in Parliament to pass legislation that will improve animal welfare and rights.

**Royal Society for the Prevention
    of Cruelty to Animals**
URL: http://www.rspca.org.uk
Phone: 0870-333-5999
Wilberforce Way
Southwater, Horsham
West Sussex RH13 9RS, UK
Animal protection organization devoted to preventing cruelty to animals, promoting kindness, and

finding new homes for abandoned animals. Consults on treatment of farm animals, animals in research, pets, and wildlife.

**Universities Federation
    for Animal Welfare**
URL: http://www.ufaw.org.uk
E-mail: ufaw@ufaw.org.uk
Phone: (0) 158-283-1818
The Old School
Brewhouse Hill
Wheathampstead
Hertfordshire AL4 8AN, UK
Provides scientific and technical expertise to help others improve the welfare of companion animals, wildlife, and animals in zoos, laboratories, and farms.

**U.S. Department of Agriculture
Agricultural Research Service**
URL: http://www.ars.usda.gov/
Jamie L. Whitten Building
1400 Independence Avenue, SW
Washington, DC 20250
The Agricultural Research Service has programs related to food animal health and welfare.

**U.S. Department of Agriculture
Animal Welfare Information
    Center**
URL: awic.nal.usda.gov/
E-mail: awic@nal.usda.gov
Phone: (301) 504-6212
National Agricultural Library
10301 Baltimore Avenue
Room 410
Beltsville, MD 20705
The Animal Welfare Information Center, part of the USDA's Na-

tional Agricultural Library, provides information for improved animal care and use in science, agriculture, and entertainment.

U.S. Department of Agriculture Animal and Plant Health Inspection Service (APHIS) Animal Welfare
URL: http://www.aphis.usda. gov/animal-welfare/
E-mail: ace@ aphis.usda.gov
Phone: (301) 734-7833
4700 River Road, Unit 84
Riverdale, MD 20737-1234
APHIS is the agency of the U.S. Department of Agriculture that administers and enforces the Animal Welfare Act and the Twenty-eight-Hour Law. This is its chief animal care site, which contains numerous resources.

World Animal Foundation
URL: http://www. worldanimalfoundation. homestead.com/index.html
5725 Liberty Avenue
Vermillion, OH 44089
Works for wildlife and habitat preservation and animals rights issues worldwide. Activities include education, research, investigations, animal rescue, legislation, events and media campaigns, and direct action.

World Animal Net
URL: http://www. worldanimal.net
E-mail: info@worldanimal.net
Phone: (617) 524-3670
19 Chestnut Square
Boston, MA 02130
World's largest network of animal protection societies, with more than 2,000 affiliates in more than 100 countries. Acts as information clearinghouse and coordinator to increase impact of animal protection campaigns and lobbying.

World Society for the Protection of Animals
URL: http://wspa.org.uk/index. asp
E-mail: press@wspa.org.uk
Phone: (0) 207-587-5000
89 Albert Embankment
London SE1 7TP, UK
This organization promotes animal welfare in countries where few laws to protect animals exist. It focuses on companion animals, commercial exploitation of wildlife, farm animals, and disaster relief for animals.

COMPANION ANIMALS

Alley Cat Allies
URL: http://www.alleycat.org
Phone: (240) 482-1980
7920 Norfolk Avenue
Suite 600
Bethesda, MD 20814-2525
Clearinghouse for information on feral and stray cats. Supports reduc-

ing feral cat population by trapping, neutering, and then returning feral cats to their colonies.

American Humane Association
URL: http://www.american
  humane.org/site/PageServer
Phone: (303) 792-9900
63 Inverness Drive East
Englewood, CO 80112
Established in 1877 as an association of more than 25 humane organizations, this group works to prevent abuse of both children and animals. It deals with farm animals and animals in entertainment as well as companion animals in shelters and elsewhere. The organization also explores links among different types of family violence, including cruelty to companion animals.

American Partnership for Pets
URL: http://www.
  americanpartnershipforpets.org
E-mail: info@
  americanpartnershipforpets.org
Prevent-a-Litter Coalition, Inc.
2579 John Milton Drive
Suite 105, PMB 143
Herndon, VA 20171
Coalition of animal, veterinarian, and fancier organizations that supports spay/neuter programs to prevent unwanted and homeless pets.

American Sanctuary Association
URL: http://www.asasanctuaries.
  org
E-mail: ASARescue@aol.com
Phone: (702) 804-8562

2308 Chatfield Drive
Las Vegas, NV 89128
Information center, accreditation establishment, and organizational network for organizations that provide sanctuaries for homeless wild and domestic animals. Also helps people locate quality facilities in which to place animals.

Maddie's Fund
URL: http://www.maddiesfund.
  org/
E-mail: info@maddiesfund.org
Phone: (510) 337-8988
2223 Santa Clara Avenue
Suite B
Alameda, CA 94501-4416
Founded by Dave and Cheryl Duffield of PeopleSoft in honor of their miniature schnauzer, this organization works for no-kill shelters and rescue of homeless dogs and cats.

National Animal Control
  Association
URL: http://www.nacanet.org
E-mail: naca@interserv.com
Phone: (913) 768-1319
P.O. Box 480851
Kansas City, MO 64148
Professional association for animal control personnel. Provides training programs, a voluntary certification program for animal control facilities, and education to promote responsible animal ownership.

National Council on Pet
  Population Study and Policy
URL: http://www.petpopulation.
  org

E-mail: ncppsp@aol.com
Sally Fekety Bolgos, Consultant
P.O. Box 131488
Ann Arbor, MI 48113-1488
Gathers and analyzes reliable data to determine the number, disposi- tion, and origin of pet cats and dogs in the United States and uses this information to encourage respon- sible stewardship of these animals and recommend methods of reduc- ing the number of unwanted pets.

ANIMALS IN AGRICULTURE

American Farm Bureau
URL: http://www.fb.org
E-mail: webmaster@fb.org
Phone: (202) 406-3600
600 Maryland Avenue, SW
Suite 1000W
Washington, DC 20024
This farm and ranch trade organiza- tion supports, among other things, reform of the Endangered Species Act to make it less hard on farmers and other private landowners.

American Meat Institute
URL: http://www.meatami.com
Phone: (202) 587-4200
1150 Connecticut Avenue, NW
12th Floor
Washington, DC 20036
Oldest and largest U.S. meat and poultry trade association. Its web site includes material on meat ani- mal welfare.

Animal Agriculture Alliance
URL: http://www.
  animalagalliance.org
E-mail: info@animalagalliance.org
Phone: (703) 562-5160
P.O. Box 9522
Arlington, VA 22209

Formerly Animal Industry Founda- tion. Works to provide positive in- formation about animal agriculture to the media and consumers.

Center for Consumer Freedom
URL: http://www.consumer
  freedom.com
Phone: (202) 463-7112
P.O. Box 34557
Washington, DC 20043
This nonprofit coalition of restau- rants, food companies, and consum- ers opposes demands from animal rights activists and others who want to reform the food industry.

Coalition to Abolish the Fur Trade
URL: http://www.caft.org.uk
E-mail: caft@caft.org.uk
Phone: (0) 845-330-7955
P.O. Box 38
Manchester M60 1NX, UK
Uses investigations, educational and political campaigns, and demonstra- tions to oppose fur farming and the fur trade in Britain and worldwide.

Compassion in World Farming
URL: http://www.ciwf.co.uk
Phone: (0) 1483-521-950

River Court
Mill Lane
Godalming, Surrey GU7 1EZ, UK
Campaigns for welfare of animals in intensive farming through peaceful protest, lobbying, and education, including scientific reports.

Compassion Over Killing
URL: http://www.cok.net
E-mail: info@cok.net
Phone: (301) 891-2458
P.O. Box 9773
Washington, DC 20016
Focuses primarily on cruelty to animals in agriculture and promotes a vegetarian diet as an alternative to eating animals, but also opposes using animals for fur, circus entertainment, and so on.

Council for Agricultural Science and Technology
URL: http://www.cast-science.org
E-mail: info@cast-science.org
4420 West Lincoln Way
Ames, IA 50014-3447
Assembles, interprets, and communicates science-based information on agricultural and related issues to policy makers, the media, and the public. Composed of scientific societies and individuals.

Farm Animal Welfare Council
URL: http://www.fawc.org.uk
Phone: (0) 207-904-6534
1A Page Street
Fifth Floor
London SW1P 4PQ, UK
Independent advisory body established by the British government in 1979 to keep under review the welfare of farm animals throughout their lives and advise the government of any legislative or other changes that may be necessary.

Farm Animal Welfare Network
URL: www.fawn.me.uk
Fax: 014-846-8408
P.O. Box 40
Holmfirth
HD9 3YY, UK
Opposes cruelty to animals imposed by intensive ("factory") farming.

Farm Sanctuary
URL: http://www.farmsanctuary.org
E-mail: info@farmsanctuary.org
Phone: (607) 583-2225
P.O. Box 150
Watkins Glen, NY 14891
Runs shelters for abused farm animals and campaigns to stop animal cruelty on farms and promote a vegan lifestyle.

Food Animal Initiative
URL: http://www.faifarms.co.uk
E-mail: enquiries@faifarms.co.uk
Phone: (0) 186-579-0880
The Field Station
Wytham, Oxford OX2 8QJ, UK
This organization was set up by farmers to encourage use of alternative farming systems that, among other things, increase the welfare of farm animals.

Food Marketing Institute
URL: http://www.fmi.org
E-mail: fmi@fmi.org
Phone: (202) 452-8444
2345 Crystal Drive
Suite 800
Arlington, VA 22202-4801
Conducts programs in research, education, industry relations, and public affairs on behalf of its member companies, which are food retailers and wholesalers throughout the world.

Fur Commission USA
URL: http://www.
furcommission.com
E-mail: info@
furcommission.com
Phone: (619) 575-0139
Teresa Platt, Executive
Director
PMB 506
826 Orange Avenue
Coronado, CA 92118-2698
Represents fur farmers in the United States. Certifies farmers who follow superior standards of animal husbandry and educates the public about responsible fur farming and the merits of fur.

Humane Farming Association
URL: http://www.hfa.org/about/
index.html
E-mail: hfa@hfa.org
Phone: (415) 771-2253
P.O. Box 3577
San Rafael, CA 94912
Aims to protect farm animals from cruelty, humans from dangerous chemicals fed to farm animals, and the environment from pollution by intensive farming. Carries out in-

vestigations, exposés, media campaigns, rescues, and lobbying.

Institute for Animal Health
URL: http://www.iah.bbsrc. ac.uk
E-mail: animal.health@bbsrc.
ac.uk
Phone: (0) 163-557-8411
Compton Laboratory
Compton, Newbury
Berkshire RG20 7NN, UK
Government-sponsored group dedicated to improving the health and welfare of farm animals and improving the efficiency and sustainability of livestock farming.

**National Cattlemen's
Beef Association**
URL: http://www.beef.org
Phone: (303) 694-0305
9110 E. Nichols Avenue #300
Centennial, CO 80112
Works to preserve and enhance the business and market climate for cattle producers by managing public policy issues, including attacks by animal rightists.

National Chicken Council
URL: http://www.national
chickencouncil.com
E-mail: ncc@chickenusa.org
Phone: (202) 296-2622
1015 15th Street, NW
Suite 930
Washington, DC 20005-2622
Nonprofit trade association representing the chicken industry in the United States that promotes and protects the industry, including defending it against criticism by animal rights activists.

National Council of Chain Restaurants
URL: http://www.nccr.net
E-mail: purviss@nrf.com
Phone: (202) 626-8183
325 7th Street, NW
Suite 1100
Washington, DC 20004
Leading trade association of chain restaurant companies that has defended the industry and its meat suppliers against accusations by animal rights groups.

National Dairy Council
URL: http://www.
nationaldairycouncil.org/
nationaldairycouncil
E-mail: ndc@dairyinformation.
com
10255 West Higgins Road
Suite 900
Rosemont, IL 60018
Carries out dairy nutrition research, education, and communication; makes scientifically sound nutrition information available to media, physicians, consumers, children, and others. Promotes dairy products as part of a healthy lifestyle.

National Farmers' Union
URL: http://www.nfuonline.com
Phone: (0) 247-685-8500
Agricultural House
Stoneleigh Park
Stoneleigh, Warwickshire CV8 2TZ, UK
Trade organization representing farmers in England and Wales. Encourages environmentally friendly and welfare-conscious farming practices and works to ensure survival of rural communities. Works

with animal welfare, environmental, and consumer groups.

National Institute for Animal Agriculture
URL: http://www.
animalagriculture.org
E-mail: NIAA@
animalagriculture.org
Phone: (270) 782-9798
1910 Lyda Avenue
Bowling Green, KY 42104
Aims to be the forum for building consensus and advancing solutions for animal agriculture and to provide continuing education to animal agriculture professionals. Works to eradicate disease, promote a safe food supply, and promote good practices in agricultural animal health and environmental stewardship.

National Pork Producers Council
URL: http://www.nppc.org
Phone: (515) 278-8012
10664 Justin Drive
Urbandale, IA 50322
Conducts public policy outreach to aid its members' business interests and build the industry's image. Works for passage and implementation of laws and regulations conducive to production and sale of pork.

National Turkey Federation
URL: http://www.eatturkey.com
E-mail: info@turkeyfed.org
Phone: (202) 898-0100
1225 New York Avenue, NW
Suite 400
Washington, DC 20005
National advocate for all segments of the turkey industry. Among other things, it defends the industry against animal rights complaints.

United Egg Producers
URL: http://www.unitedegg.org
E-mail: info@unitedegg.com
Phone: (770) 360-9220
Provides services to the egg industry including government relations, market information, and quality assurance programs for animal well-being, environmental protection, and food safety.

United Poultry Concerns, Inc.
URL: http://www.upc-online. org
E-mail: info@upc-online.org
Phone: (757) 678-7875
P.O. Box 150
Machipongo, VA 23405-0150
Addresses treatment of domestic fowl in all areas of human use, including food production and science. Actively promotes alternatives to use of poultry and educates consumers about abuses. Opposes such practices as forced molting and hatching of chicks in classrooms.

U.S. Department of Agriculture Food Safety and Inspection Service
URL: http://www.fsis.usda.gov
Phone: (202) 720-9113
The agency of the USDA responsible for inspecting slaughterhouses and enforcing the Humane Methods of Slaughter Act. It also inspects meat, poultry, and egg products to make sure that they are wholesome and packaged as required by law.

Vegetarians International Voice for Animals (VIVA)
URL: http://www.viva.org.uk
E-mail: info@viva.org.uk
Phone: (0) 117-944-1000
8 York Court
Wilder Street
Bristol BS2 8QH, UK
Europe's leading vegetarian campaigning group. It highlights the plight of farmed animals as well as the health benefits of a vegetarian or vegan diet.

World Organisation for Animal Health (OIE)
URL: http://www.oie.int/eng/ en_index.htm
E-mail: oie@oie.int
Phone: (+33) 0144-15-1888
12 rue de Prony
Paris 75017, France
This international organization works to improve health and welfare of animals all over the world. The group's main focus is livestock diseases, but treatment and welfare of farm animals are also concerns.

ANIMALS IN SCIENCE

American Anti-Vivisection Society
URL: http://www.aavs.org/home. html
Phone: (215) 887-0816
801 Old York Road
#204
Jenkintown, PA 19046-1685
Dedicated to abolition of animal use in science, which it opposes on

both scientific and ethical grounds. Includes Alternatives Research and Development Foundation.

Americans for Medical Advancement
URL: http://www.curedisease. com
E-mail: webmaster@curedisease. com
Phone: (310) 678-9076
8391 Beverly Boulevard #153
Los Angeles, CA 90048
Claims that use of animals as disease models retards biomedical research and risks human lives.

Americans for Medical Progress
URL: http://www.amprogress.org
E-mail: info@amprogress.org
Phone: (703) 836-9595
908 King Street
Suite 301
Alexandria, VA 22314
Provides resources demonstrating that biomedical research on animals is necessary and humane; opposes efforts to stop use of animals in research.

Association for Assessment and Accreditation of Laboratory Animal Care International
URL: http://www.aaalac.org
E-mail: accredit@aaalac.org
Phone: (301) 696-9626
5283 Corporate Drive
Suite 203
Frederick, MD 21703
This private, nonprofit organization promotes the humane treat-

ment of animals in science through voluntary accreditation and assessment programs.

The Boyd Group
URL: http://www.boyd-group. demon.co.uk
E-mail: mail@boyd-group. demon.co.uk
P.O. Box 423
Southsea P05 1TJ, UK
Forum for exchange of views on issues related to use of animals in science. Aims to promote dialogue among diverse groups and recommend practical steps toward achieving common goals.

British Union for the Abolition of Vivisection
URL: http://www.buav.org
E-mail: info@buav.org
Phone: (0) 207-700-4888
16a Crane Grove
London N7 8NN, UK
Opposes all experimentation on animals and seeks alternatives to use of animals in research. European Coalition to End Animal Experiments is an affiliated organization at the same address.

Coalition for Medical Progress
URL: http://www.medical-progress.org
Phone: (0) 207-921-0080
Waterloo Business Centre
117 Waterloo Road
London SE1 8UL, UK
This group defends the use of animals in medical research.

Animal Rights

European Biomedical Research Association
URL: http://www.ebra.org
25 Shaftesbury Avenue
London W1D 7EG, UK
Association of Europeans in scientific, medical, and veterinary professions. Promotes use of animals in medical and veterinary research and safety testing and works to counter the claims of antivivisection groups.

European Centre for the Validation of Alternative Methods
URL: http://ecvam.jrc.cec.eu.int
Phone: 0332-789111
E.C.-Joint Research Centre
via E. Fermi 1
I-21020 Ispra (VA), Italy
Organization created by the European Union to coordinate information on alternatives to scientific tests that use animals and to validate such tests.

European Coalition to End Animal Experiments
URL: http://www.eceae.org/english
E-mail: info@eceae.org
Phone: (0) 207-700-4888
16a Crane Grove
London N7 8NN, UK
Founded to work for laws against cosmetics testing on animals, this coalition of animal protection societies from all over Europe now also campaigns against using animals to test potentially toxic chemicals and using primates in any kind of research. It promotes scientifically

valid alternatives to animals in research.

European Partnership for Alternative Approaches to Animal Testing
URL: http://ec.europa.eu/enterprise/epaa/index_en.htm
E-mail: entr-epaa@ec.europa.eu
This organization is a collaboration between the European Union and major companies from seven industry sectors to accelerate the development, validation, and acceptance of alternative approaches to animal testing.

Federation of American Societies for Experimental Biology
URL: http://www.faseb.org
E-mail: webmaster@faseb.org
Phone: (301) 634-7000
9650 Rockville Pike
Bethesda, MD 20814-3998
Promotes the interests of biomedical scientists and disseminates information on biological research. Supports appropriate use of animals in research.

Federation of European Laboratory Animal Science Organizations (FELASA)
URL: http://www.felasa.eu/index.htm
E-mail: felasaeu@felasa.eu
P.O. Box 3993
Tamworth, Staffordshire
B783QU, UK
FELASA is composed of independent European national and regional laboratory animal science associa-

254

tions. Among other things, it makes recommendations for education and training of people responsible for the well-being of laboratory animals and scientists designing or conducting experiments involving animals.

Fund for the Replacement of Animals in Medical Experiments
URL: http://www.frame.org.uk
E-mail: frame@frame.org.uk
Phone: (0) 115-958-4740
Russell & Burch House
96-98 North Sherwood Street
Nottingham NG1 4EE, UK
Works to reduce the use of animals in research and develop and validate alternatives to animal tests but recognizes that immediate and total abolition of all animal experiments is not possible if vital medical research is to continue.

Institute for Laboratory Animal Research
URL: http://dels.nas.edu/ilar
Phone: (202) 334-2590
The Keck Center of the National Academies
500 Fifth Street, NW
Washington, DC 20001
Serves as a clearinghouse for scientific and technical information about the use and care of laboratory animals. Supports the use of animals in research.

Interagency Coordinating Committee on the Validation of Alternative Methods
URL: http://iccvam.niehs.nih. gov
Phone: (919) 541-2384

NTP Interagency Center for the Evaluation of Alternative Toxicological Methods
P.O. Box 12233
Research Triangle Park, NC 27709
Agency sponsored by the U.S. federal government to coordinate development, validation, and acceptance of toxicological test methods that do not use animals and are more accurate than present methods.

International Council for Laboratory Animal Science
URL: http://www.iclas.org
Phone: (+34) (93) 581-1848
P.O. Box 39
08193 Bellaterra, Barcelona, Spain
This international scientific organization promotes ethical care and use of laboratory animals in research as a way to improve human and animal health.

Johns Hopkins University Center for Alternatives to Animal Testing
URL: http://caat.jhsph.edu
E-mail: caat@jhsph.edu
Phone: (410) 223-1692
111 Market Place
Suite 840
Baltimore, MD 21202-6709
Seeks new methods to replace, reduce, and refine use of animals in laboratory experiments.

National Anti-Vivisection Society
URL: http://www.navs.org
E-mail: feedback@navs.org

Phone: (800) 888-6287
53 West Jackson Boulevard
Suite 1552
Chicago, IL 60604
Dedicated to abolishing use of animals in research, education, and product testing. Believes that such research is scientifically invalid as well as cruel.

**National Association for
Biomedical Research**
URL: http://www.nabr.org
E-mail: info@nabr.org
Phone: (202) 857-0540
818 Connecticut Avenue, NW
Suite 900
Washington, DC 20006
Advocates public policy that supports humane use of animals in biomedical research, education, and product testing. Connected with the Foundation for Biomedical Research.

**National Centre for the
Replacement, Refinement
and Reduction of Animals in
Research (NC3Rs)**
URL: http://www.nc3rs.org.uk
E-mail: enquiries@nc3rs.org.uk
Phone: (0) 207-670-5331
20 Park Crescent
London W1B 1AL, UK
Established by the British government in 2004, this organization helps to promote, develop, and implement the "3Rs" in that country.

**National Institutes of Health
Office of Laboratory Animal
Welfare**
URL: http://grants.nih.gov/
grants/olaw/olaw.htm
E-mail: olaw@od.nih.gov

Develops, monitors, and enforces compliance with Public Health Service Policy on Humane Care and Use of Laboratory Animals and related regulations in research conducted or supported by any component of the Public Health Service.

**New England Anti-Vivisection
Society**
URL: http://www.neavs.org
E-mail: info@neavs.com
Phone: (617) 523-6020
333 Washington Street
Suite 850
Boston, MA 02108
Opposes use of animals in research, education, and testing and seeks alternative methods. Uses education, lobbying, and litigation to support these aims.

Nuffield Council on Bioethics
URL: http://www.nuffield
bioethics.org
E-mail: bioethics@nuffield
bioethics.org
Phone: (0) 207-681-9619
28 Bedford Square
London WC1B 3JS, UK
The Nuffield Council on Bioethics examines ethical issues raised by new developments in biology and medicine, including issues related to laboratory animal welfare. They maintain a neutral stance on these issues.

**Physicians Committee
for Responsible Medicine**
URL: http://www.pcrm.org
E-mail: pcrm@pcrm.org
Phone: (202) 686-2210

5100 Wisconsin Avenue, NW
Suite 400
Washington, DC 20016
Opposes most use of animals in science and promotes nonanimal alternatives in research and education.

Pro-Test
URL: http://www.pro-test.org.uk
E-mail: contact@pro-test.org.uk
Pro-Test was formed in January 2006 by Laurie Pycroft, a 16-year-old British schoolboy, to raise public awareness of the usefulness of animals in medical research and counter the claims of animal rights activists who oppose research involving animals. Specifically, it has defended a new animal research laboratory at Oxford University that was the target of animal rights protests.

Research Defence Society
URL: http://www.rds-online.
    org.uk
E-mail: info@rds-net.org.uk
Phone: (0) 207-287-2818
25 Shaftesbury Avenue
London W1D 7EG, UK
Represents and supports biomedical researchers and appropriate use of animals in science. Provides information about the need for animal research to media, government, and the public and promotes best practice in laboratory animal welfare.

Scientists Center
    for Animal Welfare
URL: http://www.scaw.com
E-mail: info@scaw.com
Phone: (301) 345-3500

7833 Walker Drive
Suite 410
Greenbelt, MD 20770
Supports use of animals in science; provides scientific information about and promotes humane treatment and care of laboratory animals through conferences, seminars, and publications.

SPEAK: The Voice for the
    Animals
URL: http://www.speakcampaigns.org
E-mail: info@speakcampaigns.
    org
Phone: (0) 845-330-7985
P.O. Box 6712
Northampton NN2 6XR, UK
This group's specific focus is opposition to primate research. It grew out of the protest that stopped Cambridge University from building a primate research laboratory, where it was SPEAC (Stop Primate Experiments at Cambridge). It is also trying to stop primate research at Oxford University.

Win Animal Rights (W.A.R.)
URL: http://www.war-online.org
E-mail: centcom@war-online.org
This organization opposes experimentation on animals in general and the British contract testing laboratory Huntingdon Life Sciences in particular, but it claims not to be associated with the controversial SHAC (Stop Huntingdon Animal Cruelty) or SHAC-USA and not to promote or condone illegal activity.

ANIMALS IN ENTERTAINMENT

American Horse Council
URL: http://www.horsecouncil. org
E-mail: AHC@horsecouncil.org
Phone: (202) 296-4031
1616 H Street, NW
Seventh Floor
Washington, DC 20006
National trade association of the horse industry. Represents interests of owners, breeders, and others involved with horses in shows, races, rodeos, and the like to legislators and regulatory agencies.

Association of Zoos and Aquariums
URL: http://www.aza.org
E-mail: G.e.n.e.r.a.l.I.n.q.u.i.r.y. @aza.org
Phone: (301) 562-0777
8403 Colesville Road
Suite 710
Silver Spring, MD 20910-3314
Dedicated to advancement of zoos and aquariums in conservation, education, science, and recreation. Accredits zoos and aquariums that follow organizational guidelines to maintain high standards. Coordinates members' captive animal and field-based projects.

Equine Protection Network
URL: http://www.equine protectionnetwork.com
E-mail: info@equineprotection-network.com
Phone: (570) 345-6440
P.O. Box 232
Friedensburg, PA 17933

Rescues and provides sanctuaries for abused and neglected horses; provides education and information about horse welfare and the equine industry.

Greyhound Protection League
URL: http://www.greyhounds.org
Phone: (800) 446-8637
P.O. Box 669
Penn Valley, CA 95946
Protects greyhounds from the abuses it sees as inherent in the greyhound racing industry and works to help the public see greyhound racing as cruel.

National Greyhound Association
URL: http://www. ngagreyhounds.com
E-mail: nga@ngagreyhounds.com
Phone: (785) 263-4660
P.O. Box 543
Abilene, KS 67410
Official registry of racing greyhounds and association of greyhound racing.

National Thoroughbred Racing Association
URL: http://www.ntra.com
E-mail: ntra@ntra.com
Phone: (859) 223-5444
2525 Harrodsburg Road
Lexington, KY 40504
Governs and provides information about horse racing. Also provides information about horse ownership and has an adoption referral program for retired racehorses.

Outdoor Amusement Business Association
URL: http://www.oaba.org
Phone: (800) 517-6222
1035 South Semoran Boulevard
Suite 1045A
Winter Park, FL 32792
Represents and advances the interests of the outdoor amusement industry. The circus unit represents circuses, animal exhibits, and animal shows. Works toward preservation of endangered species to which many circus animals belong and encourages shows to increase public awareness of these species' plight. Stresses responsible animal care and training methods.

Performing Animal Welfare Society
URL: http://www.pawsweb.org
E-mail: info@pawsweb.org
Phone: (209) 745-2606
P.O. Box 849
Galt, CA 95632
Investigates, rescues, and provides sanctuaries for abandoned or abused performing animals and victims of the exotic animal trade. Works for legislation that will ban ownership of wild animals, restrict their breeding, and ban painful discipline techniques.

Professional Rodeo Cowboys Association
URL: http://prorodeo.org
E-mail: prorodeo@prorodeo.com
Phone: (719) 593-8840
101 Pro Rodeo Drive
Colorado Springs, CO 80919

Chief trade organization governing rodeo standards and personnel.

Thoroughbred Owners and Breeders Association
URL: http://www.toba.org
E-mail: toba@toba.org
Phone: (888) 606-TOBA
P.O. Box 910668
Lexington, KY 40591
This national trade organization for thoroughbred horse owners and breeders has the mission of improving the economics, integrity, and pleasure of the sport.

Thoroughbred Retirement Foundation
URL: http://www.trfinc.org
Phone: (518) 226-0028
P.O. Box 3387
Saratoga Springs, NY 12866
The Thoroughbred Retirement Foundation's mission is to prevent the possible neglect, abuse, and slaughter of thoroughbred horses no longer able to compete on the racetrack.

World Association of Zoos and Aquariums
URL: http://www.waza.org/home/index.php?main=home
E-mail: secretariat@waza.org
P.O. Box 23
CH-3097 Liebefeld-Bern, Switzerland
Umbrella organization for the world zoo and aquarium community. Guides and supports member organizations' animal welfare, environmental education, and global conservation programs.

ANIMALS IN THE WILD

Animals Asia Foundation
URL: http://www.animalsasia.org
E-mail: info@animalsasia.org
Phone: (888) 420-2327
PMB 506
584 Castro Street
San Francisco, CA 94114-2594
Headquartered in Hong Kong, this group works to improve the lives of all animals in Asia. One of their chief concerns is bears farmed for body parts used in Asian medicine.

Association of Fish and Wildlife Agencies
URL: http://www.fishwildlife. org
E-mail: info@fishwildlife.org
Phone: (202) 624-7890
444 North Capitol Street, NW
Suite 725
Washington, DC 20001
Quasi-governmental organizaton of public agencies charged with protection and management of North America's fish and wildlife resources. Includes federal and state or province agencies in Canada, the United States, and Mexico. Promotes sound resource management and strengthens cooperation among federal, state, and private entities. Supports sustainable use of natural resources.

Audubon Society
URL: http://www.audubon.org
E-mail: education@audubon. org
Phone: (212) 979-3000

700 Broadway
New York, NY 10003
Dedicated to protecting birds and other wildlife and their habitat. Supports nature centers, environmental education programs, and preservation of areas sustaining important bird populations.

Boone and Crockett Club
URL: http://www.boone-crockett.org
E-mail: bcclub@boone=crocket. org
Phone: (406) 542-1888
250 Station Drive
Missoula, MT 59801
Founded by Theodore Roosevelt in 1887, this organization supports both hunting and conservation of wildlife and habitat.

Born Free USA
URL: http://www. bornfreeUSA.org
E-mail: adam@bornfreeusa.org
Phone: (202) 337-3123
P.O. Box 32160
Washington, DC 20007
U.S. office of international wildlife charity working to phase out traditional zoos and conserve rare species in their natural habitats.

British Association for Shooting and Conservation
URL: http://www.basc.org.uk
Phone: (0) 124-457-3000
Marford Mill
Rossett, Wrexham LL12 0HL, UK

This group promotes all kinds of hunting and sport shooting.

Center for Biological Diversity
URL: http://www.biological
diversity.org
E-mail: center@
biologicaldiversity.org
Phone: (520) 623-5252
P.O. Box 710
Tucson, AZ 85702-0710
Combines conservation biology with litigation, political advocacy, and strategic vision to aid plants and animals on the brink of extinction and preserve their habitats.

Center for Wildlife Law
URL: http://ipl.unm.edu/cwl
Phone: (505) 277-5006
University of New Mexico
School of Law
Institute of Public Law
MSC 11 6060
University of New Mexico
Albuquerque, NM 87131
Provides research and analysis, education and training, and policy development related to laws affecting wildlife.

Coalition Against Duck Shooting
URL: http://www.duck.org.au
E-mail: info@duck.org.au
Phone: (03) 9645-8879
304, 78 Eastern Road
South Melbourne
Victoria 3205, Australia
Opposes duck shooting and rescues and rehabilitates ducks injured by hunters.

Convention on International Trade in Endangered Species of Wild Fauna and Flora
URL: http://www.cites.org
E-mail: info@cites.org
Phone: (02) 917-8139
CITES Secretariat
International Environment House
Chemin des Anémones
CH-1219 Châtelaine, Geneva, Switzerland
Organization that implements international treaty limiting trade in endangered species worldwide. Website contains materials describing the convention and how it works, including a database of endangered species and import limits.

Countryside Action Network
URL: http://www.
countrysideaction.net
E-mail: info@countrysideaction.
net
Phone: (0) 129-165-0962
Coordinates resistance to attempts to ban or restrict country pursuits, including hunting with hounds.

Countryside Alliance
URL: http://www.countryside-
alliance.org
Phone: (0) 207-840-9200
The Old Town Hall
367 Kennington Road
London SE11 4PT, UK
This organization supports hunting and the balancing of wildlife conservation with private property rights.

Defenders of Wildlife
URL: http://www.defenders.org

E-mail: defenders@mail.
defenders.org
Phone: (800) 385-9712
1130 17th Street, NW
Washington, DC 20036
Works to slow the accelerating rate of extinction, loss of biological diversity, and habitat alteration and destruction. Includes Endangered Species Coalition, which calls itself the "guardian of the Endangered Species Act."

Ducks Unlimited
URL: http://www.ducks.org
Phone: (800) 453-8257
One Waterfowl Way
Memphis, TN 38120
Duck hunters' organization. Conserves, restores, and manages wetlands and associated waterfowl habitats.

European Federation Against Hunting
URL: http://www.efah.net
E-mail: info@efah.net
Phone: (0) 6552-61729
Via Angelo Bassini 6
00149 Roma, Italy
Federation of associations and individuals working to abolish hunting in developed countries. Does not oppose subsistence hunting in undeveloped countries.

Federation of Hunters Associations of the European Union
URL: http://bch-cbd.
naturalsciences.be/belgium/
services/face.htm
Phone: (0) 2-627-4343

Belgian National Focal Point to the Convention on Biological Diversity
Royal Belgian Institute of Natural Sciences
Vautier Street 29
1000 Brussels, Belgium
Federation of national hunters' associations in Europe. Works to promote responsible hunting and lobbies against legislation that bans or excessively regulates hunting.

The Fund for Animals
URL: http://www.fundfor
animals.org
Phone: (888) 405-3863
200 West 57th Street
New York, NY 10019
Works to protect every individual wild animal, whether endangered or not, including members of so-called pest species, from suffering and death.

Game Conservancy Trust
URL: http://www.gct.org.uk
Phone: (0) 142-565-2381
Fordingbridge, Hampshire SP6 1EF, UK
The trust conducts scientific research into Britain's game animals and wildlife. It supports both hunting and conservation and advises farmers and landowners on improving wildlife habitat.

Hunt Saboteurs Association
URL: http://hsa.enviroweb.org/
hsa.shtml
E-mail: info@huntsabs.org.uk
Phone: (0) 845-450-0727

Organizations and Agencies

BM HSA
London WC1N 3XX, UK
Works directly but nonviolently in the field to protect wildlife from hunters.

International Elephant
Foundation
URL: http://www.elephant conservation.org/
P.O. Box 366
Azle, TX 76098
The foundation promotes conservation of African and Asian elephants in both management facilities and the wild.

International Fund for Animal
Welfare
URL: http://www.ifaw.org
E-mail: info@ifaw.org
Phone: (508) 744-2000
411 Main Street
P.O. Box 193
Yarmouth Port, MA 02675
Mounts rescue and relief operations to help animals in distress; works with local communities to preserve wilderness habitat; promotes economically viable alternatives to commercial exploitation of wildlife; and supports animal sanctuaries worldwide. Advocates strong laws to protect animals.

International Primate
Protection League
URL: http://www.ippl.org
E-mail: info@ippl.org
Phone: (843) 871-2280
P.O. Box 766
Summerville, SC 29484

Works to protect primates in their natural habitats through creation of national parks and sanctuaries, as well as bans on primate hunting and trapping and local and international trade. Supports sanctuaries for primates rescued from poaching, laboratories, and other abusive situations.

International Wildlife Coalition
URL: http://www.iwc.org
E-mail: iwchq@iwc.org
Phone: (508) 457-1898
70 East Falmouth Highway
East Falmouth, MA 02536
Works to save endangered species, protect wild and domestic animals, and preserve habitat worldwide. Projects include rescuing whales and other marine mammals and fighting cruel conditions around the world.

Izaak Walton League
of America
URL: http://www.iwla.org
Phone: (301) 548-0150
707 Conservation Lane
Gaithersburg, MD 20878
Works to protect wildlife and the environment. Supports hunting and fishing as well as nonconsumptive uses of wildlife such as outdoor photography.

League Against Cruel Sports Ltd.
URL: http://www.league.org.uk.
Phone: (0) 845-330-8486
Sparling House
83-87 Union Street
London SE1 1SG, UK

Investigates and exposes the abusive nature of hunting and works to ban it. Purchases land to establish sanctuaries for hunted wildlife.

National Trappers Association
URL: http://www.
  nationaltrappers.com
E-mail: ntaheadquarters@
  nationaltrappers.com
Phone: (812) 277-9670
2815 Washington Avenue
Bedford, IN 47421-5310
Protects and promotes the interests of trappers and promotes sound conservation and wildlife management to produce a continued annual fur harvest.

National Wildlife Federation
URL: http://www.nwf.org
Phone: (800) 822-9919
11100 Wildlife Center Drive
Reston, VA 20190-5362
Works for wildlife conservation and habitat protection worldwide and educates people about the need to conserve and protect the environment.

Orion (the Hunters' Institute)
URL: http://www.huntright.org
E-mail: orionhi@bresnan.net
Phone: (406) 449-2795
219 Vawter
Helena, MT 59604-5088
The institute works to sustain ethical hunting and preserve the natural resources necessary for it.

Pacific Legal Foundation
URL: http://www.pacificlegal.org
E-mail: plf@pacificlegal.org

Phone: (916) 419-7111
3900 Lennane Drive
Suite 200
Sacramento, CA 95834
This group of attorneys protects private property, free enterprise, and individual rights in the courts. It opposes use of the Endangered Species Act and other environmental regulations to limit property rights and individuals' freedom of action.

Republicans for Environmental
  Protection (REP America)
URL: http://www.
  repamerica.org
Phone: (505) 889-4544
3200 Carlisle Blvd. #114
Albuquerque, NM 87110
REP America was formed by Republicans who want to maintain both a healthy environment and a sound economy. It advocates the separation of the National Wildlife Refuge System from the U.S. Fish and Wildlife Service and creation of a separate U. S. National Wildlife Refuge Service within the Department of Interior.

SCI (formerly Safari Club
  International)
URL: http://www.safariclub.org
Phone: (520) 620-1220
4800 West Gates Pass Road
Tucson, AZ 85745-9490
Advocate for hunters and wildlife conservation worldwide.

Sea Shepherd Conservation
  Society
URL: http://www.seashepherd.org
E-mail: info@seashepherd. org

Phone: (360) 370-5650
P.O. Box 2616
Friday Harbor, WA 98250
Works to halt illegal fishing activities and killing of marine mammals worldwide and uphold international treaties and laws through investigation and documentation of violations and, where legal, enforcement.

Showing Animals Respect and Kindness
URL: http://www.sharkonline.org
Phone: (630) 557-0176
P.O. Box 28
Geneva, IL 60134
Works to stop hunting and the use of animals in entertainment; also conducts animal rescues and education projects.

Species Survival Network
URL: http://www.ssn.org
E-mail: info@ssn.org
Phone: (301) 548-7769
2100 L Street, NW
Washington, DC 20037
This international coalition of non-governmental organizations (NGOs) is committed to promotion, enhancement, and strict enforcement of the Convention on International Trade in Endangered Species of Wild Fauna and Flora (CITES) and to preventing overexploitation of animals and plants through international trade.

U.S. Fish and Wildlife Service Endangered Species Program
URL: http://www.fws.gov/ endangered

Phone: (800) 344-9453
1849 C Street, NW
Washington, DC 20240
Website provides information about the program, news, and information about particular species.

U.S. Sportsmen's Alliance
URL: http://www.ussportsmen. org
E-mail: info@ussportsmen.org
Phone: (614) 888-4868
801 Kingsmill Parkway
Columbus, OH 43229
Formerly Wildlife Legislative Fund of America. Provides lobbying, legal defense, and grassroots support for hunters, fishers, trappers, and wildlife management professionals. Also sponsors education and research programs.

The Wildlife Society
URL: http://www.wildlife.org
E-mail: TWS@Wildlife.org
Phone: (301) 897-9770
5410 Grosvenor Lane
Suite 200
Bethesda, MD 20814-2144
Promotes continuing education of wildlife professionals and sustainable management and use of wildlife and habitat resources.

World Conservation Union (IUCN)
URL: http://www.iucn.org
E-mail: webmaster@iucn.org
Phone: (+41) 22-999-0000
Rue Mauverney 28
Gland 1196, Switzerland

The world's largest conservation network, including 82 nations and numerous government agencies, nongovernmental organizations, and individual scientists and experts. It works to help societies around the world conserve the integrity and diversity of nature and use natural resources in an equitable and ecologically sustainable way.

World Wildlife Fund
URL: http://www.worldwildlife. org
Phone: (202) 293-4800
1250 24th Street, NW
P.O. Box 97180
Washington, DC 20090-7180
Works to protect the world's wildlife, especially endangered species such as the panda, and to establish and manage parks and reserves worldwide.

PART III

APPENDICES

APPENDIX A

───────■───────

ANIMAL WELFARE ACT, 1970

As Amended: 7 U.S.C. 2131-2156 [includes amendments passed in 1976, 1985, and 1990]

[Note: Some portions have been omitted.]

Section 1. (a) This Act may be cited as the **"Animal Welfare Act"**.

(b) The Congress finds that animals and activities which are regulated under this Act are either in interstate or foreign commerce or substantially affect such commerce or the free flow thereof, and that regulation of animals and activities as provided in this Act is necessary to prevent and eliminate burdens upon such commerce and to effectively regulate such commerce, in order—

1. to insure that animals intended for use in research facilities or for exhibition purposes or for use as pets are provided humane care and treatment;

2. to assure the humane treatment of animals during transportation in commerce; and

3. to protect the owners of animals from the theft of their animals by preventing the sale or use of animals which have been stolen.

The Congress further finds that it is essential to regulate, as provided in this Act, the transportation, purchase, sale, housing, care, handling, and treatment of animals by carriers or by persons or organizations engaged in using them for research or experimental purposes or for exhibition purposes or holding them for sale as pets or for any such purpose or use. The Congress further finds that—

1. the use of animals is instrumental in certain research and education for advancing knowledge of cures and treatment for diseases and injuries which afflict both humans and animals;

2. methods of testing that do not use animals are being and continue to be developed which are faster, less expensive, and more accurate than traditional animal experiments for some purposes and further opportunities exist for the development of these methods of testing;

3. measures which eliminate or minimize the unnecessary duplication of experiments on animals can result in more productive use of Federal funds; and

4. measures which help meet the public concern for laboratory animal care and treatment are important in assuring that research will continue to progress.

Section 2. When used in this Act—

(a) The term "Person" includes any individual, partnership, firm, joint stock company, corporation, association, trust, estate, or other legal entity;

(b) The term "Secretary" means the Secretary of Agriculture of the United States or his representative who shall be an employee of the United States Department of Agriculture;

(c) The term "commerce" means trade, traffic, transportation, or other commerce

(1) between a place in a State and any place outside of such State, or between points within the same State but through any place outside thereof, or within any territory, possession, or the District of Columbia;

(2) which affects trade, traffic, transportation, or other commerce described in paragraph (1),

(d) The term "State" means a State of the United States, the District of Columbia, the Commonwealth of Puerto Rico, the Virgin Islands, Guam, American Samoa, or any other territory or possession of the United States;

(e) The term "research facility" means any school (except an elementary or secondary school), institution, organization, or person that uses or intends to use live animals in research, tests, or experiments, and that (1) purchases or transports live animals in commerce, or (2) receives funds under a grant, award, loan, or contract from a department, agency, or instrumentality of the United States for the purpose of carrying out research, tests, or experiments: *Provided,* That the Secretary may exempt, by regulation, any such school, institution, organization, or person that does not use or intend to use live dogs or cats, except those schools, institutions, organizations, or persons, which use substantial numbers (as determined by the Secretary) or live animals the principal function of which schools, institutions, organizations, or persons, is biomedical research or testing, when in the judgment of the Secretary, any such exemption does not vitiate the purpose of this Act;

(f) The term "dealer" means any person who, in commerce, for compensation or profit, delivers for transportation, or transports, except as a carrier, buys, or sells, or negotiates the purchase or sale of, (1) any dog or other animal whether alive or dead for research, teaching, exhibition, or use as a pet, or (2) any dog for hunting, security, or breeding purposes, except that this term does not include

Appendix A

(i) a retail pet store except such store which sells any animals to a research facility, an exhibitor, or a dealer; or

(ii) any person who does not sell, or negotiate the purchase or sale or any wild animal, dog, or cat and who derives no more than $500 gross income from the sale of other animals during any calendar year;

(g) The term "animal" means any live or dead dog, cat, monkey (nonhuman primate mammal), guinea pig, hamster, rabbit, or such other warmblooded animal, as the Secretary may determine is being used, or is intended for use, for research, testing, experimentation, or exhibition purposes or as a pet; but such term excludes horses not used for research purposes and other farm animals, such as, but not limited to livestock or poultry, used or intended for use as food or fiber, or livestock or poultry used or intended for improving animal nutrition, breeding, management or production efficiency, or for improving the quality of food or fiber. With respect to a dog the term means all dogs including those used for hunting, security, or breeding purposes;

(h) The term "exhibitor" means any person (public or private) exhibiting any animals, which were purchased in commerce or the intended distribution of which affects commerce, or will affect commerce, to the public for compensation, as determined by the Secretary, and such term includes carnivals, circuses, and zoos exhibiting such animals whether operated for profit or not; but such term excludes retail pet stores, organizations sponsoring and all persons participating in State and country fairs, livestock shows, rodeos, purebred dog and cat shows, and any other fairs or exhibitions intended to advance agricultural arts and sciences, as may be determined by the Secretary;

(i) The term "intermediate handler" means any person including a department, agency, or instrumentality of the United States or of any State or local government (other than a dealer, research facility, exhibitor, any person excluded from the definition of a dealer, research facility, or exhibitor, an operator of an auction sale, or a carrier) who is engaged in any business in which he receives custody of animals in connection with their transportation in commerce; and

(j) The term "carrier" means the operator of any airline, railroad, motor carrier, shipping line, or other enterprise, which is engaged in the business of transporting any animals for hire.

(k) The term "Federal agency" means an Executive agency as such term is defined in section 105 of Title 5, United States Code, and with respect to any research facility means the agency from which the research facility receives a Federal award for the conduct of research, experimentation, or testing, involving the use of animals;

(l) The term "Federal award for the conduct of research, experimentation, or testing, involving the use of animals" means any mechanism (including a grant, award, loan, contract, or cooperative agreement) under which Federal funds are provided to support the conduct of such research;

(m) The term "quorum" means a majority of the Committee members;

(n) The term "Committee" means the Institutional Animal Committee established under section 13(b); and

(o) The term "Federal research facility" means each department, agency, or instrumentality of the United States which uses live animals for research of experimentation.

Section 3. The Secretary shall issue licenses to dealers and exhibitors upon application therefore in such form and manner as he may prescribe and upon payment of such fee established pursuant to section 23 of this Act: *Provided,* That no such license shall be issued until the dealer or exhibitor shall have demonstrated that his facilities comply with the standards promulgated by the Secretary pursuant to section 13 of this Act: *Provided, however,* That any retail pet store or other person who derives less than a substantial portion of his income (as determined by the Secretary) from the breeding and raising of dogs or cats on his own premises and sells any such dog or cat to a dealer or research facility shall not be required to obtain a license as a dealer or exhibitor under this Act. The Secretary is further authorized to license, as dealers or exhibitors, persons who do not qualify as dealers or exhibitors within the meaning of this Act upon such persons complying with the requirements specified above and agreeing, in writing, to comply with all the requirements of this Act and the regulations promulgated by the Secretary hereunder.

Section 4. No dealer or exhibitor shall sell or offer to sell or transport or offer for transportation, in commerce, to any research facility or for exhibition or for use as a pet any animal, or buy, sell, offer to buy or sell, transport or offer for transportation, in commerce, to or from another dealer or exhibitor under this Act any animal, unless and until such dealer or exhibitor shall have obtained a license from the Secretary and such license shall not have been amended or revoked.

Section 5. No dealer or exhibitor shall sell or dispose of any dog or cat within a period of 5 business days after the acquisition of such animal or within such other period as way be specified by the Secretary: *Provided,* that operators of auction sales subject to section 12 of this Act shall not be required to comply with the provisions of this section.

Section 6. Every research facility, every intermediate handler, every carrier, and every exhibitor not licensed under section 3 of this Act shall reg-

Appendix A

ister with the Secretary in accordance with such rules and regulations as he may prescribe.

Section 7. It shall be unlawful for any research facility to purchase any dog or cat from any person except an operator of an auction sale subject to section 12 of this Act or a person holding a valid license as a dealer or exhibitor issued by the Secretary pursuant to this Act unless such person is exempted from obtaining such license under section 3 of this Act. . . .

* * *

Section 10. Dealers and exhibitors shall make and retain for such reasonable period of time as the Secretary may prescribe, such records with respect to the purchase, sale, transportation, identification, and previous ownership of animals as the Secretary may prescribe. Research facilities shall make and retain such records only with respect to the purchase, sale, transportation, identification, and previous ownership of live dogs and cats.

* * *

Section 13. (a) Promulgation of standards, rules, regulations, and orders; requirements; research facilities; State authority

(1) The Secretary shall promulgate standards to govern the humane handling, care, treatment, and transportation of animals by dealers, research facilities, and exhibitors.

(2) The standards described in paragraph (1) shall include minimum requirements—

(A) for handling, housing, feeding, watering, sanitation, ventilation, shelter from extremes of weather and temperatures, adequate veterinary care, and separation by species where the Secretary finds necessary for humane handling, care, or treatment of animals; and

(B) for exercise of dogs, as determined by an attending veterinarian in accordance with the general standards promulgated by the Secretary, and for a physical environment adequate to promote the psychological well-being of primates.

(3) In addition to the requirements under paragraph (2), the standards described in paragraph (1) shall, with respect to animals in research facilities, include requirements—

(A) for animal care, treatment, and practices in experimental procedures to ensure that animal pain and distress are minimized, including adequate veterinary care with the appropriate use of anesthetic, analgesic or tranquilizing drugs, or euthanasia;

(B) that the principal investigator considers alternatives to any procedure likely to produce pain or distress in an experimental animal;

(C) in any practice which could cause pain to animals—

(i) that a doctor of veterinary medicine is consulted in the planning of such procedures;

(ii) for the use of tranquilizers, analgesics, and anesthetics;

(iii) for presurgical and postsurgical care by laboratory workers in accordance with established veterinary medical and nursing procedures;

(iv) against the use of paralytics without anesthesia; and

(v) that the withholding of tranquilizers, anesthesia, analgesia, or euthanasia when scientifically necessary shall continue for only the necessary period of time;

(D) that no animal is used in more than one major operative experimenta from which it is allowed to recover except in cases of—

(i) scientific necessity; or

(ii) other special circumstances as determined by the Secretary; and

(E) that exceptions to such standards may be made only when specified by research protocol and that any such exception shall be detailed and explained in a report outlined under paragraph (7) and filed with the Institutional Animal Committee.

(4) The Secretary shall also promulgate standards to govern the transportation in commerce, and the handling, care, and treatment in connection therewith, by intermediate handlers, air carriers, or other carriers, of animals consigned by a dealer, research facility, exhibitor, operator of an auction sale, or other person, or any department, agency, or instrumentality of the United States or of any State or local government, for transportation in commerce. The Secretary shall have authority to promulgate such rules and regulations as he determines necessary to assure humane treatment of animals in the course of their transportation in commerce including requirements such as those with respect to containers, feed, water, rest, ventilation, temperature, and handling.

(5) In promulgating and enforcing standards established pursuant to this section, the Secretary is authorized and directed to consult experts, including outside consultants where indicated.

(6) (A) Nothing in this Act—

(i) except as provided in paragraph (7) of this subsection, shall be construed as authorizing the Secretary to promulgate rules, regulations, or orders with regard to design, outlines, guidelines or performance of actual research or experimentation by a research facility as determined by such research facility;

(ii) except as provided in subparagraphs (A) and (C)(ii) through (v) of paragraph (3) and paragraph (7) of this subsection, shall be construed as authorizing the Secretary to promulgate rules, regulations, or orders with regard to the performance of actual research or experimentation by a research facility as determined by such research facility; and

(iii) shall authorize the Secretary, during inspection, to interrupt the conduct of actual research or experimentation.

(B) No rule, regulation, order, or part of this Act shall be construed to require a research facility to disclose publicly or to the Institutional Animal Committee during its inspection, trade secrets or commercial or financial information which is privileged or confidential.

(7) (A) The Secretary shall require each research facility to show upon inspection, and to report at least annually, that the provisions of this Act are being followed and that professionally acceptable standards governing the care, treatment, and use of animals are being followed by the research facility during actual research or experimentation.

(B) In complying with subparagraph (A), such research facilities shall provide—

(i) information on procedures likely to produce pain or distress in any animal and assurances demonstrating that the principal investigator considered alternatives to those procedures;

(ii) assurances satisfactory to the Secretary that such facility is adhering to the standards described in this section; and

(iii) an explanation for any deviation from the standards promulgated under this section.

(8) Paragraph (1) shall not prohibit any State (or a political subdivision of such State) from promulgating standards in addition to those standards promulgated by the Secretary under paragraph (1).

(b)(1) The Secretary shall require that each research facility establish at least one Committee. Each Committee shall be appointed by the chief executive officer of each such research facility and shall be composed of not fewer than three members. Such members shall possess sufficient ability to assess animal care, treatment, and practices in experimental research as determined by the needs of the research facility and shall represent society's concerns regarding the welfare of animal subjects used at such facility. Of the members of the Committee—

(A) at least one member shall be a doctor of veterinary medicine;

(B) at least one member—

(i) shall not be affiliated in any way with such facility other than as a member of the Committee—

(ii) shall not be a member of the immediate family of a person who is affiliated with such facility; and

(iii) is intended to provide representation for general community interests in the proper care and treatment of animals; and

(C) in those cases where the Committee consists of more than three members, not more than three members shall be from the same administrative unit of such facility.

(2) A quorum shall be required for all formal actions of the Committee, including inspections under paragraph (3).

(3) The Committee shall inspect at least semiannually all animal study areas and animal facilities of such research facility and review as part of the inspection—

(A) practices involving pain to animals, and

(B) the condition of animals, to ensure compliance with the provisions of this Act to minimize pain and distress to animals. Exceptions to the requirement of inspection of such study areas may be made by the Secretary if animals are studied in their natural environment and the study area is prohibitive to easy access.

(4) (A) The Committee shall file an inspection certification report of each inspection at the research facility. Such report shall—

(i) be signed by a majority of the Committee members involved in the inspection;

(ii) include reports of any violation of the standards promulgated, or assurances required, by the Secretary, including any deficient conditions of animal care or treatment, any deviations of research practices from originally approved proposals that adversely affect animal welfare, any notification to the facility regarding such conditions and any corrections made thereafter;

(iii) include any minority views of the Committee; and

(iv) include any other information pertinent to the activities of the Committee.

(B) Such report shall remain on file for at least 3 years at the research facility and shall be available for inspection by the Animal and Plant Health Inspection Service and any funding Federal agency.

(C) In order to give the research facility an opportunity to correct any deficiencies or deviations discovered by reason of paragraph (3), the Committee shall notify the administrative representative of the research facility of any deficiencies or deviations from the provisions of this Act. If, after notification and an opportunity for correction, such deficiencies or deviations remain uncorrected, the Committee shall notify (in writing) the Animal and Plant Health Inspection Service and the funding Federal Agency of such deficiencies or deviations.

(5) The inspection results shall be available to Department of Agriculture inspectors for review during inspections. Department of Agriculture inspectors shall forward any Committee inspection records which include reports of uncorrected deficiencies or deviations to the Animal and Plant Health Inspection Service and any funding Federal agency of the project with respect to which such uncorrected deficiencies and deviations occurred.

. . . .

Appendix A

Section 16. (a) The Secretary shall make such investigations or inspections as he deems necessary to determine whether any dealer, exhibitor, intermediate handler, carrier, research facility, or operator of an auction sale subject to section 12 of this Act, has violated or is violating any provision of this Act or any regulation or standard issued thereunder, and for such purposes, the Secretary shall, at all reasonable times, have access to the places of business and the facilities, animals, and those records required to kept pursuant to section 10 of any such dealer, exhibitor, intermediate handler, carrier, research facility, operator of an auction sale. The Secretary shall inspect each research facility at least once each year and, in the case of deficiencies or deviations from the standards promulgated under this Act, shall conduct such follow-up inspections as may be necessary until all deficiencies or deviations from such standards are corrected. The Secretary shall promulgate such rules and regulations as he deems necessary to permit inspectors to confiscate or destroy in a humane manner any animal found to be suffering as a result of a failure to comply with any provision of this Act or any regulation or standard issued thereunder if (1) such animal is held by a dealer, (2) such animal is held by an exhibitor, (3) such animal is held by a research facility and is no longer required by such research facility to carry out the research, test or experiment for which such animal has been utilized, (4) such animal is held by an operator of an auction sale, or (5) such animal is held by an intermediate handler or a carrier.

. . . .

APPENDIX B

ENDANGERED SPECIES ACT, 1973

16 U.S.C. 1531-1554 (1973)

[Note: Some portions have been omitted.]

Section 2.

(a) FINDINGS.—The Congress finds and declares that—

(1) various species of fish, wildlife, and plants in the United States have been rendered extinct as a consequence of economic growth and development untempered by adequate concern and conservation;

(2) other species of fish, wildlife, and plants have been so depleted in numbers that they are in danger of or threatened with extinction;

(3) these species of fish, wildlife, and plants are of aesthetic, ecological, educational, historical, recreational, and scientific value to the Nation and its people;

(4) the United States has pledged itself as a sovereign state in the international community to conserve to the extent practicable the various species of fish or wildlife and plants facing extinction, pursuant to—

(A) migratory bird treaties with Canada and Mexico;

(B) the Migratory and Endangered Bird Treaty with Japan;

(C) the Convention on Nature Protection and Wildlife Preservation in the Western Hemisphere;

(D) the International Convention for the Northwest Atlantic Fisheries;

(E) the International Convention for the High Seas Fisheries of the North Pacific Ocean;

(F) the Convention on International Trade in Endangered Species of Wild Fauna and Flora; and

(G) other international agreements; and

(5) encouraging the States and other interested parties, through Federal financial assistance and a system of incentives, to develop and maintain conservation programs which meet national and international standards is a key to meeting the Nation's international commitments and to better safe-

guarding, for the benefit of all citizens, the Nation's heritage in fish, wildlife, and plants.

(b) PURPOSES.—The purposes of this Act are to provide a means whereby the ecosystems upon which endangered species and threatened species depend may be conserved, to provide a program for the conservation of such endangered species and threatened species, and to take such steps as may be appropriate to achieve the purposes of the treaties and conventions set forth in subsection (a) of this section.

(c) POLICY.—

(1) It is further declared to be the policy of Congress that all Federal departments and agencies shall seek to conserve endangered species and threatened species and shall utilize their authorities in furtherance of the purposes of this Act.

(2) It is further declared to be the policy of Congress that Federal agencies shall cooperate with State and local agencies to resolve water resource issues in concert with conservation of endangered species.

Section 3. For the purposes of this Act— . . .

(3) The terms "conserve," "conserving," and "conservation" mean to use and the use of all methods and procedures which are necessary to bring any endangered species or threatened species to the point at which the measures provided pursuant to this Act are no longer necessary. Such methods and procedures include, but are not limited to, all activities associated with scientific resources management such as research, census, law enforcement, habitat acquisition and maintenance, propagation, live trapping, and transplantation, and, in the extraordinary case where population pressures within a given ecosystem cannot be otherwise relieved, may include regulated taking.

(4) The term "Convention" means the Convention on International Trade in Endangered Species of Wild Fauna and Flora, signed on March 3, 1973, and the appendices thereto.

(5) (A) The term "critical habitat" for a threatened or endangered species means—

(i) the specific areas within the geographical area occupied by the species, at the time it is listed in accordance with the provisions of section 4 of this Act, on which are found those physical or biological features (I) essential to the conservation of the species and (II) which may require special management considerations or protection; and

(ii) specific areas outside the geographical area occupied by the species at the time it is listed in accordance with the provisions of section 4 of this Act, upon a determination by the Secretary that such areas are essential for the conservation of the species.

(B) Critical habitat may be established for those species now listed as threatened or endangered species for which no critical habitat has heretofore been established as set forth in subparagraph (A) of this paragraph.

(C) Except in those circumstances determined by the Secretary, critical habitat shall not include the entire geographical area which can be occupied by the threatened or endangered species.

(6) The term "endangered species" means any species which is in danger of extinction throughout all or a significant portion of its range other than a species of the Class Insecta determined by the Secretary to constitute a pest whose protection under the provisions of this Act would present an overwhelming and overriding risk to man. . .

(8) The term "fish or wildlife" means any member of the animal kingdom, including without limitation any mammal, fish, bird (including any migratory, nonmigratory, or endangered bird for which protection is also afforded by treaty or other international agreement), amphibian, reptile, mollusk, crustacean, arthropod or other invertebrate, and includes any part, product, egg, or offspring thereof, or the dead body or parts thereof. . .

(15) The term "species" includes any subspecies of fish or wildlife or plants, and any distinct population segment of any species of vertebrate fish or wildlife which interbreeds when mature. . .

(18) The term "take" means to harass, harm, pursue, hunt, shoot, wound, kill, trap, capture, or collect, or to attempt to engage in any such conduct.

(19) The term "threatened species" means any species which is likely to become an endangered species within the foreseeable future throughout all or a significant portion of its range. . . .

Section 4.
(a) GENERAL.—
(1) The Secretary shall by regulation promulgated in accordance with subsection (b) determine whether any species is an endangered species or a threatened species because of any of the following factors:

(A) the present or threatened destruction, modification, or curtailment of its habitat or range;

(B) overutilization for commercial, recreational, scientific, or educational purposes;

(C) disease or predation;

(D) the inadequacy of existing regulatory mechanisms;

(E) other natural or manmade factors affecting its continued existence. . . .

(3) The Secretary, by regulation promulgated in accordance with subsection (b) and to the maximum extent prudent and determinable—

(A) shall, concurrently with making a determination under paragraph (1) that a species is an endangered species or a threatened species, designate any habitat of such species which is then considered to be critical habitat; and

(B) may, from time-to-time thereafter as appropriate, revise such designation.

(b) BASIS FOR DETERMINATIONS.—

(1) (A) The Secretary shall make determinations required by subsection (a)(1) solely on the basis of the best scientific and commercial data available to him after conducting a review of the status of the species and after taking into account those efforts, if any, being made by any State or foreign nation, or any political subdivision of a State or foreign nation, to protect such species, whether by predator control, protection of habitat and food supply, or other conservation practices, within any area under its jurisdiction, or on the high seas.

(B) In carrying out this section, the Secretary shall give consideration to species which have been—

(i) designated as requiring protection from unrestricted commerce by any foreign nation, or pursuant to any international agreement; or

(ii) identified as in danger of extinction, or likely to become so within the foreseeable future, by any State agency or by any agency of a foreign nation that is responsible for the conservation of fish or wildlife or plants.

(2) The Secretary shall designate critical habitat, and make revisions thereto, under subsection (a)(3) on the basis of the best scientific data available and after taking into consideration the economic impact, and any other relevant impact, of specifying any particular area as critical habitat. The Secretary may exclude any area from critical habitat if he determines that the benefits of such exclusion outweigh the benefits of specifying such area as part of the critical habitat, unless he determines, based on the best scientific and commercial data available, that the failure to designate such area as critical habitat will result in the extinction of the species concerned.

(3) (A) To the maximum extent practicable, within 90 days after receiving the petition of an interested person under section 553(e) of title 5, United States Code, to add a species to, or to remove a species from, either of the lists published under subsection (c), the Secretary shall make a finding as to whether the petition presents substantial scientific or commercial information indicating that the petitioned action may be warranted. If such a petition is found to present such information, the Secretary shall promptly commence a review of the status of the species concerned. The Secretary shall promptly publish each finding made under this subparagraph in the Federal Register.

(B) Within 12 months after receiving a petition that is found under subparagraph (A) to present substantial information indicating that the petitioned action may be warranted, the Secretary shall make one of the following findings:

(i) The petitioned action is not warranted, in which case the Secretary shall promptly publish such finding in the Federal Register.

(ii) The petitioned action is warranted in which case the Secretary shall promptly publish in the Federal Register a general notice and the complete text of a proposed regulation to implement such action in accordance with paragraph (5).

(iii) The petitioned action is warranted but that—

(I) the immediate proposal and timely promulgation of a final regulation implementing the petitioned action in accordance with paragraphs (5) and (6) is precluded by pending proposals to determine whether any species is an endangered species or a threatened species, and

(II) expeditious progress is being made to add qualified species to either of the lists published under subsection (c) and to remove from such lists species for which the protections of the Act are no longer necessary, in which case the Secretary shall promptly publish such finding in the Federal Register, together with a description and evaluation of the reasons and data on which the finding is based.

(C) (i) A petition with respect to which a finding is made under subparagraph (B)(iii) shall be treated as a petition that is resubmitted to the Secretary under subparagraph (A) on the date of such finding and that presents substantial scientific or commercial information that the petitioned action may be warranted.

(ii) Any negative finding described in subparagraph (A) and any finding described in subparagraph (B)(i) or (iii) shall be subject to judicial review.

(iii) The Secretary shall implement a system to monitor effectively the status of all species with respect to which a finding is made under subparagraph (B)(iii) and shall make prompt use of the authority under paragraph 7 to prevent a significant risk to the well being of any such species.

(D) (i) To the maximum extent practicable, within 90 days after receiving the petition of an interested person under section 553(e) of title 5, United States Code, to revise a critical habitat designation, the Secretary shall make a finding as to whether the petition presents substantial scientific information indicating that the revision may be warranted. The Secretary shall promptly publish such finding in the Federal Register.

(ii) Within 12 months after receiving a petition that is found under clause (i) to present substantial information indicating that the requested revision may be warranted, the Secretary shall determine how he intends to proceed with the requested revision, and shall promptly publish notice of such intention in the Federal Register.

(4) Except as provided in paragraphs (5) and (6) of this subsection, the provisions of section 553 of title 5, United States Code (relating to rulemaking procedures), shall apply to any regulation promulgated to carry out the purposes of this Act.

(5) With respect to any regulation proposed by the Secretary to implement a determination, designation, or revision referred to in subsection (a) (1) or (3), the Secretary shall—

(A) not less than 90 days before the effective date of the regulation—

(i) publish a general notice and the complete text of the proposed regulation in the Federal Register, and

(ii) give actual notice of the proposed regulation (including the complete text of the regulation) to the State agency in each State in which the species is believed to occur, and to each county or equivalent jurisdiction in which the species is believed to occur, and invite the comment of such agency, and each such jurisdiction, thereon;

(B) insofar as practical, and in cooperation with the Secretary of State, give notice of the proposed regulation to each foreign nation in which the species is believed to occur or whose citizens harvest the species on the high seas, and invite the comment of such nation thereon;

(C) give notice of the proposed regulation to such professional scientific organizations as he deems appropriate;

(D) publish a summary of the proposed regulation in a newspaper of general circulation in each area of the United States in which the species is believed to occur; and

(E) promptly hold one public hearing on the proposed regulation if any person files a request for such a hearing within 45 days after the date of publication of general notice.

(6) (A) Within the one-year period beginning on the date on which general notice is published in accordance with paragraph (5)(A)(i) regarding a proposed regulation, the Secretary shall publish in the Federal Register—

(i) if a determination as to whether a species is an endangered species or a threatened species, or a revision of critical habitat, is involved, either—

(I) a final regulation to implement such determination,

(II) a final regulation to implement such revision or a finding that such revision should not be made,

(III) notice that such one-year period is being extended under subparagraph (B)(i), or

(IV) notice that the proposed regulation is being withdrawn under subparagraph (B)(ii), together with the finding on which such withdrawal is based; or

(ii) subject to subparagraph (C), if a designation of critical habitat is involved, either—

(I) a final regulation to implement such designation, or

(II) notice that such one-year period is being extended under such subparagraph.

(B) (i) If the Secretary finds with respect to a proposed regulation referred to in subparagraph (A)(i) that there is substantial disagreement regarding the sufficiency or accuracy of the available data relevant to the determination or revision concerned the Secretary may extend the one-year period specified in subparagraph (A) for not more than six months for purposes of soliciting additional data. . .

(C) A final regulation designating critical habitat of an endangered species or a threatened species shall be published concurrently with the final regulation implementing the determination that such species is endangered or threatened, unless the Secretary deems that—

(i) it is essential to the conservation of such species that the regulation implementing such determination be promptly published; or

(ii) critical habitat of such species is not then determinable, in which case the Secretary, with respect to the proposed regulation to designate such habitat, may extend the one-year period specified in subparagraph (A) by not more than one additional year, but not later than the close of such additional year the Secretary must publish a final regulation, based on such data as may be available at that time, designating, to the maximum extent prudent, such habitat. . . .

(8) (c) LISTS.—

(1) The Secretary of the Interior shall publish in the Federal Register a list of all species determined by him or the Secretary of Commerce to be endangered species and a list of all species determined by him or the Secretary of Commerce to be threatened species. Each list shall refer to the species contained therein by scientific and common name or names, if any, specify with respect to such species over what portion of its range it is endangered or threatened, and specify any critical habitat within such range. The Secretary shall from time to time revise each list published under the authority of this subsection to reflect recent determinations, designations, and revisions made in accordance with subsections (a) and (b).

(2) The Secretary shall—

(A) conduct, at least once every five years, a review of all species included in a list which is published pursuant to paragraph (1) and which is in effect at the time of such review; and

(B) determine on the basis of such review whether any such species should—

(i) be removed from such list;

(ii) be changed in status from an endangered species to a threatened species; or

(iii) be changed in status from a threatened species to an endangered species. Each determination under subparagraph (B) shall be made in accordance with the provisions of subsection (a) and (b).

(d) PROTECTIVE REGULATIONS.—Whenever any species is listed as a threatened species pursuant to subsection (c) of this section, the Secretary shall issue such regulations as he deems necessary and advisable to provide for the conservation of such species. The Secretary may by regulation prohibit with respect to any threatened species any act prohibited under section 9(a)(1), in the case of fish or wildlife, or section 9(a)(2), in the case of plants, with respect to endangered species; except that with respect to the taking of resident species of fish or wildlife, such regulations shall apply in any State which has entered into a cooperative agreement pursuant to section 6(c) of this Act only to the extent that such regulations have also been adopted by such State.

(e) SIMILARITY OF APPEARANCE CASES.—The Secretary may, by regulation of commerce or taking, and to the extent he deems advisable, treat any species as an endangered species or threatened species even though it is not listed pursuant to section 4 of this Act if he finds that—

(A) such species so closely resembles in appearance, at the point in question, a species which has been listed pursuant to such section that enforcement personnel would have substantial difficulty in attempting to differentiate between the listed and unlisted species;

(B) the effect of this substantial difficulty is an additional threat to an endangered or threatened species; and

(C) such treatment of an unlisted species will substantially facilitate the enforcement and further the policy of this Act.

(f) RECOVERY PLANS.—

(1) The Secretary shall develop and implement plans (hereinafter in this subsection referred to as "recovery plans") for the conservation and survival of endangered species and threatened species listed pursuant to this section, unless he finds that such a plan will not promote the conservation of the species. The Secretary, in development and implementing recovery plans, shall, to the maximum extent practicable—

(A) give priority to those endangered species or threatened species, without regard to taxonomic classification, that are most likely to benefit from such plans, particularly those species that are, or may be, in conflict with construction or other development projects or other forms of economic activity;

(B) incorporate in each plan—

(i) a description of such site-specific management actions as may be necessary to achieve the plan's goal for the conservation and survival of the species;

(ii) objective, measurable criteria which, when met, would result in a determination, in accordance with the provisions of this section, that the species be removed from the list; and

(iii) estimates of the time required and the cost to carry out those measures needed to achieve the plan's goal and to achieve intermediate steps toward that goal.

(2) The Secretary, in developing and implementing recovery plans, may procure the services of appropriate public and private agencies and institutions, and other qualified persons. Recovery teams appointed pursuant to this subsection shall not be subject to the Federal Advisory Committee Act.

(3) The Secretary shall report every two years to the Committee on Environment and Public Works of the Senate and the Committee on Merchant Marine and Fisheries of the House of Representatives on the status of efforts to develop and implement recovery plans for all species listed pursuant to this section and on the status of all species for which such plans have been developed.

(4) The Secretary shall, prior to final approval of a new or revised recovery plan, provide public notice and an opportunity for public review and comment on such plan. The Secretary shall consider all information presented during the public comment period prior to approval of the plan.

(5) Each Federal agency shall, prior to implementation of a new or revised recovery plan, consider all information presented during the public comment period under paragraph (4).

(g) MONITORING.—

(1) The Secretary shall implement a system in cooperation with the States to monitor effectively for not less than five years the status of all species which have recovered to the point at which the measures provided pursuant to this Act are no longer necessary and which, in accordance with the provisions of this section, have been removed from either of the lists published under subsection (c).

(2) The Secretary shall make prompt use of the authority under paragraph 7 of subsection (b) of this section to prevent a significant risk to the well being of any such recovered species. . . .

Section 9. PROHIBITED ACTS
(a) GENERAL.—
(1) Except as provided in sections 6(g)(2) and 10 of this Act, with respect to any endangered species of fish or wildlife listed pursuant to section 4 of this Act it is unlawful for any person subject to the jurisdiction of the United States to—

(A) import any such species into, or export any such species from the United States;

(B) take any such species within the United States or the territorial sea of the United States;

(C) take any such species upon the high seas;

(D) possess, sell, deliver, carry, transport, or ship, by any means whatsoever, any such species taken in violation of subparagraphs (B) and (C);

(E) deliver, receive, carry, transport, or ship in interstate or foreign commerce, by any means whatsoever and in the course of a commercial activity, any such species;

(F) sell or offer for sale in interstate or foreign commerce any such species; or

(G) violate any regulation pertaining to such species or to any threatened species of fish or wildlife listed pursuant to section 4 of this Act and promulgated by the Secretary pursuant to authority provided by this Act. . . .

[(2) makes similar stipulations for plants]

Section 11. Penalties and Enforcement. . .

(g) CITIZEN SUITS.—

(1) Except as provided in paragraph (2) of this subsection any person may commence a civil suit on his own behalf—

(A) to enjoin any person, including the United States and any other governmental instrumentality or agency (to the extent permitted by the eleventh amendment to the Constitution), who is alleged to be in violation of any provision of this Act or regulation issued under the authority thereof; or

(B) to compel the Secretary to apply, pursuant to section 6(g)(2)(B)(ii) of this Act, the prohibitions set forth in or authorized pursuant to section 4(d) or section 9(a)(1)(B) of this Act with respect to the taking of any resident endangered species or threatened species within any State; or

(C) against the Secretary where there is alleged a failure of the Secretary to perform any act or duty under section 4 which is not discretionary with the Secretary.

The district courts shall have jurisdiction, without regard to the amount in controversy or the citizenship of the parties, to enforce any such provision or regulation or to order the Secretary to perform such act or duty, as the case may be. In any civil suit commenced under subparagraph (B) the district court shall compel the Secretary to apply the prohibition sought if the court finds that the allegation that an emergency exists is supported by substantial evidence. . . .

APPENDIX C

ANIMAL LEGAL DEFENSE FUND V. GLICKMAN I, 154 F.3D 426, 1998

U.S. COURT OF APPEALS, DISTRICT OF COLUMBIA CIRCUIT, FILED SEPTEMBER 1, 1998

ANIMAL LEGAL DEFENSE FUND, INC., ET AL., APPELLEES, V. DANIEL R. GLICKMAN, SECRETARY OF AGRICULTURE, ET AL., AND NATIONAL ASSOCIATION FOR BIOMEDICAL RESEARCH, APPELLANTS

(Note: Excerpted. Footnotes, most citations, dissent, and some other matter have been omitted.)

Appeals from the United States District Court for the District of Columbia (No. 96cv00408)

Before: Edwards, Chief Judge, Wald, Silberman, Williams, Ginsburg, Sentelle, Henderson, Randolph, Rogers, Tatel and Garland, Circuit Judges.

Argued in banc May 13, 1998

The opinion of the court was delivered by: Circuit Judge Wald.
Dissenting Opinion filed by Circuit Judge Sentelle, with whom Silberman, Ginsburg and Henderson, Circuit Judges, join.

Appendix C

Wald, Circuit Judge:

The 1985 amendments to the Animal Welfare Act ("AWA") direct the Secretary of Agriculture to "promulgate standards to govern the humane handling, care, treatment, and transportation of animals by dealers, research facilities, and exhibitors." (1985) (codified at 7 U.S.C. § 2143(a) (1994)). They further provide that such standards "shall include minimum requirements" for, inter alia, "a physical environment adequate to promote the psychological well-being of primates." Id. Pursuant to this authority, the United States Department of Agriculture ("USDA") issued regulations for primate dealers, exhibitors, and research facilities that included a small number of mandatory requirements and also required the regulated parties to "develop, document, and follow an appropriate plan for environment enhancement adequate to promote the psychological well-being of nonhuman primates. The plan must be in accordance with the currently accepted professional standards as cited in appropriate professional journals or reference guides, and as directed by the attending veterinarian." 9 C.F.R. § 3.81 (1997). Although these plans must be made available to the USDA, the regulated parties are not obligated to make them available to members of the public. See id.

The individual plaintiffs, Roseann Circelli, Mary Eagan, and Marc Jurnove, challenge these regulations on the ground that they violate the USDA's statutory mandate under the AWA and permit dealers, exhibitors, and research facilities to keep primates under inhumane conditions. The individual plaintiffs allege that they suffered aesthetic injury during their regular visits to animal exhibitions when they observed primates living under such conditions. A divided panel of this court held that all of the plaintiffs lacked constitutional standing to pursue their claims. See *Animal Legal Defense Fund, Inc. v. Glickman*, 130 F.3d 464, 466 (D.C. Cir. 1997).

This court subsequently vacated that judgment and granted rehearing in banc.

We hold that Mr. Jurnove, one of the individual plaintiffs, has standing to sue. Accordingly, we need not pass on the standing of the other individual plaintiffs. . . .

I. BACKGROUND

A. MARC JURNOVE'S AFFIDAVIT

Mr. Jurnove's affidavit is an uncontested statement of the injuries that he has suffered to his aesthetic interest in observing animals living under humane conditions.

For his entire adult life, Mr. Jurnove has "been employed and/or worked as a volunteer for various human and animal relief and rescue organizations."

Jurnove Affidavit ¶ 3. "By virtue of [his] training in wildlife rehabilitation and [his] experience in investigating complaints about the treatment of wildlife, [he is] very familiar with the needs of and proper treatment of wildlife." Id. ¶ 6. "Because of [his] familiarity with and love of exotic animals, as well as for recreational and educational purposes and because [he] appreciate[s] these animals' beauty, [he] enjoy[s] seeing them in various zoos and other parks near [his] home." Id. ¶ 7.

Between May 1995 and June 1996, when he filed his affidavit, Mr. Jurnove visited the Long Island Game Farm Park and Zoo ("Game Farm") at least nine times. Throughout this period, and since as far back as 1992, the USDA has not questioned the adequacy of this facility's plan for the psychological well-being of primates.

Mr. Jurnove's first visit to the Game Farm, in May 1995, lasted approximately six hours. While there, Mr. Jurnove saw many animals living under inhumane conditions. For instance, the Game Farm housed one primate, a Japanese Snow Macaque, in a cage "that was a distance from and not in view of the other primate cages." Id. ¶ 14. "The only cage enrichment device this animal had was an unused swing." Id. Similarly, Mr. Jurnove "saw a large male chimpanzee named Barney in a holding area by himself. He could not see or hear any other primate." Id. ¶ 8. Mr. Jurnove "kn[e]w that chimpanzees are very social animals and it upset [him] very much to see [Barney] in isolation from other primates." Id. The Game Farm also placed adult bears next to squirrel monkeys, although Jurnove saw evidence that the arrangement made the monkeys frightened and extremely agitated.

The day after this visit, Mr. Jurnove began to contact government agencies, including the USDA, in order to secure help for these animals. Based on Mr. Jurnove's complaint, the USDA inspected the Game Farm on May 3, 1995. According to Mr. Jurnove's uncontested affidavit, however, the agency's resulting inspection report "states that [the USDA inspectors] found the facility in compliance with all the standards." Id. ¶ 18. Mr. Jurnove returned to the Game Farm on eight more occasions to observe these officially legal conditions.

On July 17, 18, and 19, 1995, he found "virtually the same conditions" that allegedly caused him aesthetic injury during his first visit to the Game Farm in May. Id. ¶ 20. For instance, Barney, the chimpanzee, and Samantha, the Japanese Snow Macaque, were still alone in their cages. This time, Mr. Jurnove documented these conditions with photographs and sent them to the USDA. See id. WW19–20. Nevertheless, the responding USDA inspectors found only a few violations at the Game Farm; they reported "nothing" about many of the conditions that concerned Mr. Jurnove and that he had told the agency about, such as "the fact that numerous primates were being housed alone" and the lack of adequate stimulation in their cages. Id. ¶ 21.

Appendix C

Mr. Jurnove devoted two trips in August and one in September to "videotaping the conditions that the inspection missed," and on each trip he found that the inhumane conditions persisted. Id. WW 22-28. At the end of September, the USDA sent three inspectors to the Game Farm in response to Mr. Jurnove's continued complaints and reportage; they found violations, however, only with regard to the facility's fencing.

Mr. Jurnove returned to the Game Farm once more on October 1, 1995. Indeed, he only stopped his frequent visits when he became ill and required major surgery. After his health returned, Mr. Jurnove visited the Game Farm in April 1996, hoping to see improvements in the conditions that he had repeatedly brought to the USDA's attention. He was disappointed again; "the animals [were] in literally the same conditions as [he] had seen them over the summer of 1995." Id. ¶ 33. Mr. Jurnove's resulting complaints prompted the USDA to inspect the Game Farm in late May 1996. For the fourth time, the agency found the facility largely in compliance, with a few exceptions not relevant to the plaintiffs' main challenge in this case. In June 1996, Mr. Jurnove filed the affidavit that is the basis of his claim here. He concluded this affidavit by stating his intent to "return to the Farm in the next several weeks" and to "continue visiting the Farm to see the animals there." Id. ¶ 43.

B. THE PLAINTIFFS' COMPLAINT

The plaintiffs' complaint elaborates a two-part legal theory based on the factual allegations in the individual plaintiffs' affidavits. First, the plaintiffs allege that the AWA requires the USDA to adopt specific, minimum standards to protect primates' psychological well-being, and the agency has failed to do so. . . . ("Instead of issuing the standards on this topic, USDA's regulation [at 9 C.F.R. § 3.81] simply states that the 'plans' must be in accordance with currently accepted professional standards."); id. ¶ 107 ("By providing that animal exhibitors and other regulated entities shall develop their own 'plans' for a physical environment adequate to promote the psychological well-being of non-human primates, USDA has failed to satisfy the statutory requirement that it set the 'minimum' standards.").

Second, the plaintiffs contend that the conditions that caused Mr. Jurnove aesthetic injury complied with current USDA regulations, but that lawful regulations would have prohibited those conditions and protected Mr. Jurnove from the injuries that he describes in his affidavit. See id. ¶ 53 ("Marc Jurnove has been and continues to be injured by USDA's failure to issue and implement standards for a physical environment adequate to promote the psychological wellbeing of primates because this harms the non-human primates he sees at the Long Island Game Farm and Zoo which in turn caused and causes him extreme aesthetic harm and emotional and physical distress."); id. ("[B]ecause USDA regulations permit the nonhuman primates in zoos, such as the Long Island Game Farm and Zoological Park to be housed in isolation, Marc Jurnove was exposed to and will be exposed in the future to behaviors exhibited by these animals which indicate the psychological debilitation caused by social deprivation. Observing these behaviors caused and will cause Marc Jurnove personal distress and aesthetic and emotional injury."); id. ¶ 58 ("Marc Jurnove experienced and continues to experience physical and mental distress when he realizes that he, by himself, is powerless to help the animals he witnesses suffering when such suffering derives from or is traceable to the improper implementation and enforcement of the Animal Welfare Act by USDA.").

C. Procedural History

The United States District Court, Judge Charles R. Richey, held that the individual plaintiffs had standing to sue, finding in their favor on a motion for summary judgment. See 943 F. Supp. at 54-57. On the merits, the district court held that 9 C.F.R. § 3.81 violates the Administrative Procedure Act ("APA") because it fails to set standards, including minimum requirements, as mandated by the AWA; that the USDA's failure to promulgate standards for a physical environment adequate to promote the psychological well-being of primates constitutes agency action unlawfully withheld and unreasonably delayed in violation of the APA; and that the USDA's failure to issue a regulation promoting the social grouping of nonhuman primates is arbitrary, capricious, and an abuse of discretion in violation of the APA.

A split panel of this court held that none of the plaintiffs had standing to sue and accordingly did not reach the merits of their complaint. See 130 F.3d at 466. This court granted rehearing in banc, limited to the question of Marc Jurnove's standing.

II. ANALYSIS

"The question of standing involves both constitutional limitations on federal-court jurisdiction and prudential limitations on its exercise." Bennett v. Spear, 117 S. Ct. 1154, 1161 (1997). To meet the "case or controversy" requirement of Article III, a plaintiff must demonstrate: (1) that she has suffered "injury in fact;" (2) that the injury is "fairly traceable" to the defendant's actions; and (3) that a favorable judicial ruling will "likely" redress the plaintiff's injury. Id.; see also *Lujan v. Defenders of Wildlife*, 504 U.S. 555, 560-61 (1992). In addition, the Supreme Court has recognized prudential requirements for standing, including "that a plaintiff's grievance must arguably fall within the zone of interests protected or regulated by the statutory provision or constitutional guarantee invoked in the suit." Bennett, 117 S. Ct. at 1161.

We find that Mr. Jurnove's allegations fall well within these requirements.

A. INJURY IN FACT

Mr. Jurnove's allegations solidly establish injury in fact. As his affidavit indicates, Mr. Jurnove "enjoy[s] seeing [animals] in various zoos and other parks near [his] home" "[b]ecause of [his] familiarity with and love of exotic animals, as well as for recreational and educational purposes and because [he] appreciate[s] these animals' beauty." Jurnove Affidavit ¶ 7. He decided to tour the primate cages at the Game Farm "in furtherance of [his] appreciation for exotic animals and [his] desire to observe and enjoy them." Id. During this tour and the ones that followed, Mr. Jurnove suffered direct, concrete, and particularized injury to this aesthetic interest in observing animals living under humane conditions. At this particular zoo, which he has regularly visited and plans to keep visiting, he saw particular animals enduring inhumane treatment. He developed an interest, moreover, in seeing these particular animals living under humane treatment. As he explained, "[w]hat I observed [at the Game Farm] was an assault on my senses and greatly impaired my ability to observe and enjoy these captive animals." Id. ¶ 17. "I want to observe, study, and enjoy these animals in humane conditions." Id. ¶ 43.

Simply put, Mr. Jurnove has alleged far more than an abstract, and uncognizable, interest in seeing the law enforced. See *Allen v. Wright*, 468 U.S. 737, 754 (1984) ("This Court has repeatedly held that an asserted right to have the Government act in accordance with law is not sufficient, standing alone, to confer jurisdiction on a federal court."). . . . To the contrary, Mr. Jurnove has made clear that he has an aesthetic interest in seeing exotic animals living in a nurturing habitat, and that he has attempted to exercise this interest by repeatedly visiting a particular animal exhibition to observe particular animals there. This interest was allegedly injured, however, when Mr. Jurnove witnessed the actual living conditions of the primates described and named in his affidavit. . . .

The Supreme Court has repeatedly made clear that injury to an aesthetic interest in the observation of animals is sufficient to satisfy the demands of Article III standing. . . .

The key requirement, one that Mr. Jurnove clearly satisfies, is that the plaintiff have suffered his injury in a personal and individual way—for instance, by seeing with his own eyes the particular animals whose condition caused him aesthetic injury. . . .

[Court cases proving these points are cited and described.]

Myriad cases recognizing individual plaintiffs' injury in fact based on affronts to their aesthetic interests in observing animals living in humane habitats, or in using pristine environmental areas that have not been despoiled, articulate a second principle of standing. It has never been the law, and is not so today, that injury in fact requires the elimination (or threatened elimination) of either the animal species or environmental feature in question. . . .

[T]he Animal Welfare Act, with which we deal here, is explicitly concerned with the quality of animal life, rather than the number of animals in existence. . . . Quite naturally, suits alleging violations of this statute will focus on the conditions under which animals live. . . . Along these lines, this court has already noted in *Animal Welfare Institute*, which recognized injury in fact based on an aesthetic interest in seeing animals living under humane conditions, that "[w]here an act is expressly motivated by considerations of humaneness toward animals, who are uniquely incapable of defending their own interests in court, it strikes us as eminently logical to allow groups specifically concerned with animal welfare to invoke the aid of the courts in enforcing the statute." 561 F.2d at 1007. Moreover, and perhaps more importantly, it does not make sense, as a matter of logic, to suppose that people suffer aesthetic injury from government action that threatens to wipe out an animal species altogether, and not from government action that leaves some animals in a persistent state of suffering. To the contrary, the latter seems capable of causing more serious aesthetic injury than the former.

Mr. Jurnove has adequately alleged injury to an aesthetic interest in observing animals living under humane conditions. His affidavit describes both the animal exhibition that he regularly visits, and the specific animals there whose condition caused Mr. Jurnove injury. It requires no expansion of existing standing doctrine to find that he has established a cognizable injury in fact.

B. Causation

Plaintiffs allege that the AWA, 7 U.S.C. § 2143, requires the USDA to adopt explicit minimum standards to govern the humane treatment of primates, and that the agency did not do so. They further contend that the conditions that caused Mr. Jurnove injury complied with current USDA regulations, but that lawful regulations would have prohibited those conditions and protected Mr. Jurnove from the injuries that his affidavit describes. We find that these allegations satisfy the causation prong of Article III standing.

As Mr. Jurnove's affidavit elaborates, he allegedly suffered aesthetic injury upon observing conditions that the present USDA regulations permit. Mr. Jurnove, for instance, "saw a large male chimpanzee named Barney in a holding area by himself. He could not see or hear any other primate."

Jurnove Affidavit ¶ 8. Mr. Jurnove also "viewed a monkey cage [containing one Japanese Snow Macaque] that was a distance from and not in view of the other primate cages." Id. ¶ 14. As the plaintiffs observe, see First Amended Complaint WW 84, 95, 114-17, the housing of these two primates appears to be compatible with current regulations, which state only that "[t]he environment enhancement plan must include specific provisions to address the social needs of nonhuman primates of species known to exist in social groups in nature. Such specific provisions must be in accordance with currently accepted professional standards, as cited in appropriate professional journals or reference guides, and as directed by the attending veterinarian." 9 C.F.R. § 3.81(a). Thus, an exhibition may apparently comply with the procedural requirement that this standard creates—by establishing a plan that "address[es]" the social needs of primates—and still leave a primate caged singly. Similarly, 9 C.F.R. § 3.81(a)(3) provides that "[i]ndividually housed nonhuman primates must be able to see and hear nonhuman primates of their own or compatible species unless the attending veterinarian determines that it would endanger their health, safety, or well-being." Here again, the regulation is structured so that an exhibitor that secured the approval of the veterinarian in its employ could comply with the regulation without actually housing nonhuman primates within the sight or sound of other primates. . . . Whatever the ultimate merits of the plaintiffs' case, they most definitely assert that the AWA requires minimum standards to prohibit or more rigidly restrict the occasions on which such allegedly inhumane treatment can occur.

Mr. Jurnove's affidavit also states that "[t]he pen next to the adult bears housed the squirrel monkeys. . . . I observed the monkeys repeatedly walking over to the door and sniffing and acting very upset when the bears came near." Jurnove Affidavit ¶ 11. Plaintiffs allege that the current regulations permit the housing of incompatible species next to each other. See First Amended Complaint WW 46-47. Specifically, these regulations state that "[n]onhuman primates may not be housed with other species of primates or animals unless they are compatible." 9 C.F.R. § 3.81(a)(3). This provision does not expressly regulate animals housed next to each other, but in separate cages. But even if section 3.81(a)(3) does apply to the situation that Mr. Jurnove observed, it includes the caveat that "[c]ompatibility of nonhuman primates must be determined in accordance with generally accepted professional practices and actual observations, as directed by the attending veterinarian," thus again permitting wide discretion on the part of the local veterinarian.

Similarly, Mr. Jurnove's affidavit observes that "[t]he only cage enrichment device [a Japanese Snow Macaque] had was an unused swing." Jurnove Affidavit ¶ 14. The plaintiffs allege that such a situation is perfectly legal under the present regulations, see First Amended Complaint ¶ 84, which provide only that "[t]he physical environment in the primary enclosures must be enriched by providing means of expressing noninjurious species-typical activities." 9 C.F.R. § 3.81(b). The regulations do not include any specific requirements governing the particular kind or number of enrichment devices. According to the plaintiffs, providing only a single swing, and one that the primate appears to shun, offends the AWA's mandate for minimum standards, although it is perfectly compatible with 9 C.F.R. § 3.81(b).

The USDA's own actions in this case further support the plaintiffs' allegation that the agency's current regulations allow the conditions that allegedly caused Mr. Jurnove injury. As Mr. Jurnove's affidavit makes clear, the Game Farm has repeatedly submitted to inspection by the USDA. The allegedly inhumane conditions at the Game Farm have persisted precisely because the USDA inspectors have concluded on the basis of these visits that in every important aspect the conditions at the Game Farm comply with the USDA regulations. If the USDA had found the Game Farm out of compliance with current regulations, or if the governing regulations had themselves been more stringent, the Game Farm's owners would have been forced (in order to remain in accord with the law) to either alter their practices or go out of business and transfer their animals to exhibitors willing to operate legally; either scenario would protect Mr. Jurnove's aesthetic interest in observing animals living under humane conditions. Instead, however, the USDA has not questioned the legality of the Game Farm's plan since 1992. Since May 1995, when Mr. Jurnove began visiting the Game Farm and complaining to the agency, the USDA inspectors have examined, and largely approved, the actual conditions at the facility at least four times. The USDA's first inspection report "states that [the USDA inspectors] found the facility in compliance with all the standards." Jurnove Affidavit ¶ 18. Although subsequent inspection reports identify a few conditions that Mr. Jurnove agrees violate the USDA regulations, the USDA continued—in at least three more inspection reports—to conclude that the Game Farm was in compliance with existing USDA regulations in all other respects, including presumably the existence of a plan that met the regulations' standards.

Supreme Court precedent establishes that the causation requirement for constitutional standing is met when a plaintiff demonstrates that the challenged agency action authorizes the conduct that allegedly caused the plaintiff's injuries, if that conduct would allegedly be illegal otherwise. . . . [Citation of cases establishing this point have been omitted.]

A question was raised at oral argument about whether Mr. Jurnove has nonetheless failed to satisfy the causation prong of constitutional standing, on the ground that the governing law simply permits the conditions that allegedly injured him, rather than requiring animal exhibitors to follow the allegedly inhumane practices. The background condition governing animal exhibitors, this argument proceeds, is that anything the exhibitors do is legal unless statutes and regulations make specific conduct illegal. Because neither the AWA nor the USDA's implementing regulations have changed this status quo—i.e., in no way have they affected the conditions that allegedly injured Mr. Jurnove—there is no causal link between any government action and Mr. Jurnove's injury.

This argument, however, is founded on a false premise. The proper comparison for determining causation is not between what the agency did and the status quo before the agency acted. Rather, the proper comparison is between what the agency did and what the plaintiffs allege the agency should have done under the statute. The plaintiffs' legal theory of this case, which we accept for purposes of determining Mr. Jurnove's standing, is grounded on their view that animal exhibitors are in fact governed by a mandatory legal regime. Specifically, the plaintiffs allege that the AWA requires the USDA to establish specific, mandatory requirements that establish humane living conditions for animals. . . . According to this view, the AWA itself prohibits the conditions that allegedly injured Mr. Jurnove, and the USDA regulations misinterpret the statute by permitting these conditions. Both the Supreme Court and this circuit have repeatedly found causation where a challenged government action permitted the third party conduct that allegedly caused a plaintiff injury, when that conduct would have otherwise been illegal. Neither court has ever stated that the challenged law must compel the third party to act in the allegedly injurious way. . . . [Citations of cases establishing this point have been omitted.]

Mr. Jurnove's affidavit accordingly falls well within our established causation requirement for constitutional standing. He alleges that the USDA failed to adopt the specific, minimum standards that the AWA requires. He further describes how the conditions that caused him injury complied with current USDA regulations, and alleges that regulations complying with the AWA would have prohibited those conditions and protected him from the injuries that his affidavit recounts.

C. REDRESSIBILITY

We also find that Mr. Jurnove has satisfied the redressibility element of constitutional standing. Mr. Jurnove's affidavit alleges that he has a current routine of regularly visiting the Game Farm and provides a finite time period within which he will make his next visit, stating that he plans to "return to the Farm in the next several weeks" and to "continue visiting the Farm to see the animals there." Jurnove Affidavit ¶ 43. As the plaintiffs' complaint argues, more stringent regulations, which prohibit the inhumane conditions that have consistently caused Mr. Jurnove aesthetic injury in the past, would necessarily alleviate Mr. Jurnove's aesthetic injury during his planned, future trips to the Game Farm. See First Amended Complaint WW 53, 58. Tougher regulations would either allow Mr. Jurnove to visit a more humane Game Farm or, if the Game Farm's owners decide to close rather than comply with higher legal standards, to possibly visit the animals he has come to know in their new homes within exhibitions that comply with the more exacting regulations.

The Supreme Court's recent decision in *FEC v. Akins*, moreover, rejects the possible counterargument that the redressibility element of constitutional standing requires a plaintiff to establish that the defendant agency will actually enforce any new binding regulations against the regulated third party. . . . [Description of this case has been omitted.]

Mr. Jurnove, accordingly, has met all three of the constitutional requirements for standing.

D. Prudential Standing/Zone of Interests

Mr. Jurnove also falls within the zone of interests protected under the AWA's provisions on animal exhibitions. As the Supreme Court has recently reaffirmed, the zone of interests test is generous and relatively undemanding. "[T]here need be no indication of congressional purpose to benefit the would-be plaintiff." *National Credit Union Admin. v. First National Bank & Trust Co.*, 118 S. Ct. 927, 934 (1998). Instead, the test, a gloss on APA § 10(a), 5 U.S.C. § 702 (1994), asks only "whether the interest sought to be protected by the complainant is arguably within the zone of interests to be protected by the statute," *National Credit Union Admin.*, 118 S. Ct. at 935 [76]. . . . [Citations of further cases to prove this point have been omitted.]

In this case, logic, legislative history, and the structure of the AWA, all indicate that Mr. Jurnove's injury satisfies the zone of interests test. The very purpose of animal exhibitions is, necessarily, to entertain and educate people; exhibitions make no sense unless one takes the interests of their human visitors into account. The legislative history of both the 1985 amendments to the Animal Welfare Act and the 1970 act that first included animal exhibitions within the AWA confirms that Congress acted with the public's interests in mind.

In introducing the 1985 amendments, Senator Robert Dole explained "that we need to ensure the public that adequate safeguards are in place to prevent unnecessary abuses to animals, and that everything possible is being done to decrease the pain of animals during experimentation and testing." 131 Cong. Rec. 29,155 (1985). The Congressmen who went on the House floor to introduce the act that first extended the AWA to cover animal exhibitions recognized that their bill "ha[d] been a focal point of concern among animal lovers throughout the Nation for some time" and spoke of the "great pleasure" that animals bring to the people who see them. 116 Cong. Rec. 40,159 (1970) (statement of Rep. Mizell); see also H.R. Rep. No. 91-1651, at 1 (1970) ("Beginning with the legislation passed in 1966 (Public Law 89-544), the United States Government has implemented a statutory mandate that small helpless creatures deserve the care and protection of a strong and enlightened public.") Indeed, Congress had placed animal exhibitions within the scope of the AWA after hearings documenting how inhumane conditions at these exhibitions affected the people who came and watched the animals there. . . .

Throughout, the Congressmen responsible for including animal exhibitions within the AWA encouraged the continued monitoring of humane societies and their members. They spoke, for instance, of how America had long depended on humane societies to bring the mistreatment of animals to light. See, e.g., 116 Cong. Rec. 40,305 (1970) (statement of Rep. Whitehurst). The Congressmen further acknowledged that humane societies were the moving force behind the legislation to include animal exhibitions within the AWA. See, e.g., 116 Cong. Rec. 40,156 (1970) (statement of Rep. Foley).

The structure of the AWA also makes clear that Mr. Jurnove falls within the statute's zone of interests. While the AWA establishes oversight committees with private citizen members for research facilities, see 7 U.S.C. § 2143(b)(1) (1994), it created no counterpart for animal exhibitions. But, as the legislative history shows, the AWA anticipated the continued monitoring of concerned animal lovers to ensure that the purposes of the Act were honored. Mr. Jurnove, a regular viewer of animal exhibitions regulated under the AWA, clearly falls within the zone of interests the statute protects. His interests are among those that Congress sought to benefit through the AWA, and he certainly is one of the individuals "who in practice can be expected to police the interests that the statute protects." *Mova Pharmaceutical Corp.*, 140 F.3d at 1075.

III. CONCLUSION

Mr. Jurnove has standing to sue. He satisfies the injury, causation, and redressibility elements of constitutional standing, and also falls within the zone of interests for the Animal Welfare Act. We accordingly have no need to consider the standing of the other individual plaintiffs. We leave a determination of the merits of the plaintiffs' claim to a future panel of this court.

So ordered.

APPENDIX D

ANIMAL LEGAL DEFENSE FUND V. GLICKMAN II, 204 F.3D 229, 2000

[Some case citations and other material are omitted.]

United States Court of Appeals, District of Columbia Circuit. Judge WIL-LIAMS, Circuit Judge delivered the opinion of the court.

In *Animal Legal Defense Fund, Inc. v. Glickman*, 154 F.3d 426 (D.C.Cir.1998) (en banc), we held that plaintiff Marc Jurnove has standing to challenge regulations promulgated by the Secretary of Agriculture in 1991 that purport to set "minimum requirements . . . for a physical environment adequate to promote the psychological well-being of primates." 7 U.S.C. § 2143(a)(1)-(2). The en banc court left untouched the panel's decision that Animal Legal Defense Fund lacked standing. The court referred the merits—the question whether the Secretary's regulations satisfy that statutory mandate and the Administrative Procedure Act—to a future panel. Finding that the regulations do meet the statutory and APA tests, we reverse the district court's decision to the contrary.

* * *

In 1985 Congress passed the Improved Standards for Laboratory Animals Act, Pub.L. No. 99-198, 99 Stat. 1645, amending the Animal Welfare Act of 1966. See 7 U.S.C. § 2131 et seq. The 1985 amendments directed the Secretary of Agriculture to promulgate "standards to govern the humane handling, care, treatment, and transportation of animals by dealers, research facilities, and exhibitors." Id. § 2143(a)(1). The Act specified that among these must be "minimum requirements . . . for a physical environment adequate to promote the psychological well-being of primates." Id. § 2143(a)(1)-(2).

There are over 240 species of non-human primates, ranging from marmosets of South America that are a foot tall and weigh less than half a pound to gorillas of western Africa standing six feet tall and weighing up to 500 pounds. It proved no simple task to design regulations to promote the psychological well-being of such varied species as they are kept and handled for exhibition and research. Notice of intent to issue regulations was first published in the Federal Register in 1986, 51 Fed.Reg. 7950 (1986), but the Secretary did not publish proposed regulations until 1989. 54 Fed.Reg. 10897 (1989). After receiving a flood of comments (10,686 timely ones, to be precise), the Secretary reconsidered the regulations and published new proposed regulations in 1990. 55 Fed.Reg. 33448 (1990). After receiving another 11,392 comments, he adopted final regulations in 1991. 56 Fed. Reg. 6426 (1991); 9 C.F.R. § 3.81.

The final regulations consist of two separate modes of regulation, typically known as engineering standards and performance standards. The former dictate the required means to achieve a result; the latter state the desired outcomes, leaving to the facility the choice of means. The Secretary identifies five guidelines that he considers engineering standards, which in substance require as follows: (1) restraints are generally prohibited subject to certain exceptions as determined by the attending veterinarian or the research proposal, 9 C.F.R. § 3.81(d); (2) primary enclosures must be "enriched" so that primates may exhibit their typical behavior, such as swinging or foraging, id. § 3.81(b); (3) certain types of primates must be given special attention, including infants, young juveniles, individually housed primates, and great apes over 110 pounds, again in accord with "the instructions of the attending veterinarian," id. § 3.81(c); (4) facilities must "address the social needs of nonhuman primates . . . in accordance with currently accepted professional standards . . . and as directed by the attending veterinarian," but they may individually house primates under conditions further specified in the regulations, id. § 3.81(a); and (5) minimum cage sizes are set according to the typical weight of different species, id. § 3.80(b)(2)(i).

To implement these guidelines and to promote the psychological well-being of the primates, facilities must develop performance plans:

Dealers, exhibitors, and research facilities must develop, document, and follow an appropriate plan for environment enhancement adequate to promote the psychological well-being of nonhuman primates. The plan must be in accordance with the currently accepted professional standards as cited in appropriate professional journals or reference guides, and as directed by the attending veterinarian. This plan must be made available to APHIS [Animal and Plant Health Inspection Service] upon request, and, in the case of research facilities, to officials of any pertinent funding agency. Id. § 3.81.

Jurnove primarily maintains that nothing about these regulations establishes "minimum requirements . . . for a physical environment adequate to promote the psychological well-being of primates," and that the Secretary's use of performance plans and his apparent deference to on-site veterinarians amount to an impermissible delegation of his legal responsibility.

The district court agreed. *Animal Legal Defense Fund v. Glickman ("ALDF")*, 943 F.Supp. 44 (D.D.C.1996). It held that the regulation "fails to set standards," by which the district court meant engineering standards, and that "the regulation completely delegates the establishment of such standards to the regulated entities" because "[a]t best, the regulation refers these entities to the direction of their attending veterinarians—who are not under the control of the agency." Id. at 59. The district court also concluded that the Secretary had a duty to require social housing of primates given a finding by the Secretary that "[i]n general, housing in groups promotes psychological well-being more assuredly than does individual housing." Id. at 60 (quoting 56 Fed.Reg. at 6473). As the court read the regulation "the agency delineates only when social grouping might not be provided," and therefore "the regulation does not contain any minimum requirement on a point recognized by the agency itself as critical to the psychological well-being of primates." Id.

* * *

Jurnove argues that the plain language of the statute—the Secretary shall establish "minimum requirements . . . for a physical environment adequate to promote the psychological well-being of primates"—requires that the Secretary spell out exactly how primates may and may not be housed and handled (i.e., engineering standards), or at least spell out the "minimum requirements" in this manner. The Secretary's emphatic first response is: we did.

Jurnove consistently reads the regulations, as did the district court, as if the only "requirement" of the facilities is the production of a performance plan and that, basically, anything goes—provided the facilities honor what he views as the empty formality of finding some sort of support from "currently accepted professional standards as cited in appropriate professional journals or reference guides" and from "the attending veterinarian." 9 CFR § 3.81. This reading yields an obvious parade of horribles. Facilities will find unscrupulous veterinarians to rubber-stamp outrageous practices, and fringe periodicals will be the coin of the animal realm. This, argues Jurnove, is not the setting of "standards" or "minimum requirements" that the statute plainly commands.

We need not decide when performance standards alone could satisfy a congressional mandate for minimum requirements, or whether the sort of agency deference depicted by Jurnove could ever do so. The regulations here include specific engineering standards. The most obvious example is the regulation of cage sizes, id. § 3.80, which even Jurnove grants is an engineering standard. Jurnove attempts to discount the "primary enclosure" requirements because they appear in a different section of the regulations, and the Animal Welfare Act had previously mandated standards for "housing." But the Secretary stated that the cage requirements were set as part of the standards for promoting psychological well-being, 56 Fed.Reg. at 6468, and it is perfectly permissible to implement congressional commands through complementary regulations, some of which serve multiple goals.

The Secretary's requirement bases cage size on the weight of the primate, with special provisions for great apes, whereas the previous regulations merely required "sufficient space to allow each nonhuman primate to make normal postural adjustments with adequate freedom of movement." 56 Fed.Reg. at 6469. By hiking the requirements, the Secretary addressed an issue that Congress considered one of the central elements of a primate's psychological well-being. The statutory language speaks of minimum requirements for the "physical environment" of the primate, 7 U.S.C. § 2143(a)(2)(B), and the Conference Committee noted that "[t]he intent of standards with regard to promoting the psychological well-being of primates is to provide adequate space equipped with devices for exercise consistent with the primate's natural instincts and habits." H.R. Conf. Rep. No. 99-447, at 594 (1985).

Similarly, the regulations on environmental enrichment, special consideration of certain primates (infants, juveniles, etc.), and restraint devices all plainly provide engineering standards. 9 C.F.R. § 3.81(b)-(d). The facilities "must" provide environmental enrichment and special consideration for certain primates, id. § 3.81(b), (c), and they "must not" maintain primates in restraint devices "unless required for health reasons as determined by the attending veterinarian or by a research proposal approved by the Committee at research facilities," id. § 3.81(d). The regulation on restraints then makes clear that even where a veterinarian approves of restraints, there are still limits:

Maintenance under such restraint must be for the shortest period possible. In instances where long-term (more than 12 hours) restraint is required, the nonhuman primate must be provided the opportunity daily for unrestrained activity for at least one continuous hour during the period of restraint, unless continuous restraint is required by the research proposal approved by the Committee at research facilities. Id.

Although research facilities may be allowed to restrain primates continuously, this limited exception is not offered to non-research handlers and is in keeping with the statute's bar on the Secretary from interfering with research. See 7 U.S.C. § 2143(a)(6)(A)(i)-(iii).

These "requirements" may be minimal but they are clearly mandatory. Jurnove argued, and the district court agreed, that this case begins and ends with the fact that the Secretary provided no engineering standards. ALDF, 943 F.Supp. at 59. But in fact he did.

It of course remains possible that the engineering and performance standards chosen by the Secretary are not enough to meet the mandate of "minimum requirements." We assess this issue under the familiar doctrine that if Congress has spoken to the precise question at issue, we must "give effect to the unambiguously expressed intent of Congress," but if Congress has not, we defer to a permissible agency construction of the statute. *Chevron U.S.A. Inc. v. NRDC*, 467 U.S. 837, 842-43, 104 S.Ct. 2778, 81 L.Ed.2d 694 (1984).

Here Jurnove's Exhibit A (and indeed his only serious example) is the Secretary's handling of primates' "social grouping." In 1989 the Secretary proposed to include a requirement of group housing for primates, saying that he intended to emphasize that

> *nonhuman primates must be grouped in a primary enclosure with compatible members of their species or with other nonhuman primate species, either in pairs, family groups, or other compatible social groupings, whenever possible and consistent with providing for the nonhuman primates' health, safety, and well-being, unless social grouping is prohibited by an animal care and use procedure and approved by the facility's Committee. 54 Fed.Reg. 10822, 10917 (1989).*

This proposal was based on evidence that "nonhuman primates are social beings in nature and require contact with other nonhuman primates for their psychological well-being," and that "[s]ocial deprivation is regarded by the scientific community as psychologically debilitating to social animals." Id.

The final rule, of course, refrained from imposing such a general group housing requirement. Jurnove (stating his case in the best light) would tie the agency to its 1989 proposal on two theories: He argues first under *Chevron* that because of this finding any interpretation of the statute not recognizing social grouping as one of the "minimum requirements" could not be a reasonable interpretation of the statute. And second he claims that the Secretary's decision was arbitrary and capricious because he failed to explain it adequately, in violation of the Administrative Procedure Act. . . .

The Secretary's 1989 proposal was at odds with comments already in the record. For example, comments of the American Psychological Association had noted the wide disparities in social behavior among primates, with some forming large troops of 50 to 100 or more, others living in small groups of 10 to 20, and still others spending their lives in almost solitary isolation or as pairs in the wild. The 1989 proposal itself then generated new opposing comments, most notably from the University of Chicago, which pointed out that group housing "can significantly increase the incidence of trauma, the spread of upper respiratory and gastrointestinal diseases and more recently has been responsible for the outbreak of Simian Acquired Immune Deficiency Syndrome." Moreover, according to these comments, an image of nonhuman primates blissfully coexisting in groups is a substantially incomplete depiction of species-typical behavior. Again, as the University of Chicago informed the Secretary: "Even in compatible groups in no specific distress, species typical activities include threatening, chasing, fighting, wounding, hair-pulling, food competition, dominance challenges and reversals, and displacement of subordinate animals from food, water and shelter. Such activity can threaten the animals' health and well-being."

The Secretary took account of such comments, just as the designers of "notice and comment" rulemaking intended. He pointed to expressions of concern that "social grouping would endanger the animal's [sic] welfare by increasing noise and fighting," 55 Fed.Reg. at 33491, and to contentions that differences among species (there are, recall, over 240) required "discretion be used in deciding whether to employ group housing," id. Although it is true (as the district court noted and Jurnove here argues) that even in the final rulemaking the Secretary observed that "[i]n general, housing in groups promotes psychological well-being more assuredly than does individual housing," 943 F.Supp. at 60 (quoting 56 Fed.Reg. at 6472-73), that generality was obviously qualified by the remarks just quoted.

Thus the Secretary proposed a new regulation on social grouping:

> *The environment enhancement plan must include specific provisions to address the social needs of nonhuman primates of species known to exist in social groups in nature. Such specific provisions must be in accordance with currently accepted professional standards, as cited in appropriate professional journals or reference guides, and as directed by the attending veterinarian. 55 Fed.Reg. at 33525; 9 C.F.R. § 3.81(a) (final rule same).*

The regulation then offers "exceptions" to the social needs provision if the primate is vicious or debilitated, if it carries contagious diseases, or if its potential companions are not compatible. Id. § 3.81(a)(1)-(3). Even though social grouping is no longer formally mandated (facilities must only produce a "specific" plan for action that addresses "social needs"), the Secretary rightly argues that the enumeration of the "exceptions" makes social grouping the "norm."

Contrary to the view of the district court, the statute did not force the Secretary to require social grouping and then specify exceptions. See 943 F.Supp. at 60. To the contrary, we accord agencies broad deference in choosing the level of generality at which to articulate rules. . . . [Citations proving this point have been omitted.] Nothing in the statutory mandate required greater specificity. . . . [Citations omitted.] [B]ecause the Secretary was reasonably concerned that more precise specification might cause harm, it was entirely reasonable under the statute for him to choose a relatively flexible standard.

The explanation that renders the Secretary's interpretation of the statute reasonable also serves to establish that the final rule was not arbitrary and capricious. Where "Congress delegates power to an agency to regulate on the borders of the unknown, courts cannot interfere with reasonable interpretations of equivocal evidence"; courts are most deferential of agency readings of scientific evidence. There is little question that the Secretary was forced to regulate "on the borders of the unknown" in setting the baseline of rights to "psychological well-being" for nonhuman primates, or at least how to "promote" their psychological well-being. In changing the design of the regulations, the Secretary pointed to substantial conflicting evidence on whether a stringent social grouping requirement was a good idea, 55 Fed.Reg. at 33491, and thus his final policy judgment on social grouping was reasonable.

Jurnove may well be correct that some of the Secretary's regulations may prove difficult to enforce, or even difficult to augment through subsequent "interpretation." But the requirements such as the ones on cage size and restraints are eminently enforceable, and the Secretary has begun to offer interpretations likely to assist both regulatees and enforcers. See Draft Policy on Environment Enhancement for Nonhuman Primates, 64 Fed. Reg. 38145 (1999).

[Discussion of two additional minor issues omitted.]

* * *

The decision of the district court is
Reversed.

APPENDIX E

ANIMAL ENTERPRISE TERRORISM ACT (PL 102-346), 2006

Section 1. SHORT TITLE.

This Act may be cited as the "Animal Enterprise Terrorism Act."

Section 2. INCLUSION OF ECONOMIC DISRUPTION TO ANIMAL ENTERPRISES AND THREATS OF DEATH AND SERIOUS BODILY INJURY TO ASSOCIATED PERSONS.

(a) In General- Section 43 of title 18, United States Code, is amended to read as follows:

Sec. 43. Force, violence, and threats involving animal enterprises

(a) Offense- Whoever travels in interstate or foreign commerce, or uses or causes to be used the mail or any facility of interstate or foreign commerce

(1) for the purpose of damaging or disrupting an animal enterprise; and

(2) in connection with such purpose—

(A) intentionally damages, disrupts, or causes the loss of any property (including animals or records) used by the animal enterprise, or any property of a person or entity having a connection to, relationship with, or transactions with the animal enterprise;

(B) intentionally places a person in reasonable fear of the death of, or serious bodily injury to that person, a member of the immediate family (as defined in section 115) of that person, or a spouse or intimate partner of that person by a course of conduct involving threats, acts of vandalism, property damage, trespass, harassment, or intimidation; or

(C) conspires or attempts to do so; shall be punished as provided for in subsection (b).

(b) Penalties-

(1) ECONOMIC DAMAGE- Any person who, in the course of a violation of subsection (a) causes economic damage not exceeding $10,000 shall be fined under this title or imprisoned not more than 1 year, or both.

(2) SIGNIFICANT ECONOMIC DAMAGE OR ECONOMIC DISRUPTION- Any person who, in the course of a violation of subsection (a), causes economic damage or economic disruption exceeding $10,000 but not exceeding $100,000 shall be fined under this title or imprisoned not more than 5 years, or both.

(3) MAJOR ECONOMIC DAMAGE OR ECONOMIC DISRUPTION- Any person who, in the course of a violation of subsection (a), causes economic damage or economic disruption exceeding $100,000 shall be fined under this title or imprisoned not more than 10 years, or both.

(4) SIGNIFICANT BODILY INJURY OR THREATS- Any person who, in the course of a violation of subsection (a), causes significant bodily injury to another individual or intentionally instills in another the reasonable fear of death or serious bodily injury shall be fined under this title or imprisoned not more than 5 years, or both.

(5) SERIOUS BODILY INJURY- Any person who, in the course of a violation of subsection (a), causes serious bodily injury to another individual shall be fined under this title or imprisoned not more than 20 years, or both.

(6) DEATH- Any person who, in the course of a violation of subsection (a), causes the death of an individual shall be fined under this title and shall be imprisoned for life or for any term of years.

(7) CONSPIRACY AND ATTEMPT- Any person who conspires or attempts to commit an offense under subsection (a) shall be subject to the same penalties as those prescribed for the substantive offense.

(c) Restitution- An order of restitution under section 3663 or 3663A of this title with respect to a violation of this section may also include restitution—

(1) for the reasonable cost of repeating any experimentation that was interrupted or invalidated as a result of the offense;

(2) the loss of food production or farm income reasonably attributable to the offense; and

(3) for any other economic damage, including any losses or costs caused by economic disruption, resulting from the offense.

(d) Definitions- As used in this section—

(1) the term "animal enterprise" means—

(A) a commercial or academic enterprise that uses or sells animals or animal products for profit, food or fiber production, agriculture, research, or testing;

Appendix E

(B) a zoo, aquarium, animal shelter, pet store, breeder, furrier, circus, or rodeo, or other lawful competitive animal event; or

(C) any fair or similar event intended to advance agricultural arts and sciences;

(2) the term "course of conduct" means a pattern of conduct composed of 2 or more acts, evidencing a continuity of purpose;

(3) the term "economic damage" means the replacement costs of lost or damaged property or records, the costs of repeating an interrupted or invalidated experiment, or the loss of profits;

(4) the term "economic disruption"—

(A) means losses and increased costs that individually or collectively exceed $10,000, including losses and increased costs resulting from threats, acts or vandalism, property damage, trespass, harassment or intimidation taken against a person or entity on account of that person's or entity's connection to, relationship with, or transactions with the animal enterprise; and

(B) does not include any lawful economic disruption that results from lawful public, governmental, or business reaction to the disclosure of information about an animal enterprise;

(5) the term "serious bodily injury" means—

(A) injury posing a substantial risk of death;

(B) extreme physical pain;

(C) protracted and obvious disfigurement; or

(D) protracted loss or impairment of the function of a bodily member, organ, or mental faculty; and

(6) the term "significant bodily injury" means—

(A) deep cuts and serious burns or abrasions;

(B) short-term or nonobvious disfigurement;

(C) fractured or dislocated bones, or torn members of the body;

(D) significant physical pain;

(E) illness;

(F) short-term loss or impairment of the function of a bodily member, organ, or mental faculty; or

(G) any other significant injury to the body.

(e) Non-Preemption- Nothing in this section preempts any State law.

(b) Conforming Amendment- Section 2516(1)(c) of title 18, United States Code, is amended by inserting section 43 (force, violence and threats involving animal enterprises), before section 201 (bribery of public officials and witnesses).

APPENDIX F

TABLES AND GRAPHS

HUNTERS AS PERCENTAGE OF U.S. POPULATION, 1955–2006

Year	Number of Hunters (Millions)	Total U.S. Population (Millions)	Percent
1955	11.8	118.4	10.0%
1960	14.6	131.2	11.2%
1965	13.6	142.0	9.6%
1970	14.3	155.2	9.2%
1975	17.1	171.9	9.9%
1980	16.7	184.7	9.1%
1985	16.3	195.7	8.4%
1990	14.1	190	7%
1995	14.0	201	7%
2000	13.0	212	6%
2006	12.5	250	5%

U.S. population includes people twelve years and older.

Note: 1955 was the first year that the survey was conducted. The information is based on data from surveys conducted every five years, from 1955 through 2006. Those figures for 1990 on were compiled differently and so should not be compared directly.

Source: 2006 National Survey of Fishing, Hunting, and Wildlife–Associated Recreation, U.S. Fish and Wildlife Service.

Appendix F

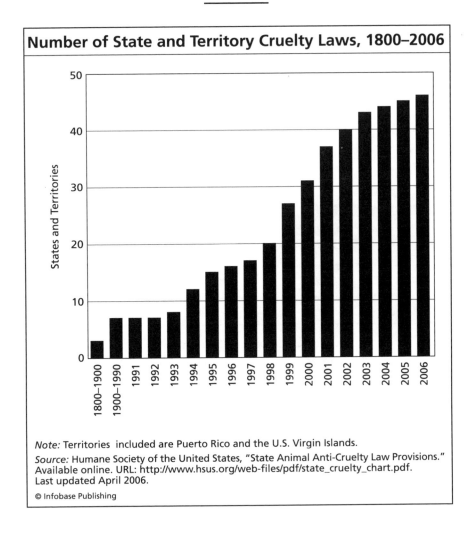

Number of State and Territory Cruelty Laws, 1800–2006

Note: Territories included are Puerto Rico and the U.S. Virgin Islands.

Source: Humane Society of the United States, "State Animal Anti-Cruelty Law Provisions." Available online. URL: http://www.hsus.org/web-files/pdf/state_cruelty_chart.pdf. Last updated April 2006.

© Infobase Publishing

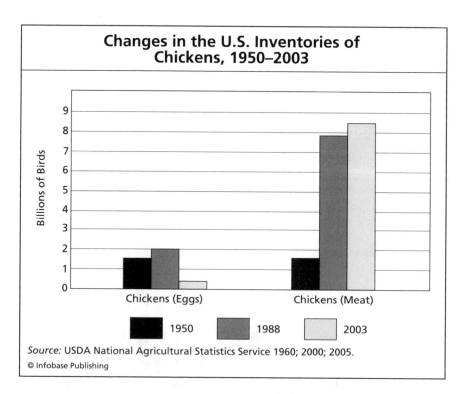

Changes in the U.S. Inventories of Chickens, 1950–2003

Billions of Birds

Chickens (Eggs)   Chickens (Meat)

■ 1950   ■ 1988   □ 2003

Source: USDA National Agricultural Statistics Service 1960; 2000; 2005.
© Infobase Publishing

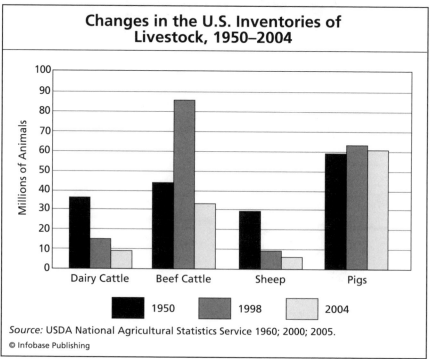

Changes in the U.S. Inventories of Livestock, 1950–2004

Millions of Animals

Dairy Cattle   Beef Cattle   Sheep   Pigs

■ 1950   ■ 1998   □ 2004

Source: USDA National Agricultural Statistics Service 1960; 2000; 2005.
© Infobase Publishing

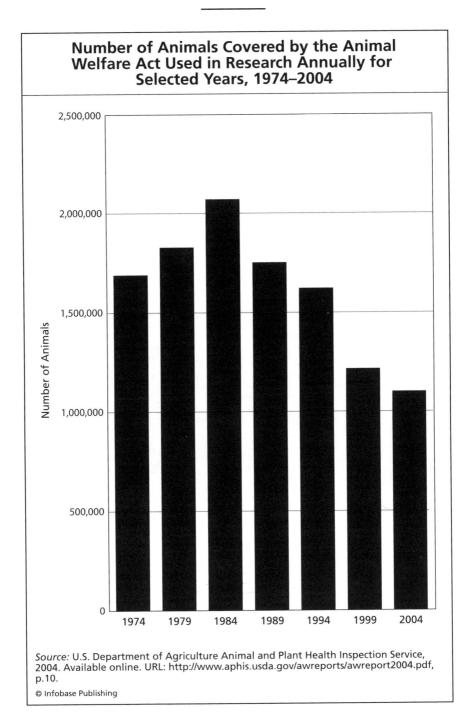

Number of Animals Covered by the Animal Welfare Act Used in Research Annually for Selected Years, 1974–2004

Source: U.S. Department of Agriculture Animal and Plant Health Inspection Service, 2004. Available online. URL: http://www.aphis.usda.gov/awreports/awreport2004.pdf, p.10.

© Infobase Publishing

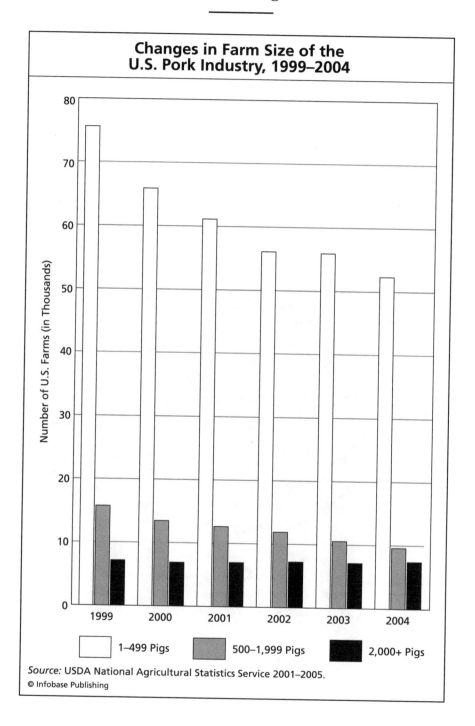

Changes in Farm Size of the U.S. Pork Industry, 1999–2004

Number of U.S. Farms (in Thousands)

1–499 Pigs   500–1,999 Pigs   2,000+ Pigs

Source: USDA National Agricultural Statistics Service 2001–2005.
© Infobase Publishing

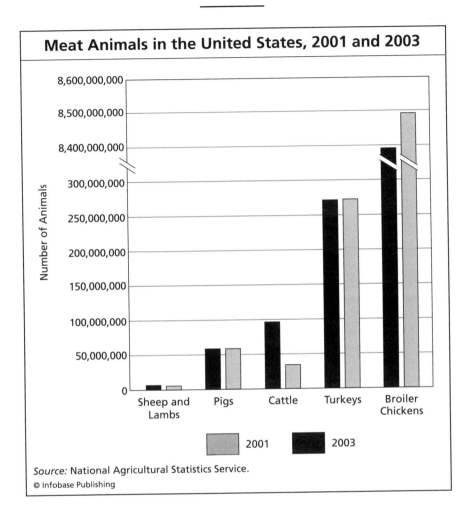

Meat Animals in the United States, 2001 and 2003

Source: National Agricultural Statistics Service.

© Infobase Publishing

INDEX

Locators in **boldface** indicate main topics. Locators followed by *g* indicate glossary entries. Locators followed by *b* indicate biographical entries. Locators followed by *c* indicate chronology entries. Locators followed by *t* indicate graphs and tables.

A

ABA. *See* American Bar Association
About.com 170
abuse of animals 92–93
  elephants 60, 133*c*
  Huntingdon Life Sciences case 17, 113
  orangutans 60, 128*c*, 129*c*
acute toxicity testing 49–50
Administrative Procedures Act 69, 108, 116
adoption 27
Advocates for Animals 240
Afognak Island, Alaska 64
agencies. *See* organizations and agencies
Agricultural Research Service 38, 245
agriculture, animals in 29–42, 166
  intensive farms 35–39
  organizations 248–252
  raising of farm animals 30–35
  resources 207–214
  transportation and slaughtering 39–42
Agriculture (Miscellaneous Provisions) Act 37, 123*c*

AgriProcessors, Inc. (slaughterhouse) 40–41, 91, 136*c*
AHA. *See* American Humane Association
AKC. *See* American Kennel Club
Alberta, Canada 34
Alcmeon of Croton 119*c*, 141*b*
ALF. *See* Animal Liberation Front
Alley Cat Allies 246–247
Alsea Valley Alliance 69, 70, 116, 117
Alsea Valley Alliance v. Evans (Alsea Valley Alliance v. Oregon Natural Resources) 69, 115–117, 133*c*, 136*c*
Altweb: Alternatives to Animal Testing 166–167
American Animal Hospital Association 77
American Anti-Vivisection Society 252–253
American Bar Association (ABA) 235
American Farm Bureau 248
American Horse Council 258
American Horse Slaughter Prevention Act 59, 133*c*, 139*c*, 140*c*, 151*g*

American Humane Association (AHA) 38, 43, 122*c*, 247
American Kennel Club (AKC) 24
American Meat Institute 35, 38, 248
American Medical Association 48
American Partnership for Pets 247
American Pet Products Manufacturers Association 22
American Sanctuary Association 247
Americans for Medical Advancement 253
Americans for Medical Progress 167, 253
American Society for the Prevention of Cruelty to Animals (ASPCA) 240–241
  origins of 14, 24, 120*c*
  on violent tactics 20, 128*c*
American Veterinary Medical Association 35, 77
Animal Agricultural Alliance 21, 248
Animal Aid 15, 241
Animal Alliance of Canada 241

316

Index

Animal and Plant Health
Inspection Service
(APHIS) 43, 59, 151*g*,
246
  Animal Welfare Act
    enforcement by 86
  and circus animal
    regulations 86
  and Laboratory
    Animal Welfare Act
    enforcement 44
  and Twenty-
    eight Hour Act
    enforcement 40
animal cruelty laws 25–26
Animal Defenders
  International 241
Animal Enterprise
  Protection Act **91–92,**
  128*c*, 151*g*
  and Public Health
    Security and
    Bioterrorism
    Preparedness and
    Response Act 134*c*
  as response to
    extremist groups 18
  and "SHAC Seven"
    trial 115, 136*c*, 138*c*,
    139*c*
Animal Enterprise
  Terrorism Act **92,** 115,
  139*c*, 151*g*, **307–309**
Animal Experiments
  Directive 46
Animal Fighting Venture
  Prohibition Act 56, 125*c*
Animal Health Institute
  33
Animal Information
  Network 164
animal law 151*g*
  courses on 130*c*
  web sites 178
Animal Legal and
  Historical Web Center
  178
Animal Legal Defense
  Fund 10, 101, 107, 108,
  241

*Animal Legal Defense Fund
  v. Glickman* I 10–11,
  101, 106–111, 130*c*,
  288–299
  analysis 292–299
  background 106–107,
    289–292
  conclusion 299
  decision 108–109
  impact 110–111
  legal issues 107–108
*Animal Legal Defense Fund
  v. Glickman* II 109–110,
  132*c*, **300–306**
Animal Liberation Front
  (ALF) 164, 241
  and Animal Enterprise
    Protection Act
    passage 91
  and Animal Enterprise
    Terrorism Act
    passage 92
  and baboon testing
    videotapes 45
  and Graham Hall
    kidnapping and
    branding 19, 131*c*
  origins of 75, 124*c*
  property damage as
    tactic of 16
  and SHAC-USA 17
  and vandalism of yacht
    club 137*c*
Animal Liberation (Singer)
  4, 12, 125*c*
Animal Machines
  (Harrison) 30, 123*c*
"animal on a chip" 151*g*
animal organizations,
  general-purpose 240–
  246
Animal People (magazine)
  20
animal protection, general
  and historical works on
  181–188
Animal Protection
  Information Service
  (APIS) 167

Animal Protection
  Institute 33, 164–165,
  242
animal protection
  organizations 23–24,
  151*g*
animal research. *See also*
  vivisection
  alternatives to 52–55
  Ingrid Newkirk on
    47
  resources on 214–223
  Peter Singer on 48
  USDA report on 55
  web sites on 166–167
Animal Rights
  International 20
animal rights movement
  152*g*
  opponents of 12–22
  resources 196–202
  Peter Singer as
    inspiration for 4
Animals and Society
  Institute 242
Animals and the Law
  (Curnutt) 9, 39, 86, 93
Animals Asia Foundation
  260
Animals Australia 242
animal shelters 202–207
animals in science 42–55
Animals (Scientific
  Procedures) Act 46,
  127*c*
Animals Voice (magazine)
  56, 61
animal testing. *See* animal
  research
Animal Welfare Act
  (AWA) 26, **85–87,** 152*g*,
  269–277
  Animal and Plant
    Health Inspection
    Service enforcement
    of 86
  and *Animal Legal
    Defense Fund v.
    Glickman* cases
    10–11, 132*c*

Animal Welfare Act
(*continued*)
  animals covered by,
    used in research
    (1974–2004) 313*t*
  and breeding facility
    regulation 24–25
  and circuses/animal
    shows 59
  classification of dealers
    28–29
  exemptions from 58,
    133*c*
  housing requirements
    for animals 62
  Improved Standards
    for Laboratory
    Animals Act as
    amendments 45
  Institutional Animal
    Care and Use
    Committees
    (IACUCs)
    established 127*c*
  and *International
    Primate Protection
    League v. Institute for
    Behavioral Research*
    98–101
  and Laboratory
    Animal Welfare Act
    43–44
  passage of 124*c*
  standing to sue for
    violation 130*c*
  and zoo regulation by
    USDA 106–107
Animal Welfare Act
  (Britain) 76, 139*c*, 152*g*
Animal Welfare Action
  Plan 138*c*
Animal Welfare Bill 138*c*
Animal Welfare
  Information Center,
  USDA 165
Animal Welfare
  Information Service
  245–246
Animal Welfare Institute
  29, 43, 58, 122*c*, 165,
  242

animal welfare organiza-
  tions 152*g*. *See also* orga-
  nizations and agencies
anthropomorphism 152*g*
anticruelty laws 92–93
antifur campaigns 124*c*
antimilk campaigns 131*c*
antislavery crusades 6
APHIS. *See* Animal and
  Plant Health Inspection
  Service
APIS. *See* Animal Protec-
  tion Information Service
Arizona 36
Arnold, Perry 74
Asian medicine, traditional
  67
ASPCA. *See* American
  Society for the
  Prevention of Cruelty to
  Animals
Association for Assessment
  and Accreditation of
  Laboratory Animal Care
  International 253
Association of Fish and
  Wildlife Agencies 260
Association of Sanctuaries
  61
Association of Zoos and
  Aquariums (AZA) 62–
  63, 258
Audubon Society 260
Austria, cosmetics testing
  ban in 51
Avanzino, Richard 141*b*
Avery, Greg 16, 131*c*,
  141*b*
Avon 127*c*
AZA. *See* Association of
  Zoos and Aquariums

B

Babbitt, Bruce 103
*Babbitt v. Sweet Home
  Chapter of Communities
  for a Great Oregon* 89,
  103–106, 129*c*
  background 103
  decision 105–106

impact 106
  legal issues 103–104
baboon testing videotapes
  45
bag limit 152*g*
Balcombe, Jonathan 52
Bald Eagle Protection Act
  65, 87
Balls, Michael 53–54
Band of Mercy 75, 124*c*
Basel Zoo 61, 122*c*
battery cage 31, 36, 37,
  131*c*, 152*g*
Beckett, Margaret 138*c*
beef cattle, "finishing" of
  31–32
Behavioral Biology Center
  98
Bentham, Jeremy 4–6,
  120*c*, 141*b*
Bergh, Henry 24, 93,
  120*c*, 141*b*–142*b*
Bernard, Claude 42, 121*c*,
  142*b*
Berosini, Bobby 60, 101–
  103, 128*c*, 140*c*, 142*b*
Best, Steven 142*b*
Best Friends (animal
  welfare group) 24
BGH. *See* bovine growth
  hormone
biblical statement 4
bibliography 180–239
  agriculture, animals in
    207–214
  animal protection and
    human relationships
    with animals 181–
    188
  animal rights
    movement 196–202
  articles 185–187,
    192–195, 198–200,
    204–206, 209–211,
    216–219, 224–225,
    231–237
  books 181–185,
    188–194, 196–198,
    202–204, 207–209,
    214–216, 223–224,
    227–231

Index

companion animals
and animal shelters
202–207
entertainment, animals
in 223–227
law, animals and the
193–195
philosophy of animal
rights 188–193
research, testing, and
education, animals in
214–223
resources, bibliographic
173
using bibliographies
174–175
web documents
187–188, 193, 195,
200–202, 206–207,
211–214, 219–223,
225–227, 237–239
wildlife 227–239
Big Cat Rescue 61
Bioscience (journal) 70
biotechnology 55
Blackmun, Harry A. 97
Black's Law Dictionary 9
blood, circulation of 119*c*
Bobby Berosini orangutan
case **101–103,** 129*c*,
140*c*
background 101–102
decision 102
impact 102–103
legal issues 102
and PETA 101–103
body-gripping trap 77,
152*g*
"Body of Liberties" 92,
120*c*
bonobo 152*g*
bookstore catalogs 174
Boone and Crockett Club
260
Born Free USA 260
bovine growth hormone
(BGH) 33, 37, 152*g*
bovine spongiform
encephalopathy (BSE)
33–34, 130*c*, 152*g*, 158*g*
in Britain 127*c*, 129*c*

Canadian case of 113,
134*c*
and cattle feed ban
130*c*
and *Texas Beef Group
v. Winfrey* case 111,
129*c*–130*c*
Texas case of 137*c*
in United States 113,
135*c*
Washington State case
of 41
The Boyd Group 253
Bradshaw, Ben 139*c*
Braithwaite, J. 20
Brambell Committee 123*c*
Brandenburg v. Ohio 114
breed-specific legislation
57
Bridge Pharmaceuticals 47
Britain 34, 37, 39, 46, 51
British Association
for Shooting and
Conservation 260–261
British Medical Journal 53
British Research Defense
Society 21
British Union for the
Abolition of Vivisection
253
broiler chickens 31, 152*g*
Brooks, Russell C. 117
Broome, Arthur 23, 120*c*,
142*b*
Bryant, John 23
BSE. *See* bovine
spongiform
encephalopathy
Buckley, Carol 60–61
bullbaiting 56
buncher 29, 153*g*
Burch, Rex 53, 123*c*, 142*b*
Burger, Warren 96–97
Burger King 36, 133*c*
Burnett, Andrew 133*c*,
142*b*
Burns Report 71–72, 74,
132*c*
Bush, George W., and
administration 69–70,
92, 115, 117, 133*c*, 139*c*

C

Cable News Network
(CNN) 168
cage-free eggs 153*g*
Cambridge University 17,
136*c*
campaign(s)
antifur 124*c*
antimilk 131*c*
"Eat the Whales"
campaign 15
"Got Beer" campaign
15
"How Many Rabbits
Does Revlon Blind
for Beauty's Sake?"
50
intimidation, and 136*c*
"Milk Gone Wild"
campaign 15
by PETA 15
spay/neuter 27–28,
124*c*
"Your Mommy Kills
Animals" 15
Campbell, Naomi 36
Canada 34, 242
Canadian Federation of
Humane Societies 242
canned hunt 74–75, 153*g*
Captive Wildlife Safety
Act 61, 135*c*, 153*g*
Carolina parakeet 64, 121*c*
Carr Securities 137*c*
Carson, Rachel 65
The Case for Animal Rights
(Regan) 6, 126*c*
Cass, Brian 19, 132*c*, 143*b*
cattle feed ban 130*c*
cattle raising 31–32
Center for Biological
Diversity 261
Center for Consumer
Freedom 15, 248
Center for Wildlife Law
261
Central Intelligence
Agency (CIA) 21
Charles I (king of
England, Scotland, and
Ireland) 42

Cheskin Research 79
Chevron U.S.A., Inc. v.
  Natural Resources Defense
  Council 105
Chicago, Illinois 36
chicken raising 31
chickens
  changes in U.S.
    inventories of (1950–
    2003) 312*t*
  raising of 134*c*
  slaughter of 137*c*
Chimpanzee Health
  Improvement,
  Maintenance, and
  Protection Act (CHIMP
  Act) 49, 132*c*, 153*g*
chimpanzees 48–49, 140*c*
China 47
Chiron (company) 16, 135*c*
Christie, Christopher J.
  115
CIA. *See* Central
  Intelligence Agency
circuses and animal shows
  59–61, 86
Circus Maximus 56
CITES. *See* Convention
  on International Trade
  in Endangered Species
  of Wild Flora and Fauna
"citizen suit" provisions
  67, 89, 110–111
civil rights 3, 12
Clark, Ward M. 13–14,
  71, 103
class A dealer 28, 153*g*
class B dealer 28–29, 153*g*
Clinton administration
  51, 131*c*
closed season 153*g*
CNN. *See* Cable News
  Network
Coalition Against Duck
  Shooting 261
Coalition for Medical
  Progress 55, 253
Coalition to Abolish the
  Draize Test 50, 124*c*
Coalition to Abolish the
  Fur Trade 248

Cobbe, Frances Power
  143*b*
cockfighting 56, 134*c*
Coetzee, J. M., 143*b*
coho salmon 69–70,
  115–117
The Columbian (newspaper)
  117
Commerce Department 89
commercial whaling
  moratorium 127*c*
Committee on
  Commerce, Science and
  Transportation 59
Community Action Plan
  on the Protection and
  Welfare of Animals 37,
  139*c*
companion animals 22–
  29, 153*g*, 202–207
  breeding and sale of
    24–25
  cruelty to 25–26
  homeless shelters for
    27–28
  Ingrid Newkirk on 23
  organizations 246–248
  theft of 28–29
  web sites 166
Compassion in World
  Farming 39, 166,
  248–249
Compassion Over Killing
  249
Conibear trap 77
Connyland (Switzerland
  marine park) 63
constitutions and
  constitutionality
  of food disparagement
    laws 112, 113
  Germany 134*c*
  Property Clause 65
Consumer Product Safety
  Commission 51
contraception 72, 124*c*
controlled atmosphere
  stunning 137*c*, 153*g*
Convention on
  International Trade in
  Endangered Species of

Wild Flora and Fauna
  (CITES) 66–67, 153*g*,
  261
  elephant ivory trade
    banned by 128*c*
  establishment of
    124*c*–125*c*
  U.S. government
    administration of
    89
Cornell Law School 176
Coronado, Rodney 20,
  143*b*
cosmetics testing bans 51,
  134*c*
Council for Agricultural
  Science and Technology
  249
Countryside Action
  Network 261
Countryside Alliance 71,
  75, 261
court cases **93–117**
  Alsea Valley Alliance v.
    Evans (Alsea Valley
    Alliance v. Oregon
    Natural Resources)
    69, 115–117, 133*c*
  Animal Legal Defense
    Fund v. Glickman I
    10–11, 101, 106–111,
    130*c*, **288–299**
  Animal Legal Defense
    Fund v. Glickman
    II 109–110, 132*c*,
    300–306
  Babbitt v. Sweet
    Home Chapter of
    Communities for a
    Great Oregon 89,
    103–106, 129*c*
  Brandenburg v. Ohio
    114
  Chevron U.S.A., Inc.
    v. Natural Resources
    Defense Council 105
  Geer v. Connecticut 64,
    121*c*
  Hunt v. United States
    65, 122*c*

Index

International Primate Protection League v. Institute for Behavioral Research **98–101**
Jones v. Butz 125c
Kleppe v. New Mexico 65, 125c
Lujan v. Defenders of Wildlife 10, 107, 128c
Palila v. Hawaii Department of Land and Natural Resources (Palila II) 104, 127c
Planned Parenthood of Columbia/Willamette, Inc., v. American Coalition of Life Activists 114
researching 177–178
Tennessee Valley Authority v. Hill **94–98**, 103, 105, 106, 125c
Texas Beef Group v. Winfrey 111–113
Creutzfeldt-Jakob disease, variant. *See* variant Creutzfeldt-Jakob disease
critical habitat 153g
cruelty laws 25–26
  in New York 93, 120c
  by state and territory (1800–2006) 311t
Cruelty to Animals Act 42, 121c
Cummings, Betsy 15
Curnutt, Jordan 9, 39, 66, 101

D

Dailey, Tim 19
"Dangerous Food" (TV broadcast) 111
Darley Oaks 18, 136c, 137c
databases 174–175
Defenders of Wildlife 261–262

DEFRA. *See* Department for Environment, Food, and Rural Affairs
Delquis, Noelle 63
DeMayo, Neda 143b
Department for Environment, Food, and Rural Affairs (DEFRA) 26, 138c, 242–243
Department of the Interior 66
Descartes, René 4, 119c, 143b
de Waal, Frans 8
dissection 52, 119c, 127c
distinct population segment 154g
DNA chip 55, 154g
dog fighting 56–57, 140c
domestic terrorist group 16
Doughney, Michael 172
"downer cattle" 41, 135c, 154g
Draize, John 50, 143b
Draize tests 50, 53, 122c, 126c, 154g
duck stamp 154g
Ducks Unlimited 73, 262

E

Earth Liberation Front (ELF) 16
EBSCOhost 175
education, use of animals in 52
  bibliography 214–223
  online resources 166–167
elephants 60, 128c
Elephant Sanctuary 61
ELF. *See* Earth Liberation Front
endangered species 64, 154g
Endangered Species Act (ESA) **87–90**, 135c, 154g, **278–287**
  and *Alsea Valley Alliance v. Evans*

(Alsea Valley Alliance v. Oregon Natural Resources) 115–117
  amended by Congress 126c
  and *Babbitt v. Sweet Home Chapter of Communities for a Great Oregon* 103–106
  and court ruling on Oregon Coast coho salmon 133c
  environmental degradation included 129c
  regulations for issued 125c
  signed into law 125c
  species delisting 69
  standing to sue granted to bird 127c
  Tellico Dam exempted from 126c
  and *Tennessee Valley Authority v. Hill* case 94–98
Endangered Species Committee 97
Endangered Species Conservation Act 88
Endangered Species Preservation Act 66–71, 88, 123c
Endangered Species Program 265
entertainment, animals in 167
  organizations 258–259
  resources 223–227
Envirolink 165
Environmental Defense Fund 94
environmental degradation 129c
Environmental Law (journal) 70, 117
Environmental Protection Agency (EPA) 51, 130c, 131c
Epstein, Richard A. 12

Equine Protection
Network 258
ESA. *See* Endangered
Species Act
Eurogroup for Animals
243
European Biomedical
Research Association
254
European Centre for the
Validation of Alternative
Methods (EVCAM) 53,
128*c*, 254
European Coalition
to End Animal
Experiments 254
European Commission
37, 62, 138*c*
European Council 41–42,
136*c*
European Federation
Against Hunting 262
European Partnership for
Alternative Approaches
to Animal Testing 254
European Union (EU) 26,
37, 42, 46, 53, 131*c*, 166
cosmetics testing ban
51, 134*c*
euthanization 28
evaluation of animals **7–9**
EVCAM. *See* European
Centre for the Validation
of Alternative Methods
evolutionarily significant
unit (ESU) 69, 116,
128*c*, 130*c*, 154*g*
extinction 64–66

F

factory farming 30–31,
37, 123*c*, 154*g*
facts, evaluation of 178
Fairfax County, Virginia
21, 138*c*
FAO. *See* Food
and Agricultural
Organization of the
United Nations
Farinato, Richard 61–63

farm animals
raising of 30–35
transportation/
slaughtering of
39–42
Farm Animal Welfare
Council 26, 249
Farm Animal Welfare
Network 249
Farm Sanctuary 41, 249
farrowing crate 32, 36,
154*g*
FDA. *See* U.S. Food and
Drug Administration
Federal Bureau of
Investigation (FBI) 16
Federation of American
Societies for
Experimental Biology
254
Federation of European
Laboratory Animal
Science Organizations
(FELASA) 254–255
Federation of Hunters
Associations of the
European Union 262
Feedstuffs (newspaper) 21
Feedstuffs Foodlink 166
FELASA. *See* Federation
of European Laboratory
Animal Science
Organizations
Feld, Kenneth 21, 131*c*,
132*c*, 138*c*, 143*b*
feminist movement 12
Fettered Kingdoms (Bryant)
23
"finishing" of beef cattle
31–32
Finsen, Lawrence 13
Finsen, Susan 13
five freedoms 155*g*
Fletcher, Kristen M. 117
Florida 35
foie gras 36, 138*c*, 155*g*
Food and Agricultural
Organization of the
United Nations (FAO)
30

Food Animal Initiative
249
food disparagement laws
38, 111–112, 129*c*–131*c*,
155*g*
Food Marketing Institute
133*c*, 250
Food Safety and Inspection
Service (FSIS) 40, 91,
155*g*, 252
forced molting 37, 155*g*
Fortuyn, Pim 19, 134*c*,
143*b*
Foundation for Biomedical
Research 16, 54–55
Fountain, Bob 21
Fox, Michael 7, 143*b*–
144*b*
Fox, Stephen 13
foxes 32, 122*c*, 123*c*, 134*c*,
136*c*
Francione, Gary 3, 11,
12, 144*b*
Fraser, David 35
"free farmed" label 38
French Resistance
comparison 20
Friedrich, Bruce 37
Friends of Animals 66,
243
FSIS. *See* Food Safety and
Inspection Service
The Fund for Animals 71,
99, 100, 262
Fund for the Replacement
of Animals in Medical
Experiments 255
fur animals 32
Fur Commission USA
250
fur farming 36, 37
Fur Farming (Prohibition)
Act 132*c*
Fur Seal Act 65, 123*c*,
155*g*
Fur Seal Treaty 65, 121*c*,
123*c*
fur trade 36
FWS. *See* U.S. Fish and
Wildlife Service

Index

G

Game Conservancy Trust 262
Gandhi, Mohandas 79
Garner, Joseph 54
Garner, Robert 78
Gay, Andrew 21
Gebel, Mark 60, 133*c*, 144*b*
Geer v. Connecticut 64, 121*c*
General Accounting Office 95
genetic engineering 55
George, Clair 21
Georgetown University law school 12, 130*c*
George Washington University 98
Germany 46, 47, 134*c*
Gesmundo, Ottavio 101
gestation stalls 32, 35–37, 39, 131*c*, 134*c*, 139*c*, 155*g*
Gillette (company) 50, 130*c*
Giuliani, Rudolph 131*c*
Glickman, Dan 10, 46, 107
Glitzenstein. Eric 12
Goodall, Jane 7, 144*b*
Goodwin, Frederick 47, 48, 144*b*
Graaf, Volkert van der 134*c*, 144*b*
Grandin, Temple 33, 38, 40, 144*b*
Great Ape Project 11, 243
great apes 129*c*, 130*c*, 155*g*
Gregory, Dick 59
Greyhound Protection League 258
greyhound racing 58

H

habitat conservation plan (HCP) 68, 90, 155*g*
Hagenbeck, Carl 61

halal slaughter 125*c*, 155*g*–156*g*
Hall, Christopher 18, 136*c*, 137*c*, 139*c*, 144*b*
Hall, David 18, 136*c*, 137*c*, 139*c*, 144*b*
Hall, Graham 19, 131*c*, 145*b*
Halverson, Marlene 20–21
Hammond, Gladys 18, 136*c*, 139*c*
Hancocks, David 62, 63, 145*b*
harm, definition of 104–106, 125*c*, 129*c*
Harper's Magazine 102
Harrison, B. 24
Harrison, Ruth 30, 37, 123*c*, 145*b*
Harvard University law school 12, 130*c*
Harvey, William 42, 119*c*, 145*b*
hatchery policy 129*c*, 156*g*
Hayre, Michael 48
HCP. *See* habitat conservation plan
Head Injury Clinical Research Laboratory 44–45, 127*c*
Hearne, Vicki 102–103
Hediger, Heini 61, 122*c*, 145*b*
high-production-volume (HPV) chemicals 51, 130*c*, 156*g*
high-technology hunting 74
Hill, Hiram 95
Hippocrates 42
HIV/AIDS 48–49
HLS. *See* Huntingdon Life Sciences
Hogan, Michael 69, 116–117, 133*c*, 145*b*
Hoggan, George 42, 145*b*
Holocaust 15
Horse Protection Act 58, 59, 124*c*, 156*g*
horse slaughter 58

House of Lords (Britain) 135*c*
HPV chemicals. *See* high-production-volume chemicals
HSA. *See* Hunt Saboteurs Association
HSUS. *See* Humane Society of the United States
Humane Farming Association 33, 250
Humane Methods of Slaughter Act 40, 41, **90–91**, 138*c*, 156*g*
  birds exempted by 137*c*, 138*c*
  enacted 125*c*
Humane Slaughter Act 40, 90, 122*c*, 125*c*
Humane Society of Santa Clara 60
Humane Society of the United States (HSUS) 165, 243
  and animal rights movement tactics 14
  captive wildlife program of 61
  on dissection 52
  on environmentalism and animal protection 79
  and greyhound racing 58
  and Humane Slaughter Act 40
  on hunting 76
  lawsuit against USDA 99
  origins of 43, 122*c*
  and poultry slaughter 41, 137*c*, 138*c*
  on tigers in United States 62
  on violent tactics 20, 128*c*
Humane USA Political Action Committee 243
Human Life Review (journal) 8

human relationships with animals, general and historical works on 181–188

Humphrey, Hubert 40, 90, 145*b*

hunting 71–76
 canned hunt 74–75, 153*g*
 federal bans on 64–65
 federal regulation of 65
 fox 122*c*, 123*c*, 134*c*, 136*c*
 with hounds 133*c*
 Internet 75
 laws 76
 regulated 135*c*
 U.S. population, hunters as percentage of (1955–2006) 310*t*

Hunting Act 76, 137*c*, 156*g*

Huntingdon Life Sciences (HLS) 21, 156*g*
 attacks on 132*c*, 135*c*, 137*c*
 and SHAC origins 16–17, 131*c*
 and "SHAC Seven" trial 113–114
 and stock exchange 138*c*
 terror tactics against 18

Hunt Saboteurs Association (HSA) 75, 123*c*, 124*c*, 262–263

Hunt v. United States 65, 122*c*

I

IACUC. *See* Institutional Animal Care and Use Committee

ICCVAM. *See* Interagency Coordinating Committee on the Validation of Alternative Methods

IES. *See* Investigation and Enforcement Services

IFAW. *See* International Fund for Animal Welfare

"If this is Kosher . . ." video 136*c*

Ill Treatment of Horses and Cattle Bill 23

Improved Standards for Laboratory Animals Act 45, 86–87

incidental take permit 126*c*, 156*g*

In Defense of Animals 244

indexes 174–175

India Project for Animals and Nature 7

Industrial Revolution 3

InfoTrac 175

inherent value 157*g*

Inhumane Trapping Prevention Act 77, 137*c*

"injury in fact" 107, 108

Institute for Animal Health 250

Institute for Behavioral Research 44, 98

Institute for Laboratory Animal Research 255

Institute of Laboratory Animal Sciences 54

Institute of Medicine of the National Academy of Sciences 48

Institutional Animal Care and Use Committee (IACUC) 45, 87, 100, 127*c*, 157*g*

intensive farms and farming 30–31, 35–39, 122*c*, 157*g*

Interagency Coordinating Committee on the Validation of Alternative Methods (ICCVAM) 53, 129*c*, 132*c*

International Council for Laboratory Animal Science 255

International Elephant Foundation 263

International Fund for Animal Welfare (IFAW) 67, 263

International Fur Trade Federation 36

The International Institute for Animal Law 178, 244

International Primate Protection League 99, 100, 263

International Primate Protection League v. Institute for Behavioral Research **98–101**
 background 98–99
 decision 99–100
 impact 100–101
 legal issues 99
 and PETA 98–101
 and Silver Spring monkey case 127*c*

International Society for Animal Rights 166

international treaty for animal protection 121*c*

International Whaling Commission 127*c*

International Wildlife Coalition 263

Internet hunting 75

In the Company of Animals (Serpell) 22

intimidation campaigns 136*c*

Investigation and Enforcement Services (IES) 46

Iovino, Shelli Lyn 106

irritation testing. *See* Draize tests

Irwin, Paul G. 76

IUCN. *See* World Conservation Union

Izaak Walton League of America 75, 263

Index

J

James, Heather 16, 131c, 145b–146b
Jane Goodall Institute 244
Jarboe, James 16
Jasper, James 13
Jensen, Patricia 29
Jewish Defense League 15
Jewish (kosher) ritual slaughter 40–41, 91
Jewish Orthodox Union 41
Johns Hopkins University Center for Alternatives to Animal Testing 255
Johnson, Lyndon 123c
Jonas, Kevin. See Kjonaas, Kevin
Jones, Edith L. 112
Jones, Grant 62, 124c, 146b
Jones v. Butz 125c
Journal of the American Medical Association 46
Judeo-Christian tradition 4
Jurnove, Marc 146b
  as *Animal Legal Defense Fund v. Glickman* plaintiff 10–11, 132c
  standing to sue 62, 130c
Justice Department (animal rights group) 16, 131c

K

Kentucky Fried Chicken 134c
Kerasote, Ted 72
Kjonaas, Kevin 18, 92, 113–114, 136c, 146b
Klamath River 115–116
  salmon fishery 68–70
Kleppe v. New Mexico 65, 125c
kosher slaughter 40–41, 91, 125c, 157g
Kraft, Jonathan 60
Kyprianou, Markos 146b

L

Laboratory Animal Welfare Act (LAWA) 43, 86, 123c, 124c
Lacey Act 61, 65, 121c, 135c, 157g
landscape immersion 124c, 157g
Lardner, Mitchell 17
Las Vegas, Nevada 101
LAWA. *See* Laboratory Animal Welfare Act
law of animal rights **9–12**
  and animals as legal persons 11–12
  resources 193–195
  and standing to sue 9–11
  in United States 85–92
LD50 ("lethal dose for 50 percent") test 50–51, 53, 122c, 157g
League Against Cruel Sports 75, 122c, 123c, 263–264
Leahy, Michael T. 7
legal databases 178
The Legal Information Institute 177
legal issues. *See also specific court cases*
  in *Alsea Valley Alliance v. Evans (Alsea Valley Alliance v. Oregon Natural Resources)* 116
  in *Animal Legal Defense Fund v. Glickman* 107–108
  in Bobby Berosini orangutan case 102
  in *International Primate Protection League v. Institute for Behavioral Research* 99
  in *Tennessee Valley Authority v. Hill* 96
  in *Texas Beef Group v. Winfrey* 112
  in Trial of the "SHAC Seven" 114
legal personhood 11–12, 157g
legal research **175–178**
  state law codes 176
  U.S. Code 176
legal standing 157g
legislation, pending 176–177
Lewis, John 16, 146b
Lewis and Clark College 110
Lexis 178
Liberty 92 (law against animal cruelty) 120c
library catalogs 173–174
Library of Congress 176
Life (magazine) 43, 123c
Life Sciences Research 17, 18, 113, 137c, 138c. *See also* Huntingdon Life Sciences (HLS)
Little Tennessee River 94, 123c, 125c
Liverpool Society for Preventing Wanton Cruelty to Brute Animals 23, 120c
Live-Shot.com 75, 157g
livestock
  cattle feed ban 130c
  cattle raising 31–32
  changes in the U.S. inventories of (1950–2004) 312t
  European Council directive on transport of 136c
logging industry 67
Long Island Game Park Farm and Zoo 106, 107
Louisiana 56
Lujan v. Defenders of Wildlife 10, 107, 128c
Lyman, Howard 34, 111, 130c, 146b

M

MacNeil, Jane Salodof 54
mad cow disease. *See*
bovine spongiform
encephalopathy (BSE);
variant Creutzfeldt-
Jakob disease
MADD. *See* Mothers
Against Drunk Driving
Maddie's Fund 247
Maine 93, 120*c*
Mallalieu, Anne 71
Manhasset Bay Yacht Club
17, 137*c*
Man in Nature
(organization) 165
Mann, Keith 19
Marine Mammal
Protection Act 65, 87
Martin, Richard 23, 147*b*
Martin Act 23, 29, 120*c*,
158*g*
Mary Kay Cosmetics 50,
131*c*
Massachusetts Bay Colony
92, 120*c*
Massachusetts Society
for the Prevention of
Cruelty to Animals 39
mastitis 158*g*
Matfield, Mark 21
McBurnett, Sara 147*b*
McDonald's
chicken slaughter
review by 41, 137*c*
egg guidelines
enforced by 131*c*
McLibel case
(England) 38, 113,
130*c*
meat supplier
guidelines 36, 40,
132*c*
McNerny, Jerry 71, 139*c*
meat animals, in United
States (2001 and 2003)
315*t*
Meat Inspection Act 125*c*
meat supplier guidelines,
issued by chain
restaurants 36

media sites 168
metasearch programs 172
Michigan State University
20
Migratory Bird Treaty Act
65, 121*c*, 158*g*
mink 32
Misguided Compassion
(Clark) 103
Mississippi-Alabama Sea
Grant Legal Program
117
Monash University 12
Montpelier PLC 17–18,
136*c*
Morrison, Adrian 45, 48,
52, 147*b*
Morton, Rogers 10
Mothers Against Drunk
Driving (MADD) 15,
131*c*
Munro, Lyle 15, 42
on animal
experimentation 42
animal rights activist
interviews of 13
on animal rights
activists 12, 14
companion animals,
influence of 23
on strategy of animal
rights activists 15, 20
Muslim (halal) ritual
slaughter 40–41, 91,
125*c*

N

NABR. *See* National
Association for
Biomedical Research
NAIA. *See* National
Animal Interest Alliance
National Agricultural
Statistics Service (NASS)
30, 166
National Animal Control
Association 247
National Animal Interest
Alliance (NAIA) 165,
244

National Anti-Vivisection
Society 255–256
National Association for
Biomedical Research
(NABR) 21, 29, 46, 54,
256
National Association of
Biology Teachers 52
National Cattlemen's Beef
Association 41, 250
National Center for
Animal Law 244
National Center for
Research Resources
(NCRR) 49, 140*c*
National Centre for
the Replacement,
Refinement, and
Reduction of Animals in
Research (NC3Rs) 53,
136*c*, 167, 256
National Chicken Council
38, 250
National Corn Growers
Association 39
National Council of Chain
Restaurants 133*c*, 251
National Council on Pet
Population Study and
Policy 166, 247–248
National Dairy Council
251
National Environmental
Policy Act 94
National Farmers' Union
251
National Geographic
(magazine) 63
National Greyhound
Association 258
National Institute for
Animal Agriculture 251
National Institute of
Mental Health 47
National Institutes of
Health (NIH) 45, 49,
98, 100, 129*c*, 167, 256
National Institutes of
Health Revitalization
Act 128*c*–129*c*

Index

National Marine Fisheries
Services (NMFS)
in *Alsea Valley Alliance
v. Evans (Alsea Valley
Alliance v. Oregon
Natural Resources)*
115–117
environmentally
significant unit
defined by 128*c*
hatchery policy
established by 129*c*
Oregon Coast coho
salmon classified by
69, 130*c*, 133*c*
role in endangered
species protection 89
National Pork Producers
Council 251
National Research Council
33
National Resources
Defense Council 51
National Science Teachers
Association 52
National Society for
Medical Research 43
National Thoroughbred
Racing Association 258
National Trappers
Association 77, 264
National Turkey
Federation 251
National Wildlife
Federation 73, 264
NCRR. *See* National
Center for Research
Resources
NC3Rs. *See* National
Centre for the
Replacement,
Refinement, and
Reduction of Animals in
Research
Netherlands 51, 53
Nevada 60, 102
New England Anti-
Vivisection Society 256
Newkirk, Ingrid 15, 44,
98, 147*b*
on animal research 47

on companion animals
23
and PETA 126*c*
New Mexico 56
Newsweek (magazine) 26
New York State 93, 120*c*
New York Stock Exchange
(NYSE) 17, 138*c*
New York Times 20, 50,
128*c*, 168
NIH. *See* National
Institutes of Health
Nixon, Richard 66, 125*c*
NMFS. *See* National
Marine Fisheries Services
Nobel Prize 47–48
no-kill shelter 28, 127*c*,
158*g*
NORINA. *See* Norwegian
Inventory of Alternatives
Norris, Scott 70
North American Animal
Liberation Press Office
244–245
northern fur seal 64
northern spotted owl 67
Northwest Center of the
Pacific Legal Foundation
117
Northwestern School of
Law 110
Norwegian Inventory of
Alternatives (NORINA)
167
"No Surprises" rule 68,
90, 126*c*, 158*g*
NTP Interagency Center
for the Evaluation of
Alternative Toxicological
Methods 255
Nuffield Council on
Bioethics 256
NYSE. *See* New York
Stock Exchange

O

O'Connor, Sandra Day
105–106
Oderberg, David S. 8

Office of Laboratory
Animal Welfare 167,
256
Office of the Inspector
General (OIG) 46
Ohio 57
OIE. *See* World
Organization for Animal
Health
OIG. *See* Office of the
Inspector General
online resources 164–173
agriculture, animals
in 166
animals in research,
testing, and
education 166–167
animal welfare general
sites 164–168
companion animal
sites 166
entertainment, animals
in 167
media sites 168
organization and
people finding
172–173
search engines 171–
172
web-based research
169–173
web portals 169–170
wildlife 167
*On the Movement of the
Heart and Blood in
Animals* (Harvey) 119*c*
Open Range Zoo 62
open season 158*g*
orangutans 60, 128*c*, 129*c*,
158*g*. *See also* Bobby
Berosini orangutan case
Oregon Coast coho
salmon 130*c*, 133*c*, 136*c*
organizations and agencies
240–266
agriculture, animals in
248–252
companion animals
246–248
entertainment, animals
in 258–259

organizations and agencies
(*continued*)
general-purpose
organizations
240–246
online resources
172–173
science, animals in
252–257
wild, animals in the
260–266
Orion (the Hunters'
Institute) 264
Outdoor Amusement
Business Association
259
overpopulation, of wildlife
72
Oxford University 17, 61,
135*c*, 138*c*

P

Pacelle, Wayne 147*b*
Pacheco, Alex 44, 98, 101,
126*c*, 147*b*
Pacific Coast Federation of
Fishermen's Associations
68–69, 115
Pacific Legal Foundation
70, 264
palila (Hawaiian native
bird) 67
*Palila v. Hawaii
Department of Land and
Natural Resources (Palila
II)* 104–106, 127*c*
Parliamentary Affairs
(journal) 78
passenger pigeon 64, 121*c*
PAWS. *See* Performing
Animal Welfare Society
pending legislation
176–177
People for the Ethical
Treatment of Animals
(PETA) 140*c*, 245
AgriProcessors
videotape released
by 91
and ALF 20

animal research
opposed by 47
antifur campaign of 36
antimilk campaign of
131*c*
and Bobby Berosini
orangutan case 60,
101–103, 128*c*, 129*c*,
140*c*
criticism of chicken
slaughter by 41
elephant abuse lawsuit
by 60
founding of 126*c*
goals of 37
and Head Injury
Clinical Research
Laboratory scandal
45
and HPV chemicals
testing 51
and Huntingdon Life
Sciences 17, 113
and *International
Primate Protection
League v. Institute for
Behavioral Research*
98–101
and Kenneth Feld case
21, 138*c*
Kentucky Fried
chicken lawsuit by
134*c*–136*c*
kosher slaughterhouse
videotapes of 91
McDonald's animal
cruelty campaign of
132*c*
membership claims
of 13
on no-kill shelters 28
and PETCO 25, 137*c*
and Silver Spring
monkey case 98–
101, 127*c*
tactics of 14
Performing Animal
Welfare Society (PAWS)
21, 101, 167, 259
periodical indexes 175
Perron, Brian J. 70, 117

PETA. *See* People for the
Ethical Treatment of
Animals
PETCO 25, 137*c*
Pet Protection Act 29, 87,
128*c*, 158*g*
Petrinovich, Lewis 8–9,
147*b*
pets, protection of 86
Pet Safety and Protection
Act 29
Philadelphia, Pennsylvania
44–45
philosophy of animal
rights **4–9,** 188–193
and evaluation of
animals 7–9
Tom Regan and 6–7
Peter Singer and 5–6
Physicians Committee for
Responsible Medicine
52, 256–257
pig raising 32
*Planned Parenthood of
Columbia/Willamette, Inc.
v. American Coalition of
Life Activists* 114
Pombo, Richard 71, 138*c*,
139*c*, 147*b*–148*b*
Pope, Al 36
Pope, Carl 73–74, 148*b*
pork industry, changes in
farm size of U.S. 314*t*
Port Washington, New
York 137*c*
Postville, Iowa 40, 91
Pottker, Janice 21, 131*c*,
148*b*
poultry slaughter 91,
137*c*, 138*c*
pounds 43, 122*c*, 158*g*
pound seizure laws 158*g*
Powell, Lewis F., Jr. 97
predators, ban on
interstate transport of
135*c*
Pribiloff Islands 64
primates 7, 98–101,
106, 136*c*, 158*g*. *See
also specific species, e.g.:*
chimpanzees

Index

The Principles of Humane Experimental Technique (Russell and Burch) 53, 123c
print sources **173–178**
  bibliographies, indexes, and databases 174–175
  bookstore catalogs 174
  library catalogs 173–174
  periodical indexes 175
Procter and Gamble 50, 131c
product testing 49–52
Professional Rodeo Cowboys Association 57, 259
Property Clause (of U.S. Constitution) 65
Protecting Animals in Democracy 245
Protection of Animals Act 26, 56
Pro-Test 257
Public Health Security and Bioterrorism Preparedness and Response Act 18, 134c
Public Health Service 45
puppy mills 24–25, 158g
PZP vaccine (porcine zona pellucida vaccine) 72, 124c, 158g

R

racing animals 58
"random sources" 28
REACH (Registration, Evaluation, Authorisation and Restriction of Chemicals) 55, 135c, 159g
Recreational Hunting Safety and Preservation Act 75, 129c, 159g
Redwood Shores, California 79

Regan, Tom **6–7**, 14, 126c, 148b
Regulation (journal) 70
Rehnquist, William H. 97, 105
remote control hunting 75
Republicans for Environmental Protection (REP America) 264
research, doing **163–179**. *See also* animal research
  online resources 164–173
  print resources 173–178
  and verification of sources 179
Research Defence Society 257
Reuters 168
Revlon 50, 126c, 127c
Revolutionary Cells 16, 135c
Rhode Island 57
Rice, Glenn 47
Richey, Charles R. 108, 109
Ringling Bros. and Barnum & Bailey Circus 133c, 138c, 167
  elephant abuse case 133c
  lawsuit against 21, 131c
  wiretapping case against 132c–133c
ritual slaughter 40–41, 91
road rage incident 133c
Robinson, Erik 117
Robinson, Mary Lou 112
rodeos 57
Roman Empire 56
Roosevelt, Franklin D. 26
Rowan, Andrew N. 14, 20, 79, 148b
Royal Society for the Prevention of Cruelty to Animals (RSPCA) 23–24, 26, 42, 120c, 245

Russell, W. M. S. 53, 123c, 148b
Ryder, Richard 5, 6, 124c, 148b

S

St. Jude Children's Research Hospital 48
Sales and Marketing Management 15
Sandler, Jessica 47
San Jose, California 60, 131c
SAPL. *See* Society for Animal Protective Legislation
Sara the Tiger Whisperer 60
Scalia, Antonin 10, 105
SCI (formerly Safari Club International) 264
science, animals in (list of organizations) 252–257
Science News (newsmagazine) 33
scientific researchers 99
The Scientist (magazine) 49, 54
Scientists Center for Animal Welfare 257
Scotland 133c
Scotland Yard 16
Scruton, Roger 8
Scully, Matthew 8, 148b–149b
Sea Shepherd Conservation Society 264–265
sentient being 159g
Serious Organised Crime and Police Act (Britain) 136c, 137c, 159g
Serpell, James 22
SHAC. *See* Stop Huntingdon Animal Cruelty
"SHAC Seven," trial of the 113–115
  background 113–114
  decision 114
  impact 115
  legal issues 114

SHAC-USA
and Animal Enterprise
Protection Act 92
Animal Liberation
Front (ALF), ties
to 17
and law enforcement
agencies 18–19
trial of "SHAC Seven"
113–115, 136*c*, 138*c*,
139*c*
Shaklee (company) 16
sheep raising 32
shelter 159*g*
Showing Animals Respect
and Kindness 265
Shupp, Lee 79
Sierra Club 74
Sierra Club v. Morton
aesthetic interest
protected 109
"injury in fact" 100
standing to sue in 10,
99, 101, 107, 124*c*
sign language, primates'
use of 7
Silver Spring monkey case
44, 126*c*, 127*c*, 159*g*.
*See also International
Primate Protection League
v. Institute for Behavioral
Research*
and Animal Welfare
Act 98–101
and PETA 98–101,
127*c*
Simmons, Daniel R. 70
Simmons, Randy T. 70
Singer, Peter **5–6,** 124*c*,
149*b*
Animal Liberation
published 124*c*
on animal research 48
animal rights
movement, origins
of 4
call to action by 12
slaughter of farm animals
39–42
slavery 6
Smith, Richard 53

Smith, Rob Roy 11, 110
snail darter 68, 94, 95,
125*c*, 159*g*
snare 77, 159*g*
Society for Animal
Protective Legislation
(SAPL) 29, 58
Society for the Prevention
of Cruelty to Animals
(SPCA) 23, 120*c*
Solomon, Gina 51
soring 57–58, 159*g*
Sparshott, Shan 132*c*–
133*c*
spay/neuter campaigns
27–28, 124*c*
SPCA. *See* Society for the
Prevention of Cruelty to
Animals
SPEAK: The Voice for the
Animals 257
speciesism 6, 124*c*, 159*g*
Species Survival Network
265
Species Survival Plan 63
Spira, Henry 20, 50, 124*c*,
126*c*, 149*b*
standing to sue 62, 159*g*
in *Animal Legal Defense
Fund v. Glickman*
107, 110, 130*c*
in *Lujan v. Defenders of
Wildlife* 128*c*
in *Sierra Club v.
Morton* 10
Stanley, Valerie 110
Stardust Hotel and Casino
101
state laws **92–93,** 176
The State of the Animals
(Fraser) 35
steel-jawed leghold trap
77, 159*g*
Stephens, Martin 45
sterilization 27–28
Stevens, John Paul 105
Stevenson, Peter 39
Stop Huntingdon Animal
Cruelty (SHAC) 16–17,
92, 113, 131*c*
stress study 38

stunning of poultry prior
to slaughter 137*c*
Sumitomo Corporation
17
"sustainable use" 72–73
Sweden 37
Sweet Home Chapter
of Communities for a
Great Oregon 67
Switzerland 37

T

"take," ESA's definition of
103–104
Tampa, Florida 61
Taub, Edward 44, 98–101,
126*c*, 149*b*
Tellico Dam (Tennessee)
68, 94, 123*c*, 125*c*, 126*c*
Tennessee Valley Authority
(TVA) 123*c*
*Tennessee Valley Authority
v. Hill* **94–98,** 103, 105,
106, 125*c*
background 94–95
decision 96–97
impact 97–98
legal issues 96
Tennessee walking horse
57
"terror tactics" 136*c*
tertiary targeting 159*g*–
160*g*
TESRA. *See* Threatened
and Endangered Species
Recovery Act
Texas 34, 38
Texas Beef Group v. Winfrey
111–113
background 111–112
decision 112–113
impact 113
legal issues 112
Texas False Disparagement
of Perishable Foods Act
111
Thomas, Clarence 105
Thomas Aquinas 4, 119*c*,
141*b*
Thomas web site 176

Index

Thoroughbred Owners
and Breeders Association
259
Thoroughbred Retirement
Foundation 259
Threatened and
Endangered Species
Recovery Act (TESRA)
71, 138c, 139c, 160g
threatened species 160g
three Rs 53, 160g
Thurman, Duane 21
Time (magazine) 168
tort 160g
toxicity testing 49–50
Tracy, California 71, 138c
transgenic animal 55,
160g
transportation
of farm animals 39–
42, 140c
truck 139c
of vertebrate animals
in European Union
139c
trapping regulations
77–78
Trenton, New Jersey 114
Trull, Frankie 149b
Turner, John F. 103
TVA. *See* Tennessee Valley
Authority
Twenty-eight Hour Act
39–40, 160g
enactment of 121c
and exhibited animals
59
expansion of 129c
and racing animals 58
and rodeos 57
and truck
transportation 139c
Tyler, Andrew 15

U

UnCover Web 174
Underground Railroad
comparison 20
"Unhappy Meals" PETA
campaign 15

United Egg Producers
(UEP) 35, 36, 39, 132c,
252
United Poultry Concerns,
Inc. 252
Universities Federation for
Animal Welfare 245
University of California,
Davis 54
University of Pennsylvania
44–45
Unti, Bernard 79
U.S. Code 176
U.S. Department of
Agriculture (USDA) 41,
43–44, 107, 245–246
Agricultural Research
Service 38, 245
Animal and Plant
Health Inspection
Service 245–246
animal law
enforcement by 40
and *Animal Legal
Defense Fund v.
Glickman* 10–11,
107–111, 132c
animal testing report
by 55
Animal Welfare Act
enforcement 24,
43–45, 86
Animal Welfare
Information Center
245–246
and Bobby Berosini
orangutan case
101–102
and bovine spongiform
encephalopathy 34
Food Safety and
Inspection Service
252
Humane Methods
of Slaughter Act
enforcement 90
and *International
Primate Protection
League v. Institute for
Behavioral Research*
case 98–101

lawsuits against 46
National Agricultural
Statistics Service
166
and poultry slaughter
137c, 138c
primate regulations
109
primates in research
report 49
stress study 38
U.S. Fish and Wildlife
Service (FWS) 66, 88,
98, 125c, 126c, 154g, 265
U.S. Food and Drug
Administration (FDA)
49, 51, 113
U.S. Forest Service 10,
89
U.S. National Academy of
Sciences 33
U.S. News and World Report
(magazine) 63
U.S. Sportsmen's Alliance
75, 265
utilitarianism 5–6, 160g

V

variant Creutzfeldt-Jakob
disease 34, 111, 160g
veal crates 36, 37
vegan 160g
vegetarian 160g
Vegetarians International
Voice for Animals
(VIVA) 252
veggie libel law 111–112,
160g
Veneman, Ann 41, 135c
Vick, Michael 140c
Victoria, Australia 62
Victoria (queen of Great
Britain and Ireland) 23,
42, 149b
Victoria Street Society
for the Protection
of Animals from
Vivisection 42
*Villanova Environmental
Law Journal* 106

VIVA. *See* Vegetarians International Voice for Animals
vivisection 42–43, 119*c*, 121*c*, 160*g*
Vlasak, Jerry 149*b*

W

W. A. R. *See* Win Animal Rights
Wald, Patricia 11, 108–109
Ward, Nathaniel 92, 120*c*, 149*b*–150*b*
Washington and Lee Law Review (journal) 52
Washington Post (newspaper) 40
Washington State 34, 41, 135*c*
Washlaw Web (web site) 178
web-based research 169–173
Wendy's 36, 133*c*
West Germany 46, 47
Westlaw (web site) 178
whales and whaling
  "Eat the Whales" campaign 15
  moratorium 127*c*

Whaling Convention Act 65
White, Caroline 150*b*
White, Edward 64
wild, animals in the (list of organizations) 260–266
Wild Free-Roaming Horses and Burros Act 65
wildlife and wildlife management 72–73, 167, 227–239
Wildlife Legislative Fund of America 75
The Wildlife Society 265
Will, George F. 26
Win Animal Rights (W. A. R.) 257
Winfrey, Oprah 34, 38, 111, 129*c*–131*c*, 150*b*
wiretapping 132*c*
Wisconsin 26
Wise, Steven 11, 150*b*
Woodland Park Zoo (Seattle, Washington) 62, 124*c*
World Animal Foundation 246
World Animal Net 246
World Animal Net Directory 165

World Association of Zoos and Aquariums 259
World Conservation Union (IUCN) 265–266
World Health Organization 32–33
World Organisation for Animal Health (OIE) 41, 42, 252
World Society for the Protection of Animals 246
worldwide standards for animal welfare 137*c*
World Wildlife Fund 266
Wurbel, Hanno 54
Wynne, Clive D. L. 8, 150*b*

Y

Yahoo! (search engine) 168, 169
Yellowstone National Park 65
Yoxhall, England 18

Z

zoos 61–64